DRUG WAR PATHOLOGIES

Drug War Pathologies

Embedded Corporatism and
U.S. Drug Enforcement in the Americas

HORACE A. BARTILOW

THE UNIVERSITY OF NORTH CAROLINA PRESS | CHAPEL HILL

Designed by April Leidig
Set in Minion and Meta by Copperline Book Services, Inc.

The University of North Carolina Press has been a member
of the Green Press Initiative since 2003.

Cover illustrations: Dollar bill with handcuffs, iStockphoto.com/Ligorka;
pesos, iStockphoto.com/AlexRaths; Wall Street sign, iStockphoto.com
/RightFramePhotoVideo; background, fotolia.com/© 123dartist

Library of Congress Cataloging-in-Publication Data
Names: Bartilow, Horace A., author.
Title: Drug war pathologies : embedded corporatism and U.S. drug
    enforcement in the Americas / Horace A. Bartilow.
Description: Chapel Hill : University of North Carolina Press, [2019] |
    Includes bibliographical references and index.
Identifiers: LCCN 2019009780| ISBN 9781469652542 (cloth : alk. paper) |
    ISBN 9781469652559 (pbk : alk. paper) | ISBN 9781469652566 (ebook)
Subjects: LCSH: Drug control—Economic aspects—United States. |
    Drug control—Economic aspects—Latin America. | Corporations—
    Political activity—America. | Corporate state—United States. | Latin
    America—Politics and government. | Human rights—Latin America.
Classification: LCC HV5825 .B364 2019 | DDC 362.8/40973—dc23
LC record available at https://lccn.loc.gov/2019009780

In memory of my mother,
Carmen Monica Bartilow

CONTENTS

ILLUSTRATIONS

FIGURES

GRAPHS

My journey in writing this book began in the 1970s when I attended high school in my native Jamaica. Back then the symbol of the U.S. drug war on the island was the Vietnam-era Huey helicopters that flew over my house, in the mornings, en route to the mountainous Cockpit Country for their ritual spraying of Monsanto-manufactured herbicide to eradicate marijuana. The experience reminded me of the "Ride of the Valkyries"—the iconic scene from the movie *Apocalypse Now* where Huey helicopter gunships blasted villages with napalm and sprayed Agent Orange to eradicate crops and forest cover used by Vietcong guerrillas during the Vietnam War. For me, this symbolized the Americanization of the drug war in Jamaica. But this was not Vietnam, and there were no Vietcong guerrillas, just a few small-time peasant farmers, and Rastafarian marijuana growers who cultivated the crop for personal and religious ceremonial consumption. I also wondered why Jamaica's ganja (marijuana) engendered the sustained cooperation of successive Jamaican governments with the DEA to suppress its production and consumption. But as a high school teenager, I lacked the knowledge to make sense of this phenomenon. It was through the process of research and the writing of this book that I learned that what I observed as a teenager was the operation of a well-oiled drug enforcement regime whose principal members are major American corporations like Monsanto and whose effectiveness requires the cooperation of overseas state and nonstate actors.

During the 1980s and 1990s, Jamaica became a strategic transit hub for South American cocaine, and Colombian drug cartels became a greater existential threat to U.S. security than the island's local marijuana growers. In meeting this threat, drug enforcement in Jamaica shifted its emphasis from marijuana eradication to interdicting cocaine smuggled in go-fast boats, which exited the island's many coastal enclaves en route to markets in North America. While the Americanization of the drug war was effective in suppressing local marijuana production, it was woefully ineffective in arresting the flow of South American cocaine from the island. According to the island's local narrative, marijuana suppression incentivized local criminal organizations, such as drug lord Christopher "Dudus" Coke's notorious Shower Posse that operated out of the West Kingston community of Tivoli Gardens, into becoming transit middlemen for South American cocaine. The cocaine trade expanded the Posse's power and global distribution networks and at the time was considered by the DEA to be one of the world's most dangerous narco-trafficking organizations. At the conclusion of a violent and bloody incursion into Tivoli Gardens by the security forces in 2007, which resulted in gross human rights violations, Coke was extradited to the United States on drug and gun trafficking charges after being indicted by the district court grand jury of the Southern District of New York. In the end, just as the Americanization of the Vietnam war failed to defeat the Viet Cong, the Americanization of the drug war in Jamaica did not solve the island's drug and crime problems—it only made them worse.

It took four years to write, develop the theoretical arguments, and collect and analyze the data used in producing this book. I hope that this research will give readers a deeper understanding of the role that corporate power plays in the operations of the drug enforcement regime and that, by becoming aware of the subsequent income inequities and class dimension of the drug war, readers will question the regime's prohibition logic and demand reform to mitigate its damage to democracy and human rights in the Americas.

ACKNOWLEDGMENTS

Colleagues from the University of Kentucky provided support, insights, and sound advice while I wrote this book. Ernie Yanarella frequently indulged me, while he was department chair and had little time, in talking through the construction of my theoretical arguments that pertained to the work of C. Wright Mills. Charles Davis, Donald Gross, and Ellen Riggle provided valuable comments on early drafts and chapters of the book. Bob Olson made me aware of how the book's empirical findings relate to how the drug enforcement regime operates in the Middle East and Central Asia. Joanne Pope Melish and Stephen Voss encouraged me to situate aspects of my empirical findings in the border literature of race and mass incarceration in the United States.

This book also benefited from the insights and comments of the anonymous reviewers at the University of North Carolina Press. My editor, Elaine Maisner, has been very supportive throughout the entire process and helped improve the manuscript. I thank her and all the other people at the University of North Carolina Press who helped bring this project to publication.

Financial support for this project came from the University of Kentucky. I am grateful to the Office of the Executive Vice President for Research and Ms. Bessie Guerrant for providing funding to student coders through the Bucks for Brains Summer Research Program. I am also grateful to the Department of Political Science and the Office of the Associate Dean for Research for providing funding to defray the publication costs of the book.

I want to express my deepest gratitude to my family. My son, Pascal, sacrificed much of the summer of 2015 to code the data used in generating the findings in chapter 7. My wife, Dale, and our six-year-old daughter, Jasmine, put up with me and the long hours it took to complete this project. I am indebted to Christ, who gave me the strength and the discipline to overcome the obstacles of writing and research and to see this project to completion.

Finally, I dedicate this book to my mother, Carmen Monica Bartilow, who served the community of Water House in Kingston, Jamaica, as principal of Balmagie Elementary School. Known in the community as Mother B, she was a fierce defender of the human rights and dignity of the poor and working people against the excesses of the anticrime strategies of the security forces that patrol the community locally known as Fire House. My mother taught me the importance of social justice and the empowerment of women, who are often the socioeconomic pillars of underserved communities throughout the developing world. It is her spirit for social justice and respect for human rights that undergird the research of this book.

AMA	American Medical Association
AS&E	American Science and Engineering (company)
ATPDEA	Andean Trade Promotion and Drug Eradication Act
AUC	Autodefensas Unidas de Colombia (United Self-Defense Forces of Colombia)
BACRIM	Bandas Criminales (criminal bands)
BFTIA	bilateral free-trade and investment agreement
BOMCA	Border Management Program in Central Asia
CAP	Center for American Progress
CARICOM	Caribbean Community
CBC	Congressional Black Caucus
CEIP	Carnegie Endowment for International Peace
CEO	chief executive officer
CFI	Committee on Foreign Intelligence
CFR	Council on Foreign Relations
CIA	Central Intelligence Agency
CIRI	Cingranelli–Richards human rights index
CSDI	Colombia Strategic Development Initiative
CSIS	Center for Strategic and International Studies
CTT	Committee on Transnational Threats
DEA	U.S. Drug Enforcement Administration
DFCR	Doctors for Cannabis Regulation

DHS	U.S. Department of Homeland Security
DTO	drug trafficking organization
ECLAC	Economic Commission for Latin America and the Caribbean
ELN	Ejército de Liberación Nacional (The National Liberation Army of Colombia)
EMP	environmental management plan
EMU	end-use monitoring (agreement)
FARC	Fuerzas Armadas Revolucionarias de Colombia (Revolutionary Armed Forces of Colombia)
FBI	Federal Bureau of Investigation
FDA	U.S. Food and Drug Administration
FDI	foreign direct investment
GDP	gross domestic product
GOP	Grand Old Party (Republican Party)
IMF	International Monetary Fund
JAA	Juan Andrés Álvarez (Front)
MPRI	Military Professional Resources Inc.
NACC	North American Competitiveness Council
NAFTA	North American Free Trade Association
NBCI	National Black Church Initiative
NGO	nongovernmental organization
NSA	National Security Agency
NSA47	National Security Act of 1947
NSC	National Security Council
ODA	official development aid
OECD	Organization for Economic Co-operation and Development
PAC	Political Action Committee

P&G	Proctor & Gamble
PNAC	Project for the New American Century
PTS	Political Terror Scale
RMSEA	root mean square error of approximation
SAIC	Science Applications International Corporation
SCEEPA	Shirley Chisholm Educational Exchange Program Authorization
SEM	structural equation model
SIGAR	special inspector general for Afghanistan reconstruction
SME	Sindicato Mexicano de Electricistas (Mexican labor union)
SPP	Security and Prosperity Partnership of North America
SRMSR	standardized root mean squared residual
TSCS	time-series cross section
UNODC	U.N. Office on Drugs and Crime
USAID	U.S. Agency of International Development
USCBP	U.S.-Colombian Business Partnership
USDA	U.S. Department of Agriculture
WOLA	Washington Office on Latin America

DRUG WAR PATHOLOGIES

CHAPTER 1

Embedded Corporatism

A Theoretical Perspective of U.S. Drug Enforcement
and Its Pathologies in the Americas

The Embedded Corporatist Drug Enforcement Regime

A major threat to capitalism is the criminal version of itself: illicit capitalism. Drug trafficking is the oldest form of illicit capitalism, whose retail value is estimated to rival those of legitimate industries (Reuter and Greenfield 2001). Drug trafficking and the financial proceeds that it generates pose a threat to neoliberal capitalism. Drug front companies whose proceeds come from money laundering have little incentive to be financially efficient and can operate in the red for extended periods of time and in consequence will undermine market prices and distort economic competition. And if the level of drug-related violence increases, which is often the case in many developing countries and urban U.S. cities, legitimate businesses will liquidate their investments and move their capital to other countries or other cities, leaving behind economic and financial blight. Criminal business enterprises may try to fill the investment void, but since they have very little incentive to operate efficiently, they are less likely to provide sustainable economic growth and employment (U.N. International Drug Control Programme 1998).

Drug trafficking also poses a threat to privatization—the holy grail of neoliberal capitalism. The essential paradox is that privatization is encouraged to increase the efficiency of the market, but if it is financed by drug trafficking proceeds, then it can be extremely inefficient. Drug trafficking financing of privatization can quickly evolve into anticompetitive approaches to business (Keh 1996). Once established in the licit economy, criminal enterprises have the ability to use intimidation and violence to erect a type of nontariff barrier to eliminate legitimate competition, which can lead to monopolistic behavior in how prices are set (Arlacchi 1986, 91). Essentially, when privatization becomes the conduit for money laundering, its corruptive effects will undermine not only the integrity of governments that initiate neoliberal reforms but also the integrity of markets that suffer from the criminal hijacking of such reforms.

While drug prohibition is an important component of the U.S. national security state (National Security Act of 1947, P.L. 114-113, Sec 101, 50 U.S.C. 3001), it has evolved into a larger corporatist regime that is predicated on protecting the operations of free market capitalism. American drug enforcement has now become the security face of corporate capitalism and is an important vehicle for leveraging corporate penetration into foreign markets (see table 3.2A in the data appendix), as well as facilitating international cooperation to combat threats to capitalism that arise from drug trafficking. The principal actors in this corporatist regime are American transnational corporations. The regime also includes policy think tanks, some members of Congress, civil society organizations, religious and political leaders in the African American community, and foreign governments that partner with the United States in the overseas prosecution of the drug war.

American transnational corporations view U.S. drug enforcement in countries that host their investments as vital to underwriting the security of corporate assets and personnel who are threatened by drug cartels and narcoterror organizations. In the United States, the regime includes think tanks whose policy and research papers consistently support drug prohibition, which not only reflect the policy preferences of their corporate sponsors but also, more importantly, influence public opinion in ways that build and maintain domestic and international consensus for prohibition. The regime includes those members of Congress, such as the Congressional Black Caucus (CBC), who support drug prohibition because drug-related violent crime and addiction have destroyed the lives of people in communities they represent. The support for prohibition by other members of Congress reflects the policy preferences of corporations that finance their election campaigns or generate jobs in the voting districts they represent. The regime also comprises civil society groups, such as the AMA, that oppose the legalization of marijuana even for medical use. Within the African American community, the regime includes the leadership of the middle-class-oriented National Urban League, the Nation of Islam, and African American churches that during the crack epidemic of the 1980s wanted strong drug enforcement to end the scourge of drug addiction and to serve as a conduit for attracting private investment to their communities. In other words, drug enforcement was needed to clear urban communities of drug dealers and, in the process, create new markets for corporate expansion. Internationally, where drug trafficking cartels represent an existential threat to the state and undermine investor confidence, the regime includes foreign governments and local business leaders that partner with American policy makers in prosecuting the drug war overseas.[1]

Together, these domestic and international actors have evolved into a regime (Nadelmann 1990, 1993; Andreas and Nadelmann 2006) because the convergence of their disparate security and economic interests builds consensus around prohibition, which makes drug enforcement cooperation among them possible. Corporatism is an embedded feature of the regime because, although the interests of the actors are disparate, their interests convergence and align in ways that produce policy outcomes conducive to corporate capital accumulation. While drug enforcement cooperation and consensus are produced by the convergence and alignment of actors' interests, this process takes place within the context of how corporate power shapes drug enforcement decision making and reflects the underlying power structure of the regime. Through the use of corporate lobbies, corporate financing of federal elections, corporate funding of policy think tanks, and corporate interlocks with the federal government and the military (discussed in chapters 3 and 4), American corporations drive drug enforcement decision making. Corporate power in the regime provides the underlying structure that facilitates how the convergence and alignment of actors' disparate interests with the need for capital accumulation produce consensus and cooperation in the domestic and international prosecution of the drug war. This, in essence, defines the nature of embedded corporatism in U.S. drug enforcement.

The nature of embedded corporatism, and the power that American corporations wield within the regime, does not suggest that there are no challengers to the policy preferences of the regime. As chapter 2 shows, human rights organizations, labor unions, and even some members of Congress were opposed to legislative funding for the drug wars in Colombia and Mexico. Nonetheless, the institutional nature of corporate power in drug enforcement decision making made the regime resilient in the face of challenges to its policy preferences.

While corporate power provides the structure that facilitates consensus and cooperation within the regime, the power of the U.S. government is also needed to manage drug enforcement cooperation with foreign governments. The idea that American hegemony is necessary for managing international cooperation has been a source of debate among international relations scholars. While realist scholars recognize that American hegemony was necessary for the initial building of postwar international cooperation (Kindleberger 1981; Krasner 1976), liberal scholars postulated that continued cooperation did not require American power (Keohane 1984). I argue here that American power is needed to manage drug enforcement cooperation because the nature of the underground economy and the unobservability of illicit drug trafficking make it difficult to effectively monitor the behavior of foreign governments to determine if they are shirking their responsibilities in executing the policies of the regime (Bartilow and Eom 2012).

American power is also needed to manage prohibitive cooperation even when the security and economic interests of foreign governments converge and align with the policy preferences of the regime. Even under these circumstances, as shown in chapter 4, foreign governments will attempt to manipulate the rules of cooperation in ways that give them a voice in how the power of the regime is used in drug enforcement (Walt 2005, 217). Therefore, an important feature of the embedded corporatist drug enforcement regime is that American power is necessary for managing cooperation with foreign governments by utilizing a combination of economic incentives and coercive sanctions to respectively reward observance of regime rules and punish violations of such rules. And as discussed in chapter 7, American power, along with the agency of foreign governments, has been very instrumental in managing drug enforcement cooperation by establishing a drug-war national security state for the purpose of prosecuting the drug war overseas. This book provides an analysis of the corporatist origins of U.S. drug enforcement policy and its paradoxical effects on human rights and democracy in the Americas.

The Nature of the Problem: The Paradox of Human Rights and Democratization in the Americas

While Latin America's relations with the United States are often defined in terms of its political and economic interdependence, Latin America and the United States are also intertwined in terms of the unintended consequences of policy choices that emerge from embedded corporatism. Latin America is considered to be the leader of democracy's third wave, since the spread of democratization has been more widespread in Latin America than in any other region in the developing world (Huntington 1991b). Relative to other regions in the developing world, Latin America is more open to international trade and is a major destination for American foreign direct investment (FDI), both of which are said to improve human rights. However, regardless of these factors, Latin America's human rights record is no better than other regions in the developing world that have not adopted democracy, and for some Latin American countries it is even worse. What has emerged in many Latin American countries is what I call "democracies without rights"—democracies that administer free elections but have a penchant for violence and human rights repression.

A Comparative Perspective of Latin America's Democratization and Human Rights Paradox

Table 1.1 displays regional averages of the Polity, Freedom House, Cingranelli-Richards (CIRI) human rights data index, and Political Terror Scale (PTS) databases, as well as FDI and the level of U.S. counternarcotic aid to the region from 1980 to 2005, capturing the period of democratization's third wave.[2] With a regional Polity score of 6.0, Latin America leads the developing world in the number of governments that are democracies. Governments in the Middle East and in North Africa and sub-Saharan Africa are autocratic, while governments in South Asia, in East Asia and the Pacific, and in eastern Europe and central Asia are semiautocratic. The Freedom House index of political rights and civil liberties tells a similar story. Although a Freedom House score of 2.8 places Latin America close to the "partly free" category, its citizens enjoy much higher levels of political rights and civil liberties than other citizens in the developing world. While FDI flows to eastern Europe and central Asia are greater than flows to Latin America, FDI flows to the region are equivalent to those found in East Asia and the Pacific and sub-Saharan Africa but significantly greater than flows to South Asia, the Middle East, and North Africa.

Given Latin America's levels of democracy, political freedoms, and ability to attract transnational corporate investment, extant theories of state repression predict that respect for human rights should be higher in this region than in the rest of the developing world. Yet the PTS and the CIRI indices both tell a different story. The PTS indicates that, along with South Asia, Latin America has the highest level of human rights repression. Similarly, the CIRI human rights index indicates that Latin America's level of repression is equivalent to repression levels among autocratic regimes in South Asia, sub-Saharan Africa, and the Middle East and North Africa and higher than repression levels among semiautocratic regimes in eastern Europe and central Asia and in East Asia and the Pacific.

The Andes and the Golden Triangle in Regional Perspective

Since the U.S. State Department defines Latin America's Andes region (Colombia, Peru, and Bolivia) and Southeast Asia's Golden Triangle (Myanmar, Laos, and Thailand) as major cocaine and opium trafficking corridors in the International Narcotics Control Report, the average democracy and repression scores for countries in these regions are shown in table 1.2.[3] As indicated by its Freedom House score, Latin America's Andes region enjoys higher levels of democracy and political freedoms than countries in the Golden Triangle, with the exception

Table 1.1. Average democracy and repression scores for Latin America and the developing world, 1980–2005

Measure	Latin America	Eastern Europe and central Asia	East Asia and Pacific	South Asia	Sub-Saharan Africa	Middle East and North Africa
Theoretical determinants of repression						
Polity index	6.0	2.4	1.2	0.5	−2.0	−4.9
Freedom House index	2.8	4.0	4.0	5.0	5.0	5.5
Foreign direct investment	3.0	4.0	3.1	1.0	3.0	1.4
Measures of repression						
Political Terror Scale index	3.0	2.4	2.3	3.3	2.7	2.8
Cingranelli–Richards (CIRI) human rights index	4.2	5.1	5.0	4.0	4.4	4.0
U.S. drug enforcement						
Counternarcotic aid flows (US$)	$28.7 million	$0.64 million	$2.6 million	$7.7 million	$0.36 million	$2.9 million

of Thailand. However, as a consolidated democracy, Colombia has the highest level of repression, as indicated by both the PTS and CIRI indices, significantly higher than those found in Myanmar's military dictatorship and the autocratic regime in Laos.

While citizens in Bolivia's consolidated democracy enjoy higher levels of political freedoms than citizens of Myanmar, Laos and Thailand, they face a level of repression equivalent to that of Thailand's or Laos's autocratic government. The level of political freedom in Peru's semidemocracy is equivalent to that of Thailand and is significantly higher than in Myanmar and Laos, and yet Peru has levels of repression equivalent Thailand's or Myanmar's military regime and significantly higher than Laos's autocratic government.

In recent years, the paradox of Latin America's democracy and human rights has given rise to a series of anthropological inquiries that focus on how the lived experience of ordinary people who reside in violent democracies affects the quality of citizenship (Arias and Goldstein 2010; Calderia 2000; Holston 2009). This literature conceptualizes democracies in Latin America as

Table 1.2. Average democracy and repression scores for illicit-drug-producing countries, 1980–2005

Measure	Latin America's Andes			Southeast Asia's Golden Triangle		
	Colombia	Peru	Bolivia	Myanmar	Laos	Thailand
Theoretical determinants of repression						
Polity index	8.0	5.4	8.0	−7.0	−5.0	6.0
Freedom House index	3.2	3.2	2.6	6.9	5.6	3.1
Measures of repression						
Political Terror Scale index	5.0	4.0	3.0	4.0	3.4	3.0
CIRI human rights index	0.8	2.1	5.3	2.0	5.0	5.0
U.S. drug enforcement						
Counternarcotic aid flows (US$)	$158.7 million	$46.8 million	$42.7 million	$3.7 million	$3.1 million	$5.1 million

disjunctive and incomplete when violence and human rights violation erode citizen security (Caldeira and Holston 1999; Holston 2008, 311). In this regard, O'Donnell (1993, 1361) argued that "even a political definition of democracy should not neglect posing the question of the extent to which citizenship is really exercised in a given country." Goldstein (2012) argues that, when the rule of law is either absent or ineffective to provide citizen security, the response to citizen insecurity is vigilantism. This perspective highlights the fact that states in disjunctive democracies do not monopolize the use of violence; violence is also deployed by citizens in an effort to create security for themselves and their communities.

Another response to citizen insecurity is one in which citizens create their own self-defense groups, which can be integrated into the larger security apparatus of embedded corporatism. Declassified documents from the National Security Archives known, as *The Chiquita Papers*, show that in Colombia peasant organizations created this type of paramilitary group, called Convivir (translated as "living together"). Before it was disbanded in 1989, Convivir was institutionalized by the Colombian government and given training and military assistance to not only provide security for their communities but also to help clear rural areas of narcoguerrillas who would often demand "revolutionary taxes" from large landowners and American transnational corporations like Chiquita and Dole. Chiquita provided security payments to Convivir to provide intelligence on the movements of narcoguerrillas. Senior officers in the Colombian

Graph 1.1. Per-capita GDP and Gini coefficients for Latin America and the developing world, 1980–2005. *Source*: World Bank 2016.

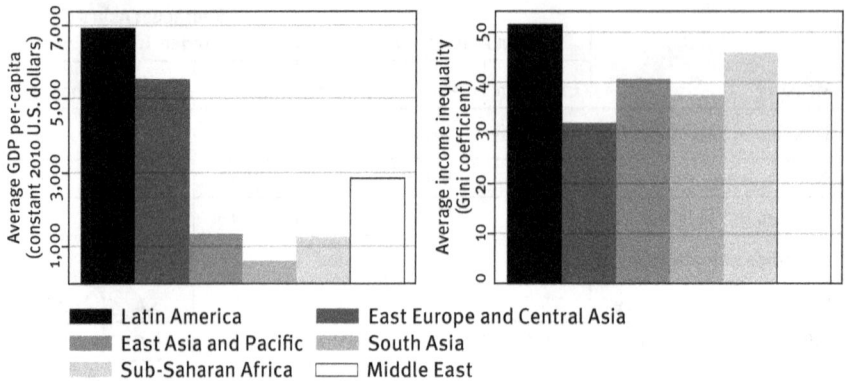

Latin America
East Asia and Pacific
Sub-Saharan Africa
East Europe and Central Asia
South Asia
Middle East

military and Álvaro Uribe, then governor of the Department of Antioquia, established a *convivir* organization in Urabá—the hub of Chiquita's operations in Colombia. In return, Chiquita made substantial campaign donations to Uribe, which were instrumental in his successful bid for the presidency in 2002 (Evans 2011). In this case, citizen insecurity was formalized into paramilitarism (as discussed in chapters 5 and 6) and was integrated into the larger security architecture of embedded corporatism where international cooperation of state and nonstate agents are vital to the realization of the objectives of the regime.

Graph 1.1 shows that per-capita GDP in Latin America during democratization's third wave was significantly higher than in the rest of the developing world. And yet, in terms of income inequities, Latin America is significantly more unequal relative to the rest of the developing world. What, then, explains Latin America's human rights and democratization paradox? How can democracy's third wave coexist with state repression? And why are some consolidated democracies in Latin America more repressive than consolidated autocracies in the developing world? How can the wealthiest region in the developing world also have higher levels of income inequality than other regions of the developing world?

In this book I argue that the paradox of democratization and human rights in Latin America stems from the fact that the region is the epicenter of the U.S. drug war.[4] As table 1.1 indicates, Latin America receives larger allocations of U.S. counternarcotic aid than any other region in the developing world. Table 1.2 shows that counternarcotic aid flows to the Andes are significantly higher than aid flows to the Golden Triangle. Latin America's paradox is symptomatic of U.S. drug enforcement aid flows that finance a drug war driven and shaped

Graph 1.2. Prison populations of the United States and seven autocracies, 2013.
Source: Walmsley 2013.

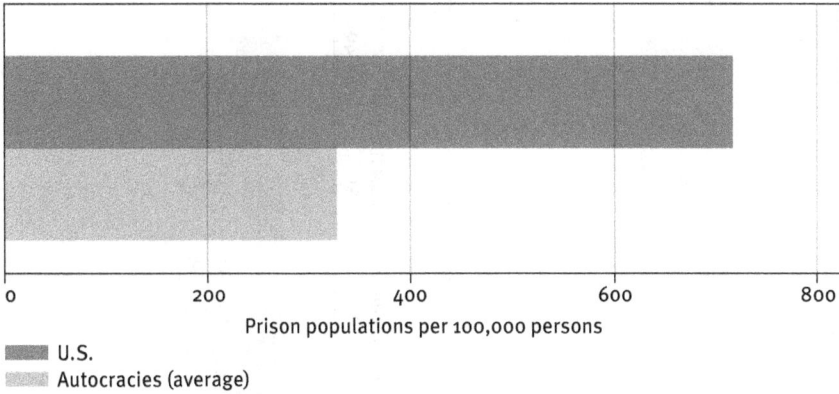

Prison populations per 100,000 persons

- U.S.
- Autocracies (average)

by the policy preference of embedded corporatism, in which human rights repression, the establishment of illiberal democratic governments, and income inequality have become the unintended pathological consequence of embedded corporatism's drive to accumulate capital.

The Paradox of Democracy in the United States

The United States is regarded as the undisputed leader of the free world. Its democratic creed is enshrined in constitutional guarantees such as the Bill of Rights, the separation of powers, the openness of the institutions of government, the administration of free elections, and the protection of individual civil liberties. In all quantifiable measures of democracy, such as the Polity index and the Freedom House index of political rights and civil liberties, the United States exceeds all other countries, yet it also leads the world in the number of its citizens that are incarcerated. According to the Sentencing Project, there are 2.2 million people in U.S. prisons and jails. This represents a 500 percent increase over the last forty years. It is widely accepted that it is the laws and policies of the criminal justice system and not increases in crime that explain this phenomenon (Sentencing Project 2017). Graph 1.2 shows that the rate of mass incarceration in the United States is significantly higher than the combined prison populations of Russia, China, Iran, Saudi Arabia, Syria, Cuba, and Vietnam—seven autocratic countries with an average Polity score of −6. In consequence, the number of disenfranchised individuals in the United States has increased from an estimated 1.7 million in 1976 to 6.1 million in 2016 (Sentencing Project 2016).

Graph 1.3. Per-capita GDP and Gini coefficients for the United States and OECD countries, 1960–2016. *Source*: World Bank 2016.

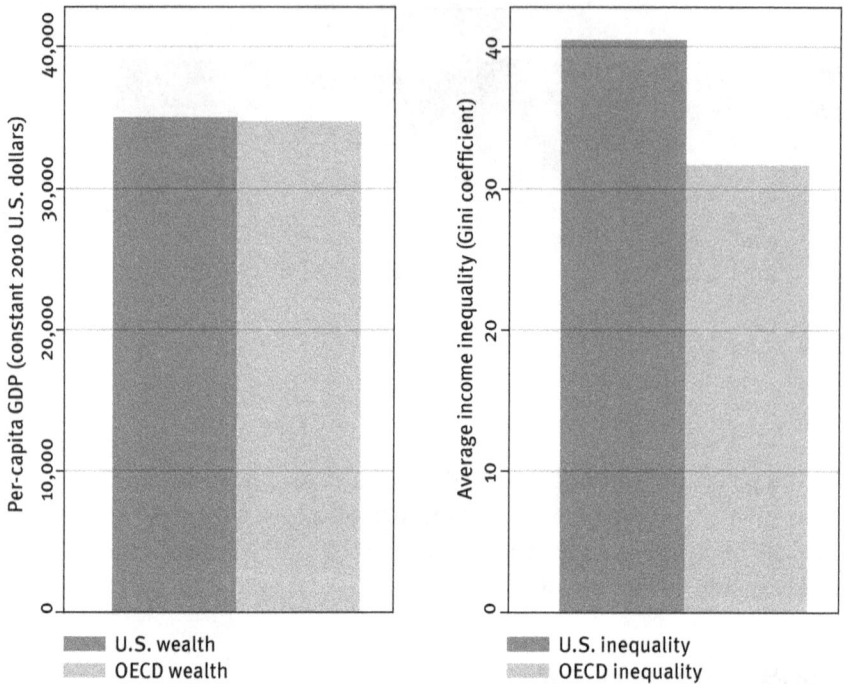

Graph 1.3 shows that from 1960 to 2016 the average per-capita GDP in the United States was equivalent to the average combined wealth of the other OECD countries. And yet, in terms of income inequality, as measured by the Gini coefficient, the United States has higher levels relative to the combined inequities of its OECD counterparts.

What explains the paradox of democracy in the United States? How can the world's leader of democracy and freedom be also the leader of mass incarceration, where 6.1 million people are disenfranchised from its democratic process? How can one of the world's wealthiest countries have consistently higher levels of income inequality than other wealthy countries? And more important, what is the connection between mass incarceration and growing income inequality in the United States? In this book I argue that the paradox of democracy in the United States is a product of the operations of the embedded corporatist drug enforcement regime, where widening class disparities along with mass incarceration have become the unintended pathological consequences of capital accumulation.

In essence, the paradox of human rights and democracy in the Americas, along with widening class cleavages, is the product of the natural operation of the embedded corporatist drug enforcement regime. I empirically demonstrate in chapter 8 that the drug war produces income inequities throughout the Americas. In Latin America, this is done through the repression of the rights of workers. In the United States, this is done through mass incarceration, as well as through budgetary priorities that privilege drug enforcement over social programs that were once ladders of upward mobility for the working class and the poor. In this sense, the United States and Latin America are conjoined twins since the pathologies that plague their democracies stem from their active participation in a drug enforcement regime where the norms of corporate capitalism are embedded.

As far as the United States is concerned, there are scholars who would challenge this argument on grounds that it ignores the role that race plays in U.S. drug enforcement and mass incarceration. In their view, racism is what drives the drug war in the United States (Hari 2015; Alexander 2012; Lusane 1991; Tonry 2011). Scholars who write in this tradition argue that racial discrimination is seen in the ways in which the policies of the criminal justice system and the implementation of drug enforcement unfairly target African American and Hispanic communities more than it does whites, even though drug use is the same across all racial categories. There is no denying that racial bias is intertwined with the operations of the criminal justice system and the ways in which drug enforcement is used in the mass incarceration of people of color. However, while racial bias is necessary for explaining the drug war's effect on mass incarceration, it is not sufficient to explain the operations of the larger embedded corporatist regime, which drives drug enforcement.

The racial bias thesis by itself does not explain why, in response to the heroine epidemic that ravaged the African America community in the 1970s, three of the nation's ten African American lawmakers voted in favor of Nixon's Comprehensive Drug Abuse and Prevention Act (P.L. 91-513), the first major piece of federal legislation to establish the rules of the war on drugs. Senator Edward Brooke from Massachusetts, Representative Shirley Chisolm from New York, and Robert Nix Sr. from Pennsylvania supported the measure. The racial bias thesis does not explain why in response to the crack epidemic, a decade later, black church leaders, prominent members of the African American middle class, and the CBC (Murch 2015) supported the Anti-Drug Abuse Act of 1988 (P.L. 100-690). Sixteen of the nineteen African American members of the House cosponsored that bill, which established a 100-to-1 disparity in the punishment for crack cocaine, the drug of choice in the African American community, compared with the more expensive powdered form of the drug, which was largely consumed by whites. The bill toughened prohibition against drug trafficking by adding the death penalty in certain instances and created the Office of National Drug Control Policy, which established, for the first time, the so-called drug czar. After President Reagan signed the bill into law, representative Charles B. Rangel, former chair of the CBC and then chairman of the House Select Committee on Narcotics Abuse and Control, praised the law, especially the provision that established the office of the drug czar, noting that "now Congress and the American people will know who is in charge of dealing with the nation's drug crisis, because this individual will be responsible full time for developing and coordinating all aspect of our war on drugs" (Johnson 1988). The racial bias thesis fails to explain why African American lawmakers supported the Clinton administration's Violent Crime and Law Enforcement Act of 1994 (H.R. 3355) that established the "three strikes and you're out" sentencing rules, expanded the death penalty for drug trafficking crimes, and eliminated federal funding for inmate education programs. The law also allocated US$9.8 billion in federal funds for the construction of state prisons nationwide. The racial bias thesis also does not explain why Eric Holder, the first African American attorney general, initially opposed efforts to decriminalize drugs and downscale the war on drugs.

In *The New Jim Crow* Michelle Alexander (2012, 210) argues that "the fact that some black people endorse harsh responses to crime is best understood as a form of complicity with mass incarceration—not support for it." The CBC, the middle-class-orientated National Urban League, African American church, and the Nation of Islam would hardly constitute "some black people"—they represent the backbone of the political, economic, and religious leadership of the African American community. Nevertheless, whether African American leaders were complicit with robust counternarcotic legislation or directly supported such legislation, they were ultimately in agreement with the operations of the embedded corporatist drug enforcement regime. In response to the heroine and crack epidemics, African American leaders provided consensus for the Nixon-, Reagan-, and Clinton-era drug war laws as a way to restore stability to communities plagued by drug addicts and terrorized by drug-dealing gangs. But robust drug enforcement was also seen as a vehicle to attract corporate investment into their communities, to spur urban economic growth and development, which facilitated the problems now associated with gentrification of the inner cities.

Notwithstanding the limitations of the racial bias thesis, it should be acknowledged that, once the drug war's pathology of mass incarceration became glaringly evident by the late 1990s, many African American church leaders and African American members of Congress, and even Eric Holder, who once supported robust drug enforcement, supported major reforms to the drug war and its sentencing laws. But even if the calls for drug war reform were implemented, they would only strengthen the regime's domestic consensus and the legitimacy of its operations (discussed in chapter 9) and would have little if any impact in changing the underlying prohibitive operations of embedded corporatism. The drug war is about providing both human security and the security of the market. It is the intersectionality of security and capital that underscores the nature of embedded corporatism where race, class, and capital accumulation are interwoven into the operational fabric of the drug enforcement regime.

The Methodological Structure of the Book

In this book I empirically demonstrate how the various actors of the embedded corporatist regime influence drug enforcement policy, in two ways: by case study analyses of the congressional deliberations of Plan Colombia and the Mérida Initiative, which represent two of the largest American drug enforcement initiatives in the developing world; and by econometric estimators that analyze cross-national panel data for thirty-three corporations and eighty counternarcotic-aid-recipient countries in Latin America and the Caribbean, the Middle East and North Africa, sub-Saharan Africa, Asia, and Eurasia and eastern Europe, during 2003–12.

The pathological effects of the embedded corporatist drug war on Latin America's human rights and democracy were discovered by using a series of advanced econometric estimators that also analyze cross-national panel data for thirty-one countries from Latin America and the Caribbean during 1978–2012. Finally, I supplement substantive and illustrative examples of various aspects of the theoretical argument by drawing on declassified U.S. government documents, as well as secondary sources, that chronicle the pathologies of the embedded corporatist drug war in the Americas. The drug war's pathological effects on the quality of democracy in the United States were discovered by using various econometric estimators that analyze the causal mechanisms of how corporate congressional lobbying for domestic drug enforcement is related to income inequality and mass incarceration, and how mass incarceration, in turn, is related to both income inequality and corporate capital accumulation.

The Organizational Structure of the Book

The analyses in this book are presented in eight chapters, divided into two parts. The question that the chapters in part 1 address is, How do the actors in the embedded corporatist regime shape drug enforcement decision making?

Since answering this question requires analyzing the domestic political process of the regime, I draw on theories of the state in advanced capitalist societies to generate competing hypotheses that are empirically tested. Armed with these theories, chapter 2 provides case study analyses of the deliberations that led to congressional funding for Plan Colombia and the Mérida Initiative. These analyses illustrate how American corporations not only shape the militarization of drug enforcement but also drive perennial increases in the federal government's drug war budget. These analyses also illustrate why civil society groups such as the AFL-CIO and human rights organizations failed in their attempts to block congressional funding for the drug war initiatives in Colombia and Mexico. The case study analyses also highlight why the CBC supported funding for the drug war initiatives in Colombia and Mexico and how they helped build drug enforcement cooperation with Afro-Colombian leaders and leaders from the Caribbean. Chapter 3 extends the analysis of chapter 2 by providing a comprehensive analysis of institutional theories of states' decision-making processes and applies these theories to explain U.S. drug enforcement policy. In addition, an econometric analysis of U.S. drug enforcement aid flows determines whether the dominance of corporations and the relative weakness of labor unions and human rights organizations seen in congressional deliberations on Plan Colombia and the Mérida Initiative are generalizable to countries beyond Colombia and Mexico. Chapter 4 provides an analysis of elite theories of the state and their application to U.S. drug enforcement policy. Since Plan Colombia and the Mérida Initiative demonstrate that corporate elite networks also influence congressional funding for drug enforcement aid, the chapter employs an econometric analysis of U.S. drug enforcement aid flows to ascertain if corporate elites' influence in shaping drug enforcement policy is also generalizable to countries beyond the region.

The chapters in part 2 analyze the unintended effects of the embedded corporatist regime on human rights repression, democratization, and income inequality in the Americas. Building on the arguments made in part 1, chapter 5 considers the ways in which U.S. drug enforcement aid facilitates American FDI in Latin America and how the process of drug-war-induced capital penetration of the region creates the conditions that facilitate human rights repression. Chapter 6 provides an econometric analysis of the various components of the theoretical argument developed in chapter 5. Chapter 7 shows that the policies of the drug enforcement regime have contributed to the creation of a "drug-war national security state" in Latin America whose modus operandi is antithetical to liberal democratic norms and practices. Chapter 8 examines the various causal mechanisms through which the drug enforcement regime produces income inequality throughout the Americas. Chapter 9 concludes by examining the endurance of the drug enforcement regime and why it is difficult to dismantle even when it fails to realize its raison d'être. In developing this argument the chapter acknowledges that, while the Obama administration's "safe harbor" policy has changed federal domestic marijuana policy by choosing not to prosecute marijuana offenses in states that have legalized marijuana—which represents a major policy shift from past administrations—the administration continued enforcement policies overseas that encouraged the prosecution of marijuana and other drugs and in this respect facilitated the endurance of the drug enforcement regime. The chapter discusses the continuity of the overseas drug enforcement policies of the Obama and Trump administrations within the context of critiquing the ways in which the forty-eight-year-old drug war has failed to slow the flow of illicit drugs into the United States. The chapter shows how the endurance of the regime is in part due to the competing nature of drug policy reforms promoted by various U.S. civil society organizations and a number of Latin American governments, which undermine the ability to galvanize domestic and international support around a cohesive policy alternative to the prohibition norm of the existing regime. The chapter concludes by examining existing drug policy reforms, such as decriminalization and legalization, and shows their limits in addressing the pathological effects of the corporatist drug enforcement regime.

PART 1

Embedded Corporatism and the
Making of U.S. Drug Enforcement

CHAPTER 2

Drug War Profiteers

U.S. Drug Enforcement Decision Making
and Plan Colombia and the Mérida Initiative

To say that the war on drugs has failed is not understanding something. It is true that for 40 years, the war on drugs has failed in its
stated objectives. Everyone knows that prevention and treatment is
the most efficient way to address the drug problem, and that foreign
operations are the most inefficient way. One has to wonder just what
is in the minds of the planners given the amount of evidence that
what they are trying to achieve doesn't work. . . . The drug war has
not failed. . . . Its consequences are intentional both within the United
States and in the hemisphere.—**Noam Chomsky,** 2012

The puzzle of the four-decade-long drug war, first declared by President Nixon
in 1971, is this: Why do American policy makers continue to increase funding
for a drug war that has failed to realize its objectives, and how does this per-
sistent failure justify implementing with even greater vigor more of the same
policies? Further, why do they consistently give greater priority to reducing the
supply of illicit narcotics from foreign countries than reducing demand in the
United States? While numerous policy analysts have consistently documented
the various policy failures of the drug war (Currie 1993; Duke and Gross 1993;
Kleiman 1992; Bertram et al. 1996, 9–11), it is resilient in its persistence.

As I sought a solution to this puzzle, I was motivated by Noam Chomsky's
skepticism about the so-called failure of American drug enforcement, but I dis-
agreed with his assertion about the "planners" of the drug war and that the drug
war's "consequences are intentional both within the United States and in the
hemisphere" (*La Jornada* 2012). American drug enforcement decision making
is not simply an artifact of the machinations of the political planners in the U.S.
government; more important, these planners are part of a larger corporatist

drug enforcement regime where American corporations play an instrumental role in shaping the policies of the drug war and where the consequences of the policy choices of the regime, as discussed in later chapters, are unintentional. In this chapter, I draw on theories of the state to highlight the role that corporate capital, and its political allies, plays in shaping the federal government's budgetary allocations for drug enforcement. The chapter highlights how corporate influence shapes the pattern of the drug war's strategy, how these strategies justify the provision of large government contracts to corporate members of the regime, how drug enforcement foreign aid is used to provide security for American oil companies that operate in Latin America, and how that aid is also used to market the defense industry's military hardware to countries in the region for the purpose of executing the war on drugs.

American policy makers have openly admitted the drug war's failure. In response to a question by a reporter from the Associated Press in Mexico City, Obama's drug czar Gil Kerlikowske conceded the drug war's failure, noting that, "in the grand scheme, it has not been successful. . . . Forty years later, the concern about drugs and drug problems [in the United States] is, if anything, magnified, intensified" (Fox News 2010). Former U.S. secretary of state and presidential candidate Hillary Clinton was even more forthcoming in her admission of the drug war's failure. While traveling to Mexico in March 2009, she stated that U.S. efforts to ban drugs such as cocaine had clearly failed and that it was unfair to blame Mexico for its drug cartel problem. She went on to say, "I feel very strongly we have a co-responsibility. . . . Our insatiable demand for illegal drugs fuels the drug trade. Our inability to prevent weapons from being illegally smuggled across the border to arm these criminals causes the death of police officers, soldiers and civilians" (*Telegraph* 2009).

The drug czar's and Secretary Clinton's admissions of failure are certainly correct. Since President's Nixon's 1971 declaration of the drug war, America's drug problems have intensified due to the drug war's failure to achieve the central component of its policy objectives; namely, reducing the availability of illicit drugs in the United States (Domestic Council Drug Abuse Task Force 1975, 50). While the cocaine market has shrunk in recent years, the United States continues to be the largest consumer of South American cocaine, accounting for 36 percent of international consumption (UNODC 2011).

The U.S. drug war in Afghanistan has become a US$7.6 billion debacle. According to the 2014 report by the SIGAR, Afghan poppy cultivation reached an all-time high in 2013 and continued to increase in 2014, despite the expenditure of over US$7 billion in counternarcotics operations (Sopko 2014, 1). At the conclusion of his report to former secretary of state John Kerry, former defense secretary Chuck Hagel, former attorney general Eric Holder, and former USAID administrator Rajiv Shah, the former SIGAR John Sopko recommended: "Given the severity of the opium problem and its potential to undermine U.S. objectives in Afghanistan, I strongly suggest that your departments consider the trends in opium cultivation and the effectiveness of past counter-narcotics efforts when planning future initiatives" (3). With the failure of U.S. drug enforcement in Afghanistan, heroin availability and use has increased in the United States, replacing synthetic opioids as the drug of choice among opioid drug users (UNODC 2014).

Even while acknowledging the drug war's failure, former drug czar Kerli-kowske suggested that forty years may not be enough time for drug enforcement expenditures to produce positive results (Fox News 2010). Likewise, while Secretary Clinton acknowledged that it is America's insatiable demand for illegal drugs that fuels the drug trade and associated violence in Mexico, her policy recommendations said nothing about controlling demand in the United States but instead rationalized continuing the drug war by providing Mexico with advanced military hardware to eliminate the cartels and reduce the supply of drugs to the United States (*Telegraph* 2009). In her meeting with the Associated Press in Mexico City, Janet Napolitano, former DHS secretary, provided another rationale for the continued funding of the drug war when she affirmed that "this is something that is worth fighting for because drug addiction is about fighting for somebody's life . . . and in Mexico they are literally fighting for lives as well from the violence standpoint—the stakes are too high to let go" (Fox News 2010).

As my previous research demonstrates, the U.S.-funded drug war is partly responsible for increasing violence as well as increasing every conceivable measure of crime throughout Latin America (Bartilow and Eom 2009a; Bartilow 2007). American counternarcotics operations such as drug interdiction and the arrest or killing of drug kingpins disrupt illicit markets and create power vacuums within and between rival drug cartels. This in turn has led to an escalation of violence, which undermines governance and regional stability (Bartilow and Eom 2009a; Bartilow 2007). In this context, official justifications of continued support for the drug war may reflect the pathological addiction of the drug war's policy makers in that they are, in the words of Brian Loveman (2006, 14, 33), "addicted to failure," unable to fathom, or at least not admit publicly, that drug-related violence is partly a consequence of the U.S.-sponsored drug war (Bartilow and Eom 2009a; Bartilow 2007).

However, American policy makers, and the larger drug enforcement regime to which they belong, are addicted less to the drug war's policy failures than to its budgetary successes, in the sense that they have been largely successful in their perennial ability to increase the drug war's budget. In terms of both absolute dollars and percentages, the Obama administration increased supply-reduction spending, such as drug interdiction and crop eradication, to record levels. In 2010, US$10 billion of the administration's US$15.5 billion drug enforcement budget, or approximately 60 percent, was devoted to supply-reduction strategies, not demand-reduction strategies such as drug prevention (Fox News 2010). Even though the United States remains the largest international consumer of illicit narcotics, the 2014 drug enforcement budget was increased to US$25 billion and contained the same 3-to-2 ratio of supply- to demand-reduction funding, which continues the spending patterns of previous administrations (White House Office of National Drug Control Policy 2013, 2014, 2016). The Trump administration's 2018 budget continued the Obama-era drug enforcement spending patterns by increasing drug interdiction expenditures by 9.9 percent and cutting drug prevention expenditures by 11.1 percent relative to levels in 2017 (White House Office of National Drug Control Policy 2017, 8, 13).

If the justification for continued increases in the drug war's budget is to save lives, as some American policy makers claim, then why prioritize supply-reduction over demand-reduction strategies when existing empirical studies have shown that for every dollar invested in demand-reduction strategies such as drug treatment, taxpayers save US$7.46 in societal costs? Such a reduction would cost fifteen times more to achieve with the dominant supply-reduction expenditures of previous U.S. administrations (Miron and Waldock 2010). If the rationale for the drug war's continued budgetary expansion is to save lives, then larger proportions of the budget should be allocated for reducing the demand for illicit drugs in the United States.

In the sections that follow, I argue that the addiction to the drug war has less to do with saving lives and more to do with the drug enforcement regime's ability to underwrite the capital accumulation of American corporations. By tying drug policy to U.S. security, and by maintaining the narrative that America's foreign enemies, whether they are "drug cartels," "narcoterrorists," or "narco-insurgent" groups, are somehow responsible for America's drug problems (Ryan 1998, 2001), I show how the drug war justifies the drug enforcement regime's intervention and co-optation of Latin America and other regions around the world to reduce the supply of drugs to the United States. In the process, it creates a security context that drives the perennial increase in the federal government's drug war budget, in which large government contracts that finance the execution of the war become the feeding trough through which corporate revenues are sustained. A full discussion of theories of the state is provided in chapters 3 and 4; in the following section I engage in a summary discussion of these theories to provide a theoretical framework for analyzing the ways in which American corporate power, within the embedded corporatist regime, drives the pattern of drug enforcement and the budgetary expenditures that financed Plan Colombia and the Mérida Initiative—two of the most heavily funded and operationally extensive drug war initiatives in the developing world.

Theories of the State and U.S. Drug Enforcement

Pluralist, radical, and instrumental theories of the state offer competing explanations of the institutional power of domestic interest groups in shaping public policy. Writing in the pluralist tradition, Dahl (1961) argues that in agrarian societies political resources for influencing public officials were characterized by cumulative inequalities. In these societies "when one individual was much better off than another in one resource, such as wealth, he was usually better off in almost every other resource" (85). However, as societies modernize through industrialization, new social forces or interest groups are created. While inequalities of political resources persist, they are no longer cumulative but dispersed throughout the political system. Different interest groups may have different political resources for influencing public officials, and individuals and interest groups who have an advantage in their access to one kind of resource are disadvantaged in their access to others kinds of resources. Moreover, no political resource will dominate all other resources in influencing all the political decisions of the state. Interest groups who seek to influence government officials may find that one type of political resource maybe effective in one issue area but ineffective in other issue areas, and no one interest group is entirely weak in political resources. Since the dispersion of unequal political resources ensures that the policy preference of no interest group will dominate the political sphere, the state's role becomes one of mediating interest group competition in pluralist polities.

From 1971 to 2019, the drug war and U.S. drug policy have spurred a cottage industry of different advocacy groups whose preferences range from maintaining the current prohibition regime to completely dismantling it. Other groups advocate changing the drug war's strategy from a focus on law enforcement to one on public health, in which demand-reduction strategies such as drug treatment and prevention are given greater emphasis. In pluralist polities, if the state simply mediates interest group competition where different interest groups have different political resources, and where no one interest group is entirely weak or strong in any issue area, then there should be significant variation in U.S. drug policy in terms of both its strategies and its budgetary allocations. Instead, over the past forty-eight years we have seen successive budgetary expansions that continually emphasize supply- over demand-reduction strategies. In essence, since at least 1971—some scholars would look to the 1909

Shanghai Conference, when the United States took the lead in constructing an international drug enforcement regime to control the opium trade (Ryan 2001; Plouffe 2011)—prohibitionist preferences have dominated all aspects of U.S. drug policy decision making.

What explains this dominance of prohibitionism in U.S. drug policy? Radical theorists answer the question by emphasizing the ways in which corporations dominate public policy decision making. In *Politics and Markets* (1977), Charles E. Lindblom argues that private corporations in pluralist democracies occupy a privileged position within government, which allows them to shape public policy in ways that serve corporate objectives. Lindblom argues that the major decisions affecting national welfare in terms of access to jobs, domestic prices, the production of goods and services, economic growth, the standard of living, the level of technology, the external balance of payments, the organizational pattern of work, the location of industry, market structure, resource allocation, and all aspects of production and distribution are made by private corporations, not governments. In their capacity to make policy decisions that have national consequences, corporate executives take on the characteristics of government officials, not interest groups, as pluralist theory would have us believe. In a general sense, corporate executives have become public officials who perform public functions but are removed from the polyarchal controls of democracy (Lindblom 1977, 171–72).

Corporations' privileged position in government is rooted in their ability to command economic activity. In democratic polities, forms of economic distress like inflation and recession can destroy governments' credibility and legitimacy. Since elections have become referendums about how elected government officials, not corporate executives, manage the economy, government officials cannot afford the political cost of being indifferent to corporations. Therefore, they find it necessary to offer corporate inducements such as tax cuts and government contracts to stimulate investment and maintain employment and growth. Corporations maintain their privileged position in government at the expense of the position that labor unions and other civil society organizations have in the state. Labor unions are locked into an inferior position because they do not command large areas of economic life, and because their livelihood is dependent on earned wages for work they can perform without inducements from the state (Lindblom 1977, 198–99). If corporations owe their privileged position in the state to government inducements, then the dominance of prohibitionist preferences in U.S. drug policy would seem to be a natural reflection of their class interest.

According to instrumental theorists, the dominance of prohibitionist preferences in U.S. drug policy is explained not by the privileged position that corporations occupy within the state but by the dominance that the power elite exerts over the state. Instrumental theories of the state posit that a power elite exercises direct dominance of the policy-making apparatus of the state, and those public policies that have national or international consequences reflect the enduring preferences of the power elite. Writing in this tradition, C. Wright Mills (1956), G. William Domhoff (1967), and Michael Useem (1984) challenge pluralist and radical theories on the basis that they emphasize the middle strata of political activity and ignore the upper strata or the power elite who are responsible for the life-and-death decisions of the state. Pluralist and radical theories of the state, according to Mills (1956, 245–46), represent the "noisy content" of congressional, state-government, and interest-group politics. Policy decisions at this level are specialized, represent the interests of the middle class, and play a limited role in major decisions that have national consequences. The lower strata comprise individuals who are depoliticized, unorganized, apathetic, and politically invisible at the national level and are removed from the decision-making process. Since international drug control has been an important objective of U.S. foreign policy for some time, instrumental theories of the state suggest that the forty-eight-year dominance of prohibitionist tendencies in U.S. drug policy is a reflection of the shared interests of America's power elite.

But how well do theories of the state explain the contemporary policies of the embedded corporatist drug enforcement regime? To what extent did political pluralism, the institutional dominance of private corporations, or the preferences of a dominant elite shape the policy dynamics of Plan Colombia and the Mérida Initiative? In the next section, I answer these questions by applying the propositions of these theories to analyzing the policy making process behind Plan Colombia and the Mérida Initiative.

Plan Colombia

With his election in May 1998, the new Colombian president Andrés Pastrana Arango called for a "Marshall Plan" to increase economic development, introduce much-needed social reform, and enter into peace negotiations with FARC and ELN guerrillas (Friedman 2011). By aiming to reduce poverty, the plan sought to eliminate the guerrilla movements' raison d'être, which would also eliminate the need for paramilitary groups who emerged as a reaction to the guerrilla insurgency. The Pastrana plan called for manual eradication of coca and poppy crops, with guerrilla cooperation, disarmament, demobilization, rehabilitation programs, and economic development programs to compensate for the loss of drug money (Guaqueta 2005, 49).

To finance this plan the government began negotiations for a US$1.6 billion loan from the Inter-American Development Bank and received a pledge of US$750 million from the European Union (International Consortium of Investigative Journalists 2001b; Friedman 2011). President Pastrana also sought financial support from the U.S. government, but since the plan was centered on economic development, poverty alleviation, and negotiations with the guerrilla insurgency, this support would not be easy to attain. The Republican-dominated congress was hostile to development-oriented foreign aid, which made it highly unlikely that the Pastrana plan, as it was conceived, would receive congressional support. After a series of consultations with Clinton administration officials from the U.S. State, Defense, and Justice Departments, as well as senior GOP congressional leaders (Williams and Jawahar 2003, 167), the Pastrana plan morphed from a Colombian social reform program into a U.S.-funded military counternarcotic operation, which is known today as Plan Colombia.

As the perception grew that Plan Colombia was now a Washington-constructed military operation, the European Parliament in February 2001 voted 474 to 1 against participating in it and withdrew its multimillion-dollar pledge (International Consortium of Investigative Journalists 2001b; Nagle 2002, 2). Plan Colombia made Colombia the third largest recipient of U.S. military aid after Israel and Egypt (Richani 2005). In 2000, the U.S. Congress approved US$1.3 billion for Colombia and neighboring Andean countries, and of the $860 million allocated for Colombia, three-quarters financed counternarcotic and military operations (Haugaard et al. 2011).

The deliberations that surrounded Plan Colombia gave the appearance of the workings of pluralist politics in the making. While support for the drug enforcement initiative came from the Congressional Black Caucus (CBC), a significant number of human rights and policy advocacy groups, as well as some Republican and Democratic members of Congress, opposed Plan Colombia's funding and its drug enforcement strategy.

The Congressional Black Caucus and Plan Colombia

The CBC at the time, led by Representative Jim Clyburn (D-SC), supported Plan Colombia. However, as discussed in the subsequent sections, the CBC's support was not transactional in the sense that CBC members were recipients of campaign contributions from the corporations who stood to benefit from congressional approval of Plan Colombia, nor did they represent voting districts where these corporations operated manufacturing facilities that generated jobs. If transactional politics did not explain the CBC's support for Plan Colombia, then what explained the pattern of their voting behavior that led them to support the drug war in Colombia?

The CBC's support for Plan Colombia was politically strategic. The CBC support for overseas drug enforcement was salient to the long-standing interests of its members who, since the heroine epidemic in the black community in the 1960s, promoted tough domestic drug enforcement in urban cities that they represent. Their support for Plan Colombia was part of a larger domestic agenda to rid their voting districts of drug abuse and violent drug gangs and, in the process, pave the way for corporate investment, economic development, and job creation.

The strategic nature of the CBC's support for Plan Colombia was also shaped by the interests of its members to partner with the Afro-diaspora in Colombia and use drug enforcement as a conduit for facilitating economic development in Afro-Colombian communities. The CBC formed a strategic alliance with black Colombian law makers such as then vice president of the Colombia House of Representatives Dr. Edgar Torres and then governor of Chocó Dr. Julio lbarguen. During congressional deliberations on Plan Colombia, these law makers traveled to Washington to lobby members of the CBC not only to support the initiative but also, more important, to shift some resources from Plan Colombia's drug enforcement budget to promote economic development in the Chocó Department, which had the lowest per-capita government or private sector investment in health, education, and infrastructure in Colombia. To this end, the CBC introduced resolutions (House Concurrent Resolution 175) to shift greater resources from the military for economic development purposes in Afro-Colombian communities such as the Chocó Department (U.S. House of Representatives 2005, 16212–13). Although the interests of the CBC, as demonstrated in the subsequent sections, were quite different from the interests of the corporations that lobbied for congressional approval of Plan Colombia, the strategic nature of their interests converged with corporate interests in ways that ultimately facilitated overseas drug enforcement and corporate capital accumulation.

Human Rights Opposition and the U.S. Congress

In the ensuing years after Plan Colombia's approval, in their attempt to kill congressional and presidential support for the initiative Amnesty International and Human Rights Watch documented its links to widespread human rights repression committed by the Colombian military and paramilitary forces (Amnesty International 2010; Human Rights Watch 2000, 2005). Human rights think tanks such as the Fellowship of Reconciliation and the U.S. Office on Colombia also provided evidence of the pervasive links between U.S. military assistance under Plan Colombia and human rights repression. The Fellowship of Reconciliation reported that the Colombian army carried out over 3,000 extrajudicial killings within the first two years of Plan Colombia (Fellowship of Reconciliation 2010; Amnesty International and Fellowship of Reconciliation 2008). In addition, in its 2013 report, the U.N. high commissioner for human rights documented systematic and widespread cases of "false positives" whereby civilians were killed by Colombian security forces and later classified as guerrillas for the purpose of concealing mass murder (U.N. General Assembly 2013, 15–17).

Plan Colombia was also opposed on the grounds that it was ineffective in dealing with America's drug problem. In their attempt to influence policy makers, independent researchers provided evidence that demand-reduction strategies like drug treatment are approximately twenty times more effective than Plan Colombia's emphasis on supply-reduction strategies like drug interdiction and crop eradication (Reuter and Caulkins 1995; Mejia 2012).

Plan Colombia received strong criticism and opposition in the U.S. Senate Caucus on International Narcotics Control, the Senate Committee on Foreign Affairs, and the Senate and House Appropriations Committees. Some Democrats and Republicans in the U.S. House doubted Plan Colombia's ability to defeat the guerrillas and stop the drug trade. Representative John Mica (R-FL) referred to the initiative as " schizophrenic," and his colleague Benjamin Gilman (R-NY) saw the initiative as another Vietnam (Nagle 2002). Representative David Obey (D-WI) also saw Plan Colombia as a prelude to another protracted Vietnam War (Nagle 2002, 5) and attempted to cut $55 million from the budget of the Defense Department, the agency responsible for implementing the initiative (Seraffino 2001). Other House representatives also attempted to defund Plan Colombia: Nancy Pelosi (D-CA) attempted to remove US$51 million that was earmarked for the Defense Department, while James Ramstad (R-MN) attempted to remove US$1.7 billion from the counternarcotic budget (Seraffino 2001).

In the Senate, Plan Colombia faced additional opposition. The Senate Appropriations Committee considered cutting US$338 million, which was allowed by the House for the purchase of U.S.-made Bell Huey helicopters to be used in Plan Colombia's drug enforcement and military operations (Seraffino 2001). Paul Wellstone (D-MN) and Thomas Gorton (R-WA) attempted to reduce Plan Colombia's budget to just US$200 million (Seraffino 2001). However, all of the attempts by these Republican and Democratic members of Congress to defund Plan Colombia ended in failure. In fact, by 2012 U.S. aid to Colombia exploded to US$8 billion (Beittel 2012) and continued to rise even with increasing federal budgetary and fiscal constraints, reaching over US$9 billion in 2014 (Isacson 2014).

Corporate Power and the U.S. Congress

Plan Colombia raises an interesting paradox. Given the level of opposition to the initiative from human rights advocacy groups, the U.N. High Commission for Human Rights, the European Union, and some Republicans and Democrats in the House and Senate, how do we explain the perennial expansion of Plan Colombia's budget with no changes in its supply-reduction strategy of drug enforcement? If pluralist theory is correct, then the level of opposition would force legislative compromise and over time produce variation in the initiative's budgetary allocations, as well as modifications in the pattern of its drug enforcement strategy. However, since Plan Colombia's inception in 2000, neither has occurred. As Mills (1956, 9) reminds us, "By the powerful we mean, of course, those who are able to realize their will, even if others resist it." In the budgetary deliberations for Plan Colombia, American corporations with substantial investments in Colombia and those who stood to make millions of dollars through the initiative's government contracts won legislative support for the initiative by buying access to Congress. In the process, they ultimately realized their will even when others resisted it.

The perennial budgetary increases for Plan Colombia and the dominance of supply reduction in its drug enforcement strategies can be explained in terms of radical and instrumental theories of the state. As predicted by radical theorists, the "privileged position" that business occupies in the U.S. government reflected the ways in which corporations influenced congressional support for Plan Colombia. This form of influence was exercised through well-funded lobbies and through corporations' ability to generate jobs by manufacturing the military hardware required by Plan Colombia in the voting districts of those members of Congress who may have voted against the bill. As predicted by instrumental theorists, corporate power in shaping the passage of Plan Colombia was also reflected in corporate dominance over the state through a revolving door between corporate elites and government bureaucracies and through the provision of campaign financing to incumbent members of Congress, which Domhoff (1983) calls the corporate candidate selection process.

American corporations lobbied collectively for the passage of Plan Colombia through the USCBP, which on its website defines itself as "a non-profit 501(c)(6) business organization comprised of U.S. companies with over $12 billion dollars of investment collectively in Colombia. The USCBP represents a broad coalition of industries representing companies in the energy, pharmaceutical, consumer products, financial services, technology, insurance, defense/security, and transportation industries" (U.S.-Colombia Business Partnership 1996). In testimonies before the House Committee on Foreign Affairs and in congressional hearings, USCBP's executive director William Burlew urged the U.S. Congress and President Clinton to "fully fund" the bill for the purpose of creating a "sustainable democracy" in Colombia (Ripley 2014, 19). Although companies lobbied collectively through the USCBP, they also lobbied individually. Among the oil and energy companies, Occidental Petroleum took the lead in lobbying Congress.

In 1983, Occidental discovered oil in Colombia's second largest oil field, in Caño Limón. Since ELN guerrilla attacks on the pipeline and the kidnapping and murder of company employees threatened the company's operations, Occidental lobbied to obtain greater security for its pipeline. In his testimony before Congress, Occidental vice president Lawrence Meriage urged law makers to expand the scope of Plan Colombia beyond providing security for the company's oil facility in the Putumayo region by extending security along the Colombian-Venezuelan border where Occidental operates the Caño Limón oil field, and in the Catatumbo region where the oil field is operated by BP-Amoco (Mondragon 2002, 131; Richani 2005). He stated:

> We understand that the package [Plan Colombia] put forward by the [Clinton] administration targets aid for counter-narcotics activities in the southern part of the country in the Putumayo region near the Ecuadorian border. We have two concerns relating to this approach. It does not address the explosion of coca cultivation that is occurring in the other parts of the country; particularly the northern regions where the bulk of existing and prospective oil development take place. Moreover, a massive concentration of force in the Putumayo region could ultimately lead to narco-guerrilla forces [FARC] to move operations further south into Ecuador. Occidental also has operations in Ecuador some 40 kilometers from the Colombian border. Recent kidnappings near our area of operation in Ecuador have been attributed to the FARC. I would urge you to consider support of counter-narcotics operations in the northern regions as well as the south. This will help augment security for oil development operations, which as noted earlier, are fundamental to the success of Plan Colombia. (Meriage 2000, 1)

Between 1996 and 2000, Occidental spent US$8.6 million lobbying the U.S. government to provide military aid to Colombia. During the 2000 election cycle alone the company spent approximately US$551,000, with 60 percent going to Republican candidates and political action committees. J. Roger Hirl, the CEO of Occidental Chemical Subsidiary, raised more than US$100,000 in support of George W. Bush's election (Montero and Whalen 2002). After Bush's victory, Occidental oil's lobbying efforts paid dividends in 2002. The Bush administration increased the scope of Plan Colombia's counternarcotics operations to include the northern as well as the southern regions of Colombia and allocated US$98 million for the protection of Occidental's five-hundred-mile Caño Limón pipeline (Richani 2005, 132).

To improve the security of their investments, other oil companies that operated in Colombia, such as ExxonMobil, Texaco, and Britain's BP Amoco, collectively spent US$13 million to lobby Congress in the years prior to Plan Colombia's approval (Aviles 2006, 131). In 2000, ExxonMobil operated El Cerrejón Zona Norte, a thirty-mile-long coal mine near the Venezuelan border, an area that has experienced frequent insurgent activity. In 2002, FARC guerrillas in El Cerrejón Zona Norte bombed and derailed a twenty-car train transporting coal to the Caribbean export terminal (Montero and Whalen 2002).

Drummond is a coal-mining company whose headquarters are in Alabama. With the depletion of Alabama's coal reserves, the company moved its operations to Colombia in 1994 and now operates the second largest coal mine in La Loma. Drummond's La Loma facility has been a frequent target of insurgent attacks and kidnapping of the company's workers for ransom (Montero and Whalen 2002). Drummond, like the oil and energy companies, lobbied for congressional support for Plan Colombia to strengthen the security of its coal mining facilities (Hodges 2000).

The Enron Corporation, now bankrupt and discredited, played a major role in the neoliberal privatization reforms that pervaded Latin America throughout the 1990s. During the deliberations about Plan Colombia, the company owned 43 percent of Promigas, the Colombian gas distribution company, and attempted to secure contracts from the Colombian government to export gas into Panama. Enron also had financial interests in other Andean countries, and since 1994 the company had acquired 30 percent of the Bolivian-Brazilian gas pipeline (CorpWatch 2002). While Enron's gas distribution company in Colombia and its Bolivian-Brazilian gas pipeline were never attacked by FARC guerrillas, the company lobbied Congress in favor of Plan Colombia so that the increased military presence would provide greater security for its investments in Colombia. In lobbying for Plan Colombia, the argument of Jeff Loving, then spokesperson for the General Public Utilities Corporation, underscored the electrical power company's concern regarding the security of its investment in Colombia. "It all comes down to security: Let's face it, if there weren't rebels there wouldn't be a security problem" (quoted in International Consortium of Investigative Journalists 2001b).

While America's oil and energy corporations lobbied for Plan Colombia's passage to provide security for their oil and mining operations, corporations that comprised America's military-industrial complex stood to reap windfall profits from Plan Colombia's military approach to drug enforcement—an approach that emphasized reducing the production and supply of Colombian cocaine to U.S. markets through interdiction, coca eradication and fumigation, and counterinsurgency warfare against the guerrilla movement. In pushing for substantial increases in drug interdiction, Lockheed Martin lobbied members of Congress to include in the bill orders to purchase its P-3 Orion radar planes, used to track drug shipments, and its K-Max helicopters, which are used for drug interdiction (Isikoff 2000).

However, facing resistance from congressional liberal democrats, Lockheed Martin commissioned Democratic pollster Mark Mellman, whose polling data showed that the American public were inclined to blame Democrats for the rise in drug use and that this issue could be the party's Achilles heel in the presidential elections in 2000. The Mellman poll concluded that 56 percent of the electorate in the 2000 election cycle supported a US$2 billion increase in funding for tracking planes to be flown in drug producing areas around the world (Isikoff 2000; Williams and Jawahar 2003, 167). By manufacturing the Democratic Party's so-called electoral Achilles heel, Lockheed Martin ultimately garnered support for Plan Colombia from congressional liberal democrats. Representative Nancy Pelosi, who initially attempted to defund Plan Colombia, now argued, "No one wants to seem soft on drugs. . . . The White House and Congress don't ever want to be seen as not doing all they can to stop the flow of drugs—even if it's the wrong policy" (quoted in Collier 2000).

United Technologies Corporation, which has its headquarters in Hartford, Connecticut, and manufactures the Black Hawk helicopter, lobbied key congressional members who were uncommitted in their support for Plan Colombia. Between 1996 and 2000, United Technologies was one of the top contributors to federal election campaigns, providing approximately US$2 million (Center for Responsive Politics 2000b), and spent over US$8 million lobbying Congress (Center for Responsive Politics 2000a). One such member of Congress was Senator Christopher Dodd of Connecticut, a leading skeptic and opponent of U.S. military intervention in Latin America (Crandall 2008b).

The members of Connecticut's liberal congressional delegation were persuaded by the needs of their constituency, in addition to United Technologies' campaign contributions to senators like Dodd and Joseph Lieberman. Since United Technologies manufactures the Blackhawk helicopter in Connecticut, the corporation is a major employer in the senator's home state. Dodd became a strong supporter of Plan Colombia and introduced an amendment that reinstated the Blackhawk, which the Appropriations Committee had removed from the Senate's version of the bill. Although Dodd's amendment failed, it nevertheless attempted to ensure that funding for the Blackhawk would not fall below US$110 million (Vacius and Isacson 2000; Seraffino 2001).

Textron Corporation manufactures the Bell Huey II helicopter, which is used under Plan Colombia for the aerial fumigation of coca (International Consortium of Investigative Journalists 2001a). Like United Technologies, Textron was one of the top contributors to federal election campaigns, providing US$1.8 million between 1996 and 2000 (Center for Responsive Politics 2000b). To ensure that the Huey II helicopter would be included in the Plan Colombia aid package, the corporation lobbied twenty-two Texas House representatives from congressional districts where the helicopters would be manufactured. Since General Electric manufactures parts for the Blackhawk and Huey helicopters, that company also lobbied for the passage of Plan Colombia, as did Northrop Grumman and Raytheon (International Consortium of Investigative Journalists 2001b). Northrop Grumman provides maintenance, logistics, and operational support for U.S. counternarcotics drug surveillance systems throughout Latin America. Raytheon produces the Paveway-2 laser-guided bombs, which increase the Colombian air force's accuracy in strikes against insurgent targets (Brownfield 2007), and provided over US$2.2 million in federal campaign contributions between 1995 and 2000, exceeding contributions form Northrop Grumman, United Technologies, and Textron (Aviles 2006).

According to the Stockholm International Peace Research Institute's arms transfer database, under Plan Colombia from 2000 to 2013 Textron sold 134 helicopters, 12 turret tanks, 13 light transport aircraft, 14 Cessna light aircraft, and 39 wheeled armored personnel carriers; United Technologies sold 81 Blackhawk helicopters; Lockheed Martin sold 5 K-Max helicopters, 3 multimission surveillance radars, and 1 Hercules transport plane; General Electric sold 3 turboprop engines; Boeing sold 6 Scan Eagle Drones and 2 transport aircraft; and Raytheon sold 180 Paveway-2 laser guided bombs (Stockholm International Peace Research Institute 2015).

Defense contractors were not the only corporations that lobbied for Plan Colombia. Deer and Company and Caterpillar Inc., producers of engines and earth-moving equipment, also lobbied for Plan Colombia, spending a total of US$1.8 million in lobbying expenditures during the final year of the bill's congressional deliberation. Even before the conception of Plan Colombia, both companies lobbied the U.S. government to increase trade and foreign aid to Colombia, as they stood to benefit from the sale of military and nonmilitary equipment to the Colombian government and local businesses (International Consortium of Investigative Journalists 2001b).

American agrochemical corporation Monsanto and the private military contractor DynCorp also lobbied heavily for Plan Colombia and received government contracts to implement the initiative's coca crop eradication program. Monsanto produces Roundup SL and Roundup Ultra, herbicides used in Plan Colombia's coca fumigation operations (Mugge 2005). DynCorp is contracted to conduct the fumigation spraying of coca fields across Colombia and in 2002 earned 96 percent of its profits from U.S. government contracts for conducting security operations in foreign countries like Colombia (Johnson 2003).

Corporate Elite Networks and the Clinton Administration

The power that corporations exercise over the state is further revealed through the elite networks that connected Cabinet members of the Clinton administration and the corporations that profited from Plan Colombia. These networks are consistent with the theoretical predictions of instrumental theories of the state. Cabinet members who had ongoing business relationships with corporations with financial interests in the passage of Plan Colombia influenced the administration's adoption of a militarized pattern of drug enforcement in Colombia. This pattern of drug enforcement justified increasing the security of fixed corporate assets in Colombia's oil and energy sectors.

The Gore family has had a long business relationship with Occidental Petroleum. As figure 2.1 illustrates, Al Gore Sr. was the company's attorney, a former board member, and the personal friend of Armand Hammer, then president of Occidental. Throughout his term as vice president in the Clinton administration, Al Gore held Occidental Petroleum stock that was valued at US$500,000, and in 1998 he engineered the sale to Occidental of drilling rights in central California's Elk Hills—federally owned land that was protected by the Endangered Species Act and was the sacred burial site and home of the Kitanemuk Indians. Gore recommended that Elk Hills be sold as part of the Clinton administration's "Reinventing Government" National Performance Review Program, which attempted to reduce the size of the federal government through greater privatization. Elk Hills was sold to Occidental Petroleum for US$3.65 billion (Bell 2013; Mesler 2000; Montero and Whalen 2002; Department of Energy 1998).

With the sale of Elk Hills, Occidental's stock value increased by 10 percent, which, as Gore later disclosed, increased the value of his stock in the company to approximately US$1 million (Bell 2013; Mesler 2000; Department of Energy 1998; Montero and Whalen 2002).[1] Given the long-standing business relationship between the Gore family and Occidental Petroleum, Vice-President Gore had a financial interest in the administration's adoption of a militarized strategy of drug enforcement in Colombia to provide greater security to Occidental's oil pipelines against ELN and FARC guerrilla attacks, which could

Figure 2.1. The elite network of Plan Colombia

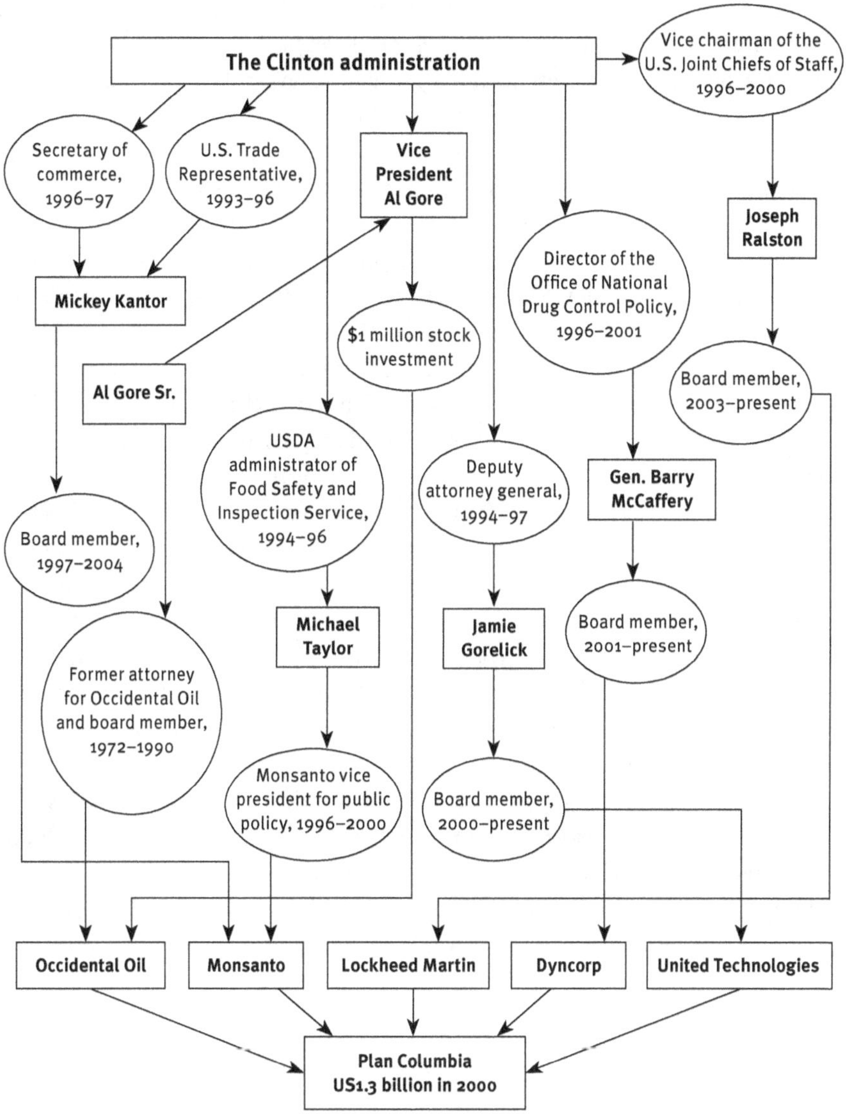

potentially affect the company's stock value. More important, figure 2.1 depicts the elite networks through which corporate Washington insiders and influence peddlers shaped the underlying drug control strategy and the accompanying military procurement for Plan Colombia.

These corporate elite networks tied the Clinton administration to corporations that had a financial interest in the congressional approval of Plan

Colombia and thus help explain the perennial budgetary increases for the drug war initiative and the dominance of its militarized drug enforcement strategy. Corporate board members who held cabinet-level positions in the Clinton administration had easy access to the administration's policy makers to lobby for government contracts and secure business opportunities through Plan Colombia (Shorrock 2008, 127). For example, after retiring from the U.S. Air Force, Joseph Ralston, the vice-chairman of the Joint Chiefs of Staff, became a member of the board of directors at Lockheed Martin (Lockheed Martin Corporation 2014, 100). After leaving the position of director of the Office of National Drug Policy, General Barry McCaffery became a member of the board of directors at DynCorp (DynCorp International Inc. 2009). After leaving her position as deputy attorney general, Jamie Gorelick became a member of the board of directors at United Technologies (United Technologies Corporation 2013, 82). After leaving his position as U.S. trade representative and secretary of commerce, Mickey Cantor became a member of the board of directors at Monsanto, receiving approximately US$100,000 per year for serving on the board, where he opened doors to the White House and pressed the administration to promote the company's financial interests in Europe and in Latin America (St. Clair 1999; Pelaez and Schmidt 2004, 234). Prior to working in the Clinton administration, Michael Taylor was an attorney for Monsanto, and after leaving his position as USDA administrator of food safety and Inspection, the company hired him as vice president for public policy (St. Clair 1999).

While radical and instrumental theories of the state, relative to political pluralism, provide stronger explanations of the decision-making process of the drug enforcement regime's deliberations over Plan Colombia, how well do they explain the Mérida Initiative, Mexico's version of Plan Colombia? And although the CBC supported Plan Colombia, did the strategic nature of their congressional voting pattern also shape their support for the Mérida Initiative?

The Mérida Initiative

Before Mérida: The Security and Prosperity Partnership

The Mérida Initiative had its origins in the Security and Prosperity Partnership of North America (SPP). Born in the post-9/11 era of the War on Terror, the SPP was launched at a meeting of U.S. president George W. Bush, Mexico's president Vicente Fox, and Canadian prime minister Paul Martin in Waco, Texas, in 2005. The SPP was not a treaty and was never submitted to the U.S., Canadian, and Mexican legislatures for ratification, but it sought to drive the integration of the three nations into a single political, economic, and security bloc. As an extension of NAFTA, the SPP sought to link NAFTA's economic integration to U.S. security objectives and institutionalize the role of transnational corporations in the privatization and deregulation of markets across the Western Hemisphere (Koulish 2010, 159).

The SPP created the North American Competitiveness Council (NACC), which served as an official trinational working group composed of representatives from Lockheed Martin, ExxonMobil, Chevron, General Electric, Ford Motor Company, General Motors, Wal-Mart Stores, Proctor and Gamble, FedEx, United Parcel Service, Whirlpool Corp, Merck, and Hewlett Packard. The NACC's recommendations supported policies that gave corporations greater access to markets and natural resources in the region, while the SPP security accords specified greater border control, military and police training, modernization of equipment, and the adoption of new technologies for prosecuting the wars on terror and drugs (Lendman 2010).

The Mérida Initiative represented the security component of the SPP. In October 2007, the United States and Mexico announced a US$1.6 billion aid package to fight the drug war in Mexico and Central America, covering fiscal years 2008–10. As proposed by the SPP, the primary objectives of the Mérida Initiative included breaking the power of drug cartels and the supply of drugs to U.S. markets; strengthening border, air, and maritime controls in Mexico and Central America and improving judicial capacity and controlling gang activity in the region (U.S. Government Accountability Office 2010, 5–6). The Mérida Initiative became the largest foreign aid package to the Western Hemisphere since Plan Colombia and formalized a new kind of security partnership among the United States, Mexico, and Central America, originated by the SPP (Seelke 2009, 2).

Like with Plan Colombia, pluralist politics characterized congressional deliberations of the Mérida Initiative, with support coming from the CBC as well as strong opposition from labor unions and human rights groups. In the end, it was corporate power and not political pluralism that determined the bill's passage and its budgetary allocations.

The Congressional Black Caucus and the Mérida Initiative

The strategic nature of the CBC's voting behavior, which shaped their congressional support for Plan Colombia, also shaped their support for the Mérida Initiative. In 2008, CBC Representative Yvette Clarke (D-NY) introduced H.R. 1504 that supported the Third Border Initiative, launched in 2001 by the Bush administration to deepen cooperation between the United States and Caribbean countries on issues such as HIV/AIDS, disaster mitigation, and law enforcement (White House 2001). The Third Border Initiative is based on the ideological belief that, behind Canada and Mexico, the Caribbean region is a sea-based border of the United States. Given this context, the CBC's introduction of H.R. 1504 called for increased cooperation between the United States and Caribbean governments to combat illicit drug trafficking (U.S. House of Representatives 2008).

The CBC's introduction of H.R. 1504 established the pretext for its members' support of H.R. 2410 of the Foreign Relations Authorization Act of 2009, which expanded the scope of drug enforcement cooperation with Mexico by adding the Caribbean Community, or CARICOM, to the Mérida Initiative. In their support for H.R. 2410, the CBC added the Shirley Chisholm Educational Exchange Program Authorization (SCEEPA) to the bill, which allowed students and scholars from the Caribbean to study in the United States in areas that support the labor market and economic developmental needs of CARICOM countries. Representative Clarke, a descendant of Jamaican immigrants and who represented a constituency that included many residents from the Caribbean diaspora and one that is often afflicted by the challenges of drug abuse, argued that the SCEEPA provisions to the bill will "promote security and education with the CARICOM region, fostering social and economic development abroad and keeping us safe here at home" (U.S. House of Representatives 2009, 15120).

Once again, it was not transactional politics but the strategic interests of the CBC that led its members to support the Mérida Initiative. The CBC's support was driven by the fact that its members sought to build foreign partnerships to prosecute the drug war overseas in order to stem the flow of drug trafficking and drug abuse in their voting districts and, in consequence, facilitate security, capital accumulation, and economic development within their constituencies, as well as in Latin American and Caribbean countries that are members of the corporatist drug enforcement regime.

Labor Unions and Human Rights Opposition

Opposition to the Bush administration's proposed Mérida Initiative came from labor unions and human rights organizations. Labor organizations such as the AFL-CIO and U.S. steelworkers wrote letters to the chair of the House Foreign Affairs Committee, Howard Berman (D-CA), and to Congressman William Delahunt (D-MA), chair of the Subcommittee on International Organizations, Human Rights, and Oversight, detailing their opposition and urging them to reject the Bush administration's request for Mérida funding (Friends of Brad Will 2008). Human rights advocacy organizations such as the Washington Office on Latin America (WOLA) argued that, in the absence of policies that reduce the demand for drugs and the easy access to guns in the United States, two factors that fuel drug violence in Mexico and Central America, Mérida, like its predecessor Plan Colombia, would fail to reduce the flow of drugs to the United States (Washington Office on Latin America 2008; House Committee on Foreign Affairs 2008, 30–32).

In 2010, the House Committee on Foreign Affairs held hearings on the progress and future of the Mérida Initiative. During these hearings, a coalition of U.S., Mexican, and international human rights organizations urged U.S. secretary of state Hillary Clinton to withhold funding until the Mexican government made concrete and measurable improvements on human rights issues, as required by the Mérida Initiative. The human rights organizations cited the U.S. State Department's 2009 Human Rights Report for Mexico, which identified human rights violations that included "unlawful killings by security forces; kidnappings; physical abuse . . . arbitrary arrests and detention; corruption, inefficiency, and [a] lack of transparency that engendered impunity within the judicial system; [and] confessions coerced through torture [as well as] multiple reports of forced disappearances by the army and police. Most occurred in the course of [executing the Mérida Initiative's] anticrime operations" (U.S. Department of State 2009a).

Writing to President Obama in 2015, the Human Rights Watch also cited the State Department's annual Human Rights Report for Mexico, which showed that these violations had in fact increased since 2009, and called on the president to withhold Mérida funding. Ignoring the State Department's reports of repression in Mexico, the Obama administration repeatedly certified that Mexico has met the Mérida human rights requirements (Vivanco 2015), and Congress has consistently increased funding for the Mérida Initiative. Mérida's initial funding of US$1.6 billion rose to US$2.4 billion in 2014, and the Obama administration requested an addition US$115 million in Mérida funding for 2015 (Seelke and Finklea 2014, 7). Opposition to the Mérida Initiative from human rights organizations and labor unions, bolstered by the State Department's own reports of state-sponsored repression in Mexico, did not convince American policy makers to reduce funding for the drug war initiative; in fact, they increased it. What explained Congress's disregard for the Mexican government's human rights practices when increasing funding for the Mérida Initiative?

Corporate Power, the U.S. Congress, and the Sacrifice of Human Rights

As with Plan Colombia, the perennial budgetary increases for the Mérida Initiative and the dominance of its militarized drug-control enforcement strategies can be explained in terms of radical and instrumental theories of the state. Radical and instrumental theoretical predictions play out in the ways in which

American defense contractors influenced congressional support for Mérida through well-funded lobbies and via elite networks that tied the Bush administration to defense contractors that profited from congressional approval of the Mérida Initiative. As discussed in the next section, American corporations, especially those in the aerospace industry, who are major employers in the voting districts of some members of Congress also influenced congressional support for Mérida.

Since 9/11 what is referred to as a "full-body scanner" lobby has developed. Such corporations as American Science and Engineering (AS&E), Rapiscan, Smith Detection, and L3 Systems retained, respectively, Washington's K Street lobby firm Wexler and Walker, former Transportation Security Administration assistant administrator for policy Chad Wolf, the lobby firm Van Scoyoc Associates, and former senator Al D'Amato to lobby Congress to secure contracts for the federal deployment of screening and scanning technology to be used not only by the DHS and the Department of Defense but also for border and maritime security under the Mérida Initiative (Ridgeway 2010).

Old-fashioned congressional pork barrel politics to secure government contracts also explain the increase in Mérida funding despite the State Department's own reports of the Mexican government's consistent pattern of human rights repression in executing Mérida's anticrime operations (U.S. Department of State 2009). The Bush administration's original three-year Mérida Initiative that began in 2007 called for eight Bell BH-412 helicopters for the Mexican Army and Navy. However, the delivery of the Bell helicopters was severely delayed. American officials attributed the delay to an outmoded bureaucratic contracting system and the challenges of creating an infrastructure to deliver an aid package involving several federal agencies. However, the delay was also rooted in traditional pork barrel politics and budgetary earmarks to purchase specific military hardware to be used in Mérida's drug war (Booth and Fainaru 2009).

The Blackhawk helicopter, manufactured by United Technologies, was excluded from the Bush administration's original Mérida funding, and given the deteriorated international economic outlook for the aerospace industry in 2009, United Technologies was forced to implement an expanded restructuring program, which eliminated 11,600 jobs in its overseas subsidiaries (Goldman 2009) and 1,500 jobs in Connecticut (Manufacturing.Net 2009b). In addition, the company announced that an additional 2,000–3,000 jobs in Connecticut would be lost if the Defense Department canceled production of the F-22 fighter jet (Manufacturing.Net 2009a).

When Congress deliberated over supplemental funding for Mexico in 2009, Connecticut's congressional delegation, led again by Senator Lieberman (then chair of the Homeland Security Committee and a senior member of the Armed

Services Committee) and Senator Dodd, who served on the Foreign Relations Committee, were faced with job losses in Connecticut and the possibility of even more to come. With the support of the Obama administration, they sought ways to include in the bill funding to purchase Blackhawk helicopters in an effort to reduce these losses. To this end, Senator Lieberman held a congressional hearing in March 2009, where he raised the specter of Mexico's drug cartels as threats to U.S. national security to justify increasing Mérida funding to the Mexican government. He asserted that "the southern border has always been on our radar screen as an entry point for narcotics and human smugglers, and others who might threaten our homeland security . . . but the recent escalation of violence along the southern border demands our immediate attention. Ideally, we can eliminate the threats and provide the Mexican government with the support it needs to win this war against the drug cartels and other dangerous actors who threaten our national security" (U.S. Senate Committee on Homeland Security 2009). In consequence, in his supplemental budgetary request President Obama requested $66 million to purchase three Blackhawk helicopters. However, the House Appropriations Committee went beyond the president's request and allocated US$470 million to purchase not just Blackhawks but all military aircraft that could be armed (Bricker 2009).

The politics that surrounded the Mérida Initiative's supplemental budgetary process raises an intriguing question: Why would Congress and the Obama White House expand Mérida funding to purchase United Technologies' Blackhawk helicopters when the sale and delivery of Textron Corporation's Bell helicopters originally requested by the Bush administration was not implemented? The delay in the sale and delivery of the Bell helicopters allowed Congress to expand Mérida's drug war expenditures by pushing contracts to United Technologies—who was excluded from the Bush administration's original Mérida contracts—and other companies in the aerospace industry that were also plagued by the international economic recession (Bricker 2009). To ensure this outcome, during the deliberations for Mérida's supplemental funding, Congress included language in the Mexico section of the bill that explicitly exempted the US$470 million in new funds from human rights stipulations and reporting requirements. This was done for the sole purpose of expediting the sale and delivery of Blackhawks and other military aircraft to the Mexican government (Bricker 2009; Seelke 2010, 5–6). Not only did the profitability of the aerospace industry and the need to preserve jobs in some congressional districts increase Mérida's drug war expenditures, but also, more importantly, these considerations took precedence over human rights repression in Mexico.

The Stockholm International Peace Research Institute (2015) reported that from 2008 to 2013 the Mérida Initiative financed Textron Corporation's sale of two Cessna transport aircraft, valued at US$1.8 million, and eight Bell-412 helicopters for US$104 million; United Technologies' sale of six Blackhawk helicopters, each valued at US$21.3 million; Northrop Grumman's sale of four air-search radar systems for US$221 million; and Lockheed Martin's sale of two Hercules transport aircraft, each valued at US$120 million. This financing all occurred as human rights requirements were bypassed to expedite underwriting the aerospace and other defense contractors' capital accumulation and to provide "pork" to congressional districts.

In addition to the aerospace industry, Mérida also financed BAE Systems' sale of twenty-six armored personnel carriers; General Motors' sale of twelve armored Suburbans; AS&E's sale of fifty-three Z Backscatter mobile X-ray vans for US$49 million; and Rapiscan system's sale of mobile X-ray screening facilities to detect contraband and illicit drugs in remote locations for US$14 million. Further, Mérida pushed contracts to Science Applications International Corporation (SAIC) and AS&E and financed Rapiscan's sale of twenty mobile Gamma Ray II trucks, which are used for interdicting contraband at Mexico's ports of entry, for US$40 million; L1 Identity Solutions' sale of biometric equipment; and Military Professional Resources Inc.'s training of military and police officers in Mexico and Central America (U.S. Government Accountability Office 2010, 8–9, 25; U.S. Embassy Mexico 2010, 4–5; 2012, 7).

Corporate Elite Networks and the Bush Administration

American corporate dominance in the federal government is also reflected in the elite networks between former Cabinet members of the Bush administration and the corporations that profited from the Mérida Initiative. These networks are consistent with the theoretical predictions of instrumental theories of the state. Figure 2.2 illustrates the elite networks through which corporate "influence peddlers" shaped the underlying drug control strategy and the accompanying military procurement for the Mérida Initiative. Corporate board members who held cabinet-level positions in the Bush administration had easy access to the administration's policy makers to lobby for government contracts and secure business opportunities through Mérida. For example, after leaving his position as CIA director, George Tenet was appointed to the board of directors at L-1 Identity Solutions, a corporation that received government contracts to provide biometric software and equipment used in the Mérida Initiative's drug war. L-1 technology is also used by the State Department and the DHS for U.S. passports, visas, driver's licenses, and transportation worker ID cards. In appointing Tenet to the board, Robert LaPenta, then chairman of the board and CEO of L-1, said, "We want the Board to contribute in a meaningful way to the success of the company. . . . George Tenet: a phone call [to the Federal

Figure 2.2. The elite network of the Mérida Initiative

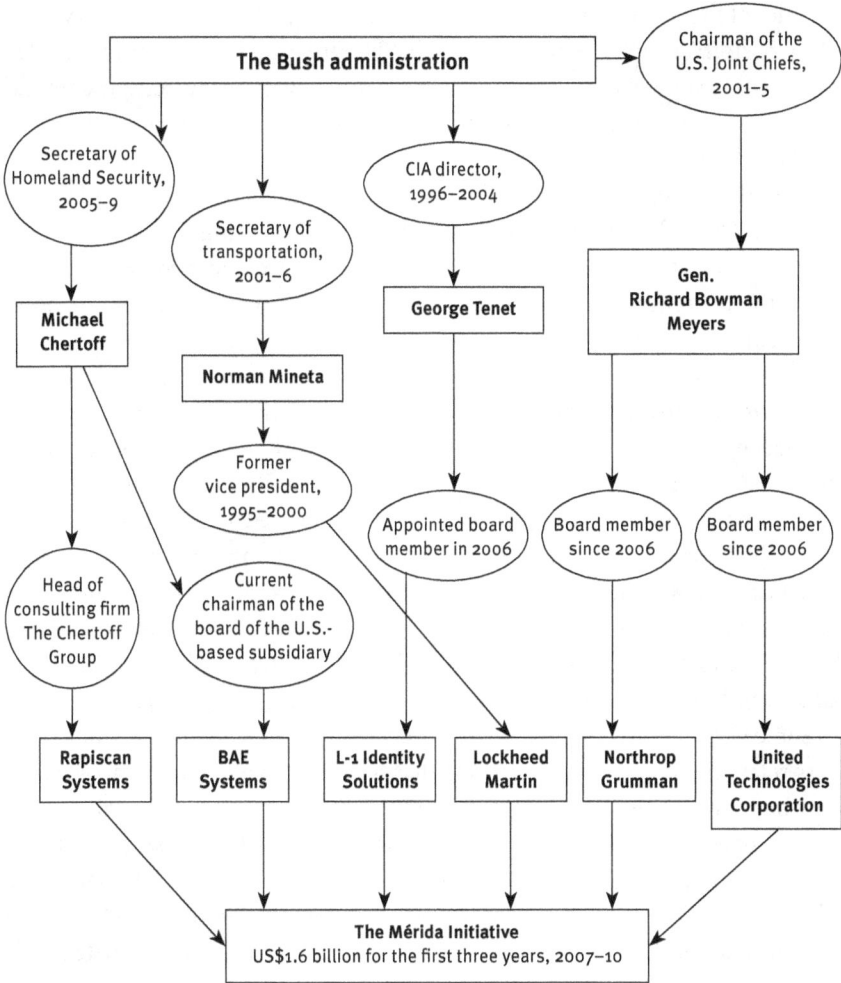

government] gets us in to see whoever we want" (Shorrock 2008, 127). Executive vice president for L-1 Communications Doni Fordyce said: "George has amazing experience. We're in the security business, right? So he's a tremendous asset" (Shorrock 2008, 128). In exchange for opening doors to the federal government, Tenet was provided with 80,000 shares of L-1 stock in 2006, which according to the Securities and Exchange Commission was worth more than US$1.5 million in 2007 when the company acquired Viisage, another biometric company, where Tenet was also a board member (Shorrock 2008, 128).

Michael Chertoff, former secretary of homeland security, is chairman and founder of the Chertoff Group, a security and risk management advisory firm. The Chertoff Group's clients have received lucrative government contracts due to the company's expertise and assistance in navigating the complex federal procurement bureaucracy. Rapiscan Systems, which received contracts under the Mérida Initiative to supply the Rapiscan 536 SV mobile X-ray screening facility to detect contraband and illicit drugs, was a client of the Chertoff Group in 2009. While the Chertoff Group has denied representing Rapiscan in communications with the U.S. government, Rapiscan secured US$118 million in government contracts for its technology between 2009 and 2010 (Baram 2010; Kane 2014).

The former secretary of homeland security is also the current chairman of the board for BAE Systems' U.S. board of directors (BAE Systems 2015). BAE Systems has received contracts under the Mérida Initiative to supply armored personnel carriers to the Mexican military.[2] General Richard Bowman Myers, former chairman of the U.S. Joint Chiefs, was appointed to the boards of directors at Northrup Grumman and United Technologies in 2006 (United Technologies Corporation 2013, 82; Northrop Grumman 2010, 90). Both companies received lucrative contracts under the Mérida Initiative to supply Blackhawk helicopters and air-search radar systems for, respectively, US$128 million and US$221 million (Stockholm International Peace Research Institute 2015).

Some Cabinet members of the Bush administration who had previous business relationships with corporations that profited from the Mérida Initiative may have also helped influence the administration's adoption of a militarized pattern of drug enforcement in Mexico. Norman Mineta, former secretary of transportation, was once a vice president for Lockheed Martin, the aerospace corporation that received $120 million for supplying Hercules transport aircraft under the Mérida Initiative (Stockholm International Peace Research Institute 2015).

Corporate elite networks thus tied the Clinton and Bush administrations to defense contractors that had huge financial stakes in the congressional approval of Plan Colombia and the Mérida Initiative. These networks exerted a powerful influence in adopting a militarized drug enforcement strategy, which in turn drove the perennial budgetary increases for the drug war initiatives in Colombia and Mexico.

Conclusion

Plan Colombia and the Mérida Initiative demonstrate the ways in which American corporations—the principal actors of the embedded corporatist regime—

shape drug enforcement decision making. Corporate lobbies, corporate financing of congressional elections, elite networks that connect corporations to the federal government, and the strategic support of the CBC for overseas drug enforcement function in concert to create a policy environment in which the drug enforcement regime facilitates the process of capital accumulation by ensuring the perennial increase in drug war funding even when "it's the wrong policy," as Representative Pelosi admitted (Collier 2000).

Is the corporatization of the drug enforcement regime's decision making generalizable to countries beyond Colombia and Mexico? In chapters 3 and 4 I answer this question via a large-sample statistical design that estimates the effects of the institutional and elite dimensions of corporate power on U.S. counter-narcotic aid flows to eighty countries from all regions of the developing world for which data are available.

CHAPTER 3

Beyond Colombia and Mérida

The Institutional Dimension of Corporate Power in the Drug Enforcement Regime

I am in this race to tell the corporate lobbyists that their days of setting the agenda in Washington are over. I have done more than any other candidate in this race to take on lobbyists—and won. They have not funded my campaign, they will not run my White House, and they will not drown out the voices of the American people when I am president.—U.S. presidential candidate **Barack Obama,** speech in Des Moines, Iowa, November 10, 2007

[The politicians] will never make America great again. They don't even have a chance. They're controlled fully—they're controlled fully by the lobbyists, by the donors, and by the special interests, fully. Yes, they control them. Hey, I have lobbyists. I have to tell you. I have lobbyists that can produce anything for me. They're great. But you know what? It won't happen. It won't happen. Because we have to stop doing things for some people, but for this country, it's destroying our country. We have to stop, and it has to stop now.—**Donald Trump,** U.S. presidential campaign announcement speech, June 16, 2015

Regardless of the different ideologies espoused by Barack Obama and Donald Trump as presidential candidates, both employed campaign rhetoric expressing disdain for corporate lobbyists and promised to banish them from making policy in their respective administrations. Despite the hyperbolic rhetoric of presidential campaigns, classic theories of the state (Miliband 1969, 1982; Poulantzas 1976, 1978; Lindblom 1977; Domhoff 1967, 1983, 1996; Mills 1956), as well as a growing body of contemporary academic research on the effects of corporate lobbies in the making of public policy (Waterhouse 2014; Drutman 2015; Gilens 2012; Katz 2015; Lessig 2012; Hula 1999), have collectively shown that corporate power not only is embedded within the economy and the structures of governance in American politics but is also firmly embedded in the institutional arrangements of the drug enforcement regime, which drives its decision making.

The case studies of Plan Colombia and the Mérida Initiative showed that the power of corporate congressional lobbies not only shaped the militarization of foreign drug enforcement but also drove the federal government's drug war expenditures. In consequence, large government contracts that finance the execution of the drug war became a feeding trough for the generation of corporate revenues. However, while these outcomes are consistent with the predictions of radical theories of drug enforcement, how generalizable are they beyond Colombia and Mexico? To what extent does the power of corporate lobbies that were instrumental in securing congressional funding for Plan Colombia and the Mérida Initiative also drive funding for the drug war in countries beyond Latin America? Labor unions and human rights organizations lobbied against the drug wars in Colombia and Mexico on grounds that both initiatives would lead to the repression of worker and human rights, but they failed to block congressional funding for drug enforcement in both countries. Will these organizations experience similar outcomes in their attempt to block drug war funding to countries beyond the region?

I use the large-sample statistical design of thirty-three corporations and eighty countries that were recipients of U.S. counternarcotic aid in the period 2003–12 to provide answers to these questions and test whether these outcomes are generalizable.[1] In answering these questions, this chapter is organized as follows. The following section discusses theories of congressional lobbying and provides an institutional analysis of the relative power of corporations and civil society organizations in shaping U.S. drug enforcement policy, and these theoretical discussions are used to generate hypotheses. The next section discusses the methodological design, which uses the Heckman selection estimator to correct for selection bias to model the decision-making process regarding counternarcotic aid disbursements. I then discuss the central variables used in these statistical models and conclude with a detailed discussion of the empirical findings.

Institutional Theories of State Decision Making

Radical Theories of Congressional Lobbies and Drug Enforcement

Radical theories of state decision making place emphasis on the institutional nature of corporate power, which is reflected in the ways in which corporate lobbies, relative to the lobbies of labor unions and other civil society organizations, dominate the legislative process. In *Lobbying America*, Benjamin C. Waterhouse (2014, 2–3) argues that the decline of liberal and progressive politics and the emergence and ultimate dominance of a corporate-oriented, neoliberal political culture embedded in America's structures of governance were not the product of economic crisis or the natural swing of the political pendulum but the result of deliberate efforts by American corporations and the political activities of their lobbies. By the mid-1970s corporate leaders from the U.S. Chamber of Commerce, the National Association of Manufacturers, and the Business Roundtable became the backbone of a powerful political coalition whose lobbyists played a vital role in stemming the tide of progressive legislation and significantly weakened organized labor and public interest groups. By the 1980s, the market-based economic solutions advanced by corporate lobbies profoundly changed public policy discourse on a wide range of issues pertaining to regulation, taxes, fiscal policy, school choice, and free trade, which ultimately culminated in NAFTA in 1994.

However, the historical narrative that supports the corporate politicization argument (Waterhouse 2014) says very little about the nature of corporate lobbies and the institutional environment in which corporate power is projected. In *The Business of America Is Lobbying*, Lee Drutman (2015, 3) fills this void. He argues that American corporations have ubiquitously inserted themselves into almost every facet of the policy-making process, which gives them a pervasive role in government and enables them to determine how public policy and, by extension, drug enforcement policy are made in Washington.

A number of elements account for the corporate infiltration of the legislative process. Chief among them are the lobbying expenditures of American corporations. These expenditures increased from US$1.82 billion in 2002 to US$3.31 billion in 2012, an increase seven times the estimated corporate lobbying expenditures of US$20 million in 1983 (Drutman 2015, 8; Reich 2007, 134). A total of 372 corporations reported lobbying expenditures of US$1 million in 2012, and the combined lobbying expenditures of another 3,587 corporations was US$1.84 billion, which is approximately 56 percent of all lobbying expenditures in 2012. If the lobbying expenditures of corporate trade associations and other businesses are included, the total combined lobbying expenditures would be US$2.57 billion, or 78 percent of all lobbying expenditures (Drutman 2015, 8–9).

Corporate lobbying expenditures are significantly larger than the lobbying expenditures of labor unions and other civil society organizations. While labor unions and other civil society organizations increased their lobbying expenditures from US$369 million and US$33.9 million, respectively, in 1998 to US$486 million and US$41.3 million in 2010, they still failed to keep pace with corporate lobbying expenditures. In fact, during 2011–12 the lobbying expenditures of labor unions and civil society groups, respectively, declined below their 1998 levels to US$45.6 million and US$29.7 million (Drutman 2015, 12). Corporate lobbyists outnumber lobbyists from other interest groups (Waterhouse 2014, 249), and relative to the lobbying expenditures of civil society groups, the sheer size of corporate lobbying expenditures allows American corporations to buy a disproportionate level of representation in Congress. Drutman (2015, 13) shows that the annual ratio of corporate lobbying expenditures to the combined lobbying expenditures of labor unions and other civil society groups increased every year since 1996, and in 2012 the ratio was 34 to 1. The substantive meaning of this ratio is that "if each dollar bought one calendar day of representation in a year [civil society organizations] . . . unions would have bought only a week-and-a-half of representation that business bought. Or if each dollar bought one minute of time in a typical eight-hour working day, [civil society organizations] would have bought just 14 minutes of time for every full eight-hour working day business interests purchased" (Drutman 2015, 13).

What are the political implications of the dominance of corporate lobbying expenditures? Drutman (2015, 33–42) argues that corporate lobbying expenditures buy access to congressional offices, which increasingly lack the institutional capacity to develop policy expertise on legislation that has become increasingly complex. To make policy, congressional offices now turn to corporate lobbyists, who provide the necessary technical expertise to draft legislation, develop its rationale, build political coalitions of cosponsors and supporters of legislation from inside and outside of government, and oversee the entire legislative process through which a bill becomes law. Another implication of the dominance of corporate lobbying expenditures is that, compared to civil society organizations, American corporations disproportionately shape the intellectual environment that informs the making of public policy. Corporate lobbying expenditures are used to fund think tank policy reports, academic research, panel discussions, advertising, and the placing of op-eds in newspapers, all for the purpose of saturating the intellectual environment with public policy arguments that are consistent with the perspectives of businesses.[2] Under these conditions, corporate preferences will likely inform policy makers' prior assumptions and shape how they frame and make policy decisions (Drutman 2015, 35–36).

Radical theories, as applied to U.S. drug enforcement policy making, explain why the lobbying efforts of American corporations had such a decisive advantage over the collective opposition of labor unions and human rights organizations in securing congressional support for Plan Colombia and the Mérida Initiative. Radical theories that emphasize the institutional nature of corporate power lend themselves to the following hypotheses:

Hypothesis 1a: Increases in corporate congressional lobbying expenditures will increase U.S. counternarcotic aid flows.

Hypothesis 1b: Increases in civil society congressional lobbying expenditures will have no effect on U.S. counternarcotic aid flows.

Pluralist Theories of Congressional Lobbies and Drug Enforcement

Dahl (1961) is often credited for advancing the theoretical propositions of political pluralism. However, these ideas actually originated with Small and Vincent (1894), who characterized society as composed of many interest groups in which no group can dominate the policy-making process and secure policy outcomes that advance only their narrow interests. In this model, the very nature of polyarchal democratic governance ensures that a constellation of interest groups with varying degrees of resources to influence policy will interact through various political processes, which involve negotiations and legislative lobbying.

Pluralist theorists (Epstein 1969, 226–28; Rose 1967; Berle 1963, 13; Truman 1951, 251, 256) have long argued that corporations do not dominate public policy because the nature of economic competition among them makes it less likely that they are politically unified and share policy preferences. Instead, variation across different industries in terms of whether firms are vertically or horizontally integrated into the economy, as well as variation in terms of economies of scale, produces cleavages among corporations that often oppose one another in their attempt to shape public policy in ways that support industry-specific interests. For example, Gibbs (1991, 28–29) observed how corporate cleavages manifest in monetary policy. Since inflation reduces the value of debt, heavily indebted corporations are more likely to prefer inflationary policies. Corporations that produce for international markets are more likely to prefer free trade, while corporations that produce for the domestic market will tend to prefer protection. Cleavages among corporations also manifest in other policy domains, including social welfare policy, fiscal policy, antitrust policy, tax policy, and environmental policy, as well as policies that regulate the trading of stocks, the sale of government bonds, and how government contracts are awarded. While corporate lobbying expenditures are significantly larger than similar expenditures by civil society groups, this does not automatically give corporations an advantage in influencing public policy decisions. This is because the lobbying expenditures of rival corporations act as a countervailing force that mitigates corporate dominance of the policy making process.

In a similar fashion, Mark S. Mizruchi (2013, 7–8) in *The Fracturing of the American Corporate Elite* argues that, after corporate success in weakening the labor movement during the 1970s and the 1980s, it became apparent that the unity of corporate collective action was no longer necessary, and as a result the corporate elite began to fragment. Corporate fragmentation was increased by the international decline of American commercial banks whose boards of directors served as a focal point for meetings among corporate leaders. With the decline of American banks the cohesiveness of the corporate elite also declined. As executive tenure among corporate CEOs dropped by 25 percent from the early 1980s to 2000, sitting CEOs no longer thought about the long-term interests of the business community but their own short-term survival, and consequently, the increasing turnover in corporate leadership undermined institutional memory and further eroded corporate cohesion.

According to Mizruchi (2013, 225–65) the fragmentation of the corporate elite undermines the policy-making process and democratic governance in America. The rise of legislative gridlock in Washington, extremist political factions in the legislative process, and the growing inability to address pressing national and international problems such as health care, the federal deficit, financial reform, and climate change all stem in part from the absence of a cohesive corporate elite that can contain and check the more destructive elements of the American political system. This aspect of the pluralist argument is an offshoot of the conventional political philosophy of the American founders who believed that democratic governance is best protected from concentrations of power when government authority is divided by a system of institutional checks and balances (Hamilton et al. 1961). However, in those instances when corporations are unified in terms of their policy preferences, is the collective strength of their lobbying expenditures a source of power that dominates public policy decision making?

In *American Business and Political Power*, Mark A. Smith (2000, 13–35) argues that even when corporations are unified in terms of their policy preferences they still do not dominate public policy decision making. This is because policy issues that galvanize corporate unity will become salient to the public and will be perceived as ideological and partisan. As a result, corporate unity will trigger the mobilization and unity of rival groups such as labor unions, human rights, environmentalists, and consumer advocacy groups. Substantial lobbying expenditures alone do not ensure that policy outcomes will reflect corporate preferences if the collective lobbying expenditures of rival groups become a countervailing check to corporate money (Baumgartner et al. 2009, 268). Because elections are important vehicles to hold legislators accountable, it is more likely that congressional legislators will respond to the policy preferences of rival advocacy groups within their constituency over the preferences of corporations. In testing the effects that corporate legislative power has on public policy outcomes, Smith (2000, 138–39) reports ordinary least square regression estimates, which show that corporate lobbying expenditures "have no systematic relationship with policy outcomes." In fact, the effects of other variables that measure corporate legislative power on policy outcomes, such as numbers of lobbyists and corporate membership within the U.S. Chamber of Commerce, all fail to reach statistical significance.

In *Lobbying and Policy Change*, Frank R. Baumgartner et al. (2009) provide evidence that corroborates the findings and arguments of Smith (2000). They argue that although money matters and corporations do enjoy greater access to congressional legislators than other civil society groups, this does not mean that they can dominate the policy-making process in government and consistently produce legislation that reflects their preferences. This is because societal interest groups, including corporations, cannot control the policy-making process, and government officials rarely have the authority to unilaterally produce the policy outcomes that lobbyists want. Corporate money is often trumped by civil society organizations with large memberships. Such organizations can provide democratic legitimacy to a legislative bill and pressure legislators who care about their own reelection to support it. Baumgartner et al. (2009, 269–70) argue that the size of the membership of an interest group, the level of public opinion supporting a particular legislative issue, and the number of other civil society organizations willing to ally with a group to fight for a particular policy outcome are sources of legislative power available to organizations even when they lack the resources to finance lobbying. They report estimates form a bivariate correlation that showed corporate political resources, which include lobbying expenditures, as having no statistical significant correlation with policy outcomes that approximate corporate preferences (Baumgartner et al. 2009, 280–81). Considering the effect of financial resources in securing policy outcomes that reflect the preference of an interest group, Baumgartner et al. (2009, 284–85) compared sets of actors who are active on the same side of an issue and asked whether the side with the most resources won. The results they report show that richer corporations won anywhere from 45 percent to 56 percent of the time, which suggests that civil society organizations with fewer resources won policy outcomes that reflected their preferences with the same probability as their wealthier corporate opponents.

When applied to U.S. drug enforcement policy making, pluralist theories suggest that corporations do not dominate U.S. drug enforcement policy making because the competitive nature of the marketplace increases the likelihood that their political activities are fragmented. Even when corporations are united, their collective political resources will only trigger countermobilization among rival civil society groups who will prevent them from achieving their policy preferences. For these reasons, pluralist theory predicts that the lobbying expenditures of American corporations, while larger than those of other civil society organizations, will give businesses no additional advantage sufficient for them to dominate drug enforcement decision making. Pluralist theoretical arguments generate the following hypothesis:

> Hypothesis 2: Relative to the lobbying expenditures of civil society organizations, increases in corporate congressional lobbying expenditures will have little to no effect on U.S. counternarcotic aid flows.

Research Design and Methodology

Modeling the Decision-Making Process of Drug Enforcement Aid Flows

This chapter and the next utilize the Heckman selection estimator (Heckman 1979) to model the two-stage decision-making process that governs counternarcotic aid flows. The first stage, the selection stage, determines whether countries are eligible to receive aid. Countries that pass through the selection stage are included in the second stage, which determines the amount of aid that they will receive.[3] Correcting for selection bias is important because certain observations are systematically censored and included in the second-stage subsample by the preceding selection process. Least-square estimation of uncensored observations risks producing biased and inconsistent estimates in the second-stage equation and could lead the analysis to misattribute causal effects to the central explanatory variables.

The Selection Stage: Determining the Eligibility to Receive Counternarcotic Aid

DEPENDENT VARIABLE: The dependent variable in the selection equation is measured dichotomously and considers whether a country received counternarcotic aid in a given year.

DEMOCRACY AND HUMAN RIGHTS COVARIATE: Existing empirical research has demonstrated that the level of democracy and the human rights practices of foreign governments are important characteristics that determine whether governments are eligible to receive aid (Poe 1991; Poe and Meernik 1995; Blanton 2000; Lai 2003; Cingranelli and Pasquarello 1985). More important, American law mandates that foreign governments' respect for human rights is a precondition to receive financial assistance. A 1974 amendment to the Foreign Assistance Act (P.L. 93-559) states: "No Security assistance may be provided to any country the government of which engages in a consistent pattern of gross violations of internationally recognized human rights. . . . Unless the President certifies in writing to the [Congress] that extraordinary circumstances exist warranting provision of such assistance" (Forsythe 1987, 383). Further, with the passage of the Leahy Amendment in 1997 (P.L. 109-102, Sec. 551), human rights preconditions are also attached to counternarcotic aid. The amendment states: "None of the funds made available by this Act may be provided to any unit of the security forces of a foreign country if the Secretary of State has credible evidence that such unit has committed gross violations of human rights, unless the Secretary determines and reports to the Committees on Appropriations that the government of such country is taking effective measures to bring the responsible members of the security forces unit to justice" (P.L 109-102, Sec. 551).

In the post–Cold War era, the promotion of democracy and human rights around the world has become a more salient objective of American foreign policy. Some scholars have argued that in the aftermath of the Cold War security has "widened beyond military threats to include socioeconomic, environmental, and especially humanitarian ones" (Weiss 1999, 500). Therefore, given the importance of democracy and human rights in American foreign policy and American law, it is expected that the democratic character and human rights practices of foreign governments are important characteristics that determine eligibility to receive drug war aid at the selection stage of the decision-making process. To capture this dynamic, the Polity and CIRI indices were used to measure countries' level of democracy and human rights practices, respectively.

PRESENCE OF NARCOTERROR ORGANIZATIONS COVARIATE: Since 9/11 American policy makers have contended that drug trafficking and terrorism are inextricably linked and represent a threat to U.S. security. In his testimony before the Senate Judiciary Subcommittee on Technology, Terrorism, and Government Information, Asa Hutchinson, a former drug enforcement administrator, noted:

> I appear before you today to testify on the nexus between international drug trafficking and terrorism, commonly referred to as narco-terrorism. As the tragic events that occurred on September 11, 2001 so shockingly demonstrated, terrorist organizations and the dependence on and relation of some of these organizations to international drug trafficking poses a threat to the national security of the United States. Consequently, the DEA has directed enforcement and intelligence assets to identify, investigate, and dismantle all organizations, including terrorist groups, engaged in the drug trafficking trade. The degree to which terrorist organizations

utilize drug profits to finance their horrific activities is of paramount concern to the DEA. (U.S. Senate Judiciary Subcommittee 2002, 1)

Therefore, in the post-9/11 international environment an important criterion affecting governments' eligibility to receive counternarcotic aid is the presence of Indigenous narcoterrorist organizations and/or drug cartels in their countries (Bartilow 2014).

BILATERAL FREE TRADE AND INVESTMENT AGREEMENTS WITH THE UNITED STATES COVARIATE: U.S. drug enforcement assistance is often used to leverage free trade agreements with recipient governments (Perl 1992). In fact, 60 percent of the countries represented in this study's sample who are recipients of U.S. counternarcotic aid have entered into or are currently negotiating a free trade or bilateral investment agreement with the United States.[4] It is therefore expected that countries that have entered into a bilateral free-trade and investment agreement (BFTIA) with the United States are more likely to be eligible to receive counternarcotic aid than countries who are not parties to these agreements.

LATIN AMERICA AND THE CARIBBEAN COVARIATE: In chapter 1, I showed that Latin America and the Caribbean receive higher levels of aid to fight the drug war than other regions in the developing world. This disparity is because the geographic proximity of these countries to the United States places them in a strategic position to serve as major producers of illicit drugs and/or drug transit areas for markets in the United States and Western Europe (Bartilow and Eom 2009b, 2012). Therefore, countries from Latin America and the Caribbean are more likely to be eligible to receive counternarcotic aid than countries in other regions of the developing world.

The Second Stage: Determining the Amount of Counternarcotic Aid

DEPENDENT VARIABLE: In the second stage, the main outcome variable of interest is the amount of U.S. counternarcotic aid disbursed. However, because there are large variations in the level of counternarcotic aid disbursed to recipient countries, the variable is not normally distributed and violates the normality assumption of regression analysis (Berry 1993, 18–22; Berry and Feldman 1985, 11). To improve the normality of its distribution, counternarcotic aid was transformed and entered into the second-stage equation as a natural log (Blanton 2005, 652).

EXPLANATORY VARIABLES: Corporate lobbying expenditures and the lobbying expenditures of the AFL-CIO, Amnesty International, and Human Rights

Watch constitute the main explanatory variables. Corporate lobbying expenditures were measured in terms of the yearly lobbying expenditures (in millions of U.S. dollars) of the thirty-three corporations in this study's sample that lobbied in support of Plan Colombia and the Mérida Initiative. The lobbying expenditures of the AFL-CIO, Amnesty International, and Human Rights Watch were measured in terms of the yearly lobbying expenditures (in millions of U.S. dollars) of these organizations that lobbied against congressional approval of Plan Colombia and the Mérida Initiative.[5]

COVARIATES

Scholars have suggested that important domestic and international security factors determine the amount of U.S. military and counternarcotic aid that foreign governments receive. These factors include the ideological orientation of the U.S. president (Fleck and Kilby 2006; Bartilow 2014), organizational inertia (Allison 1969), and the level of the Federal government's revenues and debt.

PRESIDENTIAL IDEOLOGY COVARIATE: The Office of National Drug Control Policy, which is part of the Executive Office of the President, is responsible for developing U.S. drug enforcement policy and the budget that supports it (White House Office of National Drug Control Policy 2003). Recent studies of the domestic determinants of U.S. aid have shown that, since the federal government's budget for international narcotic control is set by the executive branch, conservative presidents are far more supportive of increasing military aid and, by extension, counternarcotic aid than their liberal counterparts (Fleck and Kilby 2006; Bartilow 2014). However, as I have shown in chapter 2, the Obama administration increased drug enforcement expenditures far beyond the levels allocated by the conservative administration of George W. Bush (White House Office of National Drug Control Policy 2013, 2014). I argue that, given the power of corporations in drug enforcement policy making, successor presidents, regardless of their ideological orientation, will perennially expand drug war expenditures so that government benefits and contracts awarded to corporations for the execution of the drug war will be sustained.

ORGANIZATIONAL INERTIA COVARIATE: Theodore Sorensen observed that "presidents rarely if ever make decisions—particularly in foreign affairs—in the sense of writing their conclusions on a clean slate. . . . The basic decisions that confine their choices have all too often been previously made" (quoted in Allison 1969, 699). In building on this insight Allison (1971), in *Essence of Decision*, developed what he calls the organizational process model of foreign policy decision making. The model suggests that foreign policy decision making suffers from inertia because organizations slavishly follow routine and adhere to standard operating procedures and will thus implement foreign policy decisions that approximate prior decisions. Because organizational inertia affects foreign policy decision making when implementing foreign aid allocations, prior levels of counternarcotic aid are likely to determine current levels of aid.[6]

FEDERAL GOVERNMENT REVENUES COVARIATE: I have argued elsewhere that U.S. government revenues affect the level of foreign aid allocations (Bartilow 2014). All else being equal, increases in U.S. government revenues should make more resources available for foreign aid allocations. However, it is important to bear in mind that, since the budgetary process is highly politicized, revenue increases will not always be associated with increases in foreign aid flows (Gosling 2009). In other words, the politics of the budgetary process ensure that there is no systematic linear relationship between the revenues of the federal government and the amount of foreign aid allocated.

FEDERAL GOVERNMENT DEBT COVARIATE: As American policy makers engage in the ritual of shutting down the government as they debate their way to the perennial raising of the debt ceiling, the government's mounting debt has placed significant constraints on its domestic and international spending priorities—a phenomenon that O'Conner (2001) has aptly referred to as the fiscal crisis of the capitalist state. As a result, the federal government's debt is expected to have a negative effect on the amount of counternarcotic aid flows.

OTHER SECOND-STAGE COVARIATES: Scholars have shown that, once countries pass through the selection stage of the aid decision making process, the level of democracy, respect for human rights, bilateral trade and investment agreements with the United States, the presence of narcoterrorist and drug cartel organizations and the regional importance of Latin America and the Caribbean are also key factors that determine the amount of aid that foreign governments receive (Blanton 2000, 2005; Bartilow 2014).

Empirical Findings

Table 3.1 presents estimates from the Heckman selection model of the institutional effects of corporate and civil society organizations' lobbying expenditures on U.S. counternarcotic aid flows to eighty recipient countries. To control for the problem of heteroscedasticity in both the selection and amount equations, the regression coefficients are accompanied by robust standard errors that cluster on country (Blanton 2000, 127). In both models 1 and 2, the Wald test of the independence of the equations is statistically significant, indicating that the selection equations and the amount equations are correlated. In other words, countries' selection into the sample at stage 2 is not a random process that is unaffected by countries' eligibility to receive aid at stage 1. The Heckman technique is therefore the appropriate remedy for correcting selection bias when estimating the decision-making process of counternarcotic aid disbursements.

The main variables of theoretical interest in the amount equations support hypotheses 1a and 1b. In model 1, increases in corporate congressional lobbying expenditures are associated with increases in counternarcotic aid flows. Even when the unified lobbying expenditures of the AFL-CIO, Amnesty International, and Human Rights Watch are included in model 2, this statistical correlation does not change, which demonstrates that hypothesis 2 is not supported by the data. The lobbying expenditures of the AFL-CIO and the two the largest human rights organizations in the United States fail to achieve statistical significance.

In the control variables, notice that in the selection equations in models 1 and 2, countries from Latin America and the Caribbean are more likely to receive counternarcotic aid than are countries from outside the region. Holding all other variables constant at their mean value, the probability of being eligible to receive counternarcotic aid increases by 95 percent for countries from Latin America and the Caribbean Basin, a finding that provides additional confirmation that the region is the epicenter of the U.S. global drug war.[7]

In the selection and amount equations, having a BFTIA with the United States had no statistical significant effect on countries' eligibility to receive aid or the amount of aid that they will receive. Geographical location in Latin America and the Caribbean is positively associated with an increase in the amount of aid received. While the presence of narcoterror organizations had no statistically significant effect in determining countries' eligibility to receive aid, in the amount equations the presence of these organizations is positively associated with an increase in the level of drug war aid. The democratic characteristics of countries' governments were not a determining factor in their eligibility to receive aid, but in the amount equations, increasing levels of democracy had a reductive effect on the amount of counternarcotic aid that these governments receive. While the human rights practices of governments did not determine their eligibility to receive aid, in the amount equation in model 1 governments that are more repressive received higher levels of drug war aid than governments that respected the human rights of their citizens. In the amount equation in model 2, the variable fails to achieve statistical significance.

Table 3.1. Institutional effects of congressional lobbying expenditures on counternarcotic aid flows

Explanatory variables	Model 1	Model 2
Stage 1: The selection equation		
Presence of narcoterror organizations	−0.192 (0.290)	−0.478 (0.307)
Polity index	−0.00640 (0.00897)	−0.00727 (0.00944)
CIRI human rights index	0.0643 (0.0568)	0.0785 (0.0702)
Bilateral free-trade-investment agreements with the United States	−0.0105 (0.254)	−0.252 (0.278)
Latin America and the Caribbean Basin	0.929*** (0.278)	0.990** (0.330)
Constant	0.536+ (0.314)	−0.639+ (0.358)
Number of observations at stage 1	3432	3432
Stage 2: The amount equation		
Corporate congressional lobbying expenditures	0.00425* (0.00170)	0.00973* (0.00407)
Civil society congressional lobbying expenditures (AFL-CIO, Amnesty International, and human rights Watch)		0.00621 (0.00833)
Presidential ideology	0.351+ (0.206)	0.244 (0.243)
Organizational inertia	0.638*** (0.0536)	0.634*** (0.0577)
U.S. federal government debt (% of GDP)	−0.0134 (0.0107)	−0.00671 (0.0137)
U.S. federal government revenues	−0.00697 (0.0864)	−0.0452 (0.0769)
Presence of narcoterror organizations	0.983** (0.311)	1.531*** (0.309)
Polity index	−0.0197*** (0.00442)	−0.0162* (0.00772)
CIRI human rights index	0.0943* (0.0457)	0.00484 (0.0657)
Bilateral free-trade-investment agreements with the United States	0.0490 (0.158)	0.118 (0.251)
Latin America and the Caribbean Basin	0.630** (0.238)	−0.170 (0.327)
Constant	0.451 (1.686)	2.320 (1.830)
Number of observations at stage 2	21779	5611
Heckman model chi-square	955.60***	472.29***
Wald test of independent equations, chi-square	7.47***	23.87***

Robust standard errors are in parentheses.

Levels of statistical significance: $+p < 0.10$, $*p < 0.05$, $**p < 0.01$, $***p < 0.001$

These results are consistent with existing research, which shows that democratic governments, in the post–Cold War era, receive lower levels of U.S. arms transfers than nondemocratic regimes (Blanton 2005, 660). These results contradict the rhetoric of American policy makers (National Security Council 2002; White House 2015, 19–21) and the claims of some scholars that the promotion of democracy and human rights is an important American foreign policy goal, especially in the post-9/11 security environment (Kaufman 2007). The findings corroborate evidence from Colombia (Amnesty International 2010; Amnesty International and Fellowship of Reconciliation 2008), Bolivia (Ledebur 2005, 155–56), Mexico (Freeman and Sierra 2005, 292), Peru (Rojas 2005, 222–23), and Guatemala (Franklin 2008, 204) that documents the U.S. government's sustained support for the drug war in these countries despite reports by international human rights organizations, and in some instances the State Department's own country reports, of a consistent pattern of human rights repression (U.S. Department of State 2009). These findings also call into question the effectiveness and relevance of the so-called human rights regime in American foreign policy decision making (Sikkink 2004, 185–89), specifically the Leahy Amendment, which is intended to disqualify foreign governments that violate the human rights of their citizens from receiving counternarcotic aid.

Other variables in the outcome equations also determine the amount of counternarcotic aid disbursed. The ideology of the president matters in drug enforcement policy making, which is consistent with existing research (Fleck and Kilby 2006; Bartilow 2014). Existing research, however, reports that conservative presidents are more likely to increase military and drug enforcement assistance to recipient countries, whereas their liberal counterparts are more likely to reduce aid flows (Fleck and Kilby 2006). Contrary to existing research, in model 1 the presidential ideology variable shows that the Obama presidency, more so than the Bush presidency, is associated with increasing counternarcotic aid flows, a finding consistent with the argument developed in chapter 2.

Organizational inertia is positively associated with the amount of counternarcotic aid flows, a finding consistent with the theoretical prediction of the organizational process model of foreign policy decision making (Allison 1971). This model predicts that, since government bureaucracies have a penchant for following routine and standard operational procedures in implementing foreign aid allocations, prior levels of drug war aid are likely to determine current levels of aid. And, in models 1 and 2, the federal government's debt and revenues have no statistically significant effect on the amount of counternarcotic aid disbursed.

If corporate lobbies increase drug enforcement aid flows, then what industries are driving this phenomenon? In answering this question, table 3.2 presents estimates of the industry-level effects of corporate congressional lobbying expenditures on counternarcotic aid flows. In the amount equations, increases in congressional lobbying expenditures by corporations in the oil, the military-industrial complex, biotech, retail, and consumer industries are associated with increasing drug war aid flows. The oil industry has fixed assets in many foreign countries that are major drug producers and that host their operations, as the Colombia case demonstrates, and oil companies will lobby for counternarcotic assistance to foreign governments to underwrite the security of their assets.

Consider the example of central Asia. With the collapse of the Soviet Union, American oil companies flocked to Azerbaijan and other countries within the Caspian Basin and invested billions of dollars to access unexploited oil and gas reserves (Williams 1998). However, these oil and gas exploration and production facilities are located in the Golden Crescent, one of Asia's major opium and heroin trafficking routes at the crossroads of central, western, and South Asia (Scott 2003, 8). The foreign oil companies group, whose members include Chevron, ExxonMobil, and BP-Amoco, came into prominence at the end of the Cold War and lobbied Washington to formulate an active U.S. security policy to protect their interests in the Caspian Basin (Scott 2003, 31), including the provision of security and drug enforcement assistance to governments in the region. Chevron has now become Kazakhstan's largest private oil producer and holds important stakes in the country's two biggest oil-producing projects, the Tengiz and Karachaganak oil fields. Chevron holds a 50 percent interest in Tengizchevroil, which operates the Tengiz oil field. Tengizchevroil is a joint venture of Chevron, ExxonMobil, KazMunayGas, and LukArco. Chevron also holds an 18 percent interest in the Karachaganak oil field, which is Kazakhstan's second-largest petroleum producing reserve. The company is also the largest private shareholder in the Caspian Pipeline Consortium, which operates a 935-mile pipeline that exports crude oil from the company's Tengiz, Korolev, and Karachaganak oil fields in Kazakhstan to the Russian Black Sea port of Novorossiysk (Chevron Corporation 2015, 1–2).

In addition to its investments in Kazakhstan, since 1995 ExxonMobil has invested in oil-producing projects in Azerbaijan, where it holds an 8 percent interest in the Azerbaijan International Operating Consortium, which produces hydrocarbons from the Azeri-Chirag-Gunashli field in the Caspian Sea (Exxon-Mobil 2016a; Miraliyeva 2007). The company also has investments in natural gas production in Turkmenistan and on Russia's Sakhalin Island (Exxon-Mobil 2016b; Golubkova and Pinchuk 2014).

Table 3.2. Industry-level effects of corporate congressional lobbying on counternarcotic aid flows

Explanatory variables	Model 1: Oil	Model 2: Military industry	Model 3: Biotech	Model 4: Retail/ consumer	Model 5: Courier
Stage 1: The selection equation					
Presence of narcoter-ror organizations	−0.0993 (0.274)	−0.204 (0.294)	−0.197 (0.294)	−0.202 (0.294)	−0.202 (0.295)
Polity index	−0.0059 (0.00890)	−0.00646 (0.00899)	−0.00665 (0.00906)	−0.00653 (0.00901)	−0.00651 (0.00901)
CIRI human rights index	0.0626 (0.0567)	0.0646 (0.0568)	0.0648 (0.0569)	0.0648 (0.0568)	0.0645 (0.0569)
Bilateral free-trade-investment agreements with the United States	−0.00613 (0.253)	−0.0115 (0.254)	−0.0166 (0.253)	−0.0120 (0.254)	−0.0117 (0.254)
Latin America and the Caribbean Basin	0.936*** (0.277)	0.929*** (0.279)	0.941*** (0.280)	0.933*** (0.279)	0.929*** (0.279)
Constant	0.520+ (0.315)	0.538+ (0.315)	0.534+ (0.315)	0.536+ (0.314)	0.538+ (0.315)
Number of observa-tions at stage 1	416	936	104	208	208
Stage 2: The amount equation					
Corporate congressional lobby-ing expenditures	0.0118** (0.00443)	0.00872** (0.00274)	0.0784* (0.0306)	0.0611** (0.0236)	0.0110+ (0.00571)
Presidential ideology	0.300 (0.206)	0.360+ (0.205)	0.274 (0.210)	0.340+ (0.206)	0.287 (0.215)
Organizational inertia	0.636*** (0.0542	0.639*** (0.0534)	0.645*** (0.0521)	0.640*** (0.0533)	0.639*** (0.0533)
U.S. federal govern-ment debt (% of GDP)	−0.0111 (0.0108)	−0.0146 (0.0106)	−0.0142 (0.0105)	−0.0168 (0.0103)	−0.0120 (0.0110)
U.S. federal govern-ment revenues	−0.0133 (0.0859)	−0.00771 (0.0863)	0.0129 (0.0894)	0.0126 (0.0894)	−0.00783 (0.0861)
Presence of narcoter-ror organizations	1.018** (0.312)	0.977** (0.310)	0.955** (0.308)	0.971** (0.310)	0.972** (0.312)
Polity index	−0.0197*** (0.00445)	−0.0196*** (0.00440)	−0.0195*** (0.00437)	−0.0196*** (0.00439)	−0.0196*** (0.00446)
CIRI human rights index	0.0953* (0.0454)	0.0940* (0.0458)	0.0939* (0.0454)	0.0939* (0.0456)	0.0953* (0.0458)

Table 3.2. (*continued*)

Explanatory variables	Model 1: Oil	Model 2: Military industry	Model 3: Biotech	Model 4: Retail/ consumer	Model 5: Courier
Bilateral free-trade-investment agreements with the United States	0.0439 (0.160)	0.0476 (0.158)	0.0187 (0.159)	0.0400 (0.158)	0.0404 (0.157)
Latin America and the Caribbean Basin	0.643** (0.236)	0.629** (0.238)	0.648** (0.237)	0.633** (0.237)	0.642** (0.238)
Constant	0.280 (1.699)	0.510 (1.678)	−0.250 (1.835)	0.149 (1.739)	0.287 (1.725)
Number of observations at stage 2	2639	5940	660	1320	1320
Heckman model chi-square	910.83***	945.46***	1000.28***	996.53***	856.11***
Wald test of independent equations, chi-square	9.21**	7.33*	9.22**	7.87*	7.38*

Robust standard errors are in parentheses.

Levels of statistical significance: $+p < 0.10$, $*p < 0.05$, $**p < 0.01$, $***p < 0.001$

In response to the dramatic increase in heroin trafficking through Tajikistan, Uzbekistan, Kyrgyzstan, Turkmenistan, and Kazakhstan over the preceding two decades (Lublin 2001), the European Union in 2003 funded the creation of Border Management Program in Central Asia (BOMCA), which seeks to improve border management coordination among governments in the region, promote trade and development, and eliminate drug trafficking. In conjunction with the BOMCA program, the European Union also launched the Central Asia Drug Action Program in 2001, which promotes a public health approach to drug demand and an interdiction approach to drug supply (U.N. Development Programme 2008, 9). For its own part, the U.S. government established the Central Asian Counternarcotics Initiative, which seeks to disrupt drug trafficking from Afghanistan, promote regional cooperation for cross-border drug enforcement operations, and develop counternarcotics task forces to enable regional law enforcement cooperation (Peyrouse 2012; U.S. Department of State 2009b). With the establishment of this regional drug enforcement architecture, American arms contractors and biotech companies have an incentive for lobbying for counternarcotic aid to secure contracts to supply the military hardware and herbicides for poppy eradication initiatives.

The Obama administration pushed for the expansion of aerial poppy eradication into Afghanistan, characterizing it as a way to fight the Taliban. However, in the absence of an alternative source of income for poppy farmers, Afghan officials have repeatedly resisted poppy eradication as a viable strategy for drug enforcement and the counterinsurgency against the Taliban (Kirschke 2008).

The growth in overseas subsidiaries for retail and consumer corporations ensures that companies in this industry will increasingly depend on free trade and access to foreign customers. For example, P&G, which supported the Mérida Initiative, has operated in Russia since 1991. P&G Russia is one of the company's fastest-growing subsidiaries and exports 20 percent of P&G products to neighboring countries in central Asia (Alfa Bank 2003). With its acquisition of Lenta, a Russian retail company, Wal-Mart, also an advocate of the Mérida Initiative, has also expanded its investment in Russia (Reuters 2010).

These findings suggest that, since retail and consumer companies such as Proctor and Gamble and Wal-Mart have access to the Russian and central Asian markets, it is not surprising that the industry would lobby Washington for drug enforcement aid. This aid would strengthen existing E.U.- and U.S.-sponsored regional cross-border security arrangements that not only prosecute the drug war but also facilitate greater trade and development among countries in the region. Expanding trade is also likely to increase demand for the transportation services of companies in the courier industry, which would explain the industry's support for drug enforcement to provide security in markets where it operates. The performance of the control variables in the selection and amount equations is consistent with those reported in the previous table.

Although table 3.3 shows that the lobbying expenditures of the manufacturing, information technology, and pharmaceutical industries fail to achieve statistical significance, lobbying by specific firms within these industries drives counternarcotic aid flows. The lobbying expenditures of the Ford Motor Company, Deer and Company, Whirlpool, and Pfizer increase counternarcotic aid flows. It is also not surprising that the lobbying expenditures of SAIC, a regular recipient of U.S. government contracts to provide information technology and training used in drug enforcement, would increase counternarcotic aid flows. SAIC is regarded as a "stealth company" and in recent years received over 9,000 contracts from the federal government, most of which involve gathering intelligence. The company is also contracted to provide such products as vehicle and cargo inspection systems used in the detection of contraband. SAIC's annual revenue for fiscal year 2007 was US$8.3 billion, a 7 percent increase from 2006 (Barlett and Steele 2007; SAIC 2007, 2). In all the models, the performance of the control variables in the selection and amount equations in table 3.3 is consistent with those reported in the previous tables.

Table 3.3. Firm-level effects of corporate congressional lobbying on counternarcotic aid flows

Explanatory variables	Model 1: Manufacture industry	Model 2: Ford	Model 3: Deere & Company	Model 4: Whirlpool	Model 5: Information Tech.	Model 6: SAIC	Model 7: Pharmaceutical	Model 8: Pfizer, Inc.
Stage 1: The selection equation								
Presence of narcoterror organizations	-0.204 (0.294)	-0.181 (0.289)	-0.189 (0.293)	-0.200 (0.295)	-0.204 (0.294)	-0.199 (0.294)	-0.204 (0.294)	-0.196 (0.293)
Polity index	-0.00646 (0.00898)	-0.00752 (0.00951)	-0.00687 (0.00918)	-0.00651 (0.00899)	-0.00645 (0.00898)	-0.00658 (0.00902)	-0.00646 (0.0089)	-0.00658 (0.00903)
CIRI human rights Index	0.0646 (0.0568)	0.0646 (0.0564)	0.0646 (0.0569)	0.0642 (0.0570)	0.0646 (0.0568)	0.0650 (0.0568)	0.0646 (0.0568)	0.0651 (0.0567)
Bilateral free trade and investment agreements with the United States	-0.0112 (0.254)	-0.0105 (0.248)	-0.0194 (0.252)	-0.0167 (0.255)	-0.0112 (0.254)	-0.0151 (0.253)	-0.0113 (0.254)	-0.0145 (0.253)
Latin America and the Caribbean Basin	0.928*** (0.279)	0.954*** (0.273)	0.948*** (0.278)	0.932*** (0.280)	0.928*** (0.279)	0.940*** (0.281)	0.929*** (0.279)	0.941*** (0.279)
Constant	0.538+ (0.314)	0.524+ (0.313)	0.532+ (0.315)	0.540+ (0.315)	0.538+ (0.314)	0.534+ (0.315)	0.538+ (0.314)	0.532+ (0.314)
Number of observations at stage 1	624	104	104	104	312	104	208	104
Stage 2: The amount equation								
Corporate congressional lobbying expenditures	0.000744 (0.000659)	0.175** (0.0645)	0.346* (0.135)	0.930*** (0.283)	0.00191 (0.00840)	0.154* (0.0617)	0.00356 (0.00559)	0.0302+ (0.0156)
Presidential ideology	0.358+ (0.205)	0.306 (0.203)	0.236 (0.210)	0.222 (0.217)	0.360+ (0.205)	0.180 (0.222)	0.331 (0.215)	-0.0955 (0.309)
Organizational inertia	0.638*** (0.0535)	0.647*** (0.0527)	0.646*** (0.0516)	0.645*** (0.0521)	0.638*** (0.0535)	0.645*** (0.0525)	0.638*** (0.0536)	0.644*** (0.0532)

Table 3-3. (continued)

Explanatory variables	Model 1: Manufacture industry	Model 2: Ford	Model 3: Deere & Company	Model 4: Whirlpool	Model 5: Information Tech.	Model 6: SAIC	Model 7: Pharma-ceutical	Model 8: Pfizer, Inc.
U.S. federal government debt (% of GDP)	-0.0135 (0.0107)	-0.0119 (0.0107)	-0.0105 (0.0111)	-0.0178+ (0.0102)	-0.0137 (0.0106)	-0.00873 (0.0115)	-0.0124 (0.0111)	0.00580 (0.0161)
U.S. federal government revenues	-0.00555 (0.0864)	-0.166* (0.0738)	-0.0719 (0.0756)	0.0214 (0.0881)	-0.00545 (0.0862)	-0.0719 (0.0799)	-0.00950 (0.0865)	-0.0942 (0.0831)
Presence of narcoterror organizations	0.979** (0.311)	0.943** (0.315)	0.946** (0.310)	0.962** (0.305)	0.979** (0.311)	0.959** (0.307)	0.978** (0.311)	0.960** (0.311)
Polity index	-0.0197*** (0.00441)	-0.0195*** (0.00451)	-0.0195*** (0.00444)	-0.0195*** (0.00438)	-0.0197*** (0.00441)	-0.0195*** (0.00433)	-0.0197*** (0.00440)	-0.0195*** (0.00437)
CIRI human rights Index	0.0941* (0.0458)	0.0938* (0.0454)	0.0948* (0.0456)	0.0928* (0.0454)	0.0941* (0.0458)	0.0934* (0.0452)	0.0941* (0.0457)	0.0932* (0.0455)
Bilateral free trade and investment agreements with the United States	0.0498 (0.158)	0.0492 (0.160)	0.0181 (0.160)	0.0206 (0.157)	0.0497 (0.158)	0.0215 (0.158)	0.0491 (0.157)	0.0277 (0.159)
Latin America and the Caribbean Basin	0.627** (0.238)	0.640** (0.231)	0.658** (0.236)	0.641** (0.238)	0.627** (0.238)	0.642** (0.236)	0.627** (0.238)	0.643* (0.235)
Constant	0.458 (1.686)	1.776 (1.480)	0.758 (1.597)	-0.163 (1.762)	0.470 (1.667)	0.867 (1.605)	0.417 (1.695)	0.0842 (1.754)
Number of observations at stage 2	3336	660	660	660	1980	660	1320	660
Heckman model chi-square	926.21***	901.79***	1003.79***	935.66***	848.12***	998.07***	942.42***	899.53***
Wald test of independent equations, chi-square	7.26**	13.46***	11.32***	7.77*	7.27*	8.71**	7.30**	9.24**

Robust standard errors are in parentheses.

Levels of statistical significance: $^+p < 0.10$, $^*p < 0.05$, $^{**}p < 0.01$, $^{***}p < 0.001$.

Conclusion

The empirical evidence shows that at the institutional level of congressional lobbying, labor unions and human rights organizations collectively fail to constrain corporate preferences for an increase in drug enforcement aid flows. These results are consistent with legislative outcomes that provided drug enforcement funding for Colombia and Mexico. While the findings validate the proposition of radical theories of the state, which claim that corporations occupy a superior position within government than labor unions and other civil society organizations (Lindblom 1978), it also provide strong evidence that corporate power drives drug enforcement policy decisions because of the ways in which it is embedded within the institutional structure of the regime. The next chapter focuses on analysis at the elite level and examines the various mechanisms through which corporate elites penetrate the state and shape the regime's drug enforcement policy.

CHAPTER 4

The Corporate Elite and the
Drug Enforcement Regime

The top of the American system of power is much more unified and
much more powerful. . . . No one, accordingly can be truly powerful
unless he has access to the command of major institutions, for it is
over these institutional means of power that the truly powerful are,
in the first instance, powerful.—**C. Wright Mills,** *The Power Elite*

Mills's analysis of the projection of power by corporate elites extends to the ways in which they shape the regime's drug enforcement policy. While the legislative dimension of corporate power shapes drug enforcement policy, Plan Colombia and the Mérida Initiative suggest that corporate campaign contributions and the reciprocal relationships between corporate elites and the federal government also influence American counternarcotic aid flows to both Colombia and Mexico. However, corporate campaign contributions to policy makers and the presence of an interlocking corporate directorate with ties to the federal government by themselves do not constitute systematic evidence of the influence of the corporate elite on American drug enforcement policy. In this chapter, I use a model to empirically test instrumental theoretical perspectives of drug enforcement policy to ascertain whether these theoretical perspectives, which help explain the drug enforcement regime's policy toward Colombia and Mexico, are also generalizable across the data set of eighty countries that are recipients of American counternarcotic aid.

In describing this model I first discuss elite theoretical perspectives of the state and consider how corporate campaign contributions allow elites to control the political candidate selection process and ultimately exert a strong influence over drug enforcement policy, as argued by Domhoff (1983). I also consider how the interlocking directorate, a concept first introduced by Mills (1956, 18), affects American drug enforcement aid flows. Using principal component factor analysis, I have constructed an index that captures the concept of an interlocking directorate, which includes measures of the interconnections among members of the board of directors for the thirty-three corporations in the data set, as well as measures of the interconnections of these corporations with policy think tanks and the U.S. government. At the end of this discussion I outline several hypotheses, and the section that follows discusses how the empirical findings relate to them. Since drug enforcement policy making toward Colombia and Mexico has also shown that congressional funding for the drug war is a source of revenue for American corporations, the concluding section discusses the empirical findings concerning the effect of counternarcotic aid flows on corporate capital accumulation.

Elite Theories of State Decision Making

Instrumental Theories

Instrumental theorist C. Wright Mills (1956, 245–46) argued that theories of congressional lobbying that emphasize checks and balances and in which no one interest group dominates public policy because power is shared pay "undue attention to the middle levels of power . . . the noisy content of politics" at the cost of obscuring the power elite. According to Mills, the power elite, or what Domhoff (1983, 17–55) calls the American upper class, comprises unified members of an upper social caste whose shared values and psychological affinity for one another are shaped by their ideological indoctrination through the social institutions (prep schools, Ivy League colleges, exclusive social clubs, and interclass marriages) to which they belong (Domhoff 1983, 72–76). In his analysis of the British and American upper class, Useem (1984, 67–70) reported that Eton, Harrow, Marlborough, Rugby, and Winchester are the most frequently attended schools by British business leaders, and that Andover, Choate, Deerfield, Exeter, Groton, Hill, Hotchkiss, Lawrence, Milton, St. George's, St. Mark's, St. Paul's, and Taft are the first choice of America's business elite. Collectively, these institutions are responsible for the secondary education of over 10 percent of British and American corporate directors.

The power elite commands institutions that form a triangular structure of power in which there is an "ever increasing interlocking of economic, military, and political structures" (Mills 1956, 8), resulting in an interlocking directorate. According to instrumental theorists, this interlocking directorate controls the fundamental decisions that shape foreign policy and the nature of the economy. The creation of the postwar military-industrial complex,[1] which is a reflection of the power elites' preferences, had no input from the public

(Domhoff 1996, 218–25; Mills 1956, 19). In building on these arguments, Nomi Prins in *All the Presidents' Bankers* (2015) makes use of presidential archives to show how the corporate banking elite exercises power in American democracy. In meticulous detail, she documents the symbiotic relationships between powerful American banks and presidents from Teddy Roosevelt to Barack Obama. The decisive influence of a small number of banks over the White House and the Treasury Department played a critical role in the creation of the Federal Reserve, the U.S. response to the Great Depression, and the creation of the International Monetary Fund and the World Bank—the postwar Bretton Woods international financial institutions that wrote the rules of the contemporary international capitalist economy. This list grows if one also considers the atomic bombing of Japan during the Second World War and the U.S. entry into Vietnam, and more recently the U.S. interventions in Afghanistan and Iraq, or the multibillion-dollar bailout of the U.S. auto and banking industries during the 2008 recession. In all of these cases, the American public was merely informed of these decisions but was never involved in the decision-making process.

Corporate Campaign Contributions

There are three mechanisms through which the power elite directly involve themselves in the operations of the state and dominate the policy-making process. The first of these is the candidate selection process (Domhoff 1983, 117–29), in which members of the power elite influence election outcomes by financing the campaigns of candidates who, when elected, will represent and defend their interests. Federal election campaigns have become increasingly expensive endeavors. Between 2000 and 2006, the average cost of winning a seat in the U.S. Senate rose by 81 percent, an increase from US$5.3 million to over US$9.6 million. During the same period the average cost of winning a seat in the House increased by 50 percent, rising from US$840,000 to US$1.25 million (Juhasz 2008, 220–21). As federal election costs balloon out of control, those who seek public office will increasingly depend on the financing of powerful corporations and wealthy individuals whose influence over the candidate selection process, and ultimately over public policy outcomes, will continue to grow. As an example of this trend, chapter 2 describes how defense contractors United Technologies and Textron, respectively, made substantial campaign contributions to Connecticut liberal Democrat Senators Christopher Dodd and Joseph Lieberman and Texas Republicans who championed Plan Colombia and ensured that the bill had the necessary provisions for the sale of Blackhawk and Huey helicopters.

There has also been a long history of the power elite dominance of the candidate selection process in presidential elections. Brown and Root, Inc., which was acquired by Halliburton Energy Services in December 1962, built onshore and offshore oil platforms, petrochemical plants, and electric generators and was one of the largest construction and engineering companies in the world. The company was the chief financial backer of Lyndon Johnson's political career, pouring money into his campaigns for the House in 1937, the Senate in 1949, and the presidency in 1963. Johnson, in return, was able to influence other members of the House and Senate to obtain lucrative construction contracts and other benefits for Brown and Root from the federal government (Briody 2004, 115–41; Engler 1977, 57–58). Oil corporations financed Richard Nixon's senatorial campaign in 1950. Later, as Eisenhower's vice president he used his influence to block a full-scale investigation of the role of corporate financing in congressional elections, which was triggered by Senator Francis Case's disclosure in 1956 that he had been offered cash by an oil company in exchange for supporting legislation (Zelizer 2002, 78; Engler 1977, 58–59). In Nixon's 1972 presidential campaign, his reelection committee received US$5 million from the oil industry, which included illegal cash contributions of US$100,000 from companies such as Gulf, Phillips, and Ashland Oil. Additional contributions came from Amerada Hess, Pennzoil, Marathon, Texas Eastern Transmission, and oil companies affiliated with Brown and Root. Individual contributions came from Jake L. Hamon, then head of the American Petroleum Institute, who contributed US$25,000, and Armand Hammer, then president of Occidental Petroleum, who contributed US$100,000. Most of this money was quickly sent to Washington in April 1972, just two days before the new federal disclosure law, which ended the confidentiality of campaign contributors, went into effect (Engler 1977, 62–63).

As it did for Lyndon Johnson, the oil industry bankrolled the political career of George W. Bush. For his 1994 and 1998 campaigns for governor of Texas, the oil and gas industry contributed US$556,700, and additional contributions of US$944,733 came from individuals connected to the oil and gas industry (Palmer 2002). According to data compiled from the Center for Responsive Politics, George W. Bush received more campaign contributions from the oil industry than any other administration in America's history. Oil and gas companies contributed US$2,033,151 to Bush's presidential campaign, which made the industry among the top ten special interest contributors to his campaign in 2000 (Open Secrets 2000a). Additional contributions of US$97,235 came from PACs connected to the oil industry (Open Secrets 2000b), and another US$1 million in contributions from the oil and gas industry went to Bush's presidential inaugural committee (Palmer 2002). In his presidential reelection campaign in 2004, Bush received more than US$2.6 million from the oil and gas industry, which was more than any other politician that cycle and approximately 8.5 times more than John Kerry, his democratic presidential rival (Mayer 2007).

In return for supporting his campaigns, the oil industry played a central role in designing the Bush administration's energy policy. After his controversial presidential victory in 2000, the first priority of the Bush administration was to convene a group of executives from the nation's largest oil companies, known as the National Energy Policy Development Group, to develop a plan that would supposedly reduce U.S. dependence on Middle Eastern oil. In May 2001, the task force released its report, which argued that the Middle East and specifically the Gulf should be the primary focus of U.S. international energy policy and recommended that Middle Eastern countries open their energy sectors to foreign investment. The invasion and occupation of Iraq were a partial realization of the task force's policy recommendation. Immediately following the invasion, the Bush administration brought in representatives from the major oil industries to run and manage Iraq's postwar oil industry. Executives from ConocoPhillips, ExxonMobil, Chevron, Shell, and BP each took turns managing Iraq's oil industry. Philip Carroll, former CEO of Shell Oil's U.S. subsidiary, was one of the first energy advisers in Iraq and was given the responsibility of developing contingency plans for Iraq's oil sector. Carroll admitted to BBC reporter Greg Palast that he was asked by the Bush administration to take the job six months before the invasion (Juhasz 2008, 338–47).

The 2016 presidential primaries demonstrated that the power elite tightened their grip over the candidate selection process. Confessore et al. (2015) reported that in the first half of the campaign cycle 158 families and their companies contributed US$176 million to Republican and Democratic candidates. Most of this money came through channels legalized by the Supreme Court's *Citizens United* decision in 2010. Of these families, 138 supported Republican candidates while only 23 supported Democratic candidates. The largest contributions came from the Wilks family of Texas, who made their fortune by providing trucks and equipment to the shale oil fields; the Mercers of New York, who made millions from the hedge fund investments of Robert Mercer; and the Neugebauers of Texas, who amassed a fortune through the private equity investments of Toby Neugebauer. These families financed the campaign of Tea Party conservative senator Ted Cruz. Ray Lee Hunt of Hunt Oil, one of the largest privately held oil companies in the United States, contributed more that US$2 million to Jeb Bush. Hedge fund investor George Soros contributed US$1 million to a super PAC that supported Hillary Clinton. Contributions to Mrs. Clinton's campaign also came from Amy Goldman Fowler, who inherited a fortune from real estate in New York, and Stephen M. Silberstein, a San Francisco computer programmer who made a fortune developing computer systems for libraries. Hedge fund investor Stanley F. Druckenmiller contributed over US$300,000 to support New Jersey governor Chris Christie, Jeb Bush, and

Ohio governor John R. Kasich. The Preston Hollow neighborhood in Dallas, Texas, home to former president George W. Bush, contributed US$13 million to Republican candidates. While most of this money went to Jeb Bush, some of the neighborhood's largest contributors, including Kelcy Warren, owner of a Dallas oil pipeline, gave US$6 million to a super PAC that supported Texas governor Rick Perry. Darwin Deason, another member of the Preston Hollow community, provided another US$5 million to Mr. Perry's campaign.

Corporate Think Tanks

The second mechanism through which members of the power elite influence the operations of the state is what Domhoff (1983) calls the opinion-shaping process. In this process, elites use a wide network of think tanks and foundations, for which the corporate community provides leadership and financial support, to promote corporate interests by shaping the ideological environment in which public policy is made. By extension, this enables corporate elites to influence the beliefs and opinions of policy makers and the American public. One way in which think tanks shape public opinion is by penetrating the popular media. For example, foreign policy opinion leader Fareed Zakaria, a member of the influential Council on Foreign Relations (see Council on Foreign Relations 2015, 61–63), is the host of CNN's *Zakaria GPS*, a widely watched Sunday morning program that provides information and analysis of American foreign policy and international affairs.

Unlike lobbyists and elected lawmakers, who are subject to financial disclosure requirements, think tanks are not legally bound to reveal their donors and do so only by choice. As a result, think tanks essentially serve as unregistered lobbyists that, under the veneer of objectivity and impartiality, influence the beliefs of policy makers and the general public in ways consistent with the political and economic preferences of their corporate donors. When soliciting financial contributions from corporate donors, think tanks often give corporations access to personal briefings with their resident experts. They also provide corporations with opportunities to work directly with their senior fellows to draft research agendas with the intention of increasing the likelihood that donors' preferences will have a significant impact in shaping public policy. Moreover, to secure corporate funding, think tanks present themselves as important venues that facilitate dialogue between public and private sector leaders and help shape and build consensus around important public policy issues (Silverstein 2013).

The reputation of think tanks for producing impartial policy research and the network of contacts they provide makes them extremely useful as policy advocates for the corporations that fund them. Consider, for example, the

Center for American Progress (CAP), a liberal think tank that has been a major advocate for greater U.S.-Taiwan relations. In its 2010 report titled *Ties That Bind: U.S.-Taiwan Relations and Peace and Prosperity in East Asia* (Chen 2010), CAP argued that the stagnant relationship between the two countries threatens U.S. security interests in the region and recommended that the United States maintain arms sales to Taiwan and strengthen economic and diplomatic cooperation and that both countries should "seek ways to deepen their relationship" (Chen 2010, 3). The same year the report was published, CAP's senior fellow, Scott Lilly, gave a presentation to the American Institute in Taiwan where he characterized the U.S.-Taiwan relationship as "one of the most important bilateral relationships in the world" and called for additional U.S. arms sales to Taiwan. At the time of his presentation Lilly was also a lobbyist for Lockheed Martin, a leading arms contractor to Taiwan and one of CAP's major corporate contributors (Silverstein 2013).

Interlocking Directorate

The third mechanism by which members of the power elite influence the operations of the state is the cultivation of an interlocking directorate, which includes interlocking corporate board memberships and think tanks, as well as a "revolving door" of individual movement between corporate executiveships and influential positions in government agencies and the military (Mills 1956, 296; Useem 1984, 45–58; Domhoff 1983, 70–72). The interlocking directorate maintains the sociopolitical and economic hegemony of the American ruling elite. It reinforces their common view of reality, their common definition of ethical conduct and political correctness, and their consensus about the domestic and foreign policy priorities of the U.S. government (Koening et al. 1979, 176–77). Both the Obama and Bush administrations were replete with examples of the interlocking directorate in operation.

The ties of the interlocking directorate were particularly evident in the relationship between the Obama administration and Monsanto, the biotech giant that lobbied Congress in support of Plan Colombia. In 2009, the administration appointed Michael Taylor, Monsanto's vice president, as deputy commissioner of the FDA. Taylor's appointment is typical of the revolving door between the food industry and the government agencies that supposedly regulate it. During the 1980s, Taylor was a lawyer at the firm of King and Spalding, where he represented Monsanto. In 1991, the first Bush administration appointed him deputy commissioner for policy at the FDA, and in 1994 the Clinton administration moved him to the USDA, where he was administrator of the Food Safety and Inspection Service (Kenfield 2009). Obama's secretary of state, Hillary Clinton, was a lawyer at the Rose law firm, which represents

Monsanto. In 2009, the Obama administration appointed Roger Beachy, former director of Monsanto's Danforth Plant Science Center, to be the first director of the USAID's National Institute of Food and Agriculture. In 2010, the Obama administration appointed Islam Siddiqui, a former Monsanto lobbyist, to the position of chief agricultural negotiator in the Office of the U.S. Trade Representative (Ruskin 2010).

There were also corporate interlocks between the Obama administration and the banking and oil companies that supported Plan Colombia and the Mérida Initiative. For example, in 2011 the administration appointed William Daley, former executive at J. P. Morgan Chase, as chief of staff (Lowery 2011). In 2013 the administration appointed Chuck Hagel, then a board member of the Chevron Corporation and chairman of the think tank the Atlantic Council, as secretary of defense. Chevron is the second-largest oil company in the United States and is a major federal contractor, selling over US$501 million in fuel to the Pentagon in 2012. Chevron is also one of the largest corporate contributors to the Atlantic Council and finances its research projects in Kazakhstan, where it has invested over US$10 billion in the country's oil sector (Baker 2013; Kredo 2013).

Other members of the Atlantic Council went on to hold various positions in the Obama administration. In 2009, chairman of the Atlantic Council James L. Jones, who was succeeded by Chuck Hagel, was appointed as President Obama's national security adviser. Susan Rice was appointed as ambassador to the United Nations, Richard Holbrooke as the special representative to Afghanistan and Pakistan, General Eric K. Shinseki as the secretary of veterans affairs, and Anne-Marie Slaughter as director of policy planning at the State Department. The interlocking nature of the tripartite relationship between Chevron, the Atlantic Council, and the federal government was certainly not limited to the Obama administration. Condoleezza Rice served on Chevron's board of directors before becoming national security adviser to the Bush administration, and as a former director of the Atlantic Council she promoted greater U.S. ties to Kazakhstan (Baker 2013).

Not only does the nature of the interlocking directorate facilitate the process of capital accumulation for corporations that penetrate the decision-making apparatus of the state, but it also exerts a significant impact on the probability of interstate conflict in the international system. Consider, for example, the influence of the interlocking relationship between Lockheed Martin and the Bush administration on the decision by the latter to invade Iraq. Bruce Jackson was a former vice president for Lockheed Martin's strategy and planning division from 1999 to 2002. Prior to his tenure at Lockheed, Jackson was a U.S. military intelligence officer and held various positions in the Office of the Secretary of

Defense. Jackson is also a member of a number of think tanks, including the Council on Foreign Relations, the Center for Strategic and International Studies, and the London-based International Institute for Strategic Studies, and he was formerly a member of the American Enterprise Institute. During his tenure at Lockheed Martin, Jackson was also the director of Project for the New American Century (PNAC), a neoconservative think tank that included Paul Wolfowitz, Donald Rumsfeld, and Dick Chaney (Hartung 2012, 191).

On June 3, 1997, PNAC issued its founding statement of principles, which called for a significant increase in military spending and argued that the Clinton administration should return to the "Reaganite policy of military strength and moral clarity . . . [which] is necessary if the United States is to build on the successes of this past century and to ensure our security and our greatness in the next" (Project for the New American Century 1997). While George W. Bush was not among the twenty-five signatories of PNAC's statement of principles, his brother Jeb was.

Even before George W. Bush assumed the presidency, PNAC advocated removing the regime of Saddam Hussein from power. On January 26, 1998, PNAC published a letter to President Clinton urging him to go to war against Iraq to remove Saddam Hussein from power because his regime was a "hazard" to "a significant portion of the world's supply of oil" (Project for the New American Century 1998a). In another letter to Senate majority leader Trent Lott (R-MS) and Speaker of the House Newt Gingrich (R-GA), PNAC again called for the "removal of Saddam and his regime from power" because "Iraq has yet to provide a complete account of its programs for developing weapons of mass destruction" (Project for the New American Century 1998b).

PNAC members, as well as Lockheed Martin executives and lobbyists, went on to fill important positions in the Bush administration. These included Lockheed's former chief operating officer, Peter B. Teets, who became undersecretary of the U.S. Air Force and director of the National Reconnaissance Office. In this position Teets had the responsibility of making decisions on surveillance satellites and space-based elements of missile defense. Vice President Dick Cheney was tied to the defense contractor through his wife, Lynne Cheney, who was a board member of Lockheed Martin and the conservative think tank the American Enterprise Institute from 1995 to 2000 (Lockheed Martin Corporation 1995, 78; 1999, 66). Lockheed's former director of the United Kingdom's Atomic Weapons Establishment, Everet Becker, became the deputy administrator for defense programs at the National Security Administration. Lockheed's former lobbyist Otto Reich, who promoted the sale of Lockheed Martin's F-16 fighter jets to Chile, became the assistant secretary for Latin American affairs.

Steven Hadley, a former Lockheed lobbyist and member of the Council on Foreign Relations, became deputy national security adviser. Lockheed Martin's former vice presidents Norman Mineta and Michael Jackson were given the number one and two positions, respectively, in the Department of Transportation. Michael Jackson would later become the deputy secretary of DHS, which became one of the major sources of revenue for Lockheed Martin. According to former DHS inspector general Clark Kent Ervin, during Jackson's tenure at DHS his "undue use of no-bid contracts" or "contracts that fail to deliver what's promised even though billions of dollars have been spent" resulted in Lockheed Martin receiving over US$650 billion in DHS contracts (Hartung 2012, 192–93; Cummings 2007).

The terrorist attacks on 9/11 provided former members of PNAC with an opportunity to remove Saddam Hussein from power, a policy initiative that would net Lockheed Martin billions of dollars. However, they needed a rationale for doing so, and the Bush administration called on PNAC's former director, Bruce Jackson, to construct one. In 2002 Jackson, in close collaboration with Steven Hadley, created the Committee for the Liberation of Iraq, which not only advocated military action to remove the Iraqi regime from power but also lobbied members of Congress and the media by constructing the image that Saddam Hussein was a monster, a strategic threat to U.S. interests in the Middle East, and a gross violator of human rights in the region. This rationale justified war against Iraq, and in the process Lockheed Martin was awarded US$17 billion in contracts from the Department of Defense to provide the military hardware used in Operation Iraqi Freedom. The company's revenues increased by more than 30 percent, and its stock value went from US$16.375 in October 1999 to US$71.52 in June 2002, just nine months before the United States commenced military operations against the Iraqi regime (Cummings 2007).

In describing the interlocking directorate's ability to influence and shape U.S. domestic and strategic policy, Mills (1956, 18) wrote: "By the power elite, we refer to those political, economic, and military circles, which as an intricate set of overlapping cliques share decisions having at least national [and international] consequences. In so far as national events are decided, the power elite are those who decide them."

In the following figures, the interlocking directorate is presented graphically in Venn diagrams that reflect calculated percentages of interlock that connect the boards of the Council on Foreign Relations (CFR), Center for Strategic and International Studies (CSIS), the Brookings Institution, and the RAND Corporation to the boards of directors of American corporations, other think tanks, the U.S. government, and the military.[2] Figure 4.1 shows that 28 percent

Figure 4.1. Interlocking of the Council on Foreign Relations (CFR)

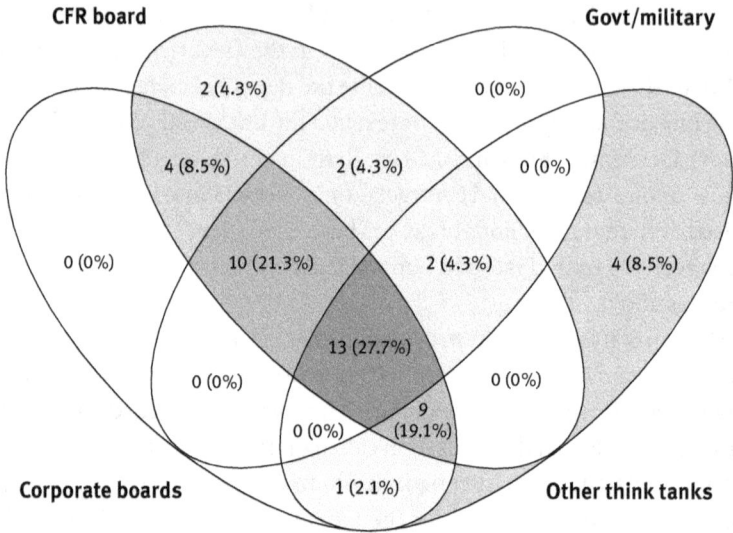

CFR board   **Govt/military**

2 (4.3%)   0 (0%)

4 (8.5%)   2 (4.3%)   0 (0%)

0 (0%)   10 (21.3%)   2 (4.3%)   4 (8.5%)

13 (27.7%)

0 (0%)   0 (0%)

9 (19.1%)

0 (0%)

Corporate boards   1 (2.1%)   **Other think tanks**

of CFR's board members are interlocked, and figure 4.2 shows that 29 percent of CSIS's board members are interlocked.

Brookings's board of directors, depicted in figure 4.3, is 10 percent interlocked. In figure 4.4, while all four elements do not intersect and evidence of an interlocking directorate is weaker, 52 percent of the members of RAND's board of directors appear interlocked with the boards of American corporations, and interlocks among RAND, the boards of American corporations, and the U.S. government and military account for another 28 percent.[3]

The forty-eight-year-old U.S. drug war has both national and international consequences, and if instrumental theorists are correct, we should find systematic evidence of the ways in which the power elite shapes and sustains drug enforcement policy. These theories suggest that corporations will finance federal election campaigns to select candidates who will be "tough on drugs" when elected and will support policy outcomes that will increase drug enforcement aid flows. These theories also suggest that, through their interlocking relationships with think tanks, corporations will provide financing and leadership to create an ideological environment that sustains and supports drug prohibition and enforcement. Instrumental theories also suggest that an interlocking directorate, which consists of interlocking corporate boards of directors,

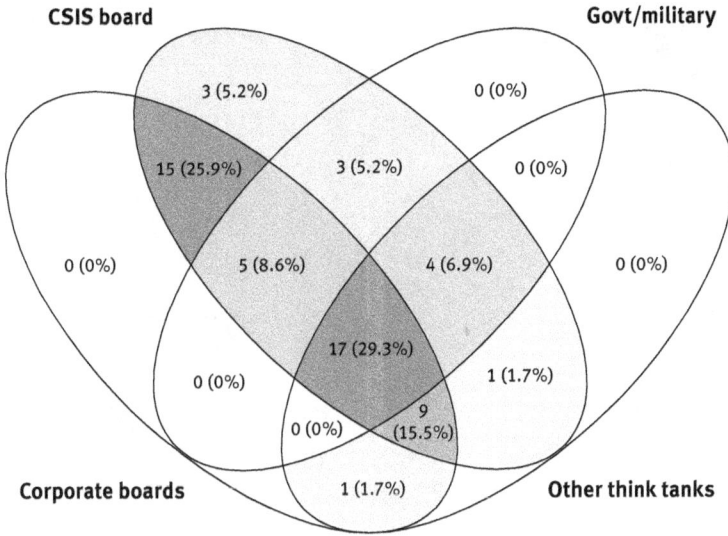

Figure 4.2. Interlocking of the Center for Strategic and International Studies (CSIS)

CSIS board   **Govt/military**

3 (5.2%)   0 (0%)

15 (25.9%)   3 (5.2%)   0 (0%)

0 (0%)   5 (8.6%)   4 (6.9%)   0 (0%)

17 (29.3%)

0 (0%)   1 (1.7%)

0 (0%)   9 (15.5%)

Corporate boards   1 (1.7%)   **Other think tanks**

corporate–think-tank interlocks, and corporate interlocks with the federal government, will also drive drug enforcement aid flows and, in the process, provide contracts and other benefits to American corporations. This discussion generates the following hypotheses:

Hypothesis 1: Increasing levels of corporate campaign contributions will increase U.S. counternarcotic aid flows.

Hypothesis 2: Increasing levels of corporate–think-tank interlocks will increase U.S. counternarcotic aid flows.

Hypothesis 3: Increasing levels of corporate-government interlocks will increase U.S. counternarcotic aid flows.

Hypothesis 4: Increasing levels of an interlocking directorate will increase U.S. counternarcotic aid flows.

Hypotheses 1 and 2 were tested by the indicators Corporate Campaign Contributions and Corporate–Think-Tank Interlocks, respectively.[4] The indicator Corporate-Government Interlocks was used to test hypothesis 3. Finally, the index of an Interlocking Directorate was created through principal component factor analysis and used to test hypothesis 4.[5]

Figure 4.3. Interlocking of the Brookings Institution

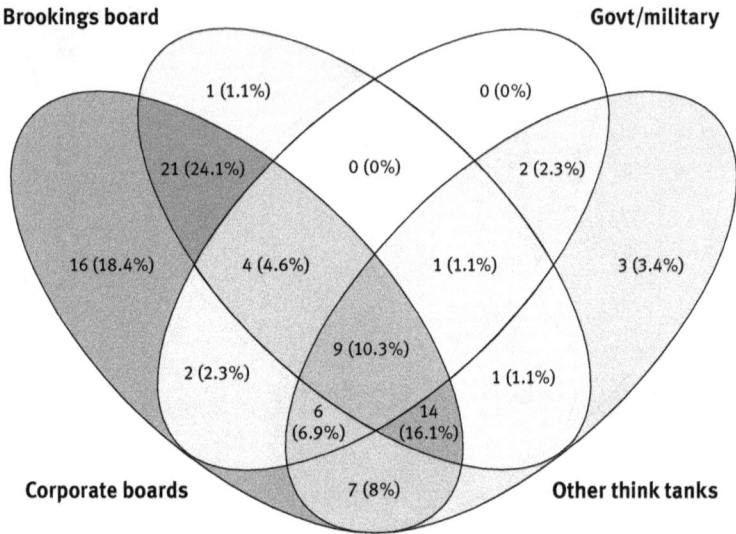

Brookings board　　　　　　　　　　　　　　　　　　**Govt/military**

1 (1.1%)　　　　　　　　　0 (0%)

21 (24.1%)　　　　0 (0%)　　　　2 (2.3%)

16 (18.4%)　　4 (4.6%)　　　1 (1.1%)　　　3 (3.4%)

9 (10.3%)

2 (2.3%)　　　　　　　　　1 (1.1%)

6　　14
(6.9%)　(16.1%)

Corporate boards　　　7 (8%)　　　**Other think tanks**

Empirical Results

Hypothesis 1 is supported by the data. As shown in table 4.1, total corporate campaign contributions and corporate contributions from individuals and PACs are all positively associated with increasing drug enforcement aid flows in the amount equations in models 1, 2, and 3. The effect of the control variables on drug enforcement in the selection and amount equations is consistent with the estimates reported in chapter 3. These results corroborate evidence from Colombia that corporate contributions to members of Congress were instrumental in sustaining congressional funding appropriations for Plan Colombia.

In 2003, former Speaker of the House Dennis Hastert (R-IL) and former representative Cass Ballenger (R-NC) galvanized support to defeat an amendment to the foreign appropriation bill that would have redirected US$75 million from the Colombian military for the prosecution of the drug war (Drug War Chronicle 2003).[6] The amendment was defeated 226 to 196. While the pattern of voting was partisan, with a majority of Republicans voting no and a majority of Democrats voting yes, eighteen Democrats and thirteen Republicans broke with their party's position on the amendment.

Some of the top corporate contributors to House members who voted no were defense contractors Lockheed Martin, United Technologies, Boeing, Ray-

Figure 4.4. Interlocking of the RAND Corporation

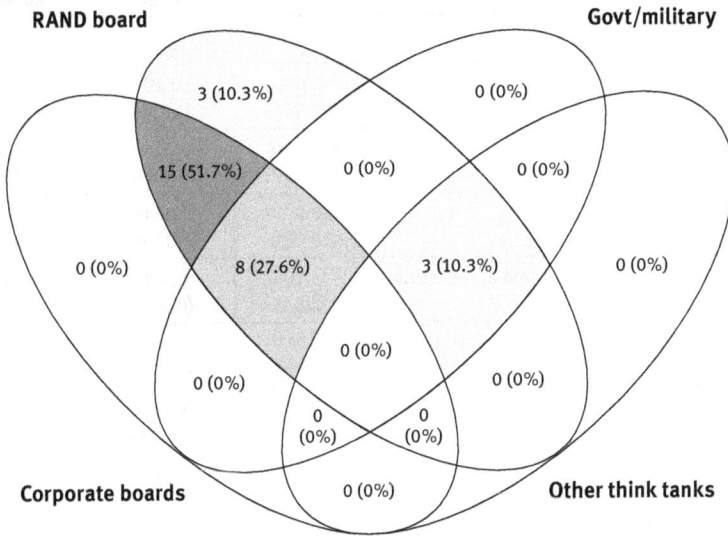

theon, General Dynamics, and Northrop Grumman—companies that success-fully lobbied lawmakers in 2000 to secure congressional funding for the drug war initiative.[7] This, however, was not the only time that Speaker Hastert pro-tected the financial interests of his corporate sponsors who operated in Colom-bia. According to declassified State Department documents from the U.S. em-bassy in Bogotá, Colombia, on November 8, 1996, the Clinton administration decertified Colombia because of the government's lack of cooperation on drug enforcement, extradition, corruption, and widespread human rights violations. A central issue surrounding Colombia's decertification was the negotiation of an end-use monitoring (EMU) agreement that would have allowed US$40.5 million in military equipment to be disbursed that year to Colombia. In his meeting with Defense Minister Guillermo González, U.S. ambassador Myles Frechette was blunt in his criticism of the Colombian military, which he char-acterized as pervasively corrupt with respect to procurement contracts and links to drug traffickers. Ambassador Frechette insisted that the emergency drawdown of equipment that was designated under section 506 of the Foreign Assistance Act would not be delivered until Colombia signed an agreement on human rights and EMU restrictions (U.S. Embassy Bogotá 1997a, 11).

While the Colombian authorities protested that decertification under-mined their ability to fight the cartels and the FARC guerrillas, Colombia's

Table 4.1. Corporate campaign contributions and counternarcotic aid flows

Explanatory variables	Model 1	Model 2	Model 3
Stage 1: The selection equation			
Presence of narcoterror organizations	−0.192 (0.290)	−0.191 (0.290)	−0.192 (0.290)
Polity index	−0.00638 (0.00897)	−0.00639 (0.00898)	−0.00638 (0.00897)
CIRI human rights Index	0.0643 (0.0568)	0.0644 (0.0568)	0.0643 (0.0568)
Bilateral free-trade-investment agreements with the United States	−0.0104 (0.254)	−0.0105 (0.254)	−0.0104 (0.254)
Latin America and the Caribbean Basin	0.929*** (0.278)	0.930*** (0.278)	0.929*** (0.278)
Constant	0.536+ (0.314)	0.536+ (0.314)	0.536+ (0.314)
Number of observations at stage 1	3328	3328	3328
Stage 2: The amount equation			
Total contributions	0.0352** (0.0126)		
Individual contributions		0.115** (0.0407	
PACs			0.0374** (0.0132)
Presidential ideology	0.363+ (0.205)	0.364+ (0.205)	0.359+ (0.205)
Organizational inertia	0.638*** (0.0536)	0.638*** (0.0536)	0.638*** (0.0536)
U.S. federal government debt (% of GDP)	−0.0139 (0.0107)	−0.0138 (0.0107)	−0.0137 (0.0107)
U.S. federal government revenues	−0.00432 (0.0867)	−0.00182 (0.0872)	−0.00634 (0.0863)
Presence of narcoterror organizations	0.983** (0.311)	0.982** (0.311)	0.983** (0.311)
Polity index	−0.0196*** (0.00443)	−0.0196*** (0.00443)	−0.0196*** (0.00443)
CIRI human rights Index	0.0943* (0.0457)	0.0943* (0.0457)	0.0944* (0.0458)
Bilateral free trade and investment agreements with the United States	0.0499 (0.158)	0.0494 (0.158)	0.0500 (0.158)
Latin America and the Caribbean Basin	0.629** (0.238)	0.629** (0.237)	0.629** (0.238)

Table 4.1. (*continued*)

Explanatory variables	Model 1	Model 2	Model 3
Constant	0.444 (1.685)	0.401 (1.692)	0.471 (1.679)
Number of observations at stage 2	21118	21118	21118
Heckman model chi-square	883.48***	929.37***	930.08***
Wald test of independent equations, chi-square	7.50*	7.61*	7.49*

Robust standard errors in are parentheses.

Levels of statistical significance: $+p < 0.10$, $*p < 0.05$, $**p < 0.01$, $***p < 0.001$.

decertification also threatened the revenue stream of U.S. defense contractors. Decertification held up the sale of Blackhawk helicopters, parts destined for the Colombian Air Force, and ground-based radar equipment used to track drug-smuggling planes. To be effective against drug traffickers the Colombian military requested thirty to forty ground-based radars, each costing US$20 million at the outset and an additional $3 million annually to keep operational (U.S. Embassy Bogotá 1997b, 11, 33). Because the Colombian military defended the oil pipelines and facilities of American oil companies from FARC and ELN guerrilla attacks, companies like Occidental Petroleum, Chevron, and Exxon-Mobil lobbied Congress to lift decertification to ensure the security of their assets in Colombia.[8]

Speaker Hastert along with congressmen Mark Sanford (R-SC), Robert Barr (R-GA), Mark Sounder (R-IN), and Rod Blagojevich (D-IL), then members of the House Oversight and Reform Committee, led a fact-finding delegation to Colombia from May 24–27, 1997, supposedly to better understand the reasons for the delay in counternarcotic aid and to determine if there were areas in the certification process that needed improvement (U.S. Embassy Bogotá 1997b, 2–3, 38). However, the real reason for the delegation's visit was to facilitate the release of the promised US$40.5 million in military equipment to the Colombian military, which ultimately undermined Ambassador Frechette's ability to negotiate an EMU agreement with the Colombian government that was consistent with U.S. human rights law.

While meeting with the ambassador, Hastert remarked that decertification was tantamount to disengagement and expressed concern that its adverse effect on the military would force the Colombian government to turn to other countries for training and equipment—a possible outcome that the delegation and their corporate sponsors clearly wanted to avoid. Congressman Barr questioned whether human rights were more important than fighting the drug trade and pressed the embassy to issue the 614 provision, which would waive human rights preconditions so that counternarcotic aid could be resumed. Nonetheless, Ambassador Frechette stood firm and insisted that the State Department must follow the human rights law passed by Congress. The ambassador noted that even before the 506 drawdown was announced he had concluded that the efficacy of the existing EMU procedures left the United States vulnerable to accusations by human rights NGOs that counternarcotic aid was not properly tracked to ensure that assistance did not go to units in the military that were implicated in human rights abuse. Therefore, given the existing EMU procedures, the ambassador refrained from issuing the 614 provision, as he could not recommend to Washington with sufficient certainty that the use of U.S. counternarcotic aid was compliant with U.S. human rights law. In his response, Hastert noted that 25,000 American youth had died in 1996 from drugs smuggled into the United States and that the U.S. government must look beyond human rights "gobbledygook" and work with all willing countries to stop drug smuggling. He concluded his meeting with the embassy by declaring that when he returned to Washington he would be holding hearings on why the embassy and the State Department had delayed providing counternarcotic assistance to the Colombian government (U.S. Embassy Bogotá 1997b, 7–17).

In meeting with members of the Colombian military Hastert promised military leaders that he and members of the House Oversight and Reform Committee would work to remove the human right conditions on counternarcotic assistance. According to declassified documents from the U.S. embassy in Bogota, Speaker Hastert said:

> That he and like-minded members of Congress are sick and tired of people who spend most of their lives living outside of the U.S. [a reference to Ambassador Frechette] inhibiting the process by placing conditions on military aid when the lives of U.S. children and youth are being destroyed by drugs. He decried the leftist-dominated Congress of years past who used human rights as an excuse to aid the left in other countries and vowed that he was committed to correcting that situation and expedite aid to U.S. allies in the war on drugs. He closed by telling the military and the police that they already knew they could bypass the U.S. executive branch and communicate directly with Congress and encouraged them to continue to do so. (U.S. Embassy Bogotá 1997b, 31)

At an impromptu press conference, when asked by a local reporter what the delegation intended to do when they returned to the United States, Congressman Sanford said that they would work to lift EMU restrictions and get the 614 waiver, which would resume counternarcotic assistance to Colombia's military and police (U.S. Embassy Bogotá 1997b, 38).

It became clear that the delegation's raison d'être was to lift restrictions on counternarcotic aid because decertification disrupted the flow of revenues to U.S. defense contractors, and the ambassador's adherence to U.S. human rights law had become an inconvenient obstacle to the process of capital accumulation. Moreover, by encouraging the Colombian military leadership to bypass the executive branch, Speaker Hastert undermined the president's constitutional authority in foreign policy decision making. In the process, he encouraged a culture of human rights impunity in Colombia for the sake of preserving the revenue stream of his corporate sponsors.

Two months after the departure of the delegation the Clinton administration succumbed to pressure from those members of Congress who were proponents of releasing aid to Colombia. Such pressure came from Hastert's congressional hearings regarding the embassy and the State Department's delay in providing counternarcotic assistance to the Colombian government. With the upcoming midterm elections in 1998, in which the president's party was expected to lose seats in Congress (Campbell 2015), these congressional hearings created the perception that the Clinton administration was soft on the war on drugs. In July 1997, despite the fact that the United States and Colombia had yet to come to an agreement regarding human rights and EMU restrictions on counternarcotic aid, the Department of Defense sent a shipment of military hardware for Colombia's security forces under the president's emergency drawdown authority. Upon learning of the delivery, Ambassador Frechette sent a cable to Washington complaining that the shipment of military equipment "will undermine the embassy's efforts to negotiate an EMU agreement." Senior officers in the Colombian military were now convinced that they had the upper hand in negotiating EMU conditions and need only take a tough line and wait for the U.S. government's insistence on human rights conditions to be overwhelmed by congressional political pressure (U.S. Embassy Bogotá 1997c, 3).

This example from Colombia and the preceding data analysis both provide strong evidence that corporations exert a powerful influence over drug enforcement policy making through the candidate selection process by means of campaign contributions to congressional lawmakers. This finding calls into question the Supreme Court's *Citizens United* decision, which effectively legalized the dominance of corporate money in shaping not only election outcomes but also, in this case, drug enforcement policy. However, the analysis testing hypothesis 2 demonstrates that the power of the corporate elite is not limited to the candidate selection process but also influences the government's drug enforcement policy making via think tanks whose research and policy papers create an ideological environment that leads policy makers as well as the public to favor drug prohibition, which in turn ultimately increases drug war aid flows.

Table 4.2 shows that hypothesis 2 is also supported by empirical data. Increasing levels of corporate think tank interlocks are positively associated with increasing drug enforcement aid flows in the amount equation in model 1. Again, the control variables in both the selection and amount equations remain consistent with those reported in previous tables. These findings are consistent with the drug enforcement policy positions adopted by leading American think tanks. A brief survey of the research that appeared in books and in policy papers published in the last thirty years by the RAND Corporation, the Brookings Institution, CFR, Carnegie Endowment for International Peace (CEIP), the Woodrow Wilson International Center for Scholars, and the CSIS, all ranked among the world's top twenty think tanks for their expertise in foreign policy and international affairs (McGann 2013, 60), shows that they have collectively contributed to creating an environment that sustains the ideology of drug prohibition. This ideological orientation emerges from the preferences of their corporate donors who receive financial and security benefits from drug enforcement.

The RAND Corporation's policy papers have consistently promoted the doctrine of prohibition and domestic and international drug interdiction. The common ideological underpinning of these policy papers is the proposition that prohibition is necessary because drug dealing and drug use are associated with violent crime. In one study RAND researchers categorized drug offenders as "violent predators" who concurrently deal drugs, engage in robbery, and commit violent assault (Chaiken and Chaiken 1982). RAND policy papers consistently promote the idea that drug enforcement is needed to reduce the societal costs associated with drug consumption. However, researchers have struggled to find consistent evidence regarding the effectiveness of drug interdiction in reducing the consumption of illicit drugs (Crawford et al. 1988; Caulkins 2000). One study has acknowledged that prohibition has not eliminated all drug use, as shown by the dramatic increase in heroin consumption in recent years. In addition, while recognizing that cocaine enforcement has now reached a point of diminishing returns in terms of reducing cocaine consumption, the study concluded that "it would be a grave mistake to turn to legalization as an alternative. . . . Prohibition must be maintained, but a 'smart prohibition' is needed to get additional results" (Caulkins 2000, 1–13).

In another study RAND researchers Reuter and Kleinman (1986, 290–91) provided evidence showing that the drug enforcement efforts of the federal government and local law enforcement have a limited effect on the retail price

Table 4.2. Corporate think tanks and counternarcotic aid flows

Explanatory variables	Model 1
Stage 1: The selection equation	
Presence of narcoterror organizations	−0.182 (0.289)
Polity index	−0.00661 (0.00900)
CIRI human rights index	0.0663 (0.0565)
Bilateral free-trade and investment agreements with the United States	−0.0363 (0.246)
Latin America and the Caribbean Basin	0.958*** (0.270)
Constant	0.522+ (0.312)
Number of observations at stage 1	3392
Stage 2: The amount equation	
Corporate think tank interlock	0.000173** (0.0000648)
Presidential ideology	0.362+ (0.206)
Organizational inertia	0.637*** (0.0537)
U.S. federal government debt (% of GDP)	−0.0135 (0.0108)
U.S. federal government revenues	−0.00357 (0.0869)
Presence of narcoterror organizations	0.984** (0.311)
Polity index	−0.0198*** (0.00443)
CIRI human rights index	0.0952* (0.0459)
Bilateral free-trade and investment agreements with the United States	0.0433 (0.158)
Latin America and the Caribbean Basin	0.640** (0.237)
Constant	0.411 (1.692)
Number of observations at stage 2	21183
Heckman model chi-square	810.27***
Wald test of independent equations, chi-square	8.74**

Robust standard errors are in parentheses.

Levels of statistical significance: $+p < 0.10$, $*p < 0.05$, $**p < 0.01$, $***p < 0.001$.

of illicit drugs because such efforts cannot alter the underlying social and cultural conditions that give rise to drug use. The massive scale of the illicit drug market and the middle-class nature of its users, they argued, are important factors that reduce the efficacy of drug enforcement. However, the study's policy recommendation does not logically flow from its central findings. Instead, the researchers concluded that "our pessimistic conclusions about the effect of cocaine and marijuana enforcement on street-level prices are not condemnations of drug enforcement generally . . . [and] . . . even if we are correct in our estimates of the relative ineffectiveness of additional Federal expenditures on cocaine and marijuana enforcement that does not imply either that less should be spent for such enforcement or that legalization is appropriate" (291).

Some readers may object to my analysis on grounds that RAND's drug enforcement research during the 1980s and early 2000s does not accurately reflect the policy nuances of the think tank's current drug policy research. This objection is valid and is deserving of inquiry by examining some of RAND's more recent drug policy research to ascertain whether the policy nuances of these studies in terms of their assessment of the effectiveness of U.S. drug enforcement are sufficient to alter the think tank's policy support for drug prohibition.

In a study titled *The Latin America Drug Trade* (2011), which specifically analyzed the effectiveness of U.S. counternarcotic assistance in prosecuting the drug war in Latin America, RAND researcher Peter Chalk argues that U.S. counternarcotic assistance has

> yet to significantly reduce or undermine the Latin American drug trade. Colombia still constitutes the principal source of cocaine for both the U.S. and global market, accounting for 90 to 80 percent of respective consumption. . . . In Mexico, the situation is even worse, with the northern border states now in the throes of what amounts to a fully-fledged narco-war. Moreover, the Mérida Initiative, at least as currently formulated, neither addresses the gap between federal and local police nor provides assistance at the municipal level to deal with everyday security issues. Finally, the trafficking routes from Colombia and the wider Andean region, by no means, been curtailed, merely shifting in response to extant [drug] interdiction approaches. Indeed, the mosaic of smuggling conduits extending from Latin America is now arguably more complex than ever before, embracing at least five principal transpacific and transatlantic corridors. (16–17)

Again, the study's policy recommendation does not flow from its assessment of the ineffectiveness of U.S. counternarcotic operations in combating Latin America's drug trade. Instead, Chalk (2011, 17) advocates for more drug enforcement and recommends that the U.S. Air Force play a role in overseas counternarcotic operations, specifically "boosting the capacity of Mexico—the geographical epicenter for much of what is occurring in the cocaine trade—to counter drug production and trafficking. Notably, these include providing reliable aerial monitoring assets, training and equipping crews to fly and maintain these platforms; enhancing intelligence, surveillance and reconnaissance capabilities; supplying accurate real-time intelligence (including satellite imagery) to facilitate ground-based and marine [drug] interdiction operations."

In a study titled *The U.S. Drug Policy Landscape* (2012), conducted by researchers from RAND's Drug Policy Research Center to provide analyses and policy recommendations regarding U.S. drug use and the efficacy of overseas drug enforcement, Kilmer et al. concluded that the "key takeaway message is that enforcement against suppliers is not a very effective way to reduce the use of drugs supplied through well-established markets; [drug] interventions in source countries appear to be particularly futile in this regard" (34). However, the acknowledgment of the futility of overseas drug enforcement did not alter their policy recommendations away from drug prohibition. In fact, they recommend that "enforcement maybe more effective at suppressing 'thin' and 'emerging' drug markets. . . . Emerging markets can be thought of as thin markets that are in transition, moving rapidly toward becoming well established. . . . . However, in broader, established markets—including those for marijuana and cocaine—there are so many suppliers that customers can readily find replacements for suppliers who are incarcerated" (34–35). In essence, the acknowledgment of the futility of overseas drug enforcement in "well-established" drug markets and the relative effectiveness of drug suppression efforts in "thin" or emerging drug markets represents a nuanced tactical policy recommendation to make the existing prohibition regime more effective.

In a RAND blog posting titled "Should California Drop Penalties for Drug Possession?" (2017), Beau Kilmer, codirector of the RAND's drug policy research, and Robert J. MacCoun, Stanford law professor, answer this question in the affirmative and recommend that all drug use should be decriminalized. Their recommendation is based on their assessment of the ways in which drug prohibition is largely responsible for increasing arrests and convictions—especially among communities of color—which makes it harder for these communities to receive federal aid for college or access public housing. They are certainly correct in recognizing how drug prohibition is associated with producing systemic inequities that flow from mass incarceration—an issue that I discuss theoretically and analyze empirically in chapter 8. However, drug users will not be penalized, under decriminalization, and enforcement will continue against drug producers and distributors; thus, while it is a nuanced approach for addressing the mass incarceration effect of drug enforcement, decriminalization is not a policy alternative to prohibition because, in the words of Kleiman et al. (2011, 27), "it gives consumers permission to buy what dealers are forbidden to sell." Decriminalization is therefore intended to reform drug prohibition and hence maintain the underlying logic and raison d'être for the existing drug enforcement regime.

Of the thirty-three corporations represented in this study, 19 percent are listed in RAND's 2014 annual report among its top corporate contributors.

These include BP, Chevron, ExxonMobil, Hewlett-Packard, Pfizer, and Wal-Mart Stores (RAND Corporation 2014, 64–65). These listed corporations also support U.S. drug enforcement initiatives in Colombia and Mexico.

Policy papers by Brookings Institution senior fellow Vanda Felbab-Brown (2014a, 2014b) also emphasize the need to maintain the existing prohibition regime, arguing that proponents of legalization incorrectly assume that it would deprive organized crime of resources, which would reduce violent crime. She argues that this assumption is erroneous because the legalization of illicit narcotics would not exclude criminal organizations from the legal drug trade. In fact, legalization might provide criminal organizations with advantages over legal companies and would more likely maintain their control over the trade through the use of violence. Legalization, Felbab-Brown contends, would also intensify violent power struggles among criminal organizations over remaining illicit economies such as human trafficking and other forms of contraband and is therefore not a solution to the problem of the drug trade and the violent crime that emerges from it. Instead, building and strengthening the law and drug enforcement apparatus of the state and its relations with marginalized communities in developing countries are the most effective ways of addressing the problems associated with illicit drugs (Felbab-Brown 2012a). In addition, Felbab-Brown (2014b, 41) argues that governments should make drug interdiction strategies more effective by implementing "focused-deterrence strategies, selective targeting, and sequential [drug] interdiction efforts, [which] are often more promising law enforcement alternatives than flow-suppression or zero tolerance approaches." The emphasis on "focused-deterrence" and "selective-targeting" as strategic mechanisms for making drug enforcement more effective is reiterated in Felbab-Brown's policy recommendations to engage criminal organizations in the context of ongoing violent conflict. Under these conditions she argues that "it is unrealistic to expect that outside policy intervention can eradicate all organized crime and illicit economies or for that matter the drug trade in the area of intervention. The priority of the international community should be to focus on the most disruptive and dangerous networks: those with the greatest links or potential links to international terrorist groups with global reach, those that are the most rapacious and detrimental to society. . . . And those that concentrate distribution of rents from illicit economies to a narrow clique of people" (Felbab-Brown 2014a, 107).

Again, some readers may object to my analysis of Felbab-Brown's work on grounds that her research is also more nuanced and has focused substantially on the unintended consequences of U.S. drug policy. It is certainly true that she is a critic of the unintended ways in which the execution of U.S. drug enforcement has undermined larger U.S. foreign policy goals such as the War on Terror and postconflict state building in such countries as Afghanistan (Felbab-Brown 2010, 2012b, 2013). However, her nuanced critique of the drug war should not be taken as a rejection of drug prohibition. To the contrary, her critique of drug enforcement is based on the failures of its tactical execution, and she consistently recommends policy changes to make the prosecution of the drug war more effective in the realization of U.S. foreign policy goals.

A careful analysis of the central argument advanced in her work underscores this point. In *Shooting Up: Counterinsurgency and the War on Drugs* (2010), Felbab-Brown is primarily concerned with how illicit economies affect military conflict and what she calls the "political capital" of insurgent groups. Through case studies of three countries, Peru, Colombia, and Afghanistan, she argues that existing drug suppression efforts in these countries have failed to deprive insurgents of financial resources from the drug trade. And since crop eradication measures have a negative impact on the livelihood of farmers, they are increasingly alienated from their governments and are unlikely to provide intelligence on insurgents, which ultimately increases the political capital of these groups. This argument is again reiterated in *Aspiration and Ambivalence: Strategies and Realities of Counterinsurgency and State Building in Afghanistan* (2013), where she argues that "eradication and bans on poppy cultivation without alternative livelihoods being in place only trust vulnerable populations—much of the rural population of Afghanistan in fact—into the hands of the Taliban" (271). While her critique of the existing practices of the drug war is indeed nuanced, her policy recommendations consistently call for selective enforcement. She contends that "counter-narcotics efforts are a key component of stabilization and development policies in Afghanistan. . . . Interdiction of drug traffickers, including by ISAF [International Security Assistance Force] forces, needs to become more selective than it has been for the past four years. Opium seizures should be limited to truly large stockpiles and not target household opium holdings . . . and inappropriate efforts to suppress the drug economy greatly complicate counterterrorism, counterinsurgency and stabilization objectives" (271).

Although Felbab-Brown's arguments are nuanced in acknowledging how the existing practices of drug enforcement undermine important U.S. foreign policy objectives, her policy recommendations seek to make the tactical execution of the drug war more effective and congruent with the goals of U.S. foreign policy in the developing world. And despite the fact that her policy recommendations are largely speculative, derived from country study narratives and not supported by systematic empirical data, her work has a significant impact on shaping the beliefs of policy makers and foreign policy opinion leaders because they come from the venerable, highly respected, and supposedly "impartial"

Brookings Institution. Brookings is ranked as the world's best think tank for its expertise in matters concerning foreign policy and international affairs (McGann 2015, 98). It is also ranked second in the world for the best external relations and public engagement programs and third in the world for the best use of both print and electronic media (McGann 2015, 142)—important avenues that allow it to effectively promote the importance of maintaining prohibition by strengthening the drug enforcement capabilities of governments in the developing world.

Other drug policy nuances should also be considered when evaluating whether the drug research of the Brookings Institution has consistently reflected the ideological preferences of its donors. In recent years research fellows at Brookings have increasingly concerned themselves with the issue of marijuana legalization. And while Brookings's research on drug legalization is limited to marijuana policy in the United States, this is still a significant departure from its attitude about drug legalization during the 1980s to early 2000s. In a paper titled *Ending the U.S. Government's War on Medical Marijuana Research* (2015), John Hudak and Grace Wallack, researchers from Brookings's Center for Effective Public Management, call on the federal government to reschedule marijuana and make it available for medical research. In another paper titled *Marijuana Legalization Is an Opportunity to Modernize International Drug Treaties* (2014), Wells C. Bennett and John Walsh, respectively fellows at the Brookings Institution and WOLA, argue that the legalization of recreational marijuana by a number of states puts the federal government at odds with international treaties that commit it to punish and criminalize the recreational use of marijuana. And they recommend that, to avoid this collision, the federal government and its treaty partners consider changing international law to better accommodate marijuana legalization. Although these researchers state that their "essay advances no claim about the desirability of legalizing and regulating marijuana" (5), their interest in marijuana legalization would seem to contradict the empirical evidence presented here (see hypothesis 2), which suggests that greater corporate–think tank interlocks—measured in terms of increases in corporate funding and corporate leadership of think tanks' boards of directors—increase public policy outcomes that support and sustain drug prohibition.

These recent developments lead to the question, What factors are driving the nuanced changes in Brookings's research interest in domestic marijuana legalization? One obvious answer is that these recent developments at Brookings reflect the think tank's response to popular initiatives on marijuana legalization, as well as efforts to decrease mass incarceration. However, upon closer examination it appears that the motivation that drove the think tank's newly acquired interest in marijuana legalization largely reflected the preference of one of its wealthy donors: insurance billionaire magnate Peter B. Lewis. In a *Washington Post* analysis that documents how corporate donors impact the research agenda of the Brookings Institution, Hamburger and Becker (2014) report that before his death in 2013 Lewis made marijuana legalization his personal mission. He financed marijuana legalization campaigns that helped secure legislative victories in Colorado and Washington, but at the federal level he was unable to get the Obama administration and congressional law makers to support his campaign. In 2012 he reached out to the Brookings Institution and other Washington-based think tanks, providing them with financial donations to "change the groundwater in Washington" to support the idea of marijuana legalization. According to Brookings officials, Lewis donated US$500,000 to the think tank, and since 2013 prominent scholars have hosted at least twenty seminars and written research papers and various op-ed pieces that consider making marijuana legal. In fact, scholars at Brookings who work on the marijuana legalization project acknowledge that they knew that Lewis was their benefactor.

Over the past decade, under the leadership of Brookings president Strobe Talbott, a former Clinton administration diplomat, the Brookings Institution has operated under a business model that has placed greater emphasis on expanding the think tank's research and influence in the public policy community through greater fund-raising. As a result, its scholars have been given a greater role in seeking money from outside donors, which include corporations, foreign governments, and wealthy individuals who have been given a voice in the think tank's research agenda (Hamburger and Becker 2014). While Brookings's research interest in marijuana legalization is certainly nuanced, it reflects the preference of one of its wealthy donors and is limited to domestic marijuana policy. However, despite Brookings's interest in domestic marijuana legalization, the ideological justification for maintaining the larger prohibition regime reflects the drug enforcement policy preferences of the corporations that fund the Brookings Institution. According to its 2014 annual report, 39 percent of the corporations in this study's data set, whose policy preferences led them to support the drug wars in Colombia and Mexico, ranked among the Brookings Institution's largest financial contributors. These companies include J. P. Morgan Chase, Chevron, ExxonMobil, Bank of America, British Petroleum, FedEx, General Electric, Northrop Grumman, Occidental Petroleum, Raytheon, United Technologies, Lockheed Martin, and Caterpillar (Brookings Institution 2014, 36–38).

In its influential journal *Foreign Affairs*, the CFR published a series of articles that reinforce the importance of prohibition, drawing on lessons from the drug war in Colombia to advance policy recommendations for defeating Mexico's drug cartels. These recommendations include using the military to destroy cocaine labs and to engage and destroy narcoterror guerrilla organizations. The recommendations also call for professionalization of law enforcement and strengthening of the capacity and integrity of state policing, prosecutorial, and judicial institutions in Latin America. Moreover, the policy recommendations in *Foreign Affairs* advocate increasing the use of electronic surveillance in counternarcotics operations and strengthening the extradition of cartel leaders to the United States (Bonner 2010, 2012; Bonner and Horton 2015). According to CFR's 2015 annual report, 55 percent of the corporations in this study's data set are corporate donors of the CFR; of these companies, 15 percent are defense contractors, including Boeing, Lockheed Martin, Northrop Grumman, Raytheon, and United Technologies (Council on Foreign Relations 2015, 64–65).

In a research report titled *Drug Trafficking on the Great Silk Road* (2000), Martha Brill Olcott and Natalia Udalova, senior associates at CEIP, called attention to the fact that the proceeds from drug trafficking in central Asia supported separatists, radical religious groups, and terrorist organizations throughout the region. Drug trafficking, they argued, supported the operations of the Kosovo Liberation Army, the Taliban, Osama Bin-Laden's Al-Qaida, and Albanian drug barons who controlled the Balkan route of the drug trade to Europe. Drug trafficking threatened not only U.S. security interests in the region, they argued, but also the economic interests of American oil companies that operated in central Asia. For example, in 1998 UNOCAL (Union Oil Company of California), which merged into Chevron in 2005, withdrew from its oil and gas development project in Turkmenistan because warring factions in Afghanistan and the subsequent lack of a recognized government in the country made it impossible to construct a pipeline across the territory. Olcott and Udalova (2000, 4–24) called on the United States to increase drug enforcement aid to the region and noted that, while the U.S. budget for international drug control and drug interdiction had increased from US$53 million in 1970 to US$8.2 billion in 1995, very little of this funding went to central Asia. While just 1 percent of the corporations in this study's data set are corporate donors of CEIP, it is not surprising that Chevron is one of the think tank's largest contributors (Carnegie Endowment for International Peace 2014).

Researchers at the Woodrow Wilson International Center for Scholars provide policy recommendations to address the problem of drug related violence and organized crime in Mexico. Contributors to the report titled *Shared Responsibility: U.S.-Mexico Policy Options for Confronting Organized Crime* (Olson et al. 2010) argue for the implementation of long-term policy solutions to reduce the consumption of drugs in the United States and build Mexico's institutional capacity to ensure that the rule of law is effectively implemented via a functioning prosecutorial and judicial system that is transparent and corruption-free. However, the report places greater emphasis on short-term solutions that call for strong drug enforcement prohibition. These include increased efforts to arrest the leadership of criminal organizations and to disrupt the logistical networks of Mexico's drug cartels by disrupting drug, money, and arms trafficking networks. The report argues that greater bilateral cooperation between the United States and Mexico is crucial to disrupting the drug trafficking and logistical operations of the cartels (Olson et al. 2010, 1–3). The Wilson Center report does not acknowledge prior empirical research demonstrating that drug enforcement efforts that attempt to disrupt the operations of cartels have directly led to increased levels of crime and violence (Bartilow and Eom 2009a). On the contrary, it recommends that an "intelligence-based" law enforcement strategy would allow both countries to identify cartel leaders and disrupt the flow of drugs smuggled into the United States and the flow of money and arms smuggled into Mexico (Olson et al. 2010, 3–4).

Much like the case with other think tanks, the Wilson Center's ideological emphasis on drug prohibition reflects the drug enforcement policy preferences of its corporate donors. According to its 2014 corporate gifts report, 30 percent of the corporations represented in this study's data set are corporate donors of the Wilson Center. These include the usual suspects: ExxonMobil, Chevron, Caterpillar, P&G, J. P. Morgan, Wal-Mart Stores, BAE Systems, Bank of America, Northrop Grumman, and Boeing (Woodrow Wilson International Center for Scholars 2014, 1–2).

In a report titled "Rebuilding the National and Global Consensus Against Illicit Narcotics: An Agenda for the Next President" (2016), Daniel F. Runde and Julie Snyder, researchers at CSIS, urged the next U.S. president to take the lead in strengthening what they refer to as "a frayed national and global consensus on illegal narcotics." Legalization, they argue, is not a policy option, since nearly 50,000 Americans died of fatal drug overdose in 2014—nearly twice as many drug-related deaths as in 2000. Instead, they argue, the next president should implement long-term counternarcotic strategies to address and reduce domestic drug consumption and addiction. Moreover, supporting long-term development in developing countries could also reduce the supply of drugs to the United States. Like the policy recommendations of other think tanks, the report emphasizes short-term drug enforcement prohibition and encourages the next president to increase counternarcotic cooperation with foreign governments and adopt "aggressive military and police strategies" to reduce the supply of illicit narcotics.

Again, like the drug enforcement policy positions adopted by other think tanks, CSIS's emphasis on drug prohibition reflects the drug enforcement preferences of its corporate contributors. According to CSIS's 2016 report, 58 percent of the corporations represented in this study are corporate donors. The corporations who are the largest contributors to CSIS, Chevron, ExxonMobil, Northrop Grumman, General Dynamics, Lockheed Martin, Boeing, and Raytheon, are also donors to the Council on Foreign Relations, the Brookings Institution, the RAND Corporation, and the Wilson Center (Center for Strategic and International Studies 2016).

Testing hypotheses 1 and 2 has produced strong evidence of the ways in which corporations' influence U.S. drug enforcement decision making through the candidate selection process and through corporate interlocks with think tanks. I next test hypothesis 3, which proposes that increases in the level of corporate-government interlocks, or a revolving door between positions as corporate executives and in government agencies and the military, will increase drug enforcement aid flows.

As predicted, the results in table 4.3 support the hypothesis. Increasing levels of corporate-government interlocks are positively associated with increasing drug enforcement aid flows. The results of the control variables in the selection and amount equations are again consistent with those reported in the previous tables. While the revolving door drives drug enforcement aid flows, this phenomenon is part of a larger process of what instrumental elite theorists refer to as an overarching interlocking directorate, which is composed of interlocking corporate boards of directors, corporate–think tank interlocks, and corporate-government interlocks. According to hypothesis 4, this interlocking directorate is also expected to increase drug enforcement aid flows.

The results in table 4.4 support the hypothesis. In model 1, increasing levels of an interlocking directorate are positively associated with increasing drug war aid flows. I also test one of the propositions of instrumental theory, which argues that, relative to the power elite's interlocking directorate, congressional deliberations at the middle strata of power, or what Mills (1956, 245–46) calls the "noisy content" of politics, does not influence policy decisions, such as drug enforcement, that have national and international consequences.

In testing this proposition, model 2 includes the variable of corporate congressional lobbying expenditures, which proxies the middle strata of corporate legislative power. If this proposition is correct, then, relative to the power elite's interlocking directorate, the influence of corporate congressional lobbying on U.S. drug enforcement aid flows should be zero. In model 2, increasing levels of an interlocking directorate and corporate congressional lobbying are both positively associated with increases in drug enforcement aid flows. Again, the

Table 4.3. Corporate-government interlocking elites and counternarcotic aid flows

Explanatory variables	Model 1
Stage 1: The selection equation	
Presence of narcoterror organizations	−0.183 (0.291)
Polity index	−0.00649 (0.00922)
CIRI human rights index	0.0712 (0.0590)
Bilateral free-trade and investment agreements with the United States	−0.0315 (0.255)
Latin America and the Caribbean Basin	1.001*** (0.279)
Constant	0.217 (0.322)
Number of observations at stage 1	3392
Stage 2: The amount equation	
Corporate-government interlocks	0.0313*** (0.00908)
Presidential ideology	0.389+ (0.205)
Organizational inertia	0.649*** (0.0526)
U.S. federal government debt (% of GDP)	−0.0151 (0.0105)
U.S. federal government revenues	0.000163 (0.0887)
Presence of narcoterror organizations	0.906** (0.314)
Polity index	−0.0200*** (0.00482)
CIRI human rights index	0.0998* (0.0467)
Bilateral free-trade and investment agreements with the United States	0.0414 (0.166)
Latin America and the Caribbean Basin	0.696** (0.249)
Constant	0.276 (1.699)
Number of observations at stage 2	14370
Heckman model chi-square	823.75***
Wald test of independent equations, chi-square	11.91***

Robust standard errors are in parentheses.

Levels of statistical significance: $+p < 0.10$, $*p < 0.05$, $**p < 0.01$, $***p < 0.001$.

results of the control variables in the selection and amount stage equations remain consistent with those previously reported.

The middle realm of power may indeed be noisy, but American corporations, as shown in chapter 3, make the loudest noise. Corporate power at both the middle and the elite level drives U.S. drug enforcement. This finding suggests that the old theoretical battle between instrumental and institutional theories over whether corporate power shapes public policy at the level of the power elite

Table 4.4. The interlocking directorate and counternarcotic aid flows

Explanatory variables	Model 1	Model 2
Stage 1: The selection equation		
Presence of narcoterror organizations	−0.190 (0.294)	−0.190 (0.294)
Polity index	−0.00657 (0.00942)	−0.00657 (0.00942)
CIRI human rights index	0.0751 (0.0607)	0.0750 (0.0607)
Bilateral free-trade and investment agreements with the United States	−0.0313 (0.259)	−0.0315 (0.259)
Latin America and the Caribbean Basin	1.030*** (0.285)	1.030*** (0.285)
Constant	0.0235 (0.329)	0.0236 (0.329)
Number of observations at stage 1	3392	3392
Stage 2: The amount equation		
Interlocking directorate	0.00109** (0.000331)	0.00126*** (0.000373)
Corporate congressional lobbying expenditures		0.00482*** (0.00146)
Presidential ideology	0.386+ (0.207)	0.373+ (0.207)
Organizational inertia	0.651*** (0.0520)	0.651*** (0.0519)
U.S. federal government debt (% of GDP)	−0.0149 (0.0104)	−0.0147 (0.0105)
U.S. federal government revenues	0.000161 (0.0893)	−0.00291 (0.0889)
Presence of narcoterror organizations	0.874** (0.322)	0.873** (0.322)
Polity index	−0.0205*** (0.00532)	−0.0205*** (0.00532)
CIRI human rights index	0.104* (0.0493)	0.104* (0.0493)
Bilateral free-trade and investment agreements with the United States	0.0378 (0.177)	0.0365 (0.177)
Latin America and the Caribbean Basin	0.754** (0.265)	0.755** (0.265)
Constant	0.160 (1.706)	0.146 (1.707)
Number of observations at stage 2	11575	11575
Heckman model chi-square	907.85***	929.18***
Wald test of independent equations, chi-square	14.56***	14.65***

Robust standard errors are in parentheses.

Levels of statistical significance: $+p < 0.10$, $*p < 0.05$, $**p < 0.01$, $***p < 0.001$.

or at the institutional level may be misguided. The empirical evidence shows that, in terms of drug enforcement policy making, corporate power dominates both the middle strata and the higher circles of power in American society.

Counternarcotic Aid Flows and Corporate Capital Accumulation

Throughout this analysis I have asserted, but have not empirically demonstrated, that American corporations dominate drug enforcement decision making for the purpose of increasing corporate revenues. I now empirically test this argument by briefly discussing important control variables, such as prior levels of corporate revenues, the U.S. corporate tax rate, foreign countries' tax rates, and economic growth, in counternarcotic aid recipient countries, all of which partially explain the dependent variable, corporate revenues.[9]

Since corporations in this study have international subsidiaries, they are subject to both U.S. and foreign corporate taxes. The U.S. worldwide tax system requires American corporations to pay taxes twice, first to the host country in which they operate and then to the Internal Revenue Service after repatriating their revenues. The U.S. worldwide tax system also requires American corporations to pay a stationary tax rate of 35 percent on revenues earned domestically or overseas, while over the past two decades the effective tax rate on foreign taxable earnings has remained constant at 26 percent (Pomerleau 2014, 1–4). Given the differences in corporate tax rates, it is expected that U.S. corporate taxes will have a negative effect on corporate revenues while lower corporate taxes in foreign countries will have a positive effect.

Yardeni and Johnson (2016) have shown that economic growth is associated with increasing corporate revenues. Economic growth in drug war aid recipient countries is also likely to affect corporate revenues. As these economies grow they will increase their demand for goods and services that are manufactured and provided by American corporations, which ultimately will increase corporate revenues. Prior levels of corporate revenues are also likely to affect corporations' current revenues.[10]

Table 4.5 shows that this argument is supported by the data. In model 1, which provides time-series cross section (TSCS) regression estimates, increases in U.S. counternarcotic aid are positively associated with increasing corporate revenues. In model 2, which provides TSCS with fixed effects estimates,[11] U.S. counternarcotic aid still drives corporate revenues. And as table 4.6 shows, this result is consistent across all industries.

The results of the control variables are consistent with theoretical expectations. Models 1 and 2 in table 4.5 show that prior levels of corporate revenues

Table 4.5. U.S. counternarcotic aid flows and corporate revenues

Explanatory variables	Model 1 TSCS	Model 2 TSCS fixed effects
Prior levels of corporate revenues	0.944*** (0.002)	2.793*** (4.21)
U.S. counternarcotic aid	273.5** (42.8)	1.087*** (4.94)
Average effective U.S. corporate tax rate	−4339.5*** (110.7)	−3.145*** (9.71)
Average effective foreign corporate tax rate	3029.4*** (158.4)	2.729*** (1.36)
Annual per-capita GDP growth in drug war aid recipient countries	195.6*** (36.2)	1.595*** (3.61)
Constant	45442.6*** (4118.4)	2.793*** (4.21)
Number of observations	27793	27793
R^2	.90	.92

Time-series cross section (TSCS) estimates. Panel-corrected standard errors are in parentheses. Regression estimates were generated using the R statistical platform.

Levels of statistical significance: $+p < 0.10$, $*p < 0.05$, $**p < 0.01$, $***p < 0.001$.

are positively associated with current levels. Increases in the annual per-capita GDP growth rates in countries that receive drug war aid are also positively associated with increasing corporate revenues.

As expected, the average effective U.S. corporate tax rate is negatively associated with corporate revenues, while the average effective foreign corporate tax rate is positively associated with revenues. As table 4.6 shows, this pattern is also consistent across all industrial sectors. These results would seem to support the contention by conservative and libertarian groups that U.S. corporate taxes discourage investment and encourage capital flight. However, since investment decisions are governed by relative rather than absolute costs, lowering the corporate tax rate by itself would not guarantee that American corporations would reinvest their foreign earnings back into the U.S. economy (Lawrence 1996).

Nevertheless, the GOP tax reform in 2017 was motivated by the ideological belief that the U.S. corporate tax rate discourages economic growth. Hence, the tax bill, which cut corporate taxes from 35 percent to 21 percent, is based on the simple "trickle-down" economic assumption that American corporations will take the money that they save and use it to grow the economy by making acquisitions, investing in equipment, and employing people. However, since the 2008 recession, American corporations have been flush with cash, and in order to stimulate the economy the Federal Reserve kept interest rates low and in 2017 predicted that unemployment would fall below 4 percent with the economy expanding by 2.5 percent in 2018 (Long 2017). Given these conditions, American corporations had sufficient incentives to invest in the economy without the GOP's large corporate tax cut. Corporate response to the GOP's tax cuts has been similar to their response to the Bush tax cuts in 2004: they used the tax savings to buy back stock in their companies, to increase dividend payments to shareholders, and to make campaign contributions—a form of political kickback—to congressional allies who shepherded the bill's passage into law.

The stock value of American corporations determines the level of compensation given to their executives. In consequence, savings from tax cuts is often used to buy the company's stock, which increases both the stock value and executives' compensation. And by reducing the number of shares that are outstanding, stock buybacks not only boost stock prices but also artificially increases corporate earnings. In the months that followed the GOP's tax cuts, stock buybacks were reported by the following companies (in US$): Apple, $100 billion; Cisco, $25 billion; Wells Fargo, $22.6 million; Pepsi, $15 billion; AbbVie, $10 billion; Amgen, $10 billion; Google's parent company, Alphabet, $8.6 billion; Visa, $7.5 billion; and eBay, $6 billion (Brumley 2018; Langone 2018).

In response to the GOP tax cuts, 940 companies increased their shareholder dividends to $19.9 billion in the first quarter of 2018, which represents a 67 percent increase from the same quarter in 2017 (Rooney 2018). Higher shareholder dividends from tax cuts could, in theory, grow the economy since shareholders could consume and invest some of their earnings in other companies. However, shareholders tend to be people at the top of the income ladder, and their propensity to spend extra income is very low compared to middle- and low-income people.

Another response to the GOP's tax reform was that some corporations used the dividends from the tax cuts to make campaign contributions to the Congressional Leadership Fund, a GOP super PAC closely aligned to former Speaker of the House Paul Ryan, who was a significant architect and proponent of the tax reform. The Congressional Leadership Fund's donors included casino magnate Sheldon Adelson, who contributed $30 million. His company, Las Vegas Sands, saved $700 million as a result of the GOP's tax reform. Other donors include Timothy Melton, chairman and majority owner of Pan Am Systems, who contributed $24 million; and Valero Services, an oil refinery company, which contributed $1.5 million after reporting saving $1.9 billion from the tax reform in the first quarter of 2018 (Tankersley and Tackett 2018).

By facilitating stock buybacks, increased dividends to shareholders, and campaign financing for the Republican Party, the GOP tax reform had little to do with generating jobs and more to do with concentrating wealth and power in hands of the corporate elite. The real effect of lowering corporate taxes is that it will increase income inequality, which will further weaken American unions and collective bargaining (Jaumotte and Buitron 2015b). The medium-to long-term threat to economic stability is that the GOP's tax cuts will contribute to increasing the national debt from $21 trillion in 2017—the beginning of the Trump administration—to $33 trillion by 2027. With the explosion of the national debt, the GOP's tax cuts will likely trigger an acute debt crisis and recession in the U.S. economy.

Conclusion

While institutional and elite dimensions of corporate power represent different mechanisms through which the corporatist regime shape drug enforcement policy, an important finding of this chapter supports the fundamental theoretical assumption of embedded corporatism; namely, that counternarcotic aid drives corporate capital accumulation, which is a central by-product of the drug enforcement regime. The chapter also shows evidence of the political dynamics of the inner workings of the corporatist regime and the significance of the agency of foreign governments in drug enforcement decision making. With the support of senior members of Congress, who represented the economic interests of their corporate donors, the Colombian military was able to resist and eventually prevail over the Clinton administration's sanctions against the government for human rights violations while prosecuting the drug war.

The findings in this chapter also provide consistent evidence of the various ways in which the corporate elite shape the decision-making process of the drug enforcement regime. Corporate campaign contributions, corporate interlocks with think tanks and the federal government, and an interlocking directorate systematically increased U.S. drug enforcement aid to eighty recipient countries. Evidence of an elite that shapes public policy will be resisted by some readers because it invokes the notion of a conspiracy. Mills (1956) was quite aware of the fact that his theory of the power elite would be charged with promoting a "conspiracy theory of history." He, however, insisted that the power elite is not a clandestine group of plotters but comprises people who have taken advantage of political and economic opportunities created by institutions.

Conspiracy theory assumes that power is concentrated in the hands of a few powerful actors who operate behind the scenes to direct the affairs of the state. There is nothing conspiratorial about corporate lobbying, corporate campaign financing, corporate funding and leadership of policy think tanks, and the revolving door between corporate executives and the federal government. None of these activities is done in secret, and they describe the political behavior of corporations who avail themselves of opportunities to dominate the institutions of the state. These opportunities are often facilitated by policy changes, such as the Supreme Court's decision in the *Citizens United* case or the recent GOP tax reform that ensures that corporate tax cuts will remain permanent relative to those for the middle and working classes. Such policy changes ultimately promote the interests of the wealthy and embed corporate power in the decision-making institutions of the state.

The embedded corporatist theory of drug enforcement is also incompatible with conspiracy theory because it explains how corporate power shapes the underlying structure of the regime to facilitate consensus and cooperation among multiple domestic and international actors with disparate security and economic interests that nevertheless converge and align in ways that are conducive to capital accumulation. Conspiracy theory also assumes that policy outcomes are "caused" by the direct actions of the conspirators. However, the econometric models used to estimate the data in this chapter and in chapter 3 provide evidence of statistical correlations, not causation. In other words, although the various mechanisms through which the corporate elite shape drug enforcement policy are indeed correlated with increasing counternarcotic aid flows, this statistical fact does not prove that the actors caused the outcome. It is simply that corporate political behavior is strongly correlated with drug enforcement decision-making outcomes.

The subsequent repression of human rights, the development of illiberal democratic regimes in Latin America, and the increase in income inequality throughout the Americas have become the unintended pathological consequences of the policy decisions of the corporatist drug enforcement regime. In the chapters that follow, I theoretically discuss as well as empirically demonstrate how the various dimensions of this pathology capture the essential paradox of democracy in the Americas.

Table 4.6. U.S. counternarcotic aid flows and corporate revenues by industry

Explanatory variables	Oil industry		Mining industry		Military industrial complex		Telecommunications	
	TSCS	TSCS fixed effects	TSCS	TSCS fixed effects	TSCS	TSCS fixed effects	TSCS	TSCS fixed effects
Prior levels of corporate revenues	0.944*** (0.00338)	5.345*** (1.334)	2.079 (2.550)	1.182 (2.54)	9.399*** (3.517)	5.902*** (7.658)	9.496*** (6.991)	7.061*** (1.535)
U.S. counternarcotic aid	273.45*** (42.95)	1.843*** (2.802)	184.4*** (2.196)	3.167*** (2.81)	8.332*** (1.501)	3.596*** (1.816)	8.741 (7.741)	6.122*** (9.972)
Average effective U.S. corporate tax rate	-4339.47*** (111.21)	-1.316*** (5.517)	-2.942*** (5.670)	-2.420*** (5.53)	-1.319*** (3.911)	-1.060*** (3.526)	-3.719*** (1.983)	-3.297*** (1.905)
Average effective foreign corporate tax rate	3029.43*** (157.75)	1.692*** (7.635)	-8.328 (8.147)	-7.530 (7.81)	3.178*** (5.451)	3.971*** (4.798)	2.230*** (2.869)	2.145*** (2.692)
Annual per-capita GDP growth in drug-war aid-recipient countries	195.60*** (36.24)	1.095*** (2.001)	-2.583 (1.855)	-3.804+ (2.06)	1.666 (1.259)	-6.957 (1.280)	8.386 (6.535)	-3.065 (7.090)
Constant	45442.64*** (4118.71)	-5.556** (2.097)	1.636*** (2.111)	1.583*** (2.15)	3.017*** (1.431)	3.930*** (1.357)	4.820*** (7.431)	4.369*** (7.409)
Number of observations	3507	3507	877	877	8500	8500	1754	1754
R^2	0.83	0.87	0.14	0.21	0.89	0.92	0.92	0.93

Table 4.6. (*continued*)

Explanatory variables	Biochemical industry		Manufacturing		Banking industry		Pharmaceutical industry	
	TSCS	TSCS fixed effects	TSCS	TSCS fixed effects	TSCS	TSCS fixed effects	TSCS	TSCS fixed effects
Prior levels of corporate revenues	0.055*** (0.01)	5.325*** (1.08)	9.704*** (3.27)	5.130*** (1.00)	8.173*** (1.34)	7.454*** (1.48)	6.881*** (1.67)	5.825*** (1.86)
U.S. counternarcotic aid	186.08*** (24.23)	3.191*** (3.11)	2.954 (5.20)	9.861+ (5.84)	7.637*** (1.085)	1.627*** (1.43)	2.514*** (5.48)	4.28*** (7.04)
Average effective U.S. corporate tax rate	−58.76 (63.52)	−1.062 (6.23)	−7.336*** (1.34)	−6.674*** (1.14)	−2.876*** (2.75)	−2.365*** (2.72)	−4.439** (1.42)	−2.702+ (1.39)
Average effective foreign corporate tax rate	223.29* (90.14)	2.322** (8.69)	4.245* (1.94)	7.269*** (1.63)	−2.020*** (3.96)	−1.871*** (3.83)	5.670** (2.07)	3.796+ (1.99)
Annual per-capita GDP growth in drug-war aid-recipient countries	−48.61** (20.55)	−6.78** (2.29)	2.737*** (4.41)	3.992*** (4.29)	−1.201 (8.99)	−2.361* (1.01)	−6.220 (4.65)	−9.23+ (5.17)
Constant	3955.7 (2336.8)	3.120 (2.39)	1.087* (5.02)	7.010*** (4.66)	1.491*** (1.02)	1.493*** (1.05)	1.105* (5.38)	1.345* (5.50)
Number of observations	877	877	5262	5262	1754	1754	1754	1754
R^2	0.10	0.17	0.94	0.96	0.71	0.72	0.50	0.54

Table 4.6. (*continued*)

Explanatory variables	Courier industry		Consumer industry	
	TSCS	TSCS fixed effects	TSCS	TSCS fixed effects
Prior levels of corporate revenues	7.646*** (1.47)	5.958*** (1.77)	9.091*** (9.45)	5.416*** (1.69)
U.S. counternarcotic aid	2.478*** (3.62)	5.386*** (4.63)	9.672** (3.16)	3.452*** (3.71)
Average effective U.S. corporate tax rate	−1.729*** (9.32)	−1.431*** (9.03)	−1.215*** (8.12)	9.484*** (7.19)
Average effective foreign corporate tax rate	1.015*** (1.33)	9.825*** (1.25)	3.624** (1.17)	3.342*** (1.01)
Annual per-capita GDP growth in drug-war aid-recipient countries	7.248* (3.03)	6.329+ (3.28)	−9.147 (2.67)	4.073 (2.66)
Constant	3.024*** (3.44)	2.846*** (3.43)	2.628*** (3.04)	3.390*** (2.80)
Number of observations	1754	1754	1754	1754
R^2	0.64	0.68	0.84	0.88

Data are time-series cross section (TSCS) estimates. Panel-corrected standard errors are in parentheses. Regressions estimates were generated using the R statistical platform.

Levels of statistical significance: $+p < 0.10$, $*p < 0.05$, $**p < 0.01$, $***p < 0.001$.

PART 2

The Pathologies of Embedded Corporatism

CHAPTER 5

The Privatization of Terror

U.S. Drug Enforcement Aid, Transnational Corporate Expansion, and Human Rights Repression

Foreign private investment . . . shares to a very high degree the
ambiguity of most human inventions and institutions: it has consider-
able potential for both good and evil. On the one hand, there are
the celebrated and undoubted contributions of private international
investment to development. . . . On the other hand, foreign investment brings not only the dangers of economic plunder and political
domination . . . but a number of other, more subtle, yet serious
effects and side effects which can handicap the development efforts
of countries. . . . It can, in fact, be argued that certain negative aspects of foreign investment do not only continue to coexist with
the positive ones, but typically tend to predominate over them as
development proceeds.—**Albert O. Hirschman**, *How to Divest in
Latin America and Why*

Albert Hirschman, former political economist at Harvard University, wrote
the above words against the backdrop of increasing expropriation of foreign
capital and rising nationalism and militancy in Latin America and the developing world. He attributed these trends to the international arrangements that
governed foreign direct investment and the resulting nationalist reaction to
their negative effects on the development of developing countries (Hirschman
1969). However, in the age of neoliberalism, when nationalist policies have
given way to greater privatization, Hirschman's thesis regarding how the negative effects of foreign capital predominate over its positive aspects as development proceeds is particularly applicable to human rights repression in Latin
America—repressive practices that take place within the context of the embedded corporatist war on drugs.

The chapters in part 1 demonstrated that, through congressional lobbying and the various mechanisms employed by the corporate elite, corporate members of the drug enforcement regime, as well as their strategic political allies, not only shape American drug enforcement policy but also drive increases in counternarcotic aid flows. Building on these arguments, this chapter is motivated by the following question: How does the drug enforcement regime's addiction to increasing counternarcotic aid facilitate the expansion of American and other transnational corporate investments in Latin America and, in the process, create the conditions that give rise to corporate-induced repression? In answering this question, I developed a theoretical framework that draws insights from the literature on foreign aid and its effect on foreign capital flows and then integrates these insights into theories of repression in dependent capitalist societies. I argue that, in addition to combating drug trafficking, U.S. counternarcotic aid facilitates the expansion of American and other transnational corporate investments in Latin America by financing countries' infrastructure development. In conjunction with neoliberal economic reforms, drug war infrastructure financing in Latin America is likely to facilitate the expansion of corporate investments by resource-seeking industries that require greater land use, which encroaches on the ancestral territories of Indigenous peoples. Further, in response to Indigenous resistance to corporate appropriation of ancestral lands, resource-seeking transnational corporations will collude with local security forces, private security firms, and paramilitary death squads to repress and eliminate resistance to capital accumulation.

Scholars have long debated the effects of foreign capital on the human rights practices in developing countries (Evans 1979, 48–49; Meyer 1996; Monshipouri et al. 2003) but often ignore the crucial prior effect that foreign aid exerts on foreign capital flows. Based on her extensive interviews throughout Latin America, Canadian journalist Dawn Paley made an attempt to draw these connections in her book *Drug War Capitalism* (2014), in which she concludes that "the war on drugs is a long-term fix to capitalism's woes, combining terror with policy making in a seasoned neoliberal mix, cracking open social worlds and territories once unavailable to globalized capitalism" (16).

However, to the best of my knowledge, no research has either theoretically or empirically used the tools of social inquiry to demonstrate a relationship between U.S. counternarcotic aid and American and other transnational corporate investments in Latin America and their subsequent impact on human rights repression. An important objective of the research presented in this chapter is to fill this theoretical lacuna in human rights research.

In presenting the components of my theoretical argument, this chapter is organized as follows: the first section discusses the security context of counternarcotic aid recipient countries in Latin America and the Caribbean. Existential threats to the state from drug cartels and narcoterror organizations tie the region's security interests to those of the United States, and the convergence of these interests encourages drug enforcement cooperation. The second section reviews the literature on foreign aid's effect on foreign direct investment (FDI). I discuss the dramatic growth in FDI in general and U.S. FDI flows in particular to Latin America and the Caribbean Basin from 1990 to 2013—the period that corresponds to the advent of democratization's third wave (Huntington 1991b) and the consolidation of neoliberal economic reforms throughout the region. I then apply theoretical insights taken from the extant aid-FDI literature to explain how U.S. counternarcotic aid facilitates the expansion of U.S. FDI in the region, especially in the natural resource industry, which requires increasing access to land. This is followed by a discussion of how resistance by Indigenous communities against resource-seeking transnational corporate penetration triggers a pattern of corporate response in which repression that is increasingly privatized becomes the by-product of capital accumulation. The chapter concludes with a brief discussion of the human rights consequences of the drug enforcement regime and its theoretical implications for the extant human rights literature, in which the existing consensus among liberal scholars is that transnational corporate expansion in developing countries improves human rights (Richards et al. 2001).

The Regional Security Context of Drug Enforcement Aid

The most prominent existential threat to governments in the region has come from drug trafficking organizations (DTOs). Some of the more sophisticated DTOs have acquired extensive paramilitary and counterintelligence capabilities. These capabilities rival the security of states and have allowed them to operate with relative impunity by penetrating governments through a dense network of corrupt officials who are centrally located in the state. Today, the most dangerous DTOs have evolved from a hierarchal, personality-driven structure of leadership, which characterized the Pablo Escobar cartels in the 1980s and 1990s, to a more networked and fluid organizational structure that is more resilient in the face of law enforcement and military pressures of the drug enforcement regime (Seelke et al. 2011, 2–3).

Drug-trafficking-related violence, which has become the primary source of citizen insecurity in the Americas, is concentrated in drug production and drug transit zones and has destabilized the Andean region as well as drug transit zones through Mexico, Venezuela, and Brazil. According to the U.N. Office on Drugs and Crime (UNODC), drug-related homicide rates in the region (discussed in more detail in chapter 7) rose to levels that are epidemic. The most violent country in the region is Honduras, where homicides have tripled since 2003, reaching an alarming 79 murders per 100,000 persons. Increases in homicides are also seen in Venezuela, Mexico, the Dominican Republic, Argentina, El Salvador, Guatemala, Bolivia, Brazil, and even Colombia, which is often touted as the successful model for drug enforcement. And with a homicide rate of 30 per 100,000 persons, the Caribbean is one of the most violent regions in the world. And it is not just homicide that has increased; extortion, sexual violence, and forced displacement have also increased in many countries in the region (UNODC 2007, 2013).

Some drug-related violence is attributed to the protection of drug trafficking routes and power struggles within cartels. Other forms of violence occur as DTOs corrupt and undermine police and criminal justice institutions in the region. In some instances, reminiscent of Colombia's Medellín cartel, Mexican DTOs have used car bombs, political assassinations, and coordinated attacks in different parts of the country to intimidate rivals, citizens, and the government. In Mexico, seven DTOs that control trafficking routes into the United States have resorted to these forms of violence: Arellano Felix Organization (Tijuana), Beltran Leyva Organization, Los Zetas, Sinaloa (La Federación), Carillo Fuentes Organization (Juárez), Gulf, and La Familia Michoacana. Since 2006, drug-trafficking-related violence has surged in Mexico when Mexican president Felipe Calderón increased enforcement measures against the country's DTOs (Seelke et al. 2011, 4–6; Linthicum 2017).

In Colombia, by the late 1990s Marxist insurgent groups became extensively involved in the drug trade. FARC and ELN increasingly used the proceeds from drug trafficking to finance military operations against the Colombian government (Crandall 2008a, 73–76). In Peru, the previously inactive insurgent group Sendero Luminoso (Shining Path) revived its involvement in drug trafficking and has executed small-scale military operations against the Peruvian police and military (Gregory 2009).

As threats to the state from DTOs and narcoinsurgent organizations increased, the security interests of governments in the region converged with those of the United States in ways that facilitated drug enforcement cooperation. The security threats from DTOs against countries beyond the Andes region and Mexico also encouraged American policy makers to increase counternarcotic aid and deepen drug enforcement cooperation with Central American and Caribbean countries via the Central American Regional Security Initiative and the Caribbean Basin Security Initiative (Meyer and Seelke 2015; USAID 2016).

Foreign Aid and Foreign Direct Investment

The conventional wisdom among many international organizations is that official development aid (ODA) complements private capital investment flows to developing countries. The U.N. 2002 Monterrey Consensus on International Financing for Development states that "ODA plays an essential role as a complement to other sources of financing for development, especially in those countries with the least capacity to attract private direct investment. A critical challenge, therefore, is to create the necessary domestic and international conditions to facilitate direct investment flows, conducive to achieving national development priorities to developing countries" (United Nations 2002, 9). However, the assumption that foreign aid facilitates or has a complementary effect on FDI has been the source of contestation among political economists. Kosack and Tobin (2006) argue that aid is unrelated to FDI because it primarily supplements governments' budgets and finances investments in human capital, while FDI is orientated toward the private sector to finance physical capital. Karakaplan et al. (2005) demonstrate that the direct effect of aid on FDI is negative and that it is only through recipient countries' good governance and the development of financial markets that aid's impact on FDI is improved.

In recent years, a consensus has emerged around the proposition that aid is more likely to attract and complement FDI if it is used to build infrastructure in developing countries (Kapfer et al. 2007; Bhavan et al. 2011; Bhavan 2014; Selaya and Sunesen 2012). This includes the building of roads, railroads, airports, ports of entry, power plants, hydroelectric dams, electricity distribution grids, renewable energy platforms, telephone networks, and other infrastructural facilities that are needed to sustain development. Kapfer et al. (2007) argue that, since infrastructure projects are the most observable of all development lending, in that they are nonfungible and cannot be used for purposes other than their intended objective, foreign investors see them as important fixed assets that are necessary for capital accumulation. Consequently, they are more likely to attract FDI. This proposition has received repeated empirical confirmation. Analyzing data for ninety-nine countries for 1970–2001, Selaya and Sunesen (2012) found that aid raises the marginal productivity of FDI when it finances public infrastructure and human capital investments such as education and training but exerts a crowding-out effect on FDI when it finances physical capital. Estimating data for a sample of South Asian countries during 1995–2012, Bhavan (2014) found that infrastructure aid is effective in facilitating FDI, and aid that finances social infrastructure is relatively more effective than other types of aid.[1] Finally, in their empirical case studies of Bangladesh,

Sri Lanka, Pakistan, and India, Bhavan et al. (2011) demonstrate that aid serves as a complementary factor to FDI when used to finance human capital and infrastructure development in South Asian economies.

Specifically, how does U.S. policy preference in bilateral aid disbursements facilitate U.S. FDI flows? U.S. congressional legislative history speaks to the relationship between U.S. bilateral aid and U.S. FDI. During the 1960s and 1970s, U.S. bilateral aid was used as a deterrent against foreign governments' expropriation of U.S. corporate assets (Hawkins et al. 1976). The Hickenlooper amendment, which was passed in 1962 and later expanded in 1963, created a statutory link between the disbursement of U.S. aid and foreign governments' repayment of expropriated U.S. corporate assets. The Hickenlooper amendment required the automatic suspension of aid unless a foreign government compensated an expropriated U.S. company or initiated the process to do so. Similarly, the Gonzalez amendment, adopted in 1972, prohibited U.S. approval of multilateral aid to foreign governments that confiscated U.S. investment (Lipson 1976, 397–98). By imposing economic sanctions on foreign governments that expropriate U.S. private investment, American legislation reduced the risk of overseas investment and thereby facilitated the expansion of U.S. FDI.

The Growth of Foreign Direct Investment in Latin America

U.S. legislation notwithstanding, FDI flows to Latin America and the Caribbean have expanded dramatically since the 1990s. As depicted in graph 5.1, overall FDI flows to the region grew from US$5 million, or 7.0 percent of the region's GDP, in 1990 to US$300 million, or 17.0 percent of GDP, by 2013.

While FDI flows from Europe and China to Latin America and the Caribbean have increased in recent years, the United States remains the largest source of FDI in the region. In 2010, U.S. FDI accounted for 17 percent of the region's inflows, followed by the Netherlands at 13 percent, China at 9 percent, and Canada, Spain, and the United Kingdom at 4 percent each (ECLAC 2010, 41). U.S. FDI accounts for 30 percent of inflows in Central America and 32 percent in Mexico (ECLAC 2013, 10).

Counternarcotic Aid and American Corporate Expansion

In this context, how is U.S. counternarcotic aid related to the growth of FDI, and especially U.S. FDI, in Latin America and the Caribbean? Specifically, how does the extant literature's theoretical and empirical conceptualization of aid's effect on FDI inform our understanding of the relationship between U.S. counternarcotic aid and U.S. FDI flows in the region? The expansion of U.S.

Graph 5.1. Latin American and the Caribbean Basin: Foreign direct investment (FDI), 1990–2013. *Source*: Author-generated time-series graph of the International Monetary Fund's International Financial Statistics database and the United Nations Conference on Trade and Development database.

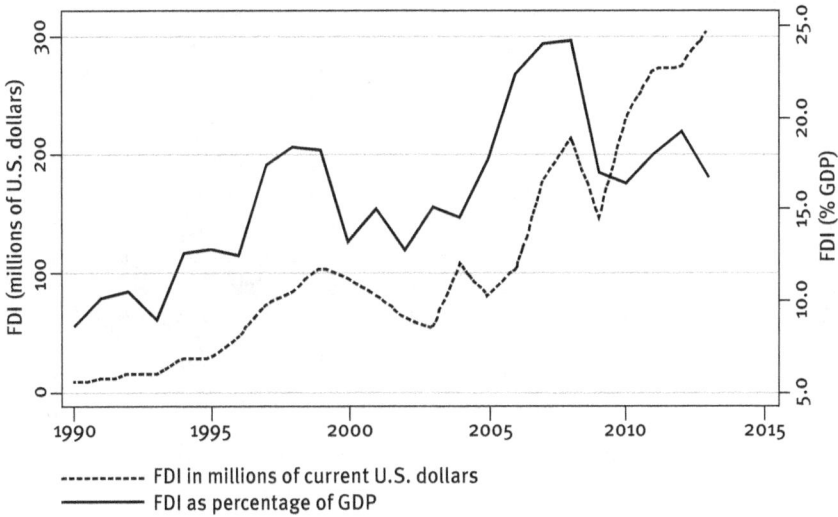

FDI flows to Latin America and the Caribbean is associated with increases in U.S. counternarcotic aid to the region. For example, from 2002 to 2011, U.S. counternarcotic aid to Colombia totaled US$3.5 billion and accounted for 39.9 percent of the country's ODA. This parallels the expansion of FDI in Colombia, which grew from US$1.3 billion in 1990 to US$12.3 billion in 2011 and peaked at US$16 billion in 2005 (Stirk 2013). This relationship is not specific to Colombia— as graph 5.2 shows, it is systematically represented in the sample of thirty-one countries from Latin America, Central America, and the Caribbean included in this study. The nonparametric LOWESS (locally weighted scatter plot smoothing) regression analysis shows that from 1988 to 2012 increases in U.S. counternarcotic aid to countries in the sample had a positive linear relationship with increases in U.S. FDI flows to the region. The 95 percent confidence interval around the fitted values for these variables suggests that U.S. counternarcotic aid is a strong linear predictor of U.S. FDI flows in the region.[2]

This finding suggests that U.S. counternarcotic aid is an important exogenous or "push" factor related to the expansion of U.S. FDI flows to countries in the region. It does not, however, detract from the importance of host country characteristics in Latin America and the Caribbean, such as the level of economic development, the regulatory nature of financial and labor markets,

Graph 5.2. U.S. foreign direct investment and counternarcotic aid in Latin America, 1988–2012. *Source*: Author-generated LOWESS scatter plot.

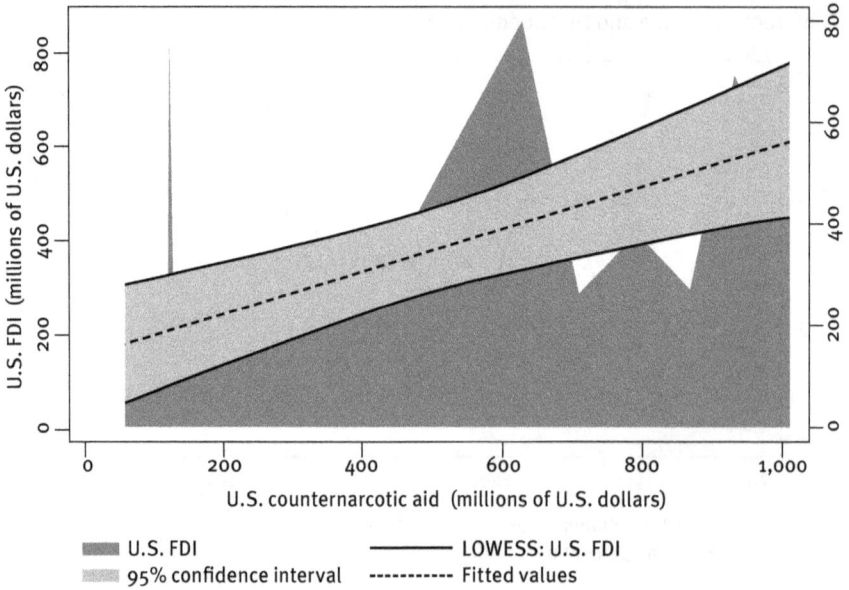

the relative openness to international trade, natural resource endowment, and government tax structure (Akinkugbe 2004, 2005; Akinkugbe and Gbenedio 2004) as endogenous or "pull" factors that also explain U.S. FDI flows to the region.

How can this empirical phenomenon be explained? U.S. counternarcotic aid shares some of the same properties as ODA; namely, in addition to drug enforcement, it also provides funding for infrastructural development, which the extant literature has shown to facilitate FDI flows to developing countries. However, the type of infrastructure development funded by U.S. counternarcotic aid specifically facilitates FDI in natural resources. The subsequent discussion of Plan Colombia and the Mérida Initiative will show that U.S. counternarcotic aid has largely funded infrastructure development projects such as roads, energy, and border and port security. By funding the development and expansion of roads, U.S. counternarcotic aid facilitates the growth of FDI in natural resources since new roads provide transnational companies with easier access to land. This enables the exploration and extraction of oil, coal, gold, and mineral deposits, as well as the expansion of agribusiness, especially the cultivation of African palm oil, which is increasingly being used in the growing biofuel industry. By enhancing border and port security, U.S. counternarcotic aid facilitates not only the exports of corporations in the manufacturing industry but also the exports of companies specializing in natural resources and agribusiness.

While FDI in natural resources accounted for 26 percent of total FDI in Latin America and the Caribbean in 2012, in South America (with the exception of Brazil), where there is a high concentration of resource endowment as well as high levels of U.S. counternarcotic aid, FDI is primarily destined for transnational corporate investment in natural resources, particularly in mining. The share of FDI in South America's natural resource sector grew to 51 percent in 2012, after averaging 44 percent in previous years. In comparison, FDI in manufacturing and services accounted for just 12 percent and 37 percent, respectively (ECLAC 2012, 38). In 2013, FDI in the oil and gas industries grew in Brazil, Colombia, Bolivia, and Trinidad and Tobago. In the last decade, FDI in mining grew in Chile, Peru, Colombia, the Dominican Republic and Mexico. In 2013, FDI in natural resources also grew in several Central American and Caribbean countries including Guatemala, Panama, Suriname, and Barbados, which now host large transnational mining and hydrocarbon projects (ECLAC 2013, 26). FDI in agroindustry totaled US$48.4 billion for 2005–11. Most of these flows went to Brazil (37.9 percent), Mexico (35.9 percent), Argentina (15.5 percent), Guatemala (12.5 percent), Costa Rica (6.7 percent), and Ecuador (7.3 percent) (ECLAC 2012, 14).

Under Plan Colombia, U.S. counternarcotic aid funded the country's "infrastructure security," which provided security for the oil pipeline that helped facilitate the expansion of the oil and mining facilities of U.S. multinational firms Occidental Petroleum and Drummond. In fiscal years 2000–2008, Plan Colombia provided funding amounting to over US$115 million to help implement the first phase of Colombia's "infrastructural security" strategy, which was designed to protect the first 110 miles of the 500-mile-long Caño Limón-Coveñas oil pipeline from FARC and ELN guerrilla attacks. U.S. counternarcotic aid funded air and ground combat support, which included two UH-60 Blackhawk helicopters and eight UH-II Bell helicopters, with logistical and ground support. Approximately US$30 million was used to fund U.S. Special Forces training and equipment for 1,600 Colombian military personnel who provided protection for the pipeline (U.S. Government Accountability Office 2008, 35).

Additionally, under the Colombia Strategic Development Initiative (CSDI), U.S. counternarcotic aid provided funding to increase and consolidate the state's presence in parts of the country plagued by armed groups and drug trafficking cartels. To this end, two major infrastructural development investments were funded under Plan Colombia: the Putumayo Road Project and the Colombia Clean Energy Project. Of the US$24 million that was needed to complete the Putumayo Road Project, Plan Colombia provided US$12 million and the Colombian government assumed responsibility for the remaining 50 percent of the project's anticipated cost. The project maintained, repaired, and paved the roads between the municipalities of Puerto Caicedo and Villagarzon, in the Department of Putumayo. The Putumayo Road Project linked domestic and foreign companies to overseas and domestic markets and facilitated the growth of transnational corporations conducting oil explorations in the towns of Orito and Mocoa. The Putumayo Road Project also helped stimulate FDI financing of the hydroelectric project on the Caquetá River (USAID 2013, 1, 3; David and Richardson 2002).

U.S. counternarcotic aid under the CSDI also invested US$18.7 million in the Colombia Clean Energy Project from 2012 to 2017. The project seeks to improve energy efficiency by attaching its finances to industries that have an interest in upgrading or converting their energy production facilities to adopt new technologies such as methane capture and gasification. With the partnership of private sector investors, the project seeks to provide renewable energy (mostly microhydro and solar energy) to eighty communities that are off grid and also to facilitate financing and remove barriers to private sector investment in renewable energy (USAID 2013, 5).

In their effort to eradicate coca, American policy makers encouraged the development of a biofuel industry through the cultivation of African palm oil, which was intended to be a replacement crop. Under Plan Colombia USAID invested US$10 million dollars to help coca growers switch to palm oil (Otis 2005). USAID's financing of palm oil production contributed to the growth of African palm tree cultivation in Colombia and other countries in Latin American. The expansion of palm oil production has been achieved by increasing areas of land planted with palm trees as opposed to increasing yields on land already under cultivation (Kongsager and Reenberg 2012, 6–7). During 2006 and 2010 the land area used for the production of African palm oil expanded significantly in Mexico, where it grew by 44 percent or 9,700 hectares, and in Central America, where it grew by 34 percent or 64,715 hectares. In 2010, Central American countries, Colombia, Ecuador, and Brazil were the region's leading African palm oil producers, respectively accounting for 36 percent, 26 percent, 15 percent, and 11 percent of the region's production (ECLAC 2012, 110).

As in Plan Colombia, key components of the Mérida Initiative also provide funding for infrastructure development. These relate to funding appropriations that seek to modernize border infrastructure to facilitate greater

FDI investment and international trade. This was an important element of the Obama administration's "Beyond Mérida" strategy, which provided funding for "Building a Twenty-First-Century Border" between the United States and Mexico. In its supplemental budget for Mérida funding during 2008 and 2009, the administration requested US$544.6 million for Mexico and US$56.6 million for Central America to upgrade border infrastructure and implement innovations in ports of entry to combat illicit trafficking and criminality along the border region while increasing the growth and international competitiveness of legitimate business (Cook and Seelke 2008, 2; U.S.-Mexico Chamber of Commerce 2011, 2).

The administration's budgetary request funded the installation at Mexico's southern borders of biometric equipment that allows Mexican officials to monitor and store data about individuals crossing into the country, which provides greater security to the porous Mexico-Guatemala and Mexico-Belize borders. Data collected from the biometric equipment is connected to Mexico's national database, which uses servers and software provided by the Mérida Initiative (U.S. Government Accountability Office 2010, 9). Half of the budgetary request for Central America provided funding for port, airport, and border security, which included equipment and training for border and law enforcement personnel (Cook and Seelke 2008, 4).

The U.S.-funded drug war in Latin America and the Caribbean complements and facilitates corporate expansion, particularly in the region's natural resource sector, in that it creates a security environment that is conducive to the logic of capital accumulation. Even though the initial process of capital expansion into the developing world under conditions of war and conflict (Mommsen 1980) appears as a historical artifact, archived in the museums of the Western industrial world, this phenomenon has reproduced itself in the ways in which the U.S.-funded drug war facilitates the expansion of American and other extractive corporations into the region. Taking this into consideration, how do domestic civil society groups, such as Indigenous communities, respond to resource-seeking corporate incursions into their ancestral lands? The answer to this question is discussed in the next section.

Domestic Resistance: Indigenous Communities

Growing Indigenous peoples' movements in Latin America have been relatively effective in resisting the expansion of transnational corporate encroachments on their lands for the purpose of resource extraction. In 2009, 300 Indigenous people in Oaxaca, Mexico, blocked the operations of the Vancouver-based mining corporation Fortuna Silver for one month (Bacon 2012).

In 2012, the Ikoots people in the Isthmus of Tehuantepec, in Oaxaca, resisted the efforts of transnational corporations to take their ancestral lands. The Ikoots people—a fishing community that depends on the ocean for its livelihood—had inhabited the Isthmus of Tehuantepec for more than 3,000 years. The proposed San Dionisio Wind Park, a wind farm that would be constructed in the ocean along the coast, would consist of 102 wind turbines in the water outside the town of San Dionisio del Mar, and 30 more outside neighboring Santa Maria del Mar, as well as two electric transformer substations, six access paths, and additional support structures. A consortium of transnational corporations, among them the Australia-based investment bank Macquarie, the Dutch investment group PGGM, and the Mitsubishi Corporation of Japan, implemented the project. It included turbines constructed by the Danish company Vestas Wind Systems and two wind power companies, Spain's Grupo Preneal and Mexico's DEMEX (Smith 2012). The San Dionisio Wind Park was largely constructed to provide a cheap source of energy to corporate giants with investments in the region. These included Coca-Cola, Heineken, Wal-Mart, Nestlé, and Mexico's FEMSA, the largest beverage company in Latin America. The Ikoots people feared that the vibration from the wind turbines would destroy the aquatic life in the area and therefore threaten their community's economic and cultural way of life. The Ikoots also contended that the wind turbines threatened migratory birds and would damage the ecosystems of the local mangrove swamps. Most important, they opposed the construction of the wind park because it would desecrate their sacred territory: the Isla de San Dionisio and the Barra de Santa Teresa (Smith 2012).

The Ikoots community did not consent to the construction of the wind park on their land, nor were they informed that the project was under consideration. The failure of the Mexican government to get the consent of the Ikoots people violated the U.N. International Labor Organization's Convention on the Rights of Indigenous and Tribal Peoples. Article 32 of the convention, which was ratified by the Mexican government in 1990, states that "states shall consult and cooperate in good faith with the Indigenous peoples concerned through their own representative institutions in order to obtain their free and informed consent prior to the approval of any project affecting their lands or territories and other resources, particularly in connection with the development, utilization or exploitation of mineral, water or other resources" (United Nations 2008, 12).

Subsequently there has been an intense resistance movement against the wind farm in San Dionisio del Mar. The Ikoots people initiated a legal battle in the Tribunal Unitario Agrario (Agrarian Unitary Tribunal), the government agency in charge of settling agrarian disputes, for the purpose of voiding the government's contract with the transnational companies involved in the construction the project. In their protest the Ikoots people, in late January 2012, took over the municipal palace in San Dionisio, removing Miguel López Castellanos, the municipal president, and created the General Assembly of the People of San Dionisio. In April, the San Dionisio communal assembly prevented workers from transnational companies from constructing access roads in the Barra de Santa Teresa and blocked the return of contractors. In September, the Ikoots people organized a national gathering in San Dionisio of 300 people representing 25 different Indigenous and activist organizations, who came from six different states in Mexico. The intent of the gathering was to raise awareness of the Ikoots' struggle and to develop a national strategy to resist megacorporate projects like wind farming that appropriate the ancestral lands of Indigenous peoples (Smith 2012).

In conjunction with neoliberal economic reforms, Mérida funding for Central America upgraded border infrastructure and encouraged the growth of FDI in Guatemala, especially in the country's mining and agribusiness industries (Cook and Seelke 2008, 2). On September 4, 2014, after ten days of widespread street protests against the American biotech giant Monsanto's expansion into Guatemalan territory, the Mayan community, with the support of labor unions, farmers, and women's organizations, won a victory when the Guatemalan Congress finally repealed legislation that would have opened up the market for genetically modified seeds. The Monsanto Law, as it was locally known, gave the biotech corporation exclusive rights to patented seeds and created a major imbalance between the Monsanto corporation and small farmers, who represent 70 percent of Guatemala's population. Moreover, the law would displace the traditional Mayan cultivation system, which is based on the diversity of natural herbs, corn, and black bean seeds—foods that are a substantial component of the Mayan diet (Sandberg 2014b).

Indigenous peoples in Guatemala also successfully resisted the expansion of transnational corporate mining in their ancestral lands. In April 2012, the general director of the Ministry of Energy and Mines granted the local company Entre Mares de Guatemala S.A., a subsidiary of the Canadian mining company Goldcorp Inc., a permit to mine for gold, silver, nickel, cobalt, lead, and zinc in Sipacapan territory. The permit was given without prior consultation with the Indigenous community. In 2014, a Guatemalan court ruled that since the government granted the permit to the mining corporation without consulting the Indigenous community, as required by the U.N. Declaration on the Rights of Indigenous People and International Labor Organization Convention 169, it was illegal and therefore the contract should be withdrawn (Sandberg 2014a).

Indigenous resistance against Yanacocha, a Peruvian gold mine operated by the Newmont Mining Corporation of Denver, Colorado, is also consistent with this growing trend of social resistance to corporate expansion into the ancestral territories of Indigenous peoples. Newmont is the largest gold mining company in the world, and its Yanacocha mine is reputed to be the world's most productive gold mine. By 2005, the mine had already produced US$7 billion worth of gold (Frontline World 2005). In June 2000, a truck that was contracted by Newmont to carry canisters of mercury from the mine spilled 330 pounds of the poisonous substance over a twenty-five-mile stretch of road around the village of Choropampa, approximately fifty-three miles from the mine. Indigenous campesinos who were exposed to the mercury became sick with symptoms of mercury poisoning and later filed a class-action suit against Newmont Mining in U.S. federal court (Frontline World 2005; Langdon 2000).

The mercury spill ignited violent confrontations between the campesino community and the police. In an attempt to reduce tensions, Newmont conducted its own environmental audit and found that local lakes and streams were contaminated. Because of the mercury spill the Quebrada Honda stream, which had thirteen fish per kilometer in 1997, had none in 2000, and rocks that were not processed for the recovery of gold were leaking hazardous acidic runoff that contaminated the ground water. Mr. Kurlander, a former legal adviser to Governor Mario M. Cuomo in New York, as well as a former Newmont executive, conducted the audit and wrote a letter to Newmont's chief executive, Wayne Murdy, in which he stated that with the expansion of the mine "we eliminated many environmental safeguards that were in the construction and environment management plans," and consequently, the environmental impacts of mining were so serious that they could jeopardize future mining operations and subject senior executives to "criminal prosecution and imprisonment" (Perlez and Bergman 2005). Newmont Mining concealed the findings of its environmental audit within the company, never publicly acknowledging them to its shareholders or making them available to the Indigenous campesino community (Perlez and Bergman 2005).

Even though the local government had approved an ordinance in 2000 that declared the Quilish region and its watershed a protected natural preserve, Newmont overturned it by convincing the court that it had legally acquired the concession to mine in the region years before the ordinance was issued. In August 2004, the company started its gold mine drilling in the Quilish region and sent several hundred armed officers from Lima to guard the mine. Campesinos responded by blocking the road from the town of Cajamarca to the mine with boulders, cars, and debris. A violent clash ensued between the security forces and the campesino Indian community in which protesters were arrested and tear gassed. The campesino resistance grew into a region-wide strike that featured street demonstrations in Cajamarca (Perlez and Bergman

2005). The resistance intensified further when thousands of farmers held a one-day strike and called for the end of Newmont's gold mining operations in the Quilish region, arguing that the company's mining operations contaminated the ecosystem and dried up water that they needed for dairy farming. The campesinos' resistance and demonstrations in Cajamarca ultimately forced Newmont to suspend its mining operations in the Quilish region (Perlez and Bergman 2005; Reuters 2004).

During 2000 and 2001, Indigenous communities and peasant farmers in Brazil and Bolivia mobilized against a 630-kilometer gas pipeline financed by U.S. energy giant Enron International and Shell International Gas Ltd. Since the gas pipeline would cut across the tropical forest and the land of Indigenous communities in both countries, it threatened both the ecosystem and the cultural integrity of the Indigenous populations. However, despite protests the pipeline was completed and the feared negative effects on the environment and Indigenous societies were fully realized (Roberts and Thanos 2003, 170).

In Ecuador, Indigenous communities from the oil-producing Amazon provinces of Orellana and Sucumbios mobilized in 2005 around what was called the Biprovincial Assembly, motivated by the communities' growing resistance to mining and oil extractions in the Amazon (Chicaiza and Hass 2013; Lopez 2012). The Chevron oil company was found guilty of the environmental destruction of portions of the Ecuadorian Amazon and was ordered by an Ecuadorian court to pay US$9.5 billion to clean up its contamination (Koening 2015). After witnessing Chevron's environmental debacle, the Indigenous community opposed the operations of Occidental Petroleum in the Amazon region.

In May 1999, Occidental Petroleum signed a twenty-year contract with the government of Ecuador and the state oil company Petroamazonas for oil exploration and extraction in the segment of Ecuador's Amazon region known as Block 15. Since Occidental bore the entire financial risk of the operation, it was contractually entitled to 70 percent of the oil produced, while the government owned the rest. The contract also stipulated that, while Occidental could sell the oil, it could not sell any portion of its oil production rights without authorization from the government. The contract clearly stated that transferring the rights to produce oil without the government's authorization "shall terminate" the contract and forfeit the company's investment. This provision explicitly enforced Ecuador's hydrocarbons law and ensured that the government had the ability to vet companies seeking to produce oil in its territory, which was viewed as essential given Chevron's earlier massive contamination of portions of the Ecuadorian Amazon (International Center for Settlement of Investment Disputes 2008, 4–7). However, in October 2000, in an attempt to generate capital and reduce the risk of its investment, Occidental sold 40 percent of its oil production rights to the Canadian firm Alberta Energy Company. After an audit in 2004, Ecuador's attorney general realized that Occidental had violated its contract, as it had failed to secure government authorization for the sale of its oil production rights and thus did not comply with Ecuador's hydrocarbons law (International Center for Settlement of Investment Disputes 2008, 7–8).

After a governmental delay in action against Occidental, the 2006 presidential election cycle provided the Indigenous movement with the opportunity to press a politically vulnerable incumbent government, urging the administration to cancel its contract with Occidental Petroleum and redistribute oil revenues to benefit the provinces of Sucumbios, Orellana, and Napo—Amazonian provinces that were adversely affected by the oil industry and were also the poorest in the region. In May 2006, the government terminated its contract with Occidental Petroleum and transferred its oil production operations to Petroamazonas (Lopez 2012).

In Colombia, the Embera Indigenous people of the Antioquia and Chocó Departments, as well as the Afro-Colombian community in the Jiguamiandó region, have successfully resisted the Mandé Norte Mining Project, which was sponsored by the U.S. Muriel Mining company. The Mandé Norte Mining Project was intended to begin copper, gold, and molybdenum exploration and production on the lands of the Embera and Afro-Colombian communities. In 2005, the Colombian government gave mining concessions to Muriel Mining without obtaining the consent of the Indigenous Embera and Afro-Colombian communities as required by the Colombian constitution. A lawsuit filed on behalf of the communities by the Inter-Church Justice and Peace Commission, a Colombian NGO, was effective in stopping plans to proceed with the Mandé Norte Mining Project. The Colombian Constitutional Court stopped the project on grounds that there had been a lack of consultation with the Indigenous communities (ABColombia 2010, 21) and that the project would destroy the ecosystem and traditional cultural and spiritual life of the Embera people, one of thirty-four Indigenous peoples in Colombia identified as being at risk of physical or cultural extinction. The Court also stopped the mining project on grounds that it would destroy the traditional livelihood of the Afro-Colombian community in Jiguamiandó (U.S. Office on Colombia 2013, 12; ABColombia 2011).

As graph 5.3 demonstrates, the number of social mobilizations by Indigenous communities against transnational corporations in Colombia's coal, gold, and oil sectors has sharply increased since 2008, and by 2010 they surpassed the number of social mobilizations that were not associated with the country's coal, gold, and oil sectors (U.S. Office on Colombia 2013, 9). A similar trend can also be seen in Peru, where the Defensoría del Pueblo (National Ombudsman

Graph 5.3. Trajectory of social mobilization associated with coal, gold, and oil extraction in Colombia, 2001–2010. *Source:* Author-generated time-series graph of data adapted from ECLAC 2013, 9.

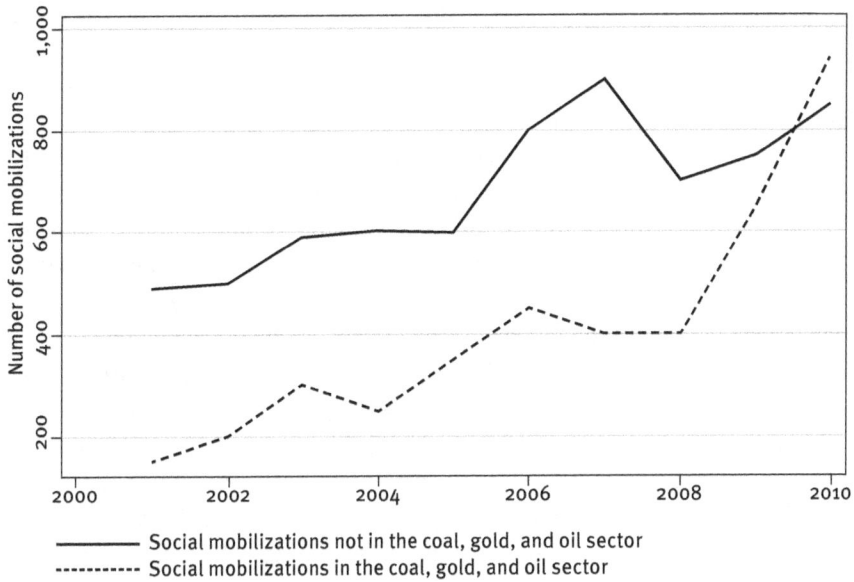

Social mobilizations not in the coal, gold, and oil sector
Social mobilizations in the coal, gold, and oil sector

Office) reported that in 2013, for just the month of September there were 223 social conflicts, over two-thirds of which were associated with transnational corporations in the mining sector. From 2006 to 2011, disputes with Indigenous communities over natural resources left 196 people dead and 2,369 injured (Defensoría del Pueblo 2013).

Increasing social resistance to the expansion of U.S. and other transnational corporations, especially in the extractive sectors in Latin America, raises questions about how corporations will respond. Will resistance from Latin America's Indigenous communities trigger patterns of repression that are corporate induced? Specifically, what are the mechanisms through which corporate-induced repression is exercised? In the following sections I answer these questions by drawing on theories of repression in dependent capitalist societies.

Neoliberalism and the Privatization of Terror

Theories of repression in dependent-capitalist societies provide important insights into the pattern of U.S. and other transnational corporate responses to civil societies' resistance to capital accumulation. While dependency theory takes countries' historical relations with the international capitalist economy as its starting point, most dependency scholarship emphasizes the internal class relations within developing countries (Evans 1979, 27).[3] For example, Cardoso and Faletto (1973, 140) argue: "There is no such thing as a metaphysical relation of dependency between one nation and another, one state and another. Such relations are made concrete possibilities through the existence of a network of interests and interactions which link certain social groups to other social groups, certain social classes to other social classes."

The interaction of class interests in dependent capitalist societies not only shapes the underlying social structure in which political power is configured but also shapes patterns of political repression. In *Dependent Development*, Peter Evans (1979, 48–49) argues that political power in these societies takes the form of a triple alliance between the state, transnational corporations, and national capital, on the basis of collective interests that lead them to create and maintain a social order conducive to the logic of capital accumulation (Cardoso 1972; Amin 1977). Repression of civil society groups is a necessary feature of capital accumulation. In Latin America this was especially true during the phase of import-substitution development, when both transnational and national capital relied on the coercive capacity of what O'Donnell (1973) calls the bureaucratic authoritarian state to control the working class and keep wages low. The importance of the state and its repressive capacity to facilitate corporate interest is also emphasized in some Marxist scholarship. Magdoff (1978, 183), for example, argues that transnational corporations not only rely on state repression in order to accumulate capital but also "will, when necessary, invest in private armies to guard their property and repress trade unions."

Corporate reliance on the state's repressive capacity will, however, vary across industries. Repression is more likely among resource-seeking transnational corporations than among transnational corporations in the service and manufacturing industries. Service and manufacturing transnational companies are more likely to develop a "social license" with their host countries to recruiting skilled labor, promote their goods and services for domestic and international markets, and reduce or prevent conflict with civil society groups (Blanton and Blanton 2009, 474), all of which reduce the likelihood that corporate alliance with the state will produce repression. On the other hand, resource-seeking transnational companies are more likely to develop a "silo mentality" in that they will not seek to broaden their integration within the host country beyond guaranteeing the security of their own facilities (Blanton and Blanton 2009, 474), which increases the likelihood that their alliance with the state will ultimately produce repression.

However, the effect of industry differences on the likelihood that the corporate-state alliance will produce repression takes place within the context of

Latin America's neoliberal reforms. Has the adoption of neoliberal reforms, with their emphasis on privatization, changed the configuration of power within the corporate-state alliance such that capital, specifically resource-seeking transnational capital, has become less reliant on the state to repress civil society groups that resist capital accumulation? I argue that neoliberal reforms that emphasize corporate subcontracting of labor have made corporate subcontracting of repression possible. As a result, the nature of power within the corporate-state alliance is reconstituted such that the use of force is increasingly privatized; resource-seeking companies will subcontract terror as a response to civil-society threats to capital accumulation. To the extent that neoliberal capitalism has privatized the state, it has also increased the tendency toward the privatization of repression among resource-seeking transnational corporations. In Latin America, there is a growing pattern of subcontracting repression to private security firms, privatized national police, and paramilitary death squads.

Subcontracting Terror: Private Security Firms and a Privatized National Police

Peru is the quintessential example of how neoliberal market reforms, in conjunction with the growth of private security firms, have facilitated the privatization of the national police force, creating conditions in which the subcontracting of repression is essential to the process of capital accumulation. The proposition that neoliberal market reform, with its shrinking of the public sector, is associated with the expansion of private security firms has received repeated empirical confirmation (Weiss 2007; Ungar 2007; Trevaskes 2007; Kontos 2004; Campbell 2006).

In 2008, a U.N. study estimated that 100,000 private security guards were in Peru, a number exceeding the country's national police force of 92,000 (del Prado 2008, 13; Kamphuis 2012, 535). Approximately half of the country's private security companies are not registered, as required by Peru's Private Security Services Act, and are therefore operating illegally (Kamphuis 2012, 535). By legislating the integration of the national police into the private sector, the Private Security Services Act created the legal framework that has helped facilitate the process of privatizing the national police. The act permits the supervision of private security companies by retired police and military officers and allows actively serving police and military officers to be employed by private security firms (Kamphuis 2012, 536). The act legally establishes the structure for an interlocking relationship among Peru's private security firms, the national police, and the military—a relationship that is consistent with Mills's (1956) and Domhoff's (1983) power elite theory of the state. In its report, the United Nations noted that "in many cases, these companies are run by former members of the Armed Forces or the Police, or they occupy senior positions. Peru also seems to experience the 'revolving door' syndrome whereby, when they retire, members of the military and police are hired by private security companies or start their own. The Ministry of the Interior apparently authorizes these companies to hire off-duty police to protect buildings" (del Prado 2008, 14).

While the Private Security Services Act legalized the establishment of an interlocking security elite, another important component of the privatization of Peru's national police was the increasing number of transnational corporations that had entered into agreements with the police for the provision of "extraordinary" security services. This meant that, in addition to normal policing, units of the national police force were authorized to provide "extraordinary additional" services for the protection of private property and corporate investments (Kamphuis 2012, 536; Human Rights without Frontiers et al. 2013, 9).

Two types of extraordinary additional services, institutional and individual, can be provided. Institutional services require a formal agreement between the director of the National Police Force and the corporation that requests protection. Individual services do not require a formal agreement with the National Police but are provided by police officers who are off duty. Individual services are arranged by agreement between individual police officers and corporations that require protection. Payments for the provision of these security services can be made in two ways. For individual services, police officers receive direct payment from corporations, which is not considered part of their normal salary or pension, nor does it contribute to their social security benefits. In the case of institutional services, corporations make direct payments to police units, which cover the logistical and administrative costs that units incur while providing security for corporate clients (Human Rights without Frontiers et al. 2013, 9).

Transnational mining corporations also provide the National Police Force with vehicles and insurance coverage against injury or death. In addition, in some cases, companies provide police units with communications and monitoring equipment and contribute to the repair, maintenance, and replacement of firearms that are damaged or lost during security operations. In 2013, the Peruvian National Police had concluded agreements with the Newmont Mining Corporation and twelve other transnational mining corporations for the protection of their mining facilities (Human Rights without Frontiers et al. 2013, 10–11).

In 2006, in response to the campesino protest against Newmont's expansion of its mining operations in the Combayo region, the company deployed 200 armed security personnel, a force composed of officers from the private security firm Forza and off-duty police officers who were employed by the company via its private security contract with the National Police Force. Within days of the demonstrations a campesino demonstrator was shot and killed by Newmont's security forces (Kamphuis 2012, 549–50). Moreover, Forza launched Operación Diablo, a program of digital surveillance, illegal wiretaps, intimidation, and death threats that targeted the personnel of GRUFIDES—the local human rights NGO—and environmental and campesino leaders who opposed the expansion of Newmont's mining operations in the Combayo. Later that year, hit men murdered one of the campesino leaders that the Forza surveillance program identified as a threat to the company's mining operations. Court documents showed that between October 2006 and February 2007 numerous telephone conversations between GRUFIDES personnel and activists from the campesino community were illegally recorded (Kamphuis 2012, 550–51, 553; Human Rights without Frontiers et al. 2013, 14).

The campesino community would again come into conflict with Newmont over its proposed plan to establish a new mining facility at Conga. The Indigenous campesinos opposed the proposal on grounds that they would lose four mountain lakes that supplied water to their communities and that the project would further exacerbate the water supply shortage in the region. In February 2012, thousands of campesinos mobilized a large-scale rally against Newmont's Conga mining proposal and organized La Gran Marcha Nacional del Agua (the Great National March for Water). President Ollanta Humala declared a state of emergency and dispatched police units to the Conga region. The ensuing conflict between the campesino protesters and police units contracted to provide security for Newmont led to police attacks on independent journalists. Police units also confiscated journalists' video recordings, some of which captured excessive use of police force that led to the deaths of 5 protesters and the seriously injury of another 150. While attending the demonstration, Marco Arana, the founder of GRUFIDES, was arbitrarily arrested and tortured while in police custody (Human Rights without Frontiers et al. 2013, 12; Claps 2013, 2014).

In 2013, Guatemala's Indigenous peoples' resistance to the mining operations of the Canadian-American mining company Tahoe Resources turned violent when the company's security firm, Alfa Uno—an affiliate of the Golan Group, an Israeli private security firm—indiscriminately shot Indigenous community members who were protesting peacefully in front of the company's mining facility in San Rafael Las Flores. When Tahoe Resources hired the Golan Group, the company had already established a reputation for human rights violations. Between 2005 and 2009, the Golan Group provided security services for Glamis Gold and HudBay Minerals at their respective Marlin and Fenix mining facilities. In both cases, the Golan Group was accused of human rights violations. HudBay Minerals is currently being prosecuted in Canada for the company's alleged murder of the teacher Adolfo Ich. On June 18, 2014, seven members of Guatemala's Indigenous community filed a lawsuit against Tahoe Resources in the Supreme Court of British Columbia on grounds that the company explicitly or implicitly authorized the conduct of its security personnel and was negligent in preventing them from using excessive force (Solano 2015).

Subcontracting Terror to Paramilitary Death Squads and Militaries

In Colombia, U.S. drug enforcement policies that encourage the cultivation of palm oil as an alternative to coca are ultimately responsible for corporations' use of paramilitary death squads to dispossess Indigenous peoples of their lands in order to expand palm oil production. By financing the cultivation of palm oil as an alternative to coca and facilitating its expansion through neoliberal trade reforms (Otis 2005), the drug war policies of the United States created the conditions that gave rise to corporate-paramilitary collusion to expropriate the lands of Indigenous communities to increase the acreage for palm oil cultivation and in the process commit gross human rights atrocities.

In 2012 Colombia's prosecutor general, Eduardo Montealegre, indicted nineteen Colombian palm oil companies for colluding with the Autodefensas Unidas de Colombia (AUC) in the forced displacement of campesino peasants and Afro-Colombians from their lands in the western Department of Choco (Kinosain 2012; Caracol Radio 2012). Urapalma S.A., Palmas de Curvarado S.A., and Palmura S.A. were among the palm oil companies that received indictments. In 2014 a Medellín court sentenced sixteen businessmen employed by these companies to prison for using paramilitary groups to illegally obtain territory to expand their palm oil business (Wojciak 2014). Drawing on interviews with several survivors, Ballvé (2011, 9) reports that the AUC came to their farms with a nonnegotiable offer: "Sell us your land or we'll negotiate with your widow." This threat was followed by an onslaught of violence that left thousands either dead or landless. Once the Indigenous population relinquished their property to the paramilitaries, these groups would make arrangements for the illegal transfer of abandoned farmland to palm oil companies. In return, as they expanded their operations onto new land many of these companies helped launder the drug trafficking proceeds of the AUC (Ballvé 2011, 16).

American transnational corporations Chiquita and Dole also colluded with the AUC and acquired large tracts of land for banana cultivation and the production of African palm oil to produce biofuels (Paley 2014, 64). In March 2007, Chiquita executives pleaded guilty before Judge Royce C. Lamberth in the U.S. District Court for the District of Columbia on the charge of providing payments to the AUC, which the U.S. government designated as a foreign terrorist organization on September 10, 2001. Chiquita made monthly payments to the AUC in two regions in Colombia, Urabá and Santa Marta, through its Colombian subsidiary, Banadex. From September 10, 2001, through February 4, 2004, Chiquita made fifty payments to the AUC totaling over US$825,000 and continued to pay the AUC even against the advice of its defense team, which was led by Eric Holder, former deputy attorney general in the Clinton administration and former attorney general in the Obama administration. The U.S. Department of Justice investigations revealed that for over six years from 1997 to February 4, 2004, Chiquita made over 100 payments to the AUC that amounted to over US$1.7 million. Chiquita's sentence included a US$25 million criminal fine, and the corporation was required to implement and maintain an effective compliance and ethics program and agreed to cooperate in the Justice Department's ongoing investigations (U.S. Department of Justice 2007; Leonning 2007). Holder protested the Justice Department's sentencing on grounds that it unfairly punished his client for making a difficult decision to voluntarily disclose an illegal activity, arguing, "Here's a company that voluntarily self-discloses in a national security context, where the company gets treated pretty harshly, [and] then on top of that, you go after individuals who made a really painful decision. If what you want to encourage is voluntary self-disclosure, what message does this send to other companies?" (quoted in Leonning 2007).

This protest was completely without merit. Consider the fact that, in addition to Chiquita's collusion with the AUC, which led to the paramilitary's murder of over 4,000 civilians in Urabá and the forced displacement of an additional 60,000, the Organization of American States found Chiquita's subsidiary Banadex guilty of facilitating the illegal diversion of 3,000 Nicaraguan AK-47 assault rifles and 5 million rounds of ammunition from Panama to Antioquia, where Banadex controlled the port of Turbo (Moore 2011, 2). Moreover, Chiquita's collusion with the AUC extended beyond the forced displacement of Indigenous peoples and illicit arms shipments to the company's implicit participation in the AUC's drug trafficking. Under the "Justice and Peace" process, initiated by the Colombian government in 2007–8, AUC leaders were encouraged to disarm and turn themselves in and were promised minimal jail time if they confessed to their terrorist crimes. Éver Veloza García, former commander of the AUC's Turbo Front in northern Urabá, testified that the paramilitary circumvented port security by smuggling narcotics in the hulls of Chiquita's banana vessels. In fact, Colombian authorities seized over 1.5 tons of cocaine, valued at US$33 million, from Chiquita ships. These crimes notwithstanding, in an April 24, 2007, meeting with Chiquita's executives, the Justice

Department concluded that the corporation would not be held liable for past misconduct. In the end, Chiquita executives walked away without having to do jail time, instead negotiating only a plea bargain fine (Moore 2011, 3).

Under the Justice and Peace process José Gregorio Mangones Lugo, who commanded the William Rivas Front of the AUC's Northern Bloc, provided sworn testimony on the nature of Dole's relationship with the AUC. Mangones testified that both Dole and Chiquita paid money to the AUC to provide services that included driving Indigenous farmers from their lands and leftist guerrillas out of the banana zones, which allowed Dole and Chiquita subsidiaries and affiliates to plant bananas and palm oil and in the process killed thousands of innocent people. In his testimony, Mangones stated: "My men were contacted on a regular basis by Chiquita or Dole administrators to respond to a criminal act . . . We would also get calls from the Chiquita and Dole plantations identifying specific people as 'security problems' or just 'problems.' Everyone knew that this meant we were to execute the identified person. In most cases those executed were union leaders or members or individuals seeking to hold or reclaim land that Dole or Chiquita wanted for banana [and palm oil] cultivation" (quoted in Robinson 2009).

Although Chiquita confessed to violating U.S. antiterrorism laws, Dole denied making payments to the AUC. However, in the case of *Mendoza Gomez et al. v. Dole Food Company, Inc.*, sixty-five Colombians brought a lawsuit against Dole for its collusion with the AUC, which led to the wrongful death of their relatives. While the California Superior Court dismissed the case, on appeal the appellate court remanded the case for further proceedings. After the case was dismissed for a second time, the plaintiffs appealed again and obtained another reversal. Dole and the plaintiffs eventually engaged in discovery and settled the case out of court (International Rights Advocates 2009b).

Corporate-paramilitary collusion behind the illegal appropriation of land was also a common practice for Colombia's mining industry. In May 2009, 529 relatives of 131 victims of violence in the Cesar mining region brought a lawsuit against the Alabama-based Drummond Mining Corporation before the U.S. District Court of Alabama. In *Balcero et al. v. Drummond Company, Inc.*, in testimonies made under oath ex-paramilitaries who operated in the region described how they forcefully removed Indigenous peoples from their lands for the purpose of expanding Drummond's mining operations (International Rights Advocates 2009a). For example, the AUC's Juan Andrés Álvarez (JAA) Front committed fifteen murders in the regions of Mechoacán and El Prado. During this period, paramilitary terror drove eighty-one families from their land. In their testimonies, ex-paramilitaries who were involved in these forced displacements claimed that the interests of the mining companies in the region motivated their actions (Moor and Sandt 2014, 75). Regarding the JAA's operations in El Prado, former AUC commander El Samario stated: "All this is done because of the coal-rich land: it brings in a lot of money, and that explains this [forced] displacement. A plot of land that is under dispute is worth nothing. Where there has been murder and people have been displaced, you can buy a hectare of land for 150,000 COP (USD 75)" (75). The eyewitness statement of ex-paramilitary El Mecánico corroborated El Samario's testimony: "We were ordered to be present there to put as many people as possible under pressure to sell their land. . . . It was a place where they knew there was much coal in the ground, and where in future Drummond or some other company, such as Prodeco, would buy these plots of land" (2014, 75).

The human rights NGO PAX Netherlands, in its study of paramilitary violence in the Cesar region, reported that from 1996 to 2006 Drummond and the Anglo-Swiss mining company Prodeco financially supported paramilitaries who murdered 3,100 people and drove 55,000 Indigenous farmers from their land. The JAA Front of the AUC committed 2,600 selective killings and massacred 499 civilians (Moor and Sandt 2014, 30–31). In their initial reaction to FARC and ELN guerrilla attacks on their mining operations in the Cesar region, Drummond and Prodeco coordinated with the Colombian army to establish security departments within their respective companies. Former Colombian army intelligence officer José del Carmen Gelvez Alvarracín, alias El Canoso, held a position in Prodeco's security department gathering intelligence for the AUC. According to his testimony his job was to "detect guerrillas and subversives [including those who resisted being dispossessed of their land] in the area and within the union at the time" (Moor and Sandt 2014, 45). Former Drummond security manager James Adkins also testified that the Colombian army had been in contact with Drummond about the possibility of financing paramilitaries in the region through the army's *convivir* system. However, when *convivires* were declared illegal by the Colombian government, many of these groups were absorbed into the AUC paramilitary organization. Adkins, who reported directly to Drummond CEO Garry Drummond, informed him that the military's plan to establish paramilitaries in the Cesar region would "bring with it egregious human rights violations" (Moor and Sandt 2014, 46). Nevertheless, Adkins testified that Garry Drummond paid the army US$1.1 million to establish paramilitaries in the mining region (Moor and Sandt 2014, 46).

In the end, Drummond and Prodeco cooperated to finance the operations of the AUC. El Canoso testified that James Adkins and Manuel Gutiérrez, the respective heads of the security departments for Drummond and Prodeco, along with himself and other representatives from both companies scheduled a meeting at Drummond's La Loma mine. According to El Canoso: "We discussed and we all agreed that we would give the AUC a monthly payment to cover the salaries, food and cost of the AUC troops. We also agreed to buy the AUC some vehicles and supply them with fuel. There was no objection to any of these agreements from anyone present" (Moor and Sandt 2014, 47). While Drummond and Prodeco agreed to share the cost of maintaining the AUC in the Cesar region, disagreement arose over the mechanism through which payments would be made. The testimony from Jaime Blanco Maya, Drummond's food service contractor, stated that Drummond used his company, Industrial de Servicios y Alimentos, to funnel money to the AUC from 1997 to 2001. Blanco testified that he paid a total of US$900,000 to the JAA division of the AUC between 1997 and 2001 (Moor and Sandt 2014, 57, 59; Bedoya 2014).

Jairo de Jesús Charris Castro, a Drummond contractor, testified that Drummond continued to finance the AUC after 2000 when the U.S. government designated the paramilitary organization a foreign terrorist organization. The private security firm Secolda was used as a front company for payments to the AUC. According to Charris Castro, Secolda was created by Tolemaida, the AUC's commander of the JAA Front, and José Alfredo Daza Ortíz, the lawyer for the AUC's Northern Bloc, specifically to allow Drummond to funnel money to the AUC. After 2000, Drummond siphoned US$1.5 million to the Northern Bloc and made monthly payments of approximately US$100,000 to the JAA Front (Moor and Sandt 2014, 60).

According to reports from the human rights NGOs Franciscans International and Dominicans for Justice and Peace, the Indigenous peoples in Mexico's Sierra Tarahumara and Selva Lacandona, regions rich in natural resources, have also been the victims of forced displacement. Through a combination of threats and physical assaults, paramilitary groups working in concert with transnational extractive corporations and Mexico's security forces perpetrated the forced displacement of the Indigenous community from their land (Delegation of the Order of Preachers to the United Nations 2000).

Indigenous communities across Guatemala face an increasing threat of extrajudicial eviction by security forces and private militaries, the latter formed by large landowners to force families from their land to make way for transnational mining and hydroelectric projects and the production of African palm oil for the international biofuel trade. The Q'eqchi' Maya territory has experienced a rapid increase in the number of extrajudicial evictions, especially along the banks of the Dolores River, which the Q'eqchi' people have traditionally relied on to water their fields and to support their livelihood. However, on August 14, 2014, more than 1,600 members of the Guatemalan National Police and elements of the Guatemalan military forcefully evicted members of the

Q'eqchi' community along the Dolores River to make way for the construction of a hydroelectric project (Abbott 2015). Then on September 19, armed actors affiliated with the cement corporation Cementos Progreso entered the territory of the Indigenous community and shot and killed a community member. This precipitated a wave of violence that caused the death of eleven people and the injury of several more. According to the human rights NGO Peace Brigade, there have been armed attacks against people, property (vehicles and a church), Indigenous community leaders, and social activists who support the Indigenous movement (Coordinator for the Rights of Indigenous Peoples 2014, 2). On February 9, 2014, in the Indigenous communities of Monte Olivio, police burned homes and destroyed property, which resulted in the internal displacement of hundreds of families. In the Indigenous community of Semococh, police shot and killed Luciano Can, Oscar Chen, and Sebastian Rax in confrontations during eviction. Sixty other people were injured and twenty-six were arrested in the operation to forcefully evict Indigenous community members (Abbott 2014, 1–2).

As seen in the Colombian and Mexican cases, the Indigenous people maintain that the Guatemalan government never consulted their communities regarding the use of their land, which violates U.N. Convention 169 on the Rights of Indigenous and Tribal Peoples—a U.N. convention to which Guatemala was a signatory since 2007 (Abbott 2014, 2). In its report Amnesty International supported the Indigenous community's contentions, noting that " the government of Guatemala is feeding the fire of conflict by not consulting with local communities before handing out mining concessions to companies; in that way, in practice, the government is increasing the risk of bloodshed and destroying the rights of the population" (Coordinator for the Rights of Indigenous Peoples 2014, 3). James Anaya, the United Nations' special rapporteur on the rights of Indigenous people, pointed to the link between the presence of transnational companies and increased violence against Indigenous communities when he noted after his mission to Guatemala in 2011 that "the presence of companies in Indigenous territories has created a situation of great conflict and has caused enormous divisions in the communities" (Coordinator for the Rights of Indigenous Peoples 2014, 2).

Conclusion

This chapter demonstrates that human rights repression is an unintended outcome of a process set in motion by the policy decisions of the corporatist drug enforcement regime. American counternarcotic aid flows to Latin America facilitate American corporate expansion into the region, and in the process of accumulating capital, drug enforcement policy decisions create the conditions that facilitate corporate-induced repression. The chapter also highlights the agency of states, security firms, and paramilitary death squads as mediators of corporate-induced repression. The theoretical implications of the argument are at variance with liberal scholarship, which views transnational corporations as agents that improve human rights in the developing world. Unlike Albert Hirschman, who acknowledged the virtues of transnational capital but also recognized that over time the negative aspects of foreign investment will predominate over these virtues (Hirschman 1969), liberal scholars claim to have debunked dependency theory by supposedly amassing repeated empirical confirmation that transnational capital improves human rights in developing countries. In the next chapter these claims are empirically tested in the context of the embedded corporatist regime's drug enforcement in Latin America.

CHAPTER 6

Corporate Hit Men

An Empirical Analysis of U.S. Drug Enforcement Aid, American Corporations, and Paramilitary Death Squads

To test the theoretical components of the argument presented in chapter 5, I developed an empirical model of how U.S. transnational corporations and paramilitary death squads mediate the U.S.-sponsored drug war's effect on human rights repression in Latin America. In outlining this empirical model, this chapter is organized as follows: I first juxtapose the theoretical arguments of dependency and neoclassical liberal theories regarding the human rights effects of transnational capital by highlighting the theoretical and empirical limitations of neoclassical liberal claims. This is followed by a discussion of the empirical model, which draws on the extant human rights literature to identify important control variables that are important predictors of state repression. I then discuss important theoretical modifications that are incorporated into the overall empirical model. This is followed by a discussion of the limitations of the indicators used to measure the model's mediating variables. The chapter concludes with a discussion of the results of the structural equation model (SEM), which estimates data for thirty-one countries in the Latin American region from 1980 to 2012.

Corporations and Repression:
Theoretical Debate and Empirical Limitations

Students of state repression have long debated the human rights effects of foreign direct investment (FDI) in developing countries. According to neoclassical liberal theory, transnational corporate investment has an indirect impact on civil and political rights. Theorists who write in this tradition assume that transnational corporate investment increases economic development, which in turn fosters a middle class that is expected to use its newfound economic power to make political demands for greater civil and political rights (Friedman 1962; Schumpeter 1950). At the end of World War II, America's foreign economic policy was based on the notion that transnational corporations were engines of economic growth and development that would ultimately facilitate the growth of democracy and improvements in government respect for human rights in developing countries. From John F. Kennedy's Alliance for Progress and Ronald Reagan's Caribbean Basin Initiative to George H. W. Bush and Bill Clinton's NAFTA, all had provisions that promoted the expansion of U.S. transnational corporate penetration into Latin America and the Caribbean Basin (Taffet 2007; Baken et al. 1993; Hufbauer and Schott 2005).

Some political economists have suggested that the effect of transnational corporate investment on state repression may be more direct. These scholars argue that transnational corporations in capital-intensive industries where assets are fixed and vulnerable to domestic violence are more likely to invest in countries that are not prone to conflict and repression (Blanton and Blanton 2009). Therefore, if governments want to attract foreign capital to grow their economies, then they are more likely to create a political environment that is not conducive to violence and thus minimizes corporate risk. State repression of unions may also prove counterproductive to governments' preference for economic growth, since the repression of labor is likely to undermine gains in corporate productivity, drive down the value of corporate stocks, and alienate customers in developed economies (Blanton and Blanton 2009; Spar 1999).

The findings of existing empirical cross-national studies have largely supported the predictions of neoclassical liberal theory. In their attempt to test dependency theory's proposition regarding state repression, Timberlake and Williams (1984) in a cross-national analysis of data from the 1960s and 1970s found no direct relationship between FDI and state repression. FDI was associated with repression only when citizens were excluded from the political process. At best, FDI may aggravate preexisting political tensions that ultimately lead to repression. Using two different measures of FDI, Meyer (1996) estimated data for 1985 and 1990 and found that FDI was positively associated with improving political rights and civil liberties, as well as economic and social rights in developing countries. Expanding the temporal domain of their research from 1981 to 1995, Richards et al. (2001) found that transnational corporate penetration was positively associated with improving physical integrity rights, as well as political rights and civil liberties. In a study that estimated data for 152 developing countries during 1990–96, Apodaca (2001) confirmed the findings of Meyer (1996) and Richards et al. (2001). In analyzing the effects of FDI on labor rights for ninety developing nations from 1986 to 2002, Mosley and Uno (2007) found that FDI flows were positively associated with improving the rights of workers.

Finally, in their analysis of the impact of labor rights on bilateral FDI flows to eighty-two developing countries for 1984–2004, Busse et al. (2011) found that transnational corporate investments were significantly higher in countries that adhered to labor rights, supposedly refuting dependency theory's proposition that repression of these rights creates an economic and political environment conducive to corporate penetration.

Dependency theory, which many liberal scholars regard as outdated, has largely been understood as an attempt to explain the ways in which the international capitalist economy produces and reproduces patterns of economic stratification that privilege advanced industrial countries while promoting underdevelopment in the least developed countries (Haggard 1990; Frank 1966). Liberal critiques have been limited to dependency theory's propositions about developing countries' external relations with international capitalism but have failed to engage dependency theory's proposition regarding how the internal political configurations and class relations within developing countries explain the conditions under which FDI promotes state repression (Cardoso and Faletto 1973).

While dependency theory is regarded as outdated, it remains a useful theoretical alternative to neoclassical liberal theories of repression and is used here as a theoretical framework to analyze how the effect of FDI on human rights repression is mediated by domestic political actors. Because foreign transnational corporations dominate the productive apparatus in developing countries, state repression becomes a rational response to make the economic and political environment conducive for foreign corporate penetration. The repression of the urban working class (analyzed in chapter 8) is necessary for the process of capital accumulation because it keeps labor costs low. Further, the repression of labor unions and political parties that represent the interests of the working class is necessary to prevent collective bargaining, which has the potential of increasing the cost of corporate foreign investment and consequently increases the likelihood of capital flight. In summary, state repression is needed to deactivate labor unions and the popular sector's demand for greater political and economic rights and in the process enhances the state's bargaining with foreign capital (Evans 1979, 48–49). Therefore, as O'Donnell (1973) has shown in his comparative analysis of Brazil and Argentina in the late 1960s, repression is useful in developing countries because it simultaneously promotes capital accumulation and maintains an authoritarian political order that is particularly suited for foreign corporate investment.

While the extant neoliberal literature claims to refute dependency theory by showing that transnational corporations actually improve human rights in developing countries, the empirical models on which these findings are based do not accurately reflect dependency theorists' conceptualization of human rights repression as produced by domestic and internal class configurations (Meyer 1996, 1998; Richards et al. 2001; Spar 1999). In this regard the extant literature is ahistorical since its modeling specifications assume that FDI has a direct effect on human rights and ignore the various domestic political configurations through which transnational corporations' effects on human rights are mediated (Azarvan 2009).

The human rights effects of American and other transnational corporate investments in Latin America and other countries in the developing world have long been mediated through military regimes that represent the class interests of state and national capitalist elites (Evans 1979). History also attests to the ways in which transnational corporations facilitate the process of state repression in developing societies. For example, ITT's role in the coup d'état of the Allende government in Chile in 1973 (Kornbluh 2000, 2013), its role in the coup d'état of the João Goulart government in Brazil in 1964 (Kornbluh 2000), and the United Fruit Company's role in "Operation PBSUCCES," which led to the coup d'état of the Arbenz government in Guatemala in 1954 (Schlesinger and Kinzer 1999). In Argentina, auto manufacturers Mercedes Benz and Ford Motor Company are under investigation for their role in Argentina's "Dirty Wars" during the 1970s, in which the military junta committed egregious human rights violations. In 2002, criminal proceedings began against Mercedes Benz, on the charge that the corporation assisted the dictatorship in the kidnapping of workers by supplying the military with a "blacklist" of union activists (Ambito.com 2014; Payne and Pereira 2016; Verbitsky and Bohoslavsky 2013). In October 2013, an appeals court in Argentina upheld criminal charges against three former Ford Motor Company executives, Pedro Muller, Guillermo Galarraga, and Hector Francisco Jesus Sibilla, for their role in targeting union leaders for kidnapping and torture. The former executives were placed under house arrest for giving the junta names, national identification numbers, photographs, and home addresses of union activists. This information constituted the intelligence that enabled the military dictatorship to seize, torture, and imprison over two dozen union workers from Ford's manufacturing plant (Centro de Información Judicial 2013; Bohoslavsky and Opgenhaffen 2010; Verbitsky and Bohoslavsky 2013).

In 2010, a lawsuit was brought against Merrill Lynch, Citibank, and the Bank of America by Garragone, the son of one of Argentina's disappeared, who argued that the banks' loans to the junta were a crucial aspect of the military's repressive infrastructure (Morini 2013). Contributors to *The Economic Accomplices to the Argentine Dictatorship* (Verbitsky and Bohoslavsky 2013) also claim that the banks were fully aware that their loans to the dictatorship would finance the illegal repressive apparatus used to commit human rights atrocities.

Argentina's national capitalist firms were also accomplices to the junta's repression. Several executives of Ledesma S.A.A.I., Argentina's largest agribusiness and food processing company, faced criminal prosecution for their complicity in human rights violations during Noche del Apagón (Night of the Blackouts), during which an estimated 400 workers, students, and professionals were allegedly kidnapped, tortured, killed, and disappeared from July 20 to 27, 1976. Ledesma executives Alberto Lemos and Carlos Pedro Blaquier were indicted for providing the trucks used in the illegal kidnappings. The company was accused of orchestrating the blackouts by cutting off the electricity to facilitate the junta's military operation, as well as allowing the military to establish an illegal detention center on company property (Movement de Unidad Popular Argentina 2013).

In 2009, Royal Dutch Petroleum Company and Shell Transport and Trading Company paid a US$15.5 million settlement for complicity in human rights abuses against the Nigerian Ogoni people. Shell collaborated with the Nigerian junta to suppress opposition to the company's operations on Ogoni land. The company was also complicit in the 1995 hanging of nine members of the Ogoni community (*Wiwa v. Royal Dutch Petroleum Co. and Shell Transport and Trading Co.*, 626 F. Supp. 2d 377 [S.D.N.Y. 2009]). In 2011, U.S. defense contractor L-3 Communications was accused of training security personnel who committed acts of genocide in Croatia (*Genocide Victims of Krajina Plaintiffs v. L-3 Services, Inc.*, Complaint Case 1:10-cv-05197 [N.D. Ill., 2010]). In 2004, the Canadian Anvil Mining company was accused of facilitating the rape, torture, and murder of civilians in the town of Kilwa by supplying trucks and other logistical support to Congolese troops for military operations to recapture the town from rebel forces (BBC News 2010). During Liberia's civil war from 2000 to 2003, Danish timber giant Dalhoff, Larsen, and Horneman illegally bought lumber from Liberian companies that financed the brutal regime of war criminal Charles Taylor (Global Witness 2009). A subsidiary of French oil giant Total SA faced civil suits in Belgian and French courts for providing logistical and financial support to Myanmar's military junta during the 1990s in order to extract forced labor from villagers for the construction of Total SA's Yadana pipeline (Sisodia and Buncombe 2009). In the case of *Bowoto v. Chevron Corp.* (481 F. Supp. 2d 1010 [2007]), in 1999 Nigerian citizens filed a lawsuit against Chevron in the U.S. federal court in San Francisco, alleging that from 1998 to 1999 the company provided helicopters and boats, as well as payments, to the Nigerian military to destroy two villages where protesters opposed Chevron's operations in the Niger Delta. A French tribunal has investigated French software manufacturer Qosmos for supplying surveillance equipment to Syrian dictator Bashar El-Assad, which has led to the targeting, monitoring, arrest, and torture of dissidents (Hansia 2015).

These cases all reflect a general pattern in which transnational corporations' effect on human rights atrocities is not direct but mediated through local militaries that represent the class interests of the ruling elite. As discussed in chapter 5, the drug war in Latin America demonstrates that resource-seeking transnational corporations' impact on human rights is exerted through local militaries, private security firms, and more often paramilitary death squads, which serve as mediators for corporate-induced repression. Ignoring the role that domestic mediators play in producing repression introduces bias that, if corrected, would undermine the neoclassical liberal claim that transnational corporations improve human rights practices in developing countries. The next section introduces a path diagram that highlights the importance of specifying an empirical model in which transnational corporations and domestic political actors mediate U.S. counternarcotic aid's effect on human rights repression.

SEM Specification: The Path Diagram

The model specification of the path diagram, shown in figure 6.1, captures three related hypotheses. The first of these states that increasing levels of U.S. counternarcotic aid will increase U.S. FDI flows to Latin America. The second hypothesis states that increasing levels of U.S. FDI will increase the activity of paramilitary organizations in Latin America. The final hypothesis states that increasing paramilitary activity will increase human rights repression. In essence, U.S. FDI and paramilitary organizations mediate U.S. counternarcotic aid's effect on human rights repression.

As discussed in chapter 1, the Political Terror Scale (PTS) captures how the human rights practices of state and nonstate actors affect overall levels of repression in countries (Gibney and Dalton 1996). Since the nonstate actor used in the SEM measures the activity of pro-government paramilitary groups that were in many cases created to be force multipliers for the military (Bartilow 2001, 2000) or, in the Colombian case, given logistical and financial support by the Colombian government (School of the Americas Watch 2007; Evans 2011), such groups proxy government's role in human rights repression. As a result, pro-government paramilitary groups make it necessary to incorporate CIRI physical integrity and civil liberty indices into the empirical model in order to capture the human rights and civil liberties practices of governments (Cingranelli and Richards 1999, 2010).[1]

Figure 6.1. The main structural model

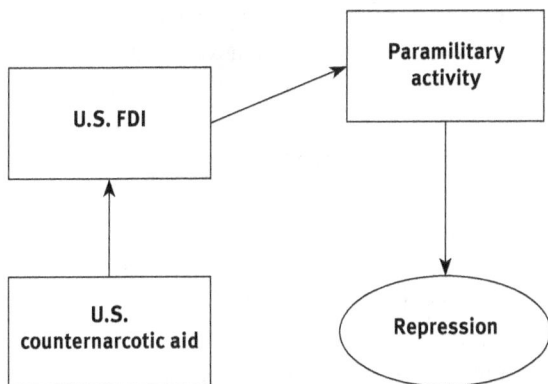

The path diagram (U.S. counternarcotic aid → U.S. FDI → paramilitary activity → repression) constitutes the SEM equations' main structural model. In addition, variables that have an independent effect on repression (not shown in figure 6.1.), such as judicial independence, the level of economic development, population size, the level of democracy, military regimes, and the presence of narcoterror organizations, are integrated into the structural model, as discussed in the next section.

The Determinants of State Repression

Independent Judiciary

Students of state repression have theorized that an independent judiciary is vital for the protection of human rights and civil liberties (Keith 2011, 2002b; Keith et al. 2009; Cross 1999). A central proposition that emerges from this scholarship is that an independent judiciary has the constitutional authority to act as a counterbalance against political leaders' abuse of power by holding security personnel accountable when the human rights of citizens are violated (Keith et al. 2009).

The notion of an independent judiciary is enshrined in international law. The Basic Principles on the Independence of the Judiciary were adopted in 1985 by the Seventh U.N. Congress on the Prevention of Crime and the Treatment of Offenders and were subsequently endorsed by the U.N. General Assembly

(United Nations 1985a, 1985b). The Basic Principles establish the notion of the institutional independence of the judiciary, which means that the judiciary must be independent of other branches of government, specifically the executive branch and the legislature. This independence must be guaranteed by the constitution or via other legal provisions (United Nations 1985a, 1985b). In addition, the Basic Principles emphasize the notion of the administrative independence of the judiciary. What this means in practice is that the judiciary must have the autonomy to manage its own administration and govern its own operations. Judicial independence also entails the relative financial independence of the judiciary (United Nations 1985a, 1985b).

To execute its functions effectively without being vulnerable to political pressure and corruption, the judiciary must be adequately funded. According to the Basic Principles, the executive branch, the legislature, and other governmental institutions must respect and abide by the decisions and judgments of the judiciary. Respect for the decisions of the judiciary is indispensable for the maintenance of the rule of law and respect for human rights. Judicial independence, according to the Basic Principles, also includes jurisdictional competence. This means that the judiciary must have exclusive authority over issues of a judicial nature and be able to decide if issues submitted for its ruling fall within its competence as governed by law (United Nations 1985a, 1985b).

Judicial independence, however, goes beyond jurisdictional competence and the institutional and administrative independence of the judiciary, extending to the individual independence of judges. Judges have a right and a duty to make judicial rulings that are based on law and must be free from fear of personal criticism or reprisals. In many countries judges are not allowed to dispatch their responsibilities in this spirit of judicial independence, as they are often the targets of undue personal criticism, transfer, and dismissal, and in some instances they are the victims of violent and fatal attacks. The independence of judges can be secured in a number of ways: (1) appointing and promoting judges based solely on professional merit and personal integrity, (2) ensuring the job security of judges through long-term tenure, (3) ensuring the financial security of judges, and (4) ensuring that judges have the right to freedom of expression and association. Judges are better equipped to defend their independence when they can freely express themselves and form their own professional associations (United Nations 1985a, 1985b).

Empirical research on the effects of judicial independence on governments' respect for human rights has consistently shown that in countries where the judiciary is independent citizens enjoy greater freedom from state repression (Keith et al. 2009). In their cross-national examination of the impact of constitutional provisions for judicial independence on the human rights practices of governments, Blasi and Cingranelli (1997) constructed an index of nine attributes of judicial independence and found that constitutional provisions for these attributes provided protection against political torture, imprisonment, and disappearances. In examining the relationship between judicial independence, constitutional protection against unreasonable searches, and governments' human rights practices, Cross (1999) found that judicial independence increased political rights and protection against unreasonable searches. Keith (2002b) examined seven key constitutional elements that have been identified as necessary to produce an independent judiciary capable of protecting human rights: institutional independence of the judiciary, the long-term tenure of judges, respect for judicial decisions, the jurisdictional competence of the judiciary, bans against exceptional or military courts, the fiscal autonomy of the judiciary, and the selection of judges on the basis of professional merit. She found that the long-term tenure of judges, the institutional independence of the judiciary, bans on exceptional or military courts, and the fiscal autonomy of the judiciary were all positively associated with the protection of human rights.

Economic Development

Theories of state repression also demonstrate that greater levels of economic development will reduce the likelihood of repression. Some scholars argue that increasing levels of poverty and scarcity increase social and political tensions, which threaten regimes and provide them with the opportunity and justification to engage in acts of repression (Poe et al. 1999; Poe and Tate 1994; Mitchell and McCormick 1988). But why do regimes choose terror when facing low or declining levels of economic development when other forms of sanctions are available? Dallin and Breslauer (1970) argue all social systems need the power to secure compliance with state directives and policies. Three types of sanctions are available as instruments of state power: normative sanctions include persuasion, socialization, education, and offers of recognition; material sanctions include financial incentives and rewards; and coercive sanctions, which are often referred to as negative coercion, include state terror, fines, and penalties. Under conditions of stagnant and declining levels of economic development and rising levels of social and political conflict, there is no effective alternative to the use of coercive sanctions to establish order. In the absence of economic development, political elites lack the material and financial resources to buy off popular resistance to the regime. Because socialization and indoctrination require time, increasing levels of economic deprivation undermine elites' ability to create normative dedication to the regime and its policies. Consequently, political terror and repression become a rational response to the decline in economic development (Dallin and Breslauer 1970, 1–7).

Population

Students of state repression have also shown that demographic factors like the size of a population or its growth is likely to increase state repression. Inspired by Malthusian catastrophic theory (Malthus 1708), human ecology theorists argue that population pressure is a major factor underlying many of the world's socioeconomic and political challenges (Catton 1982; Ehrlich and Ehrlich 1990; Hardin 1993). Scholars argue that large populations place greater demands on natural resources and the financial resources of the state. Overpopulation can lead to environmental deterioration, which in turn weakens the economy and the capacity of governments to meet the needs of their citizens. The unmet demands of large populations threaten political stability and invite state repression. Population growth can also aggravate latent ethnic conflict when the growth of an ethnic group leads it to demand a larger share of the country's economic and political benefits. Other ethnic groups will perceive these demands as attempts to marginalize them politically and will likely respond with violence, which ultimately triggers state repression (Henderson 1993, 323–25; Gupte 1984, 20–25). Extant empirical research that has investigated the direct link between population size and state repression (Henderson 1993; Frey et al. 1999) or used measures of population as control variables to explain governments' respect for human rights (Keith 1999, 2002a; Mitchell and McCormick 1988; Poe and Tate 1994; Poe et al. 1999; Zanger 2000) has consistently shown that a large population or rapid population growth increases the likelihood of state repression.

Military Regimes

The extant human rights literature has consistently demonstrated the rather intuitive empirical finding that military regimes are likely to be more repressive than other polities (McKinlay and Cohan 1976, 1975; Poe and Tate 1994).

Democracy

For theoretical reasons discussed more fully in chapter 1, students of state repression have argued, and found repeated empirical confirmation, that democratic regimes increase respect for human rights (Poe and Tate 1994; Poe et al. 1999; Davenport 1995; Henderson 1991) while autocratic regimes increase repression (Poe and Tate 1994; Boswell and Dixon 1990).

The Presence of Narcoterror Organizations

Chapter 3 introduced an empirical model that predicts U.S. counternarcotic aid flows. Subsequent chapters demonstrated that an important variable that predicts counternarcotic aid is the presence of Indigenous narcoterror organizations and international drug trafficking cartels. However, since narcoterror organizations and drug trafficking cartels wage war against the state by targeting government officials and terrorizing and killing civilian populations, their very presence in countries is likely to increase human rights violations (Bartilow 2014). The variable predicts human rights violations that are attributed to nonstate actors, an aspect of repression captured by the PTS index.

Theoretical Modifications of the Empirical Model

In building the empirical model it was necessary to consider theoretical modifications and incorporate these into the overall structural model. The presence of narcoterror organizations (Indigenous narcoinsurgent guerrilla organizations and drug cartels) is a control variable that explains levels of repression (Bartilow 2014). However, as I have argued and demonstrated in chapters 3–5, since American policy makers consider drug trafficking a security threat (Bartilow and Eom 2012), they will extend larger disbursements of counternarcotics aid to countries with Indigenous narcoterror organizations than to countries where such organizations do not exist (Crandall 2008a).

While economic development and population are control variables that explain levels of repression in Latin America, these variables also explain levels of paramilitary activity in the region. Poor countries without the resources to finance large armies turn to paramilitary organizations, which can be financed more cheaply, to intimidate and control the local population (Bartilow 2000, 2001). National wealth, therefore, can be expected to have a negative effect on the likelihood that paramilitary organizations will become active. Since large armies allow governments to exert control over large populations, paramilitaries allow governments to effectively coerce and control countries with smaller populations (Bartilow 2000, 2001). It is therefore expected that large populations will also have a negative effect on the likelihood that paramilitary organizations will become active.

An independent judiciary is a control variable that explains levels of repression (Keith 2002a, 2011). However, since an independent judiciary is the constitutional defender of citizens' civil rights, the variable is also expected to have a direct reductive effect on the violations of civil liberties (Keith 2002b).

I also consider the direct effect of repression on U.S. FDI. The extant literature has shown that repression in host countries has a negative effect on the decision of transnational corporations to invest in these countries. Blanton and Blanton (2007, 152) found that "developing countries that respect human rights are more successful in attracting FDI than those where there is widespread human rights abuse." Similarly, in examining the determinants of Japanese FDI in Latin America during 1979–93, Tuman and Emmert (1999) found that human rights conditions in the region were negatively related to FDI. Because a major component of my theoretical argument holds that increased para-military activity is associated with increased human rights repression, I also consider the direct effect of ongoing paramilitary activities on the decision of transnational corporations to invest in host countries where they are present. While CIRI's measurements of physical integrity rights and the PTS each cap-ture different aspects of human rights violations against citizens, I argue that both indexes are correlated (Cingranelli and Richards 2010, 407) and assume covariance in the error structures of these variables.

Limitations of the Mediating Variables

Data limitations regarding the measurement of FDI present challenges in es-timating the empirical model. First, disaggregated measures of FDI in natural resources and agribusiness are not available for most years and countries in Latin America.[2] Instead, the aggregated measure of U.S. FDI serves as a proxy for U.S. investment in natural resources and agribusiness. This measure serves as a good proxy for several reasons. First, the United States continues to be the largest investor in Latin America, Central America, and the Caribbean. In 2012, transnational corporations based in the United States accounted for 24 percent of inward FDI in the region (ECLAC 2012, 37). Second, chapter 5 showed that the share of FDI in South America's natural resource sector grew to 51 percent in 2012, after averaging 44 percent in previous years (ECLAC 2012, 38), and in 2013 FDI in natural resources in Central American and Caribbean countries grew in Guatemala, Panama, Suriname, and Barbados (ECLAC 2013, 26). Moreover, FDI in agroindustry in the region totaled US$48.4 billion for 2005–11 (ECLAC 2012, 14). Given that the United States is the leading source country for FDI in the region and that the bulk of FDI is invested in the natural resource and agrobusiness sectors, U.S. FDI, while imperfect, is still an effec-tive proxy for capturing the human rights effect of resource-seeking transna-tional companies.

Another central component of my theoretical argument is that, in response to Indigenous challenges to capital accumulation, corporations are likely to contract with private security firms and local militaries, as well as colluding with paramilitary organizations. However, since no measures are available for private security firms in Latin America, it is not possible to generate SEM es-timates using this indicator. While indicators measure the aggregate number of military personnel in the region, they do not distinguish between military personnel on active duty from those that are not. Consequently, such measures will likely inflate U.S. counternarcotic aid's effect on repression as mediated by U.S. FDI and the military. Given these data limitations, SEM estimates were generated for the structural model that features U.S. FDI and the activity of paramilitary organizations as mediators for the human rights effect of U.S. counternarcotic aid.[3] Following Carey et al. (2013) I define paramilitary organizations as pro-government militias.

Empirical Findings

Figure 6.2 presents an SEM diagram with levels of statistical significance of the main SEM along with control variables and the theoretical modifications of the model. Table 6.1 presents the results with standard errors and goodness-of-fit statistics. SEM estimates of the main structural model support my theoretical argument: U.S. counternarcotic aid is positively associated with increases in U.S. FDI in Latin America and the Caribbean. In addition, U.S. FDI in the region is positively associated with increased paramilitary activity, which in turn is positively associated with increased human rights repression.

However, some interesting findings emerge from the theoretical modifications of the main structural model. While existing U.S. FDI is positively associated with increased paramilitary activity, the increased activity of paramilitary organizations is negatively associated with new FDI investment in the region. It would appear that this reverse pathway is at odds with the finding that U.S. FDI is positively associated with paramilitary activity. This, however, is not the case, and in fact these results complement each other. The increased activity of paramilitary death squads represents increased levels of conflict, which will naturally discourage new investments in the region. However, prior to the outbreak of conflict, U.S. FDI that faces domestic threats to capital accumulation will encourage the activation of paramilitary death squads to repress and eliminate such threats.

Other findings that emerge from these theoretical modifications are also consistent with my theoretical expectations. The presence of narcoterror organizations is positively associated with increases in U.S. counternarcotic aid disbursements—a finding with repeated empirical confirmation in chapters 3–4. In countries that are more economically developed with larger populations, paramilitary death squads are less likely to become active.

Increasing levels of repression, which is produced by paramilitary death squads, are positively associated with increases in U.S. FDI flows in the region. This finding contradicts the extant literature's consensus that repression in host countries has a negative effect on the decision of transnational corporations

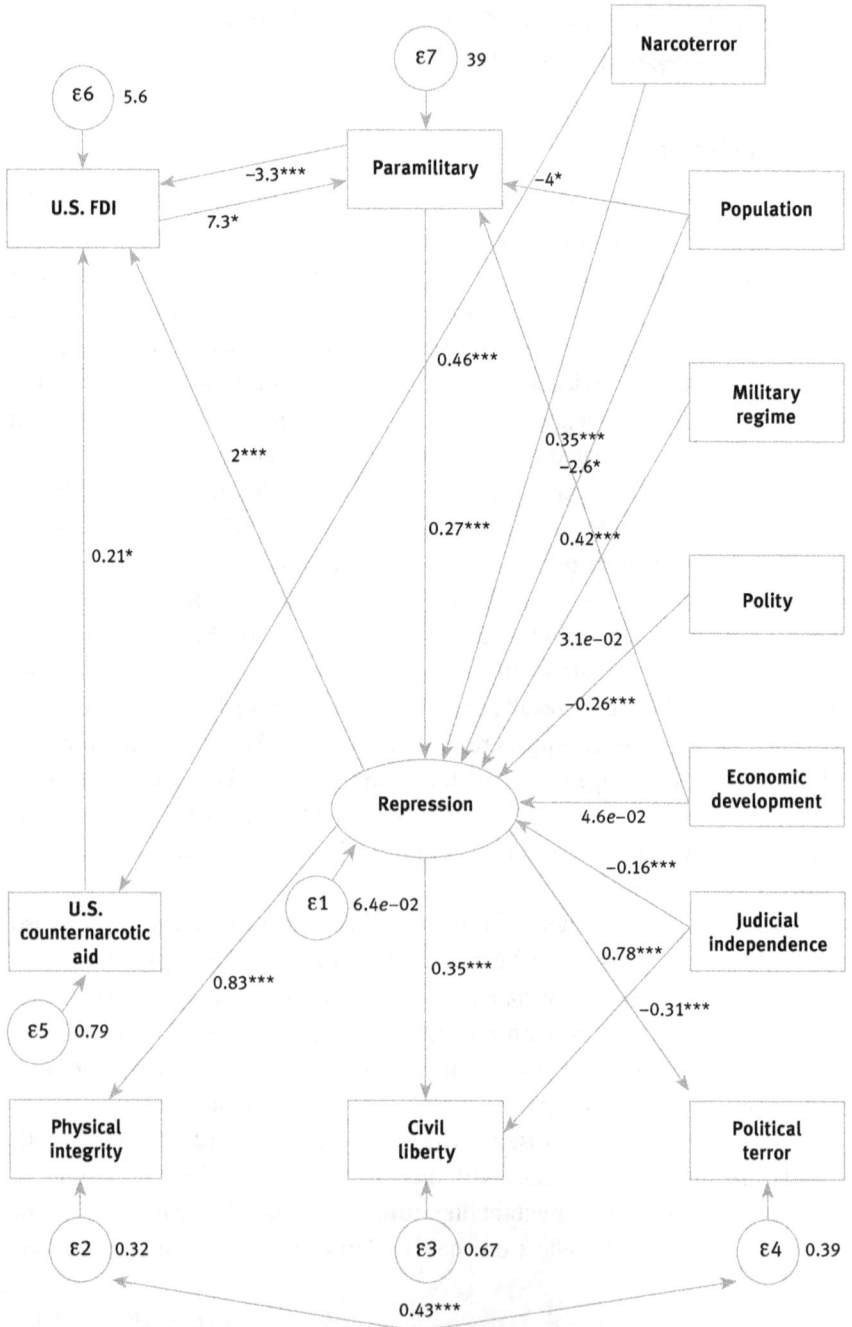

Figure 6.2. Structural equation modeling of U.S. counternarcotic aid, U.S. foreign direct investment, paramilitary death squads, and repression. The error terms (ε) are the residual variances within variables not accounted for by the pathways hypothesized in the model; they are accompanied by their coefficients. Levels of statistical significance: +*p* < 0.10, **p* < 0.50, ***p* < 0.01, ****p* < 0.001.

Table 6.1. U.S. counternarcotic aid, U.S. foreign direct investment, paramilitary death squads, and repression

Dependent variables	Explanatory variables	Estimates
U.S. foreign direct investment	U.S. counternarcotic aid	0.2106861* (0.1085024)
	Repression	2.002912*** (0.302273)
	Paramilitary activity	−3.331064*** (0.5555916)
	Constant	−4.85796*** (0.8779574)
Paramilitary activity	U.S. FDI	7.348404* (3.263802)
	Population (logged)	−3.986355* (1.872279)
	Economic development	−2.633191* (1.147628)
	Constant	33.60532* (15.59146)
U.S. counternarcotic aid	Narcoterror organizations	0.4601027*** (0.0289497)
	Constant	0.0541469 (0.0369644)
Civil liberty	Repression	0.3533673*** (0.0378883)
	Judicial independence	−0.305715*** (0.0360153)
	Constant	0.4672254** (0.1866218)
Repression	Paramilitary activity	0.2690964*** (0.0569557)
	Population (logged)	0.4229588*** (0.0281121)
	Military regime	.0312157 (0.0258032)
	Level of democracy (Polity index)	−0.2612213*** (0.0291438)
	Economic development	0.0464317 (0.0273698)
	Judicial independence	−0.1635098*** (0.0284061)
	Narcoterror organizations	0.3487291*** (0.0295313)
Measurement model estimates		
CIRI physical integrity index	Repression	0.8262914*** (0.0287968)
	Constant	−1.060531*** (0.262382)
Political terror scale	Repression	0.7841135*** (0.0286335)
	Constant	0.0224971 (0.2616107)
Covariance	Physical integrity Political terror	0.4293823*** (0.063518)
	Number of observations	663

Standard errors are in parentheses. Goodness-of-fit statistics: model chi-square, $p > \chi^2 = 0.0000$; population error: root mean square error of approximation (RMSEA) = 0.08; baseline comparison: comparative fit index = 0.90, Tucker-Lewis index = 0.92; size of residuals: standardized root mean squared residual (SRMSR) = 0.05.

Levels of statistical significance: $^+p < 0.10$, $^*p < 0.05$, $^{**}p < 0.01$, $^{***}p < 0.001$.

to invest in these countries (Blanton and Blanton 2007; Tuman and Emmert 1999). It also suggests that increasing levels of repression encourage U.S. FDI because it deactivates civil society groups and signals transnational capital that such groups will not obstruct the process of capital accumulation. Preexisting paramilitary conflict, however, discourages new investments because it signals the insecurity of corporate assets.

An independent judiciary is negatively associated with violations in civil liberties, and as predicted, the covariance between violations of citizens' physical integrity rights and the level of terror in the political environment is statistically significant and positive. With the exception of economic development and military regime, the effect of the other independent variables on repression is consistent with the findings of the extant human rights literature. Democracies and independent judiciaries are both negatively associated with repression. Large populations and the presence of an Indigenous narcoterror organization are positively associated with repression. The latent variable, repression, is positively associated with violations of physical integrity rights and civil liberties, as well as the level of political terror in the environment.

How well does the model fit the data? With the exception of the model chi-square, the model fits the data very well. The model chi-square is statistically significant and indicates poor goodness of fit. However, Kline (2011) has shown that the model chi-square statistic is overly influenced by sample size, correlations, variance that is unrelated to the model, and multivariate nonnormality. It is therefore not a reliable indicator of goodness of fit. It is standard practice to report other fit indices when reporting the results of SEM analyses, and the following goodness-of-fit statistics are worth reporting: the model's RSMEA is 0.08, which indicates a reasonable fit. The convention for the RSMEA is that 0.0, 0.05, and 0.08 indicate excellent, good, and reasonable fits, respectively (MacCallum et al. 1996). The comparative fit and Tucker-Lewis indices are respectively 0.90 and 0.92, both indicating good fits, and the SRMSR is 0.05, which also indicates a good fit (Kline 2011).

Conclusion

This chapter provides an analysis of the pathways through which American counternarcotic aid facilitates repression in Latin America. In doing so, it provides empirical support to the theoretical arguments in chapter 5 that American counternarcotic aid to Latin America facilitates the expansion of resource-seeking transnational corporations in the region and that the expansion of such transnational capital creates the conditions for corporate-induced repression in response to Indigenous resistance to capital accumulation.

The SEM estimates suggest that American counternarcotic aid's effect on human rights repression is mediated by both U.S. FDI and paramilitary death squads. This finding refutes the prediction of neoclassical liberal theory and is consistent with dependency theory's proposition that the effect of FDI on repression is not direct but mediated by domestic political actors. The finding also highlights the importance of foreign governments' agency in the corporatist drug enforcement regime and suggests that foreign governments with ties to paramilitary death squads and private security firms are not passive players in the regime's repressive pathology as they engage in the process of capital accumulation. The policy decisions of the drug enforcement regime also contribute to the production of other pathologies, which are reflected in the dysfunctional and repressive nature of democracies in Latin America, an issue discussed and analyzed in the next chapter.

CHAPTER 7

Democracy without Rights

The Drug-War National Security State and Illiberal Democracies in Latin America

In a "bifurcated system—a structure of double government" where power has shifted away from the Madisonian institutions and toward the permanent Trumanite national security and intelligence bureau-cracies, "towards greater centralization, less accountability," we face an "emergent autocracy" under the guise of a democratic republic.
—**Michael Glennon,** "National Security and Double Government"

Michael Glennon's analysis of the unchecked power of the national security state, which he characterizes as an "'emergent autocracy' under the guise of a democratic republic," describes the very essence of the illiberal democracy that has emerged not in some distant country in the developing world but here in the United States. Glennon's analysis of the national security state and its adverse effects on America's democracy provide important theoretical insights for understanding the paradox of Latin America's democratization: although the region is considered the leader of democratization's third wave (Hunting-ton 1991a, 1991b), scholarly consensus and public opinion suggest something is amiss in the practice and quality of democracy in the region.

Moreover, Latin America's democratization has not always been a linear process characterized by regime transitions from authoritarianism to liberal democracy. In many instances regime transitions have been regressive, in the sense not of sliding back to military dictatorship but of sliding back to illiberal democratic regimes that combine free elections with systematic constraints and violations of citizens' civil and human rights (Smith and Ziegler 2008). While Latin American scholars share Glennon's conceptual understanding of the es-sential nature of illiberal democracies, there is widespread disagreement about the factors that give rise to them in the region. They also recognize the pattern of regressive transitions from liberal to illiberal governance but have offered no overarching theoretical explanations for the cause of this phenomenon.

The paradox of Latin America's democratization motivates the following question: What explains the determinants of illiberal democracies in Latin America and the prevalence of regime transitions from liberal to illiberal governance? In this chapter I argue that counternarcotic aid is the financial and diplomatic mechanism through which the corporatist drug enforcement regime has replicated essential features of the U.S. national security state in aid-recipient countries in Latin America for the purpose of fighting the drug war. The replication of the national security state undermines the process of democratization and, in the process, produces illiberal regimes in the region. The drug-war-induced national security state explains not only the emergence of illiberal democracy in the region but also regressive regime transitions from liberal to illiberal governance.

In this chapter, I begin my argument with a discussion of the scholarly conceptual consensus regarding the theoretical foundations of illiberal democracy, as well as public opinion regarding the quality and practice of democracy in Latin America. This is followed by a discussion of the scholarly debate about the factors that give rise to illiberal democracy in the region. I contribute to this debate by briefly discussing the National Security Act of 1947 (NSA47), which gave rise to the U.S. national security state. I then discuss the central features of the national security state and show how the policy conditions attached to American counternarcotic aid disbursements produce a "drug-war national security state" by replicating the essential features of the U.S. national security state in aid-recipient countries in Latin America. Drawing on insights about how American counternarcotic aid encourages the development of the drug-war national security state, the section that follows explains why regime transitions from liberal democracy to its illiberal variant are more prevalent than transitions to nondemocratic authoritarian rule. After these theoretical discussions, I move to the generation of hypotheses, which is followed by a discussion of the variables incorporated into the probabilistic regression models used to estimate the data. The final section discusses my findings and concludes by considering the implications of the drug enforcement regime's prohibition policy decisions for democratization in Latin America.

Theoretical Foundations of Illiberal Democracy

Illiberal democracy, or what Uruguayan novelist Eduardo Galeano dubbed "democratatorship," describes a political system that has all the formal institutional procedures of a democracy but has simultaneously incorporated features of a dictatorship with a voracious appetite for repression (Hristov 2009, 27; Giraldo 1996). Zakaria (1997, 22–23) views these regimes as an abrogation of what is traditionally meant by *liberal democracy*— namely, a polity that is not just founded on free and fair elections but one whose authority structure is based on the rule of law, the separation of political power, and the protection of civil liberties. Illiberal democracies are democratically elected regimes that ignore the constitutional limits of their power and deny their citizens' human rights and political freedoms. A central feature of these regimes is the persistence of a weak, semi-independent judiciary. Calleros (2009) examined twelve countries in Latin America to assess the capacity of the judiciary's contribution to the process of democratic consolidation and found that, with the one exception of Costa Rica, the judiciary is the least evolved of the three branches of government. Judicial systems are persistently weak, which makes them unable, in practice, to check the power of other branches of government; namely, the executive and the military, and ineffective in protecting human rights or implementing due process under the law.

Other scholars, including Schedler (2002, 37), define these regimes as "electoral democracies" that are capable of conducting free and fair elections but fail to institutionalize vital components of democratic constitutionalism—namely, the rule of law, the accountability of public officials, bureaucratic integrity, and transparent deliberations. Gills and Rocamora (1992), Gills et al. (1993), and Kruit (2001) define these regimes as "low-intensity democracies" and emphasize the synchronization of the military and its national security doctrine (Giraldo 1996, 57) with the formal procedures and norms of democratic governance. *Low-intensity democracy* refers to the controlled transition from authoritarian rule to a type of "armored or guided democracy" under the sponsorship of the military (Kruit 2001, 412), which enables regimes to pursue repression with more impunity and less popular resistance than their authoritarian predecessors (Gills and Rocamora 1992, 505). Low-intensity democracies, as Kruit (2001, 415) observes, are "democracies whose citizens are guarded, whose politicians are advised, whose legislators are timid, and whose judges are fearful." These are regimes where democratic and civil-society institutions are permanently frozen in a stage of adolescent development.

O'Donnell (1994) conceptualizes these regimes as "delegative democracies." They are democracies in the sense that they satisfy Dahl's (1971) definition of polyarchy, but democratic governance is not institutionalized. Delegative democracies are fiercely majoritarian and thus are more democratic than representative democracies but not as liberal. Through elections, the majority chooses and empowers an individual—the president—to become the embodiment and defender of the nation's interests. Elected presidents present themselves as being above political parties and organized interest groups. They see themselves as representing a broad-based movement that is well equipped to overcome the political factionalism and conflicts associated with the myopic interests of party politics. In these regimes the winner of the presidency is entitled to govern without constraint, with the exception of those constitutional constraints that impose limits on the president's term in office (O'Donnell 1994, 59–60).

In delegative democracies the judiciary and the legislature are nuisances to the democratically elected president. Accountability to these institutions is seen not as an important aspect of democratic consolidation but as an impediment to the full authority that the majority has authorized the president to exercise. In institutionalized democracies accountability is structured both vertically and horizontally: vertically in the sense that elected officials must answer to voters, and horizontally in the sense that each branch of government has relatively autonomous powers and can veto the policies or decisions of other branches. Delegative presidents often see the institutions that make horizontal accountability effective as a threat to their mission and their paternal sense of the national interest, so they actively seek to impede and weaken the development of these institutions of government (O'Donnell 1994, 60–62). Consequently, horizontal accountability is weak or nonexistent in delegative democracies.

Public Perceptions of Democracy in Latin America

The academic consensus about the illiberal nature of democracy is also reflected in public opinion attitudes regarding the quality of democracy in the region. Graph 7.1 displays data calculated from the Latinobarómetro for a sample of South and Central American countries during the years 1995 to 2011.[1] The graph shows the aggregated averages of citizens' responses to the question: Would you say that you are very satisfied, fairly satisfied, not very satisfied, or not at all satisfied with the way democracy works in your country? Combining and comparing the responses of those who answered "not very satisfied" and "not at all satisfied" with responses of those who answered "rather satisfied" and "very satisfied" indicates that 65 percent of the citizens from South and Central America are not satisfied with democracy, versus 34 percent who report they are satisfied.

The public's dissatisfaction with the quality of democracy may also be related to their perception that democratic governance benefits the interests of the region's powerful elites. Graph 7.2 displays data calculated from the Latinobarómetro for the same sample of countries during the years 2005 to 2011,

Graph 7.1. Levels of satisfaction with the quality of democracy in Latin America, 1995–2011. *Source*: Latinobarómetro 1995.

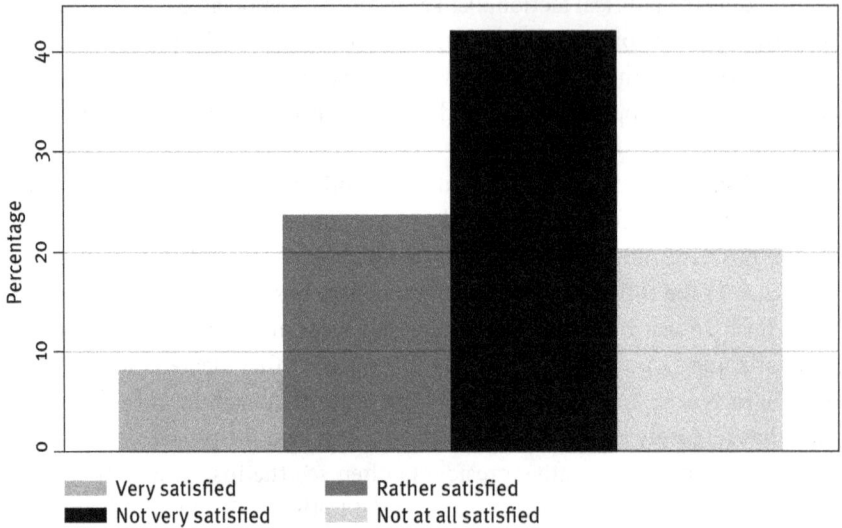

Legend:
- Very satisfied
- Not very satisfied
- Rather satisfied
- Not at all satisfied

showing the aggregated averages of citizens' response to the question: Which of the following statement do you agree with: (1) The country is governed for the benefit of the powerful; (2) the country is governed for the benefit of all. Responses indicate that 65 percent of respondents believe that their country is governed for the benefit of a powerful elite, while just 25 percent believe that their country is governed for the benefit of all.

The Determinants of Latin America's Illiberal Democracy: Competing Perspectives

What explains the evident illiberal pattern of democratization in Latin America? Gills and Rocamora (1992, 504–5) blame Latin America's illiberalism on external forces, specifically the post–Cold War changes in U.S. geopolitical and economic interests in the region. With the dissolution of the Soviet Union, American policy makers came to the realization that the Kirkpatrick Doctrine, which justified supporting anticommunist authoritarian regimes (Kirkpatrick 1982) in the region, was unsustainable and that democratization was inevitable. It was therefore necessary for the United States to guide the process of democratization so as to preempt any radical or revolutionary changes that would threaten U.S. geopolitical and economic interests. In effect, low-intensity

Graph 7.2. Central and South Americans' perception of who their countries' governments benefit, 2005–2011. *Source:* Latinobarómetro 1995.

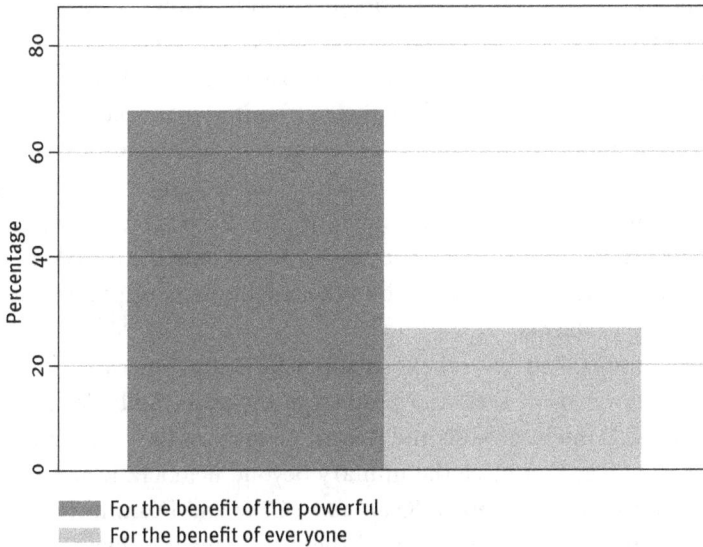

For the benefit of the powerful
For the benefit of everyone

democracy, like its militaristic cousin low-intensity conflict, is a type of intervention to prevent progressive or revolutionary change in America's so-called backyard. To the extent that low-intensity democracy demobilized Latin America's progressive Left, it also legitimized and strengthened the political position of the oligarch clients of the United States. Under the tutelage of the IMF and the World Bank, conservative elites in these regimes have allowed greater transnational corporate penetration into Latin America, ensuring that capital accumulation is unencumbered by the process of democratization in the region.

Kruit (2001, 413) attributes Latin America's tendency toward illiberal democracy to what he calls the "shadowy presence" of the military in the governance structure of civilian governments. Since ex-dictators and their juntas feared being tried by civilian governments that they could not control, they sought to guide democratization, thus producing low-intensity democracy. The military's presence in Latin American democracy is felt in terms of its control over the system of intelligence, its predominance over the police, and its establishment for itself of a legal basis for impunity and immunity against charges of human rights repression. Echoing similar sentiments, Loveman (1998, 121–27) argues that in spite of Latin America's democratization the military reserved for itself "a formal constitutional and statutory role in the new regimes." As a virtual fourth branch of government that is unconstrained by the three civilian branches, the military is immune from not only past acts of human rights abuse but also present acts of repression (Cruz and Diamint 1998, 17)

O'Donnell (1994, 63–65) explains Latin America's illiberal democracy in terms of the severity of the socioeconomic problems that the newly installed civilian governments inherited from their authoritarian predecessors. Because high levels of inflation, stagnant economic growth, and severe fiscal crisis require the implementation of IMF structural adjustment economic reforms (Bartilow 1997) and decisive government action, these circumstances justify the emergence of delegative democracies in which only the president, who is above politics and unconstrained by other institutions of government, can solve pressing problems.

These accounts offer several explanations for Latin America's illiberal democracy. It is variously seen as a product of the post–Cold War changes in U.S. geopolitical interests (Gills and Rocamora 1992), of the constitutional and political privileges that place the military beyond democratic accountability (Foweraker and Krznaric 2009; Kruit 2001; Cruz and Diamint 1998), and of economic crises that have encouraged the development of hyperpresidential or delegative systems (O'Donnell 1994). Taken together, these factors represent different components of Latin America's national security state, which U.S. drug enforcement policies have encouraged in order to prosecute an unrelenting drug war in the region.

NSA47 and the Emergence of the U.S. National Security State

The term *national-security state* refers here to the network of bureaucracies that dominate American foreign and security policy that emerged with the passage of NSA47 and, with it, the creation of the National Security Council (NSC). NSA47 brought about three major structural changes in the American foreign policy establishment. The first was the creation of the CIA, which not only made secrecy and intelligence gathering legitimate but also established it as a necessary form of government. The second change was the reorganization of the armed forces under the secretary of defense, which was accompanied by the Joint Chiefs of Staff. The third ensured that resources from the national economy would be made available for the purpose of security and national defense (Raskin 1976, 193).

The NSC is composed of the president, the vice president, the secretary of state, the secretary of defense, the secretary of energy, and the secretaries and undersecretaries of the various executive and military departments who are appointed by the president. This also includes the director of national drug control policy, who is the principal adviser to the NSC on national drug control policy. The NSC has the responsibility to "advise the President with respect to the integration of domestic, foreign, and military policies relating to national security so as to enable the military services and other departments and agencies of the government to cooperate more effectively in matters involving national security" (National Security Act of 1947, P.L.114-113, sec. 101, 50 U.S.C. 3001, 6–7). NSA47 also authorized the creation of the Committee on Foreign Intelligence (CFI), and recent amendments have led to the creation of the Committee on Transnational Threats (CTT). The CFI is responsible for identifying appropriate intelligence and establishing policies that govern the mission of the intelligence community to ensure the realization of the national security objectives of the United States. The CTT is expected to coordinate and direct all activities of the U.S. government that relate to combating transnational threats to the United States. These threats include international terrorism, narcotics trafficking, and the proliferation of weapons of mass destruction and delivery systems for such weapons. The CTT is also responsible for developing policies and procedures to ensure the effective sharing of information about transnational threats among federal law enforcement agencies and elements of the intelligence community operating outside the United States (National Security Act of 1947, P.L. 114-113, sec. 101, 50 U.S.C. 3001, 8).

Although NSA47 led to the creation of the NSC, the legislation never formulated a definition of *national security*. Instead, national security would be defined by the military and government elites who exercise power through the bureaucratic apparatus of the national security state. In the absence of a formal definition, the legislation gave the various agencies within the national security bureaucracy broad discretion to expand and interpret their own mandate. Vesting the national security state with such unchecked discretion has had the political consequence of making it incompatible with democratic norms and practices (U.S. House Committee on the Judiciary 1984) and undermining the ability of the other branches of government to restrain its growing power (Raskin 1976, 193).

The Characteristics of the U.S. National Security State

There are five essential characteristics of the national security state. The first is the exaggeration of perceived threats against the state (Nelson-Pallmeyer 1992). In the United States the exaggeration of such threats (Glennon 2014a) not only defines the purpose and the identity of the national security state but also legitimates the expansion of its budgets and programs. In *Dubious Specter* Fred M. Kaplan (1980) debunked the highly publicized claims made during the Cold War that the Soviet Union was bound to achieve "strategic superiority" and showed instead that the so-called Soviet nuclear threat was promoted by the national security bureaucracies to garner public support and congressional funding for new strategic weapons systems that were moving into development.

In *The Rise and Fall of the Soviet Threat*, Alan Wolfe (1984) similarly argued that the variation in U.S. perceptions of the Soviet threat demonstrated that this threat was more imagined than real and was largely determined by the dynamics of domestic politics. Increased presidential power, as discussed below, is not only an important aspect of the national security state but also a prerequisite for governing an advanced capitalist society whose foreign and economic policies have an international reach. However, at times Congress has attempted to curtail the power of the presidency, making it necessary for the executive branch to exaggerate external threats to hold on to the power it has accumulated. Truman, Kennedy, Carter, and Reagan all exaggerated the Soviet threat, thereby increasing presidential power and the budget of the national security state (Wolfe 1984, 50–51). The Soviet threat was also a product of the politics of interservice rivalry and was often exaggerated when the three branches of the armed forces could not agree on their proper share of the defense budget. The equilibrium between the three normally broke down when a new administration entered the White House and attempted to shift resources to its favorite service. In response, those branches of the armed forces that stood to lose resources exaggerated the Soviet threat in ways that enhanced their role in countering it. The president, not wanting to appear weak in the face of this exaggerated threat, would reestablish equilibrium among the armed forces by supporting new legislation that expanded the overall military budget (Wolfe 1984, 61).

The second characteristic of the national security state is that it often maintains the appearance of democracy, but in reality power rests with the military and the broader national security establishment (Nelson-Pallmeyer 1992). Glennon (2014a, 12) argues that, while the American public believes that the constitutionally established branches of government are the locus of power, it is in fact the national security bureaucratic establishment that makes the central decisions relating to national security. This bureaucracy often operates outside of public knowledge and the constitutional restraints of Congress and the judiciary.

The third characteristic of the national security state is what Schlesinger (1973) popularized as the imperial presidency, which extracts and relies on powers beyond those that are authorized by the Constitution. According to the Constitution, only Congress has the power to initiate war, while the president is responsible for managing existing military conflicts and ongoing foreign policy and responding to preemptive attacks on the United States if Congress is not in session. Today, the president can order American citizens killed in secret; can detain prisoners indefinitely without charges or trial; can order drone strikes on countries without a congressional declaration of war; can initiate a torture program with impunity; and, with the assistance of the Patriot Act, can conduct warrantless surveillance on tens of millions of Americans. However, Glennon (2014a, 12) reminds us that the national security state has moved beyond the imperial presidency to a structure of "double government" in which even the president has very little control over the direction of U.S. national security policy. This explains why there was very little change in the direction of U.S. national security policy during the Obama administration.

Although candidate Obama, in 2008, promised to break with the imperial presidency of the Bush era and make major changes in national security policy, his policies did not depart from those of the Bush administration, and in many respects they were more strident. The Obama administration, like the Bush administration, sent terror suspects overseas for detention and interrogation, a process commonly known as extraordinary rendition (Johnston 2009). The administration has also exercised its power to hold American citizens accused of committing acts of terror in military confinement without trial (Baker 2009), and Obama often invoked the presidential prerogative to decide whether an accused terrorist will be tried by a military tribunal or a civilian court (Kornblut and Johnson 2010). Despite Obama's 2008 election-year promise to close the military prison at Guantánamo, his administration kept it open (Martin 2013), arguing that detainees cannot challenge the conditions of their imprisonment (Glennon 2014a, 3). The administration restricted Guantánamo detainees' access to legal counsel (Savage 2012), resisted efforts to extend the rights of habeas corpus to other offshore detainees (Savage 2009a), and denied their access to the International Red Cross (Rubin 2009). Further, the administration launched military operations against Libya without the approval of Congress (Savage and Landler 2011) and expanded the use of drones in Somalia, Libya, and Afghanistan, which resulted in an estimated death toll more than four times that during the Bush administration (Bergen 2012; Downie 2016).

With the exception of ending torture, the Obama administration did not alter the CIA's operations and programs from the form they took under the Bush administration (Moughty 2011). The administration continued the program of targeted killings and even approved the killing of American citizens Anwar al-Awlaki and Samir Khan without securing judicial warrants (Mazzetti et al. 2013; Savage 2011). The Obama administration opposed legislative proposals that would force it to increase the number of lawmakers who would be informed about covert operations (Pincus 2010). In addition, it expanded the role of covert special operations (DeYoung and Jaffe 2010) and continued all of the covert action programs of the Bush administration (Mazzetti 2013, 225). The Bush administration's program of cyberwarfare against Iran, code-named Olympic Games, was continued by the Obama administration (Sanger 2013, 188–203), which would often invoke the state secrets privilege (Savage 2009b; Devereaux 2010) to block lawsuits that challenged the legality of other national security operations (Liptak 2013). The administration also continued the surveillance policies of the Bush administration. These include the homeland surveillance program of the NSA (Savage and Risen 2010) and the interception of the communications of foreign leaders, some of whom, like German chancellor Angela Merkel (Wilson and Gearan 2013), are America's allies.

In essence, the imperial presidency has become the public face of the national security state. The accumulation of presidential power relative to Congress reflects a broader power shift in favor of the national security state. In terms of national security decision making, presidential elections have become spectacles to create the appearance of democracy, allowing prospective candidates to compete over who gets to pretend that they will direct the affairs of the national security state.

The fourth characteristic of the national security state is that the influence of the legislative branch of government over national security decision making is all but nil (Glennon 2014a, 62). The constitutional power of Congress is vastly disproportionate to the actual power it has over national security. This is an example of the classic principal agent dilemma, in which Congress, the principal, has constitutional authority over the agent—the national security bureaucracy—which is constitutionally obligated to implement the policy preferences of the principal. The dilemma exists when the national security bureaucracy is motivated to pursue its own interests that are at variance with those of their congressional principals (Moe 1984).

One reason for this power imbalance is that members of Congress face a gaping structural information asymmetry on matters of national security relative to the various security experts and generals who run the national security state. Given the intensity of their work load on myriad public policy issues, members of Congress are forced to be policy generalists, while bureaucrats and generals in the national security establishment concentrate on only one issue: national security. Moreover, informational asymmetry is enhanced by the fact that the agents of national security will sometimes manipulate or misrepresent intelligence reports on which members of Congress rely to make legislative decisions, as when Congress was misled in giving approval to go to war in Iraq. In other instances, agents would often withhold national security intelligence from Congress (Glennon 2014a, 60). As David Gergen, former presidential adviser to the Nixon, Ford, Reagan, and Clinton administrations, once observed, policy experts in the national security bureaucracy "simply do not trust the Congress with sensitive and covert programs" (Brzezinski 1983, 477).

Policy experts in the national security bureaucracy also dominate the legislative process on matters concerning national security issues. National security experts lobby congressional members and often draft national security bills that members introduce. They also provide arguments and data to support members of Congress during House and Senate deliberations and debates over national security issues (Glennon 2014a, 62). Therefore, given the informational asymmetries that structure the principal-agent relationship, Congress is more likely to accept the national security bureaucracy's threat assessments and the policy prescriptions to address these threats as presumptively correct (Glennon 2014a, 60) and, in doing so, is relegated to the periphery of national security decision making.

The fifth characteristic of the national security state is that the judiciary exercises very little influence over national security decision making. Judicial presidential nominees are often former prosecutors, members of law enforcement, and national security officials. According to a *New York Times* analysis of every judge who has served in the Foreign Intelligence Surveillance Court since its establishment in 1978, 66 percent were Republican appointees and 39 percent once worked for the executive branch (Savage 2013). Some lawmakers, such as Senator Richard Blumenthal, have expressed concern that this "revolving door" through which judges with a prior relationship with the executive branch are often selected to serve on the court may be perceived as conducive to bias in favor of the executive branch's applications for warrants, as well as other activities of the national security bureaucracy. Citing his own experience as a former U.S. attorney and state prosecutor, Senator Blumenthal noted that members of the judiciary who come from the executive branch are "more likely to share a 'get the bad guys' mind-set and defer to the Justice Department if Executive Branch officials told them that new surveillance powers were justified" (Savage 2013).

This view, however, is contested. Steven G. Bradley, the Justice Department legal counsel during the second term of the Bush administration, has argued that since national security involves highly technical issues it is important that judges be former government prosecutors who understand the inner workings of the executive branch. Prior experience with the executive branch gives judges on the Foreign Intelligence Surveillance Court the necessary background to rigorously vet the government's applications for national security surveillance operations (Savage 2013).

Does prior experience working for the executive branch provide judges with the knowledge and expertise necessary to hold the government accountable in matters relating to national security surveillance? Or does surveillance court judges' prior experience with the executive branch increase the likelihood that they may be unduly accommodating to requests from the government? While the rulings of surveillance court judges are secret, documents leaked by Edward Snowden would appear to lend support to the latter contention. The documents showed that Judge Roger Vinson, a senior federal judge, while a member of the Foreign Intelligence Surveillance Court issued a court order that required Verizon's Business Network Services to provide metadata on all calls in its system to the NSA on an ongoing and daily basis and also instructed the company not to publicly disclose the court order (U.S. Foreign Intelligence Surveillance Court 2013).

There are a few instances where the judiciary has imposed restraints on the national security state. For example, the Supreme Court overturned the military commissions that had been established to try enemy combatants for war crimes and later issued a ruling that Guantánamo detainees had been unlawfully denied habeas corpus rights. The court also pushed back against the objections of the national security establishment and allowed the publication of the Pentagon papers, which revealed the Defense Department's duplicity and ineptitude during the Vietnam War (Glennon 2014a, 58).

These occasional counterexamples of the court's resistance to the national security state are not enough to overcome the general thesis that the judiciary exercises very little restraint and influence over national security decision making. Notwithstanding the numerous U.S. military operations carried out without congressional approval, with the exception of a temporary order to cease bombing in Cambodia the courts have never stopped a war. Between 1979 and 2011 the Foreign Intelligence Surveillance Court received 32,093 requests for warrants from the government; it approved 32,087 and denied only 11. In 2012 the court received 1,789 requests for electronic surveillance; virtually all requests were approved, with only one withdrawn (Glennon 2014a, 58, 60).

U.S. Drug Enforcement Aid and the Making of the Drug-War National Security State

Like its American prototype, an essential feature of Latin America's drug-war national security state is the perception of threat. The increase in drug-related violence perpetrated by cartels and narcoinsurgent groups poses a major threat to states' national security during the period of democratization. Graphs 7.3 and 7.4 present cross-regional drug-related homicide rates per 100,000 persons

Graph 7.3. Drug-related homicides worldwide, 1995–2013. *Source*: World Bank n.d.

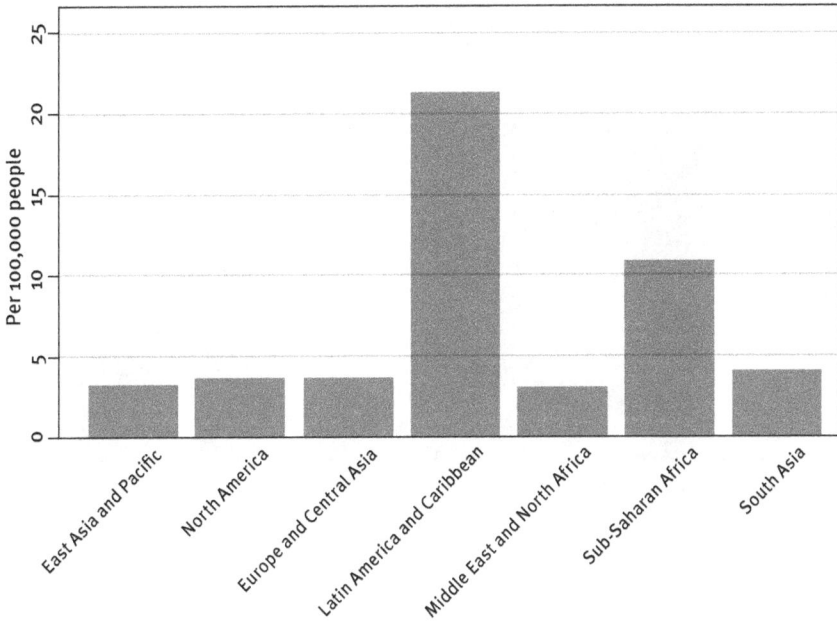

based on regional averages for 1995–2013. Graph 7.3 shows that Latin America and the Caribbean, with a homicide rate of 20.5 per 100,000 persons, is the most violent region in the world.[2]

As graph 7.4 shows, the drug-related homicide rate of 28 per 100,000 persons in South America's Andes, comprising the cocaine-producing countries of Colombia, Bolivia, and Peru, is far greater than that found in the opium- and heroin-producing countries of the Golden Triangle (Myanmar, Laos, and Thailand) and the Golden Crescent (Afghanistan, Kazakhstan, Kyrgyz Republic, Tajikistan, and Turkmenistan). Latin America and the Caribbean is the epicenter of the U.S.-funded drug war, and in consequence, the region has become the murder capital of the world.

Drug-related violence in Latin America permeates the social fabric of democracies in the region and has heightened states' perceptions of threat. On the basis of his interviews with Ecuadorian and Argentinean military officers during the 1990s, Fitch (1998, 116) reported that 46 and 37 percent, respectively, cited drug trafficking and narcoterrorist organizations as national security threats to the state. The November 2016 ratification of the revised peace accord between FARC and the Colombian government was a significant step toward peace. However, peace is still elusive due to the government's ongoing war with

Graph 7.4. Drug-related homicides in major drug-producing regions, 1995–2013. *Source*: World Bank n.d.

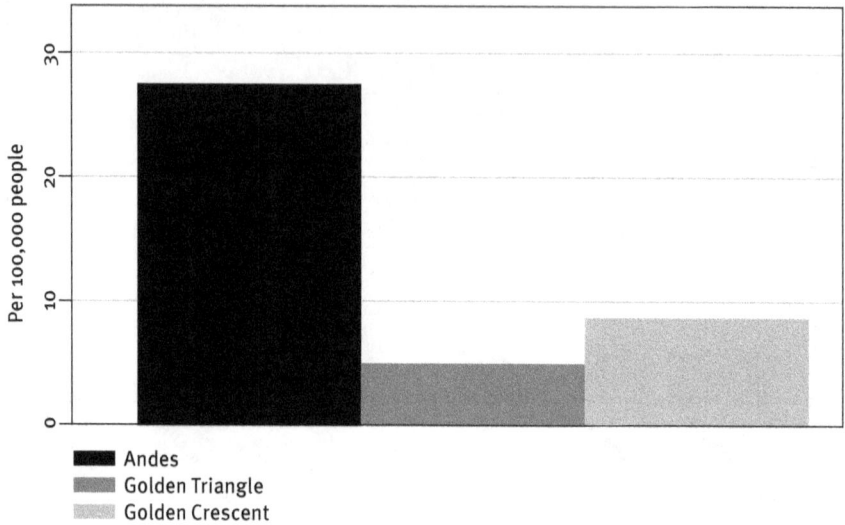

other insurgent groups, such as the ELN (McDermott 2016), and an estimated 30 percent of FARC (Ditta 2016) who did not demobilize (Yagoub 2016). There is also the government's ongoing war with narco-paramilitary groups, such as the Urabeños or the Gulf Clan and Rastrojos, and criminal organizations such as the BACRIM (Gagne 2016a; Forero 2018), all of which make peace elusive. Notwithstanding its peace accord with FARC, these ongoing conflicts will continue to have a significant impact in shaping the Colombian government's perception of threat.

There is also evidence that the peace accord has destabilized the dynamics of Colombia's drug trafficking and criminal networks and has led to a proliferation of drug-related violence throughout the Andes, which has increased the governments' threat perception. As FARC relinquishes its holdings in drug production and trafficking zones, the Urabeños have moved into these contested areas, sparking violent clashes with dissident factions of FARC along with the ELN, as well as with other drug trafficking criminal organizations (Ditta 2016; Yagoub 2016; Forero 2018). Dissident factions of FARC have formed new criminal structures in eastern Ecuador, where they engage in extortion, kidnapping, and coca production for sale to BACRIM criminal groups or to the Mexican Sinaloa cartel. This has prompted the Ecuadorian government to increase security operations along its eastern border with Colombia (LaSusa 2016). The security challenges raised by the peace accord prompted the Colombian government, on the fifteenth anniversary of Plan Colombia, to request a new aid package from the United States to confront narcosecurity threats (Gagne 2016b).

While threat perception is a necessary feature of the national security state, in the absence of a credible coercive capacity to respond to narcotrafficking threats it is not sufficient to explain the evolution of Latin America's drug-war national security state, especially during the region's transition from military dictatorship to democracy. American counternarcotic aid to Latin American governments provides them with the coercive capacity to respond to narcotrafficking threats. American policy makers attach conditions to counternarcotic aid, which replicate features of the national security state that are essential for its development in Latin America. Most significant, American policy makers stipulated that drug enforcement in the region requires the concentration of power in military and security forces, at a time when countries in the region were transitioning to democracy. In essence, American drug enforcement assistance requires its recipients to concentrate political power in the military under the guise of democratization. This dynamic has become an essential feature of Latin America's drug-war national security state, like that of its American prototype.

In 1989, the administration of George H. W. Bush, for the first time with congressional support, passed legislation that increased counternarcotic aid to foreign militaries. The Andean Initiative, a five-year counternarcotic aid package to the security forces in Colombia, Bolivia, and Peru, resulted from this legislation. As a precursor to Plan Colombia and the Mérida Initiative, the Andean Initiative was the first attempt by American policy makers to stipulate that militaries in the region would play a central role in domestic drug and law enforcement (U.S. House Committee on Foreign Affairs 1990). This policy dictate would have been unenforceable in the United States, as the Posse Comitatus Act of 1878 prohibits federal military personnel from conducting domestic law enforcement operations. Nevertheless, as a result of the Andean Initiative, militaries in the region began conducting counternarcotic operations, mounting road blocks, performing internal surveillance (including wiretaps), executing searches and seizures, forcing down suspicious civilian aircraft, conducting eradication operations on coca and marijuana crops, patrolling rivers, and arresting and interrogating civilians (Isacson 2005, 23). The Andean Initiative became the blueprint for the drug enforcement regime's militarization of the drug war throughout Latin America and the Caribbean.

Along with the financial incentive of counternarcotic aid, U.S. officials applied diplomatic pressure to militarize drug enforcement in the region. Beginning in the mid-1980s, American policy makers passed a series of legislation that required the president to certify that drug-producing and drug-transit countries were fully cooperating with the U.S. drug enforcement efforts.[3] Countries that failed to cooperate would be the targets of U.S. sanctions, which included the suspension of U.S. foreign assistance and U.S. opposition to loans in multilateral financial institutions (Storrs 2003, 1–9). To meet the demands of the annual certification process and avoid sanctions, governments throughout the region increased their militaries' role in domestic drug enforcement to demonstrate cooperation with the United States (Bartilow and Eom 2012, 63).

Counternarcotic aid created specialized counterdrug units within the militaries of recipient governments. In Bolivia, it financed the creation of the army's Green Devils and Black Devils task forces, the navy's Blue Devils task force, and the air force's Red Devils task force. In Colombia, it financed the creation of the First Army Counternarcotics Brigade and the Navy River Brigade. In Mexico, it provided funding for the Air-Mobile Special Forces Group and the Amphibious Special Forces Group. Counternarcotic aid also created specialized counterdrug units within countries' police forces. In Colombia, it financed the development of the Anti-Narcotic Division. In the Dominican Republic, it financed the creation of the National Directorate for Drug Control. In Ecuador, it provided financing that created the National Anti-Narcotic Directorate. In Guatemala, it financed the creation of the Anti-Narcotics Analysis and Information Service. In Jamaica, counternarcotic aid was responsible for the financing that created the Constabulary Force Narcotics Division. In Paraguay, it financed the creation of the Anti-Narcotic Secretariat. In Peru, it financed the Peruvian National Police Narcotic Directorate. In Bolivia, it financed the creation of the Special Drug Police Force and the Rural Mobile Patrol Unit, which specializes in jungle patrol, reconnaissance, air insertions, mobile roadblocks, and river operations. American counternarcotic aid also financed the creation of Bolivia's paramilitary counterdrug force, the Expeditionary Task Force, which during its eighteen months of operations in the Chapare region was implicated in gross human rights violations that resulted in the deaths of coca growers in the region (Isacson 2005, 25; Ledebur 2005, 151–52, 155). During the 1990s, counternarcotic aid to Mexico financed the training, equipment, and operational support of the Center of Anti-Narcotics Investigations, an elite team of Mexican soldiers who formed a specialized intelligence. The unit was responsible for developing intelligence that identified drug traffickers and designed counternarcotic strategies to dismantle drug cartels (Freeman and Sierra 2005, 277).

American counternarcotic aid also financed the training of the region's police, many of whom receive instruction from military institutions in the United States such as the Western Hemisphere Institute for Security Cooperation, formerly known as the School of the Americas. The militarization of the police undermines the process of democratization in a region that has sought to bring the police under greater civilian control and accountability. Moreover, the military tactics and skills taught to the region's police forces are antithetical to the norms and standards of democratic policing. While military doctrine emphasizes the use of overwhelming force to destroy the enemy in war, democratic policing seeks to minimize the use of force, cultivate the support and cooperation of citizens, and protect and serve them through crime prevention mechanisms while enforcing the rule of law (Neild 2005, 69–70).

While American policy makers claim to support democratic institutional accountability and shared governance in Latin America, their rhetoric is often at variance with the policies of the drug enforcement regime in the region. Since the implementation of the drug war often relies on an imperial executive, the policies of drug enforcement regime have reinforced the tradition in Latin America where the executive has stronger formal powers relative to the legislature (Mainwaring and Shugart 1997; Shugart and Carey 1992; Tseblis and Aleman 2005). In prosecuting the drug war, decree powers and urgency provisions allow Latin American presidents to directly initiate drug enforcement legislation often without the approval of the legislature (Carey and Shugart 1998; Negretto 2004). Implementing the policies of the drug enforcement regime in this context encourages the continuation of Latin America's version of the American imperial president at a time when the region is supposedly the leader of democratization's third wave (Huntington 1991b). In Bolivia, U.S. diplomatic pressure forced former president Jaime Paz Zamora to sign a number of agreements with the United States without the constitutionally mandated approval of the Bolivian Congress (Ledebur 2005, 150–51). The president unilaterally approved Annex III, which allowed the use of the military in domestic drug enforcement for the first time. The president, without congressional involvement, also approved Operations Blast Furnace and Snowcaps, which were joint counternarcotic operations conducted by the Bolivian army, the DEA, and U.S. military personnel (Central Intelligence Agency 1986; Drug Enforcement Administration 1990, 69).

In 2003, then-president Uribe of Colombia, with the support of the U.S. Department of State, blatantly disregarded the ruling of the Administrative Court of Cundinamarca, which said that the state's aerial crop fumigation program violated citizens' constitutional guaranteed rights to public health, security, and a healthy environment. The Administrative Court found that the Uribe government had not complied with the country's environmental management plan (EMP) and ordered the National Narcotics Directorate to suspend the aerial crop eradication program until the government fully complied with the

EMP and developed studies that measured the public health and environmental impact of the U.S.-sponsored crop eradication program (Lemus et al. 2005, 120–21). Not only did the national police not follow the court's order, but President Uribe denounced it and declared, "While I am President, fumigation will not be suspended" (*El Tiempo* 2003).

The perpetual cycle of violence that the policies of the drug enforcement regime facilitate in Latin America (Bartilow and Eom 2009a; Bartilow 2007) has also enabled the growth of presidential power. In fact, by virtue of being on a constant "war footing" against narcoterrorist groups, the executive branch has sought to control the judiciary in a fashion that is consistent with delegative democracy. While O'Donnell (1994) may be correct in his observation that delegative democracies emerge in the context of Latin America's economic crisis, their emergence can also be understood as the drug-war national security state's response to the existential threat of a perennial drug war. It was, for example, in the context of the drug war that the Panamanian president reduced the independence of the judiciary by creating a new Supreme Court Chamber with justices of his own choosing (Popkin 2001).

This pattern of an expansion of executive power justified by a perceived threat of drug war has played out in several Latin American countries. In response to a series of murders by Pablo Escobar's Medellín cartel in 1989, Virgilio Barco Vargas, then president of Colombia, issued several decrees that expanded the powers of the executive. Decree 1860 established an abbreviated administrative procedure for processing extradition requests from foreign governments, which bypassed the constitutional requirement for Supreme Court deliberation on cases that involved the extradition of Colombian citizens. The decree also blocked judicial review of the president's extradition orders. Decree 1859 authorized military and other security personnel engaged in counternarcotic operations to place persons in detention with no outside contact for several days. Decree 1863 authorized military judges to order searches on mere suspicion, disregarding the principle of probable cause. Decree 2013 authorized the government, for reasons of national security, to suspend the popular election of mayors and replace them with military officers. Finally, Decree 182 placed severe limits on the availability of habeas corpus (American Watch Report 1990, 32–37). The prosecution of the Mérida Initiative provided Mexican president Felipe Calderón the justification to rule by decree. With the enactment of *estados de excepción* (states of exception), without legislative approval the president was able to suspend civil liberties and habeas corpus while allowing the military to operate freely outside the limits of the constitution in the prosecution of the drug war (Tielemans 2014).

American policy makers' demands for the militarization of drug enforcement and the perception of perpetual threat from narcotraffickers provided the policy rationale for concentrating more power in the military and security forces, the intelligence bureaucracy, and the presidency, creating in the process a drug-war national security state. As their regimes strengthened executive power unconstrained by the legislature or the judiciary, recipient governments of American counternarcotic aid were more likely to become illiberal democracies under which the agents of the state increasingly violated citizens' human rights and civil liberties with impunity in the process of fighting the drug war. The above discussion leads to the following hypothesis:

> Hypothesis 1: U.S. counternarcotic aid to countries in Latin America increases the probability that recipient countries will be illiberal democracies.

Modeling the Determinants of Illiberal Democracy

THE DEPENDENT VARIABLE: The main outcome variable of interest was illiberal democracy, adapted from Smith and Ziegler (2008, 51–52).[4]

THE MAIN EXPLANATORY VARIABLE: U.S. counternarcotic aid is the main explanatory variable because it proxies the financial and diplomatic mechanisms through which essential features of the U.S. national security state are transnationalized and replicated in the form of the drug-war national security state in Latin America.

CONTEXTUAL VARIABLES: Since all regimes benefit from presiding over stable and growing economies, economic factors may determine the emergence of illiberal democracies: the level of economic growth (Huntington 1968), economic development (Przeworski 2000), inflation (Gasiorowski 1995; Kaufman 1979; Epstein 1984), and debt crisis (Remmer 1990). The debt crisis variable is proxied by whether countries are under an IMF structural adjustment program.

The extant literature on democratization has also identified political variables that may determine illiberal democracy. These variables include the duration of military rule, presidential electoral cycles, and post–Cold War changes in U.S. geopolitical and economic interests. Scholars argue that a longer duration of military rule increases the probability that the regime will be illiberal, as the military is likely to maintain control over the intelligence and surveillance apparatus of the state and establish a legal basis for immunity for its own past and present acts of repression (Kruit 2001, 49; Cruz and Diamint 1998, 17). By contrast, regular presidential electoral cycles create the conditions that expand the rights of citizens (Smith and Ziegler 2008, 41). In particular, presidential candidates who cast themselves as political outsiders above politics (O'Donnell 1994) are likely to attract new voters and increase citizen participation. Looking to external factors, scholars such as Gills and Rocamora (1992, 504–5) attribute the illiberal nature of democracy to post–Cold War changes in U.S. geopolitical and economic interests in the region. They argue that, by promoting illiberal democracies in the aftermath of the Cold War, American policy makers guided the process of democratization in order to preempt radical and revolutionary changes that would threaten U.S. interests in the region. In effect, illiberal democracy is a type of U.S. intervention to prevent progressive or revolutionary changes in America's so-called backyard. Finally, countries' prior experiences with illiberal regimes are likely to determine current experience with illiberal democracy.[5]

U.S. Drug Enforcement Aid and Regime Transitions

The growth of electoral democracies has been a central characteristic of the spread of democratization throughout much of the developing world (Huntington 1991b, 1997). In Latin America by 2004, according to Smith and Ziegler (2008, 36), seventeen of the nineteen countries in the region (all except Haiti and Venezuela) administered free and fair elections, and autocracies and semidemocracies had virtually disappeared. However, graph 7.5 shows a dramatic rise in the number of illiberal democracies in the region during the period of democratization. Moreover, their data show that "no matter what criterion—number of countries, millions of people, or accumulated country years—illiberal democracy emerged as the dominant type of political regime throughout the region" (36–37).

Why were regime transitions from liberal to illiberal democracy more prevalent than regime transitions to autocracies, which were virtually nonexistent? The answer lies in the fact that U.S. counternarcotic aid to liberal democracies, as discussed in the previous section, shifted power toward the military and the executive and away from the legislature and the judiciary—institutions that were constitutionally designed to restrain the national security bureaucracy. The outcome of this reconfiguration of power is the emergence of an ominous drug-war national security state whose autocratic practices for fighting the drug war are antithetical to liberal democratic governance. Given these conditions, U.S. counternarcotic aid is not expected to promote transitions toward

Graph 7.5. Liberal and illiberal democracies in Latin America, 1978–2004. *Source*: Author-generated time-series graph of data adapted from Smith and Ziegler (2008, 51–52).

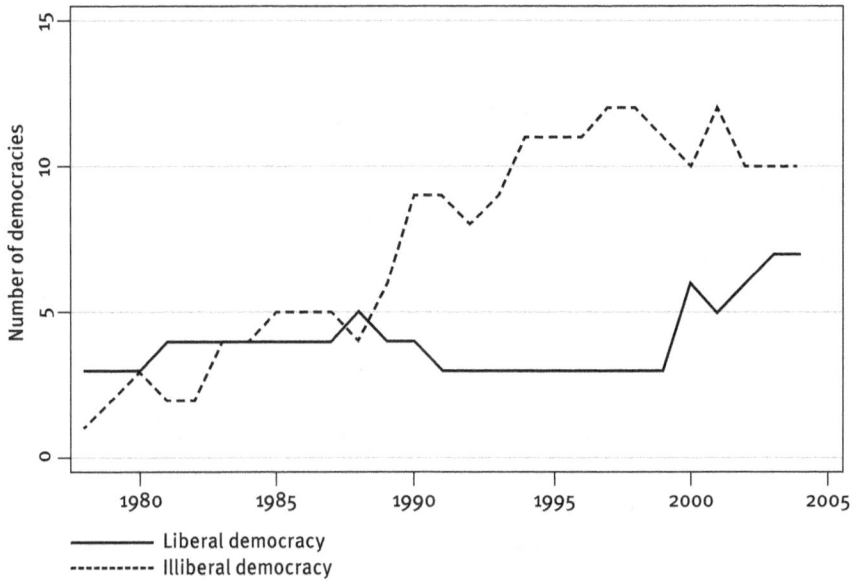

greater democratization, nor will it facilitate transitions from illiberal to liberal democracy; it will instead drive the political dynamics within recipient countries to facilitate transitions from liberal to illiberal democracy. The hypotheses that emerge from this discussion are as follows:

> Hypothesis 2: Increasing levels of U.S. counternarcotic aid flows will have no effect on regime transitions toward greater democratization.
> Hypothesis 3: Increasing levels of U.S. counternarcotic aid flows will have no effect on regime transitions from illiberal to liberal democracy.
> Hypothesis 4: Increasing levels of U.S. counternarcotic aid flows will increase the probability of regime transitions from liberal to illiberal democracy.

However, these considerations raise an important question: Wouldn't the autocratic practices of the drug-war national security state be more effective without the pretense of democracy? If so, how do we account for the fact that transitions from liberal to autocratic rule were nonexistent during the period of Latin America's democratization?

What may appear to be an anomaly is in fact consistent with an essential characteristic of the national security state, which is the centralization of power within the military and surveillance bureaucracy under the pretext of democracy. While the practices of the drug-war national security state are antithetical to the norms and practices of liberal democracy, like its American prototype it needs the facade of democracy, or what Glennon (2014b) calls "double government." This facade enables the drug-war national security state to legitimize the unconstitutional expansion of its power and make the public more accepting, more compliant, and more trusting of its operations even when it tramples on citizens' human rights and civil liberties. Double government, according to Glennon (2014a, 11), "promotes continued public deference to the efficient institutions' [the national security state] decisions and the continued belief that the dignified institutions [the judiciary and legislature] retain real power. These dual institutions, one for show and the other for real, afford . . . expertise and experience in the actual art of governing [or in this case drug enforcement] while at the same time providing a façade that generates public acceptance of the [national security state's] decisions." It is therefore expected that American counternarcotic aid will not promote transitions toward nondemocracies because such regimes do not provide the drug-war national security state with the legitimacy that it needs to prosecute the drug war. The hypothesis that emerges from this discussion is as follows:

> Hypothesis 5: Increasing levels of U.S. counternarcotic aid flows will have no effect on regime transitions from liberal democracies to nondemocracies.

Modeling Regime Transitions

DEPENDENT VARIABLES: The outcome variables that measure regime transitions were adapted from Smith and Ziegler (2008).

CONTEXTUAL VARIABLES: The regime transition models feature the subset of economic variables discussed in the previous section. Following Smith and Ziegler (2008, 40–41), the models utilize the variables of presidential election, duration of democracy, and social upheaval as predictors of regime transitions.[6] The duration of democracy variable tests whether democracies are more or less likely to undergo transitions the longer they remain in political power. Social upheavals are also said to affect regime transitions. Such developments could intensify popular demands for free elections and lead to greater democratization, or they could threaten the ruling elite and encourage greater state repression.

Empirical Findings

Table 7.1 presents time-series probit estimates of the determinants of illiberal democracy in Latin America. In model 3 these estimates are accompanied by predicted probabilities for the variables that are statistically significant and theoretically meaningful. Hypothesis 1 is supported by the data: model 3 shows that increasing levels of U.S. counternarcotic aid increase the likelihood of illiberal democracy. Graph 7.6 shows how changes in the predicted probabilities of illiberal democracy are determined by increases in U.S. counternarcotic aid flows. While holding all other variables constant at their mean value, when U.S. counternarcotic aid is at 0—meaning governments who are not recipients of counternarcotic aid—there is a 36 percent probability that these governments will be illiberal democracies. This indicates that a significant proportion of illiberal democracy is produced by domestic political and economic factors, such as the agency of political elites and structural economic conditions, that are endogenous to Latin American countries. However, when counternarcotic aid is at approximately US$260 million, the probability that a recipient government is an illiberal democracy increases to 56 percent. This finding clearly suggests that U.S. counternarcotic aid does not cause but, rather, accelerates illiberal democratic development among aid recipient countries in Latin America.

In model 2, the data also support claims that post–Cold War changes in U.S. geopolitical and economic interests in Latin America increase the likelihood of illiberal democracy in the region. However, in model 3, the variable fails to achieve statistical significance. In models 2 and 3, increases in countries' economic development (GDP per capita) reduce the likelihood of illiberal democracy. Holding all other variables constant at their mean value, when economic development is at its highest level it decreases the probability that a government will be an illiberal democracy by 29 percent.

In all models, increases in countries' economic growth increase the likelihood of illiberal democracy. Holding all other variables constant at their mean value, when economic growth is at its highest level it increases the probability of illiberal democracy by 71 percent. Likewise, in all models, increasing levels of inflation increase the likelihood of illiberal democracy. Holding all other variables constant at their mean value, when inflation is at its highest level it increases the probability of illiberal democracy by 87 percent. In models 2 and 3, military duration is negatively associated with illiberal democracy. Holding all other variables constant at their mean value, when military duration is at its highest level it decreases illiberal democracy by 10 percent. While IMF's structural adjustment programs increase the likelihood of illiberal democracy in models 1 and 2, the variable fails to achieve statistical significance in model 3

Table 7.1. U.S. counternarcotic aid and the determinants of illiberal democracy in Latin America

Explanatory variables	Model 1	Model 2	Model 3	Changes in predicted probabilities
Illiberal democracy (lagged)	2.614*** (0.151)	2.531*** (0.123)	2.512*** (0.121)	0.7110004 (0.1385477)
GDP growth	0.0179** (0.00568)	0.0154* (0.00637)	0.0143* (0.00614)	−0.2896677 (0.0664995)
GDP per capita	−0.0000180 (0.0000277)	−0.0000783* (0.0000364)	−0.0000793* (0.0000400)	0.8695717 (0.1463099)
Inflation	0.000153** (0.0000519)	0.000159* (0.0000702)	0.000181* (0.000739)	
IMF structural adjustment program	0.432*** (0.120)	0.259* (0.127)	0.212 (0.132)	
Military duration		−0.0554* (0.0231)	−0.0500* (0.0224)	−0.0660458 (0.1012282)
Presidential election vote (percentage of population that voted)		−0.000146 (0.00463)	−0.00238 (0.00487)	
Post–Cold War international system		0.418* (0.210)	0.411 (0.231)	
U.S. counternarcotic aid			0.100* (0.0405)	0.5605257 (0.0685228)
Constant	−1.636*** (0.147)	−1.488*** (0.233)	−1.427*** (0.244)	
Number of observations	645	645	642	

Time-series probit with population-averaged estimator. Robust standard errors are in parentheses.
Changes in predicted possibilities were calculated using the Margins command in STATA 14.

Levels of statistical significance: $^+p < 0.10$, $^*p < 0.05$, $^{**}p < 0.01$, $^{***}p < 0.001$.

Graph 7.6. U.S. counternarcotic aid and illiberal democracy in Latin America, 1978–2011: Predictive margins with 95 percent confidence intervals

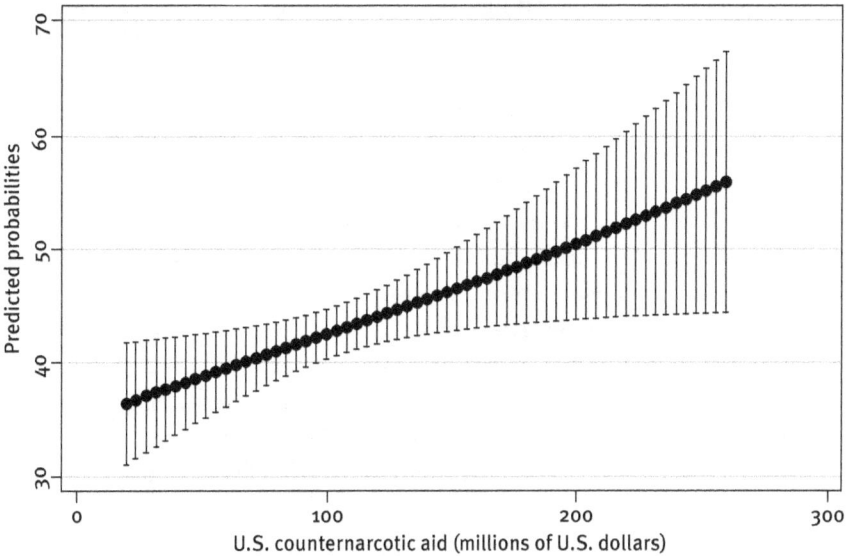

when U.S. counternarcotic aid is included in the model. This finding suggests that in the age of democratization the policy decisions of the drug enforcement regime trump economic structural adjustment intervention as a determinant of illiberal democracy in Latin America. In all models, countries' prior experience with illiberal governance increases the likelihood that their governments will be illiberal democracies. And finally, voter turnout for presidential elections fails to achieve statistical significance in all models.

Table 7.2 presents rare event logit estimates of regime transitions in Latin America,[7] and in model 4 these results are accompanied by relative risk estimates for the variables that are statistically significant and theoretically meaningful. The data support hypotheses 2, 3, and 4. As predicted, model 1 shows that U.S. counternarcotic aid has no effect on regime transitions toward greater liberal democracy. Similarly, model 2 shows that U.S. counternarcotic aid has no effect on regime transitions toward greater authoritarianism, nor does it affect transitions from illiberal to liberal democracy, as shown in model 3. However, as the financial and diplomatic mechanism through which the U.S. national security state is both transnationalized and replicated in the form of the drug-war national security state, U.S. counternarcotic aid is the principal driver of regime transitions from liberal to illiberal democracy. For liberal democracies that are recipients of U.S. counternarcotic aid, the relative risk of becoming an illiberal democracy increases by 44 percent. Graph 7.7 shows how the changes in the predicted probabilities of regime transitions from liberal to illiberal democracy are determined by increases in U.S. counternarcotic aid.

Moving to a consideration of the contextual variables, GDP growth is negatively associated with transitions to nondemocracy but fails to achieve statistical significance in models 1, 3, and 4. High levels of economic development (GDP per capita) have no effect on regime transitions in models 1, 2, and 3. In model 4 the variable predicts transitions from liberal to illiberal democracy. Increasing levels of economic development in liberal democracies increase their relative risk of becoming illiberal democracies by 15 percent. This finding appears to corroborate the central proposition of Samuel P. Huntington in *Political Order in Changing Societies* (1968, 41), where he argued that political stability and regression from democracy to authoritarianism could be explained by the ways in which the development of political institutions lagged behind modernization and the rate of economic development: "If poor countries appear to be unstable it is not because they are poor, but because they are trying to become rich."

Inflation has no statistical significance in explaining regime transitions toward nondemocracy, as shown in model 2, but in models 1 and 3, respectively, it predicts transitions toward greater liberal democracy and transitions from illiberal to liberal democracy, findings that are consistent with those reported by Smith and Ziegler (2008, 42). In model 4, inflation also predicts regressive transitions from liberal to illiberal democracy. Inflationary pressures in liberal democracies increase their relative risk of becoming illiberal democracies by 39 percent. Because inflation increases income inequality, reduces investment, and encourages capital flight, it increases the likelihood that the working and middle classes will seek to replace an incumbent regime by supporting opposition parties. Whenever domestic support for governments is based on their ability to provide economic stability, the destabilizing force of inflationary pressures on the economy will drive changes in the governing regime.

In model 1, regime transitions toward liberal democracy are more likely in countries that undergo IMF structural adjustment economic reforms. In all other models the variable fails to achieve statistical significance. In model 1, the longer the duration of democracy reduces the likelihood of regime transitions toward liberal democracy, which is another way of saying that countries with longer histories of being democracies are less likely to become more democratic. In all other models the variable fails to achieve statistical significance. In all the models voter turnout for presidential elections, organized nonviolent protest and organized violent opposition against governments fail to achieve statistical significance.

Table 7.2. U.S. counternarcotic aid and regime transitions

Explanatory variables	Model 1 Transitions toward liberal democracy	Model 2 Transitions toward nondemocracy	Model 3 Transitions from liberal to illiberal democracy	Model 4 Transitions from liberal relative to illiberal democracy	Risk estimate
U.S. counternarcotic aid	-0.0129 (0.0117)	0.0157 (0.0205)	0.0129 (0.00778)	0.0300** (0.00951)	43.6
GDP growth	0.00604 (0.0170)	-0.134* (0.0532)	-0.0212 (0.0328)	0.0329 (0.0185)	
GDP per capita	-0.00000983 (0.0000722)	0.000173 (0.000116)	0.000143 (0.000111)	0.000267* (0.000128)	14.5
Inflation	0.000184* (0.0000924)	0.00110 (0.000597)	0.00202*** (0.000409)	0.000507** (0.000169)	39.4
IMF structural adjustment program	0.820* (0.338)	-0.120 (0.784)	0.743 (0.696)	-0.0271 (0.637)	
Democratic duration	-0.0904** (0.0301)	-0.0822 (0.0784)	-0.0354 (0.0273)	0.00419 (0.0202)	
Presidential election vote (percentage of population that voted)	-0.00381 (0.00617)	0.0120 (0.0107)	0.0106 (0.0137)	0.0205 (0.0257)	
Organized nonviolent government protest	0.273 (0.321)	-0.294 (0.592)	-0.158 (0.899)	1.612 (1.076)	
Organized violent government opposition	0.168 (0.310)	0.337 (0.673)	-0.313 (0.820)	0.0970 (0.823)	
Constant	-1.999*** (0.432)	-3.695*** (0.825)	-4.603*** (0.925)	-7.257*** (2.110)	
Number of observations	646	646	646	646	646

Rare event logit estimates. Robust standard errors are in parentheses.

Levels of statistical significance: $^+ p < 0.10$, $^* p < 0.05$, $^{**} p < 0.01$, $^{***} p < 0.001$.

Graph 7.7. U.S. counternarcotic aid and the predicted probability of transitions from liberal to illiberal democracy in Latin America, 1978–2011

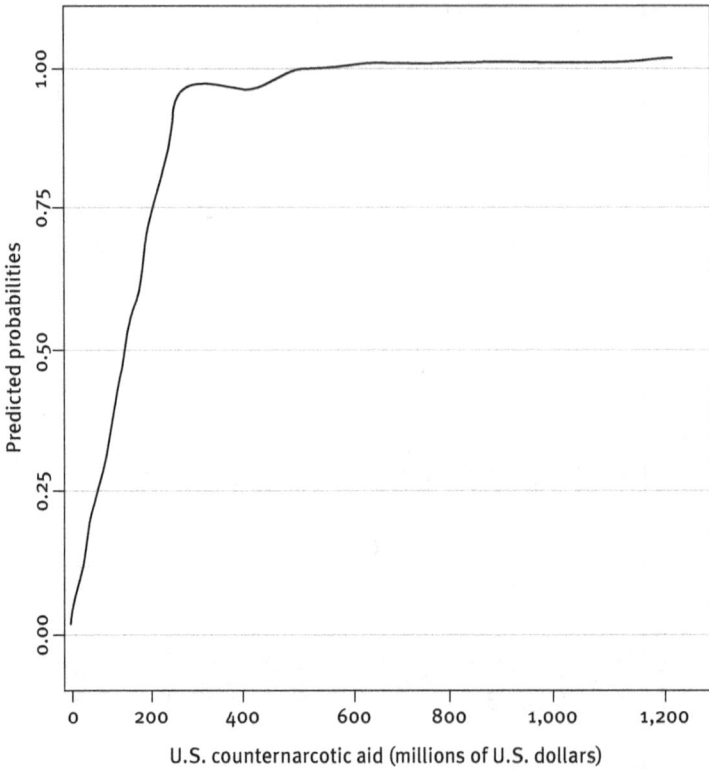

X-axis: U.S. counternarcotic aid (millions of U.S. dollars)

Y-axis: Predicted probabilities

Conclusion

This chapter has demonstrated that the paradox of Latin America's democratization is attributed to the ways in which U.S. counternarcotic aid has not only accelerated the development of illiberal democracies but also serves as the principal driving force behind regime transitions from liberal to illiberal democracy—increasing such transitions by 44 percent. However, when counternarcotic aid to recipient Latin American countries is at 0, there is a 36 percent probability that a government will be an illiberal democracy. In other words, the findings show that a significant part of illiberal democratic development in Latin America is driven purely by the agency of Latin American governments and structural economic factors, such as inflation and economic growth. For example, Venezuela, which is not a recipient of U.S. counternarcotic aid, has descended into illiberal governance that borders on outright authoritarianism. In recent years, falling oil prices have led to hyperinflation, which has decimated wages, produced widespread food shortages, and forced significant cuts in popular social programs. President Nicolás Maduro's reelection in 2018 was marred by low voter turnout and opposition abstention. In the year prior to his reelection he used the security forces to repress popular protest, imprisoned some of his political opponents, and convened a rubber stamp constituent assembly.

The evidence in this chapter also shows the importance of the diplomatic and economic power of the United States in facilitating foreign country cooperation in constructing the drug enforcement regime. In consequence, the U.S.-induced drug-war national security state is not compatible with the norms of liberal democratic governance, and given its need for public legitimacy, it is also incompatible with outright autocracy. This explains why U.S. counternarcotic aid has no statistically significant effect on regime transitions toward either liberal democracy or nondemocracy, only toward illiberal democracy. While these results do not prove that regime transitions to illiberal democracy reflect the intentional policy preference of American policy makers, the policy outcome nonetheless supports the interest of the drug enforcement regime because it produces a form of "double government" where free and fair elections create public deference to the autocratic operations of the drug-war national security state. This is why democracies in the region, as I have argued elsewhere, are more repressive than their military predecessors (Bartilow 2014).

This double government, one for show and the other for real, is the unintentional outcome of the policy conditions that are attached to U.S. counternarcotic aid, which has undermined Latin America's democratization and reduced the likelihood that progressive governments would threaten the interest of the drug enforcement regime by developing alternate approaches to drug policy. For example, in 2008, the Morales government in Bolivia ejected the DEA (Kraul 2009), and subsequently, according the UNODC, Bolivia reduced coca production by 34 percent between 2010 and 2014 (UNODC 2015) by deemphasizing the militarization of drug enforcement. The stark possibility of a domino effect whereby other countries in the region could follow Bolivia's example and develop alternate drug policies undermines the drug enforcement regime's ability to promote international consensus and cooperation in the prosecution of the drug war in Latin America.

In short, the paradox of Latin America's democratization reflects an unintended political pathology of the corporatist drug enforcement regime, which has transnationalized and replicated important features of the U.S. national security state in the region and, in the process, has accelerated the development of illiberal governments. These "democracies for show," without rights guarantees, suit the autocratic tendencies of the drug-war national security state. In the next chapter, I examine the pathological class contradictions of the corporatist drug enforcement regime and its impact on income inequality in Latin America and the United States.

CHAPTER 8

Drug War Capitalism and Class Conflict in the Americas

The history of all hitherto existing societies is the history of class struggles . . . contests between exploiting and exploited, ruling and oppressed classes.—**Karl Marx and Friedrich Engels,** *The Communist Manifesto* (1848)

Actually, there's been class warfare going on for the last 20 years, and my class has won. We're the ones that have gotten our taxes reduced dramatically . . . down from 29 percent of income. So, there's class warfare, all right, but it's my class, the rich class, that's making war, and we're winning.—**Warren E. Buffett,** 2011

When one thinks about contemporary philosophical equivalents to Marx and Engels, corporate billionaire Warren Buffett does not usually come to mind. However, like Marx and Engels, Buffett recognizes that class conflict between the owners of capital and labor not only emerges from their different social relations to the means of production but also underscores the dialectical nature of capitalism. In this chapter, I consider the drug war as a manifestation of class conflict in the Americas and provide an analysis of the ways in which the embedded corporatist drug enforcement regime has produced and reproduced patterns of class conflict in Latin America and the United States. The chapter is therefore motivated by the following questions: Under what conditions is the drug war used to repress labor unions and, in the process, increase income inequality in Latin America? What political mechanisms in the United States create linkages among drug enforcement, income inequality, poverty, mass incarceration, and corporate capital accumulation? In other words, does the embedded corporatist drug war in Latin America and the United States provide evidence of class conflict that is consistent with the proclamations of Marx, Engels, and Buffett?

To answer these questions, the next section discusses the relationships among U.S. counternarcotic aid, the repression of workers' rights, and income inequality in Latin America. The following section examines the relationship between drug enforcement and income inequality in the United States. This is followed by an analysis of the drug war's effect on poverty and mass incarceration in the United States and the ways in which the exploitation of prison labor increases corporate revenues. These analyses are followed by a brief discussion of the theoretical determinants of income inequality to identify control variables to be used in the empirical models. The hypotheses that emerge from these discussions are tested via a time-series cross section (TSCS) statistical analysis of twenty-one countries from Latin America, which covers 2003–12, and TSCS statistical analysis as well as a structural equation model (SEM) of data collected from the United States for 2000 to 2012. The chapter concludes with a discussion of the empirical results and a consideration of their policy implications.

U.S. Drug Enforcement, Labor Rights, and Income Inequality in Latin America

As chapter 7 has demonstrated, U.S. drug enforcement aid to governments in Latin America is partially responsible for increasing the coercive capabilities of the drug-war national security state (Bartilow 2014). This makes it possible for the state to repress labor unions when collective bargaining, strikes, and other industrial action activate the progressive political sector, threaten the political interests of the ruling elite, and impede the ability of domestic and transnational corporations to accumulate capital. Graph 8.1 shows that the number of strikes in Latin America has increased from 1990 to 2008. Between 1990 and 1994, the years that coincide with the introduction of neoliberal reforms, there was very little strike activity. The number of strikes rose sharply from 1995 to 1997 and then declined from their 1997 level and remained constant between 1998 and 2005, but since then they have shown a dramatic increase.

The pattern in the number of strikes suggests that, in addition to the increasing flexibility of domestic and transnational capital, which introduced temporary contracts, reduced workdays, and increased subcontracting (Patroni and Poitras 2002, 212), all of which weaken union membership, union industrial actions were also affected by state repression (O'Donnell 1973). It should come as no surprise that Colombia, which was the world's largest recipient of U.S. counternarcotic aid, was also ranked as one of the worst countries in the world for trade unionists in the Global Rights Index of the International Trade Union

Graph 8.1. Strikes in Latin America and the Caribbean Basin, 1990–2008.
Source: ILOSTAT n.d.

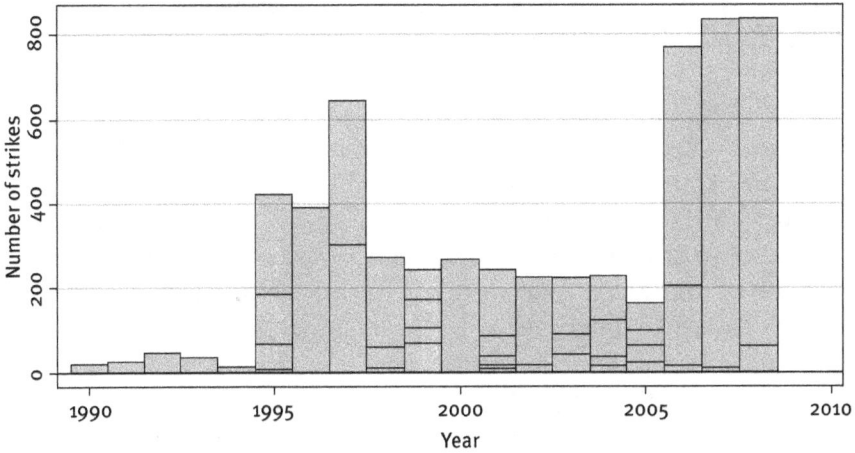

Confederation. Although the country's national legislation formally acknowledges specific labor rights, Colombia's workers are de facto denied access to these rights and are routinely exposed to assassinations, threats, and unfair labor practices (International Trade Union Confederation 2016).

Justice for Colombia, the British-based nongovernmental human rights organization, report that since 1977, there have been 3,062 assassinations, 233 kidnappings, 342 attacks, 6,572 threats, 1,890 forced displacements, and 725 arbitrary detentions of trade unionists (Justice for Colombia 2016). Of the 527 worldwide murders of trade unionists from 2005 to 2009, Colombia accounted for 54 percent. Since 1985, 2,700 unionists have been murdered in Colombia, and the immunity rate for murderers of trade unionists remained at 965 as new murders outpaced convictions for old murders (Escuela National Sindical 2010).

The Colombian government has often participated in the repression of trade unionists. It was revealed that in 2006 the now defunct Administrative Department of Security, Colombia's version of the FBI, provided paramilitaries with a hit list of twenty-three trade unionists and leftist political leaders who were subsequently killed or displaced (Colectivo de Abogados José Alvear Restrepo 2007). Under the government's Justice and Peace process, the testimonies of demobilized AUC members provided additional evidence of the Colombian government's collusion with paramilitaries in the murder of unionists, confirming the paramilitary's connections to Congress members as well as military and police officers (Alsema 2015). In 2007, Salvatore Mancuso, the former commander of the AUC, testified that the Colombian government had supported paramilitaries since their creation in the 1980s and that high-ranking military officers and government officials such as General Rito Alejo del Río, General Martín Carreño Sandoval, General Harold Bedoya Pizarro, General Fernando Landazabal, Colonel Alfonso Manosalva Flores, and Minister of Defense Juan Manuel Santos provided training and logistics to the paramilitary organization (School of the Americas Watch 2007).

Central American recipients of the Mérida Initiative have also seen, in recent years, an increase in violence targeting unionists. Between 2009 and 2012, fifty-seven rural workers were murdered in Honduras because they opposed forced evictions by large landowners who wanted to increase the cultivation of African palm trees (International Trade Union Confederation 2013, 49). Similarly, in Guatemala, fifty-three trade unionists were murdered between 2007 and 2013 (International Trade Union Confederation 2013, 7).

In Mexico, employers and the government systematically violate trade union rights. The Mexican labor union SME struggled against the government's attempt to privatize the state-run electric company, Luz y Fuerza del Centro (Central Light and Power), which employed some 44,000 workers, most of whom belonged to the SME. In 1999, the SME staged a successful grassroots campaign that blocked President Ernesto Zedillo's attempt to reform the Mexican constitution to privatize Luz y Fuerza del Centro. By emphasizing how prior attempts to privatize the banking sector, toll roads, and airlines had been ineffective in terms of improving efficiency and reducing costs, the SME collected 2.4 million signatures against privatization (Friedland 1999). The Mexican government continued its attempt to privatize Luz y Fuerza del Centro when pro-business President Felipe Calderón, backed by drug war funding from the Mérida Initiative, ordered the military takeover of Luz y Fuerza del Centro in 2009 and decreed the liquidation of the company, which effectively resulted in the mass firing of 44,000 workers and reduced SME membership by two-thirds (Miller 2009). On December 16, 2013, the Mexican Congress approved an energy bill that modified Articles 25, 27, and 28 of the Mexican Constitution to allow the participation of private capital in the generation and commercialization of electric power in Mexico (Parra 2013).

Independent trade unions throughout Mexico have also been the targets of violent attacks, intimidation, and repression. These unions include Sindicato Nacional de Trabajadores Mineros, Metalúrgicos y Similares de la República Méxicana, SME, the Pemex workers union (representing professional and technical workers at the state oil company), Unión Nacional de Técnicos y Profesionistas Petroleros, Sindicato Nacional de Trabajadores de General Tire de México, Sindicato Único de Trabajadores de la Universidad Autónoma de la Ciudad de México (the union that represents the staff at the Universidad Autónoma de la Ciudad de México), Sindicato de Telefonistas de la República Mexicana (telephone workers' union), Frente Auténtico del Trabajo (Authentic Labor Front), and other organizations that are affiliates of the umbrella Unión Nacional de Trabajadores (National Union of Workers). With the support of the Mexican government, private employers have increased the level of anti-union repression and threats by hiring criminal thugs to prevent workers from organizing (International Trade Union Confederation 2016).

This drug-war-induced repression of workers' rights is primarily intended to erode union membership. In Mexico, Guatemala, and Colombia—Mérida Initiative and Plan Colombia recipient countries—union members represent respectively 17 percent, 1.6 percent, and 4 percent of the labor force, respectively (Otis 2012; Bevan 2013). In a recent study of labor markets and inequality in advanced economies during 1980–2010, Jaumotte and Buitron (2015a), economists from the orthodox neoliberal IMF, found that the decline in unionization is correlated with the rise in income of the corporate rich and a significant decline in income redistribution. They also found that the erosion of minimum wages, against which the labor movement has traditionally organized, is also correlated with significant increases in overall inequality. Financial deregulation and lower tax rates for the top income earners—the mantras of neoliberal capitalism—are also correlated with higher levels of inequality. Based on these findings, Jaumotte and Buitron argue that policies that reduce the collective bargaining power of unions increase the income of corporate CEOs and shareholders and that a weakened labor movement reduces the bargaining power of the working class relative to the owners of capital, which ultimately increases the share of corporate income. Lower levels of unionization, moreover, will reduce workers' influence over corporate decisions such as the size and structure of CEO compensation, which again benefits the corporate rich (Jaumotte and Buitron 2015b, 30–31).

If the repression of unionists in Latin America reduces union membership, then the union movement's ability to effectively engage in collective bargaining with private corporations and influence corporate decision making is significantly diminished. Under these conditions, Jaumotte and Buitron's (2015a) research suggests that the share of corporate income in Latin America will increase in proportion to the income of the working class. Therefore, by facilitating the repression of trade unions, the drug war indirectly increases income inequality and, in the process, exacerbates class contradictions in Latin America. This discussion leads to the following conditional hypothesis:

Hypothesis 1: Increasing levels of U.S. counternarcotic aid to recipient governments in Latin America will increase income inequality under conditions of increased repression of workers' rights.

Drug Enforcement and Income Inequality in the United States

Overall income inequality in the United States has increased in recent years. Income inequality was 7 percentage points higher in 2015 than in 1980, and the top decile of earnings had risen from 150 percent of the median in 1950 to 244 percent in 2012 (Atkinson and Morelli 2014, 63). From 1999 to 2012, the income of middle-class Americans declined by more than 9 percent, while the average income of the top 5 percent grew by 52 percent (Madland and Miller 2013). The academic and policy debates regarding the factors that explain income inequality in the United States have largely focused on the ways in which the process of international integration through bilateral free trade agreements such as NAFTA (Caulfield 2010; Burfisher et al. 2001) has led to the deindustrialization of the U.S. economy (Stone and Harrison 1982). However, this debate lacks any consideration of the drug war's impact on income inequality in the United States.

While the previous section argued that the repression of the working class in Latin America is an important causal mechanism through which the drug war increases income inequality throughout the region, in the United States the perennial increases in drug enforcement expenditures, which reflects the policy preferences of corporate lobbies, corporate elite networks, and their congressional allies, exacerbate income inequality through budgetary priorities that privilege the drug war over the various social programs that were once ladders of upward mobility for the working class and the poor. Graph 8.2 shows that the federal government's budgetary priority for drug enforcement is significantly larger than domestic expenditures for job training programs, social services, public housing and rent assistance programs, low-income energy assistance, and various public health care services. Since expenditures on social programs are central to the ability of the working class to improve their level of income (Madland 2015), federal budgetary outlays that privilege the drug war over existing social programs have the effect of removing the social foundations of upward mobility, in the process creating increasing levels of income inequality and a permanent underclass in the United States. This discussion suggests the following hypothesis:

Hypothesis 2: Increases in the federal government's drug enforcement (narcotic supply reduction) expenditures will increase income inequality in the United States.

Graph 8.2. U.S. government domestic expenditures, 2003–2012.
Source: Drug War Facts n.d.; House Committee on the Budget 2003–2012.

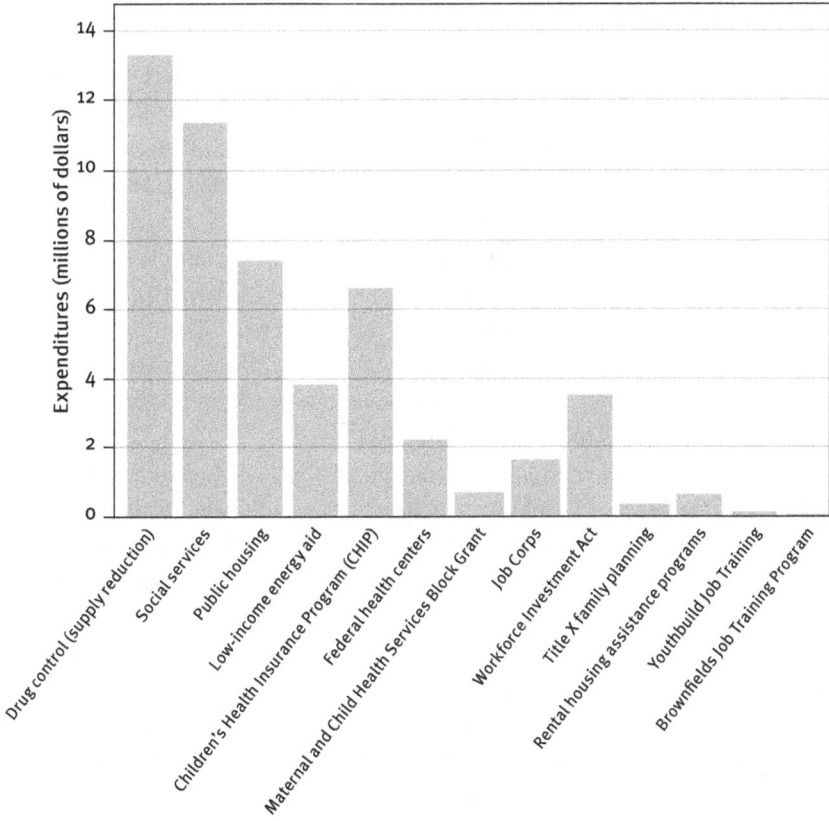

Drug Enforcement, Mass Incarceration, Poverty, and Corporate Profits in the United States

While the consequences of the policy decisions of the corporatist drug enforcement regime have produced various political pathologies in Latin America, it has also produced increased rates of incarceration in the United States. High levels of incarceration have become the primary mechanism for generating prison labor, which reduces production costs and the need for unions and maximizes corporate revenues. Corporate revenues generated with the use of prison labor are used to increase corporate lobbying expenditures. This allows corporate lobbies to buy greater access to congressional lawmakers and influence their decision to continue increasing federal drug enforcement expenditures, and hence reproduces the cyclical process of corporate-convict capital

Drug War Capitalism and Class Conflict | 191

accumulation. In the following sections, I discuss the sequential and relational ordering of the various components of this argument.

Drug Enforcement and Mass Incarceration

First, this argument depends on the recognition that the growth of the prison population is partly the consequence of the prosecution of the forty-eight-year drug war in the United States (Mauer and King 2007; Fellner 2009). Although the prison population has decreased by 3 percent between 2010 and 2014 (Carson and Sabol 2012; Guerino et al. 2011; Carson 2014, 2015), 2.2 million people are still incarcerated in the United States, making the country the world's leader in the number of people who are imprisoned (Sentencing Project 2013, 1–2; Walmsley 2013, 1). Drug offenders comprise 50 percent of the population of federal prisons and 60 percent of the population of state prisons. The vast majority of drug felons have no history of violent behavior, nor are they high-profile drug kingpins (Mauer and King 2007, 2).

Since federal welfare legislation enacted in 1996 prohibits convicted drug offenders from receiving welfare benefits, drug-war-induced incarceration impoverishes the poor and deepens income inequality by creating an underclass of millions of Americans who are barred from voting, obtaining licenses, and accessing public assistance, as well as myriad other social services. These prohibitions contribute to why people who have served time in prison have lower lifetime earnings and are far less likely to move out of poverty than their peers who were never incarcerated (Western and Pettit 2010). Further, given the racial disparities of drug enforcement sentencing, these prohibitions are disproportionately borne by people and communities of color (Mauer and King 2007, 14).

The increase of mass incarceration has the effect of pushing states' budgetary priorities away from education and toward building more prisons, a shift that reinforces the drug war's tendency to undermine the social mobility of the working class and further increase income inequality. Since the 1990s, states have spent more on correction than they spend on state colleges and universities (Irwin et al. 1999, 8–9; Ambrosio and Schiraldi 1997). States have imposed deep budgetary cuts on higher education, K-12 and early education, and public health programs (Johnson et al. 2011) while simultaneously expanding expenditures for corrections (Stephan 2004, 1–2). In 2008, taxpayers spent US$68.7 billion to feed, clothe, and provide medical care to prisoners in county jails and state and federal prisons. State and federal expenditures for corrections, not adjusting for inflation, increased by 423 percent between 1982 and 2002. From 1986 to 2001, correction expenditures, as a share of state budgets, grew faster than health care and education (Kirchhoff 2010, 49). In 2010, the average total taxpayer cost per inmate was US$31,286, which ranged from a low of

US$14,603 in Kentucky to a high of US$60,076 in New York (Henrichson and Delaney 2012, 9). The drug war has effectively altered states' spending priorities such that the cost of incarceration is now significantly greater than the average cost of tuition at state colleges and universities (U.S. Department of Education 2015, 626).

The Prison-Industrial Complex and Corporate Profits

The second component of my main argument is that a disproportionate share of public expenditure is used to subsidize the operations of an expanding prison-industrial complex, whose growth is sustained in part by corporate lobbies that support increased drug enforcement expenditures. Corporations increasingly rely on prison labor to generate profit, meaning that, by extension, public expenditures that finance the operations of the prison-industrial complex subsidize corporate profits. To this end, 56 percent of the corporations represented in this study are involved with the operations of the prison-industrial complex and make use of prison labor.

Corporate involvement with the operations of the prison-industrial complex takes three forms. In the first, corporations directly employ inmate labor to manufacture products (Sloan 2015). Sixty percent of the corporations in this study that are members of the military-industrial complex use prison labor for the assembly of components used in various weapons systems. The defense industry's support for increased drug enforcement has created the evolution of what I call the military-prison-industrial complex, characterized by the insourcing of defense contracting jobs to inmates at UNICOR, which until 1977 was known as Federal Prison Industries. UNICOR comprises a network of over 100 factories located at 70 federal penitentiaries throughout the United States and is a self-sustaining, self-funded company owned by the U.S. government. UNICOR was created by congressional legislation in 1934 to operate as a rehabilitative institution that would teach practical work skills to federal inmates.

Approximately 21,836 inmates work in UNICOR's programs. Inmates assemble the electronic components for Lockheed Martin's Patriot Advanced Capability (PAC-3) missile, which costs US$5.9 million. Inmates at UNICOR, however, earn between US$0.23 and US$1.15 an hour for their work on the missile. UNICOR inmates also make the cable assemblies for the McDonnell Douglas/Boeing F-15 fighter jet, as well as the cable assemblies for General Dynamics's F-16 fighter jet. Inmates assemble the parts for Textron's Cobra attack helicopter, and they also assemble the electro-optical equipment for the Bradley Fighting Vehicle's laser rangefinder, which is manufactured by BAE Systems. The majority of UNICOR's products and services come from the contract orders of the Department of Defense, which earned the company US$772 million in 2011. Approximately 53 percent of UNICOR's sales are derived from the Department of Defense (Shachtman 2011; Rohrlich 2011).

By purchasing parts that are assembled by UNICOR's prison labor and then reselling the finished weapons components to the Pentagon and other customers from around the world, defense contractors like Lockheed Martin significantly reduce the production costs of their weapons systems and maximize their profit margins (Flounders 2011). The military-prison-industrial complex conceptualizes the ways in which the defense industry and the federal government exploit prison labor to maximize profit. As approximately 50 percent of the inmates in federal prisons are nonviolent drug offenders, the growth of the prison population is in part a testament to the ways in which corporate lobbies drive drug enforcement policy making, which in the end makes prison labor increasingly available for corporate exploitation.

British Petroleum, Hewlett-Packard, IBM, Motorola, Microsoft, AT&T Wireless, Texas Instruments, Dell, Compaq, Honeywell, Nortel, Lucent Technologies, 3Com, Intel, Northern Telecom, TWA, Nordstrom, Revlon, Macy's, Pierre Cardin, Target Stores, Whole Foods, and many other companies have taken advantage of the Bush administration's Work Opportunity Tax Credit (Scott 2013), which rewards companies with a tax credit of US$2,400 for every work-release inmate that they hire. For example, after the Deepwater Horizon oil spill, British Petroleum employed Louisiana prisoners to clean up the contaminated beaches in the Gulf of Mexico (Young 2010).

Corporate involvement with the prison-industrial complex can also takes the less direct form of contracting with other companies to purchase products and services made by prison labor. The third category of corporate involvement is investment in companies that directly use prison labor or investment in private prison corporations such as the Corrections Corporations of America and the GEO Group. The vast majority of corporations in this study invest in companies that use prison labor or companies in the private prison industry. These corporations include Bank of America, J.P. Morgan, Chevron Corporation, ExxonMobil Corporation, Merck and Company, Pfizer, Caterpillar, Deere and Company, Proctor and Gamble, UPS, Newmont Mining Corporation, and Wal-Mart Stores (Sloan 2015).

Regardless of the nature of their involvement with the prison-industrial complex, corporations use their lobbies to drive increases in drug enforcement expenditures, which consequently increase mass incarceration and, in the process, create a "third world" labor market within the United States. State governments' financing of the operations of the prison-industrial complex, as well as inducements such as the federal government's Work Opportunity Tax

Credit, provide corporations with incentives to exploit cheap prison labor and thereby boost corporate profits. It is estimated that corporate profits from the use of prison labor increased from US$392 million to US$1.31 billion between 1980 and 1994, the only years for which data are available (Pelaez 2014). However, the prison population has grown substantially since then, along with the number of private corporations that directly or indirectly manufacture products made by prison labor, meaning that corporate profits generated by prison labor are likely to far exceed their 1980s and 1990s levels.

Corporate Revenues and Corporate Lobbying

The third component of the argument is that corporate revenues are used not only to pay dividends to their investors but also to finance lobbies that exert political influence in Congress. Students of corporate lobbying have made several attempts to identify the determinants of corporate lobbying. One important predictor is corporate revenues. Brown et al. (2006) have shown that corporations with growing revenues are able to afford larger lobbying expenditures and are more active in lobbying legislators than companies whose revenue streams are much smaller. Therefore, since corporations have a financial incentive to maintain the drug enforcement regime, corporate revenues will be used to increase corporate lobbying expenditures to ensure that policy makers continue to increase drug enforcement expenditures. Considering that corporations seek to influence public policy decision making, it is no accident that the growth in corporate lobbying expenditures, which increased from US$1.45 billion to US$3.30 billion between 1998 and 2012 (see Open Secrets, Lobbying Database), mirrors the growth in corporate profits (Waldron 2013).

The sequential and relational components of the argument in this section highlight the path through which the effects of corporate lobbying on corporate revenues are mediated by drug enforcement expenditures and the rate of mass incarceration in the prison-industrial complex. The argument in this section is formalized by the following hypotheses:

Hypothesis 3: Increasing levels of corporate lobbying expenditures will increase drug enforcement expenditures.
Hypothesis 4: Increasing levels of drug enforcement expenditures will increase the rate of incarceration.
Hypothesis 5: Increasing levels of incarceration will increase corporate revenues.
Hypothesis 6: Increasing levels of corporate revenues will increase the level of corporate lobbying expenditures.

Modeling the Income-Inequality Effects of the Drug War

The Dependent Variable

Income inequality is measured in terms of the Gini index. Data on the distribution of income and consumption come from nationally representative household surveys obtained from government statistical agencies.

The Central Explanatory Variable

To test hypothesis 1, the primary explanatory variable is the interaction (Jaccard and Turrisi 2003) between U.S. counternarcotic aid and the rights of workers in South America, Central America, and the Caribbean Basin. The U.S. federal government's yearly drug enforcement expenditures for reducing the supply of narcotics to the United States is the primary explanatory variable that tests hypothesis 2.

Contextual Variables

Existing research suggests that important contextual factors have an independent effect in determining the level of income inequality across countries. These factors include the annual growth rates of countries' GDP, countries' level of integration into the international capitalist economy, and institutional factors such as the level of democracy, property rights, government spending, the level of corruption, and labor freedoms.[1]

GDP ANNUAL GROWTH: In his seminal article, Kuznets (1955) argued that as countries develop from rural agricultural to urban industrial societies, income inequality will increase in the early stages of economic growth and then decrease once the economy has reached a mature level of development. Kuznets's (1955) hypothesis is that economic growth has a nonlinear or a concave U-shaped relationship with income inequality. Other economists have challenged this hypothesis and have argued that income inequality decreases in the early stages of economic growth and then increases at a later stage of development (Barro 2000). Graph 8A in the data appendix is a nonparametric LOWESS graph showing that neither Kuznets's hypothesis of an inverted U-shaped relationship between income inequality and economic growth nor Barro's hypothesis of a U-shaped relationship is supported by the data. From 2000 to 2012, the level of income inequality remained constant as economic growth increased in Latin America.

INTERNATIONAL ECONOMIC INTEGRATION: The impact of international economic integration on income inequality is one of the most contentious issues facing policy makers in developing and developed countries. There is no consensus among scholars regarding its effect on levels of inequality. Dependency and world-systems theorists argue that growing levels of integration into the international capitalist economy not only increase the distribution of wealth and income between developed and developing countries but also increase income inequality within countries (Wallerstein 1974, 1984; Evans 1979).

Studies of the effects of trade liberalization on income inequality across countries have also been inconclusive. Scholars who are motivated by the "labor pauperization theory" of trade argue that international free trade causes poor wage performance and declining incomes in advanced developed countries because high-wage countries cannot compete with low-wage developing countries (Tulchin and Bland 2005). Others, however, argue that the effect of trade liberalization on income inequality is not uniform across countries because trade is driven not by absolute advantage but by comparative advantage. If trade decreases the comparative advantage in one country, it will increase it in another (Lawrence 1996). The effects of FDI, another measure of international economic integration, on income inequality are also inconclusive. According to Obstfeld (1998) the influx of FDI from developed to developing countries is likely to reduce income inequality by creating jobs. With the transfer of advanced technology, labor productivity should also improve. Other scholars, however, challenge these claims, arguing instead that FDI distorts host countries' production and employment, worsens the trade deficit, and widens the income gap between skilled and unskilled labor, thereby increasing income inequality (Graham and Krugman 1995).

Finally, there is no consensus on how to quantify international economic integration. In an attempt to capture the various components of international economic integration, existing studies have used separate indicators for trade, FDI, and openness to portfolio investment (Li and Reuveny 2003; Lee et al. 2013) and, in doing so, risk complications that arise from multicollinearity among these variables (Voss 2004). Therefore, to avoid issues of multicollinearity, the measure of international economic integration in this analysis is restricted to the KOF Swiss Economic Institute's index of economic globalization (Dreher 2006, 1092–93).

INSTITUTIONAL FACTORS: In addition to these considerations of international economic integration, some scholars emphasize the role that institutions play in shaping income inequality, arguing that the type of government and the legal system, particularly with respect to property rights, government social expenditures, and levels of corruption, explains cross-country patterns of income inequality. Sokoloff and Engerman (2000) explain income disparities between North and South American countries in terms of the different property-rights regimes that were instituted in each under colonialism. It is reasonable to assume that governments that guarantee property rights are likely to facilitate investment and economic growth. This, however, could come at the expense of widening the distribution of income since investment is inherently risky and higher risks ensure greater profits for the owners of capital relative to labor. On the other hand, when economic bargaining takes place between capital and labor, governments that guarantee the rights of workers can help prevent the exploitation of labor by the wealthy and thereby reduce income inequality. Moreover, structures of governance that facilitate social spending and limit corruption are more likely to reduce income inequality (Gyimah-Brempong 2002; Foster 2012) than institutional arrangements that cut social expenditures, and in which government corruption has become entrenched in the operations of the state.

It is possible to include separate variables to measure the type of government, property rights, government spending, corruption, and labor freedom. However, issues of multicollinearity among these variables will likely produce regression estimates that are inefficient (Voss 2004). Therefore, following Levine et al. (2000), these institutional dimensions of income inequality are captured by the indices that measure economic freedom (Heritage Foundation 2016), and government type (alternatively democracy), which is captured by the Polity index.[2]

Empirical Findings

For hypothesis 1, table 8.1 presents TSCS regression estimates of the interactive effect of U.S. counternarcotic aid and the repression of workers' rights on income inequality in Latin America. Model 1 provides estimates of the direct effect of these variables on income inequality. While prior levels of income inequality are positively associated with current levels, all other variables fail to rise to the level of statistical significance. The interactive effect, which is featured in models 2 and 3, supports hypothesis 1. In model 2, while U.S. counternarcotic aid (the constituent element of the interaction term) is negatively associated with income inequality, its interaction with the repression of workers' rights is positively associated with increasing income inequality.

And while prior levels of income inequality are again positively associated with current levels, democratic governments have a reductive effect on income inequality. All other variables fail to rise to the level of statistical significance. This finding remains robust in model 3, which features fixed effects.[3] While both constituent elements of the interaction term are negatively associated with

Table 8.1. U.S. counternarcotic aid, the repression of workers, and income inequality in Latin America

Explanatory variables	Model 1: TSCS No interaction	Model 2: TSCS With interaction	Model 3: TSCS Interaction with fixed effects
Prior levels of income inequality	0.746*** (0.141)	0.725*** (0.143)	0.199 (0.123)
U.S. counternarcotic aid × repression of workers' rights		0.293* (0.119)	0.294** (0.101)
U.S. counternarcotic aid	0.187 (0.118)	−0.219+ (0.125)	−0.231+ (0.128)
Repression of workers' rights	0.567 (0.446)	0.254 (0.397)	−0.469+ (0.282)
GDP annual growth rate	−0.030 (0.039)	−0.0382 (0.0403)	−0.0642 (0.0489)
Polity index	−0.218 (0.135)	−0.249+ (0.138)	−0.118 (0.0847)
Index of economic freedom	0.045 (0.068)	0.0344 (0.0665)	−0.0388 (0.0524)
Index of international economic integration	−0.002 (0.032)	0.00882 (0.0294)	0.131*** (0.0196)
Constant	11.050 (5.844)	12.72* (6.114)	38.13*** (6.002)
Number of observations	197	197	197
R^2	0.68	0.69	0.88

Time-series cross section (TSCS) estimates. Panel-corrected standard errors are in parentheses.

Levels of statistical significance: $+p < 0.10$, $*p < 0.05$, $**p < 0.01$, $***p < 0.001$.

income inequality, their interactive effect is still positively associated with increasing income inequality. Increasing levels of Latin America's integration into the international capitalist economy are also positively associated with increasing income inequality. All other variables fail to rise to the level of statistical significance.

Graph 8.3 presents the marginal effect of U.S. counternarcotic aid on income inequality at changing levels of worker repression in Latin America. At levels where the rights of workers are fully protected, counternarcotic aid has a reductive effect on income inequality. However, it is only when worker repression is greater than 0.8, or increases to the level where the rights of workers are somewhat restricted, that U.S. counternarcotic aid increases income inequality in Latin America.

Graph 8.3. U.S. counternarcotic aid and income inequality at changing levels of worker repression in Latin America. Dashed lines show 95 percent confidence interval.

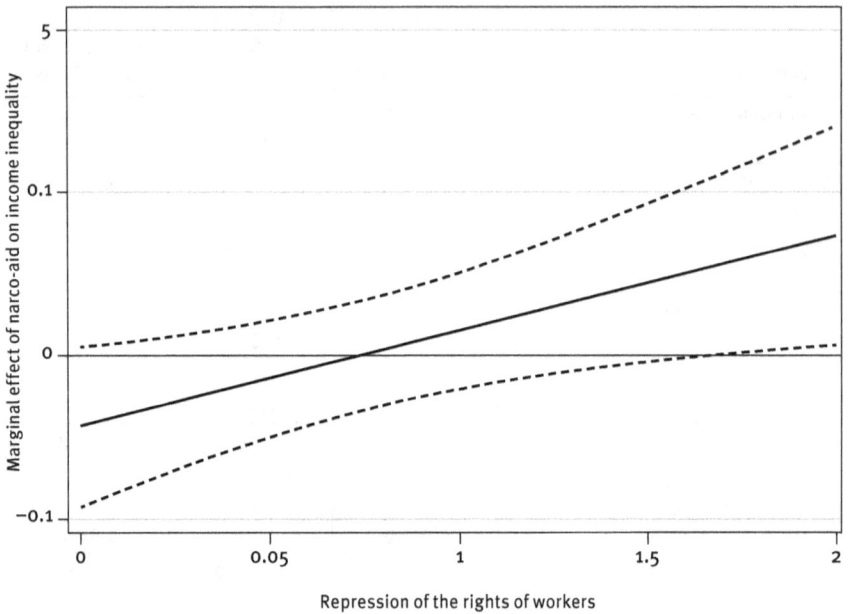

Table 8.2, which tests hypothesis 2, provides time-series regression estimates of the effects of drug enforcement expenditures on five measures of income inequality in the United States.[4] The empirical results support hypothesis 2. The federal government's drug enforcement budget is positively associated with increasing overall income inequality as measured by the Gini index in model 1. While drug enforcement expenditure increases poverty in model 2, it also increases the income shares for the top 1 percent in model 3 and the top 0.1 percent in model 4, and as a percentage of the median income, it increases the earnings of the top decile as shown in model 5.

Moving to a consideration of the control variables, increases in the annual growth rate of GDP are positively associated with income inequality in all models. These results capture the nature of the jobless recovery of the U.S. labor market. This is characterized by stagnant unemployment, high levels of underemployment, and the declining income of middle- and working-class Americans despite the growth in real GDP that followed the recession in 2001 and the collapse of the U.S. financial sector in 2008.

Table 8.2. Drug enforcement and income inequality in the United States

Explanatory variables	Model 1: Gini index	Model 2: % below poverty line	Model 3: Top 1% share of gross income	Model 4: Top 0.1% share of gross income	Model 5: Top decile as % median income
Federal drug enforcement expenditure (supply reduction)	0.000318*** (0.0000825)	0.000572*** (0.0000916)	0.000774*** (0.000147)	0.000484*** (0.000975)	0.00274*** (0.000714)
GDP annual growth rate	0.175** (0.0634)	0.327*** (0.0719)	0.478*** (0.124)	0.293*** (0.0818)	1.960*** (0.559)
Index of economic freedom	0.0539 (0.0400)	0.129** (0.0455)	0.175 (0.101)	0.0858 (0.0691)	1.357** (0.509)
Index of international economic integration	−0.103 (0.0558)	−0.268*** (0.0673)	0.299*** (0.0539)	0.219*** (0.0361)	−1.254*** (0.351)
Constant	42.69*** (6.268)	11.41 (7.096)	−26.16** (8.041)	−19.81*** (5.372)	162.5*** (40.98)
Number of observations	13	13	13	13	13
R^2	0.75	0.88	0.72	0.70	0.77

Time-series estimates. Panel corrected standard errors are in parentheses.

Levels of statistical significance: $^+ p < 0.10$, $^* p < 0.05$, $^{**} p < 0.01$, $^{***} p < 0.001$.

Increasing levels of economic freedom enjoyed by private corporations and investors are positively associated with increasing poverty in model 2, and as a percentage of the median income, increasing levels of economic freedom increase the earnings of the top decile in model 5. These results run counter to the predictions of supply-side economists (Friedman 1962), who believe that regressive tax policies that privilege the corporate rich, the privatization of state enterprises, and the deregulation of capital and labor markets will unleash market forces and that the private wealth produced will "trickle down" to the poor and lift them out of poverty. In all other models, the variable fails to achieve statistical significance.

The results concerning the effects of international economic integration on income inequality are mixed. In model 1, increasing levels of international economic integration have no statistically significant effect on overall income inequality but are positively associated with increasing income shares for the top 1 percent in model 3 and the top 0.1 percent in model 4. International economic integration is negatively associated with poverty in model 2, and as a percentage of the median income it decreases the earnings of the top decile in model 5. While these results appear to contradict the notion that international economic integration exerts a "race to the bottom" effect on the incomes of the poor, Rudra (2008) reminds us that domestic institutions in developing countries have historically ignored the needs of the poor, and thus international economic integration poses a greater threat to the income of the middle classes that have benefited the most from the social programs of the welfare state. However, these results suggest that a similar argument can be made regarding the United States, where the upper middle class is the most vulnerable to international economic integration's reductive effect on income, as shown in model 5.

Are there any discernible racial patterns of income inequality induced by the federal government's drug enforcement expenditures? The regression estimates presented in table 8.3 suggest that there isn't, which underscores the importance of class and not the racial dimension of the drug war. While drug enforcement expenditures have no statistically significant effect on income inequality among Asian Americans, they are positively associated with increasing income inequality among whites, blacks, and Hispanics. Nevertheless, with a statistical significance of 0.05, drug enforcement has a weaker impact on income inequality among whites relative to blacks and Hispanics.

The estimates of the control variables show that increases in the annual growth rate of GDP are positively associated with increasing income inequality among whites and blacks but fail to achieve statistical significance for Asians and Hispanics. Again, this finding speaks to the nature of the jobless recovery

Table 8.3. Drug enforcement and income inequality by race in the United States

Explanatory variables	Model 1 Gini index for whites	Model 2 Gini index for blacks	Model 3 Gini index for Asians	Model 4 Gini index for Hispanics
Federal drug enforcement expenditure (supply reduction)	0.0180* (0.00715)	0.0360*** (0.00951)	0.00963 (0.0138)	0.0225*** (0.00532)
GDP annual growth rate	18.94*** (5.646)	18.79** (7.200)	−17.81 (14.74)	5.823 (5.562)
Index of economic freedom	0.0587 (3.283)	−7.184 (4.881)	28.58* (12.77)	−4.575 (5.203)
Index of international economic integration	−4.821 (3.809)	1.735 (3.596)	−15.68 (12.14)	−15.39*** (3.301)
Constant	4623.4*** (457.9)	4784.0*** (531.9)	3229.5* (1586.9)	5502.8*** (521.5)
Number of observations	13	13	13	13
R^2	0.62	0.64	0.51	0.76

Time-series estimates. Panel corrected standard errors are in parentheses.

Levels of statistical significance: $^+p < 0.10$, $^*p < 0.05$, $^{**}p < 0.01$, $^{***}p < 0.001$.

of the U.S. labor market that followed the 2001 and 2008 recessions and suggests that it had a much greater impact on income inequality among whites and blacks than it did among Asian and Hispanic Americans. While international economic integration has no statistical significant effect on income inequality among whites, blacks, and Asian, it reduces income inequality among Hispanics. This suggest that the liberalization of trade and cross-border capital flows significantly improve the distribution of income among Hispanic Americans. And while economic freedom increases inequality among Asian Americans, its fails to achieve statistical significance among white, black, and Hispanic Americans.

To test the sequential and relational order of the argument from which hypotheses 3, 4, 5, and 6 emerge, I used SEM to estimate the data. Since an important component of the main argument is that increases in drug enforcement expenditures and the rate of mass incarceration increase levels of poverty, estimates of these relationships are provided as well. Table 8.4, along with its visual representation in figure 8.1, shows that the data support the hypotheses' sequential and relational ordering of the argument.

Increasing levels of corporate lobbying expenditures are positively associated with increases in drug enforcement expenditures. An increase in drug enforcement expenditures is positively associated with an increasing rate of

Table 8.4. The drug enforcement regime, corporate revenues, poverty, and the prison-industrial complex in the United States

Dependent variables	Explanatory variables	SEM estimates
Federal drug enforcement expenditures	Corporate lobbying expenditures	96.18*** (15.48)
	Constant	12574.1*** (125.2)
Mass incarceration	Federal drug enforcement expenditures	0.00222*** (0.000327)
	Constant	460.7*** (4.337)
Percent below the poverty line	Federal drug enforcement expenditures	0.000492*** (0.0000227)
	Mass incarceration	0.0186*** (0.00326)
	Constant	−2.480 (1.527)
Corporate revenues	Incarceration	676.7+ (375.9)
	Constant	−255245.9 (184199.3)
Corporate lobbying expenditures	Corporate revenues	0.0000175*** (0.00000275)
	Constant	4.577*** (0.335)
	Number of observations	408

Standard errors are in parentheses. Goodness-of-fit statistics: model chi-square, $p > \chi^2 = 0.650$; population error: root mean square error of approximation (RMSEA) = 0.000; baseline comparison: comparative fit index = 1.000, Tucker-Lewis index = 1.003; size of residuals: standardized root mean squared residual (SRMSR) = 0.035.

Levels of statistical significance: $+p < 0.10$, $*p < 0.05$, $**p < 0.01$, $***p < 0.001$.

mass incarceration within the prison-industrial complex. Increases in the rate of mass incarceration are positively associated with the increasing revenues of American corporations. The results also show that increases in corporate revenues are positively associated with increases in corporate lobbying expenditures. Finally, increases in the drug war's budgetary expenditures and the rate of mass incarceration to which it gives rise are both positively associated with an increase in the percentage of Americans who live below the poverty line. In essence, domestic drug enforcement in the United States creates the conditions that facilitate the growth of poverty and mass incarceration while increasing corporate revenues. The drug war drives the process of capital accumulation through the prison-industrial complex, and the revenues produced by this process increase the power of corporate lobbies that reproduce the process of capital accumulation.

Any interpretation of SEM results must be done in the context of the model fitting the data. By all the measures of goodness of fit, the model fits the data very well. The statistic for the model's chi-square is 0.650, which indicates a good

Figure 8.1. The drug enforcement regime, corporate revenues, poverty, and the prison-industrial complex in the United States. The error terms (ε) are the residual variances within variables not accounted for by the pathways hypothesized in the model; they are accompanied by their coefficients. Levels of statistical significance: $+p < 0.10$, $*p<0.05$, $**p<0.01$, $***p < 0.001$.

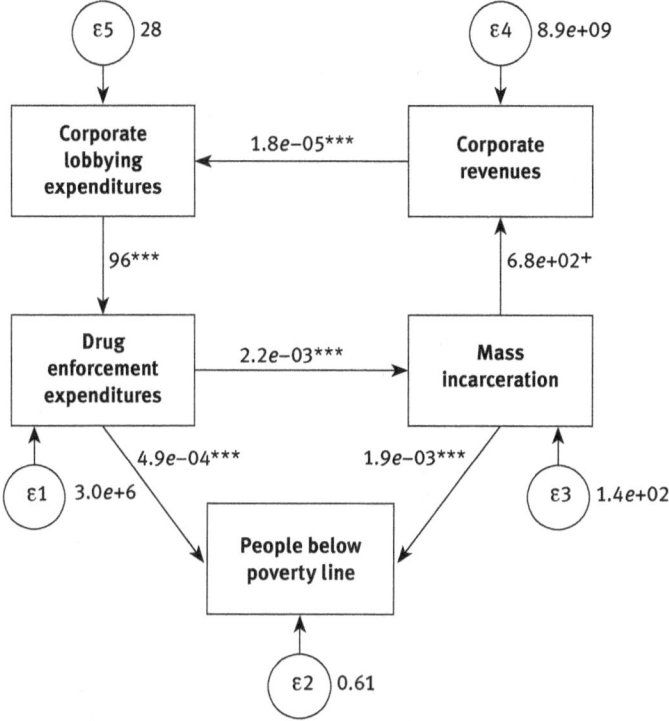

fit. The model's RMSEA is 0.000, which indicates an excellent fit (MacCallum et al. 1996). The comparative fit and Tucker-Lewis indices are both 1.0, indicating excellent fits. The SRMSR is 0.04, also indicative of a good fit (Kline 2011).

Is racial bias the primary explanation, as some scholars have argued (Tonry 2011; Alexander 2012; Lusane 1991), of how the drug enforcement regime operates in the United States? SEM estimates presented in table 8.5 again suggest that this is not the case.[5] The statistically significant correlated pathways in models 1 and 2, which provide estimates for whites and people of color, are identical. Increases in corporate lobbying expenditures are positively associated with increasing drug enforcement expenditures. Increases in drug enforcement expenditures are positively associated with an increasing rate of mass incarceration among whites and people of color. An increasing rate of mass incarceration among whites and people of color is positively associated

Table 8.5. The drug enforcement regime, corporate revenues, the prison-industrial complex, and income inequality by race in the United States

Dependent variables	Explanatory variables	SEM estimates	
		Model 1: Whites	Model 2: People of color
Federal drug enforcement expenditures	Corporate lobbying expenditures	94.96*** (15.54)	93.09*** (15.67)
	Constant	12581.4*** (125.5)	12592.4*** (126.0)
Mass incarceration of whites	Federal drug enforcement expenditures	4.750*** (0.493)	
	Constant	442313.4*** (6535.5)	
Mass incarceration of people of color	Federal drug enforcement expenditures		15.91*** (0.959)
	Constant		85490.3*** (12718.0)
Income inequality among whites	Federal drug enforcement expenditures	0.000000747*** (0.000000124)	
	Mass incarceration of whites	6.95e–08*** (1.12e–08)	
	Constant	0.415*** (0.00516)	
Income inequality among people of color	Federal drug enforcement expenditures		0.00000204*** (0.000000164)
	Mass incarceration of people of color		4.93e–08*** (6.52e–09)
	Constant		0.409*** (0.00176)
Corporate revenues	Mass incarceration of whites	0.473* (0.238)	
	Constant	−162231.1 (120232.2)	
Corporate revenues	Mass incarceration of people of color		0.214* (0.106)
	Constant		13207.7 (31551.9)

Table 8.5. (*continued*)

		SEM estimates	
Dependent variables	Explanatory variables	Model 1: Whites	Model 2: People of color
Corporate lobbying expenditures	Corporate revenues	0.0000173*** (0.00000276)	0.0000170*** (0.00000279)
	Constant	4.594*** (0.335)	4.618*** (0.336)
	Number of observations	408	408

Model 1: Standard errors are in parentheses. Model 1 goodness-of-fit statistics: model chi-square, $p > \chi^2 = 0.798$; population error: root mean square error of approximation (RMSEA) = 0.000; baseline comparison: comparative fit index = 1.000, Tucker-Lewis index = 1.011; size of residuals: standardized root mean squared residual (SRMSR) = 0.029. Model 2 goodness-of-fit statistics: model chi-square, $p > \chi^2 = 0.834$; population error, RMSEA = 0.000; baseline comparison, comparative fit index = 1.000, Tucker-Lewis index = 1.006; size of residuals, SRMSR = 0.027.

Levels of statistical significance: $+p < 0.10$, $*p < 0.05$, $**p < 0.01$, $***p < 0.001$.

with increases in corporate revenues, which in turn are associated with increasing corporate lobbying expenditures. And finally, increases in the drug war's budgetary expenditures and the rate of mass incarceration of whites and people of color are positively associated with increasing income inequality among both racial groups.

Regardless of race, the drug war drives the process of corporate capital accumulation and income inequality through the prison-industrial complex. In essence, the bias that drives how the drug enforcement regime operates in the United States is class, not race. This, however, does not mean that racial bias does not shape mass incarceration in the way in which drug war sentencing laws are used to discriminate against people of color. But it does suggest that racial bias, while important, is not sufficient to explain the operations of the larger embedded corporatist regime where American corporations use the prison-industrial complex to appropriate capital from convict labor, which in consequence increases income disparities among whites and people of color.

Conclusion

This chapter has demonstrated that the operations of the corporatist drug enforcement regime in the Americas increase income inequality and reflect the class bias of the drug war. In Latin America, it does so through the repression of workers' rights. In the United States, it does so through budgetary priorities that privilege the drug war at the expense of social programs that have traditionally provided upward mobility to the working class and poor. Moreover, in the United States, corporations are both benefactors and beneficiaries of drug enforcement, while corporate capital accumulation rests on the backs of the incarcerated and the poor. What are the implications of these findings for the Americas?

Drug-war-induced repression of the working class and its resultant effect of increased income inequality reinforce the repressive impulse of the drug-war national security state in Latin America and severely undermine the possibilities of democratic governance by excluding the socioeconomic and political aspirations of the working class from countries' development. In the United States, the corporatist drug enforcement regime's impact on mass incarceration, poverty, income inequities, and the use of prison labor for corporate profits undermines liberal democracy and facilitates illiberal governance. The operations of the regime via the prison-industrial complex has reproduced the sordid history of the convict leasing system known as the "Yankee invention," in which states leased prisoners to private companies, either within prison walls or in outside (work-release) workshops, factories, and fields (McLennan 2008). As it is today, and as it was during the Jim Crow era, the primary objective of the convict leasing system is the generation of profits for corporations that exploit leased prison labor, and revenues for state governments that lease out their prisoners (McLennan 2008; Sellin 1976).

These pathological class contradictions are natural outcomes of the policy choices of the drug enforcement regime. In the United States, the increasing reliance on incarcerated laborers—those who have been caught in the dragnet of its drug enforcement policies—will contribute to the continued demise of the labor movement and collective bargaining. While the Obama administration curtailed the use of private prisons, the Trump administration has rolled back this Obama-era policy and in consequence has strengthened the process of corporate-convict capital accumulation, which only deepens the class bias of the corporatist drug enforcement regime.

CHAPTER 9

Drug War Policy Reforms and the Endurance of the Embedded Corporatist Regime

The drug war I think is over. Certainly, calling it the drug war should be over. But the battle against the narcotic problem in this country has to go on. But we need to take some different approaches. . . . It ought to be a public health issue. . . . I certainly think it [marijuana] ought to be rescheduled. You know, we treat marijuana in the same way that we treat heroin now, and that clearly is not appropriate.
—Former U.S. attorney general **Eric Holder,** PBS interview, 2016

Our policy is the same, really fundamentally, as the Holder-Lynch policy, which is that the federal law remains in effect and a state can legalize marijuana for its law enforcement purposes but it still remains illegal with regard to federal purposes.
—Former U.S. attorney general **Jeff Sessions,** House Judiciary
 Committee oversight hearing, 2017

Regime Endurance: Drug Enforcement Policy Continuity from Obama to Trump

Given the pathologies of the corporatist drug enforcement regime, has it become malleable to proposed policy reforms of its operations? The comments above by Holder and Sessions suggest that, regardless of the pathologies of the regime, its prohibition logic will endure. The regime endures regardless of the fact that it places few constraints on illicit drug trafficking penetrating the U.S. market. And notwithstanding an elaborate anti-money-laundering regime, traffickers' ability to compromise the integrity of America's financial institutions has proven impossible to eliminate. Consider how drug cartels used the money transfer industry in states like South Carolina to launder drug money. During the years when South Carolina's money transfer industry (dominated by Western Union, MoneyGram, and Vigo) was unregulated, fewer than 10 percent of the 3,000 money transfer services that operated out of Horry and Georgetown Counties were registered with the state. It is estimated that businesses operating out of these counties laundered approximately US$700 million a year to criminal cartels and terror organizations in Mexico, Colombia, and the Middle East (RAYCOM News Network 2015). House Bill 4554, South Carolina's Anti-Money Laundering Act, attempted to "provide regulation and oversight of the money transmission services business most commonly used by organized criminal enterprises to launder the monetary proceeds of illegal activities" (South Carolina Money Services and Illicit Finance Abatement Act, S. 1230, sec 1), and was passed in June 2016 after being introduced to the state senate in 2012. For four years the bill languished in the legislature as local business lobbies blocked its passage, perceiving the legislation as more government regulation of their industry (RAYCOM News Network 2015).

Further, consider how Wells Fargo and HSBC laundered the drug proceeds of Mexico's cartels.[1] Wells Fargo paid a US$160 million fine to avoid prosecution. HSBC ultimately evaded criminal prosecution by paying a fine of almost US$2 billion (Murphy 2013; Smith 2010) and later attempted to repair its public image by hiring former U.S. deputy attorney general and former FBI director James Comey to serve as an independent board member on its Financial Systems Vulnerabilities Committee (Brinded 2013). All of these cases highlight the drug enforcement regime's inability to preserve the integrity of the American banking and financial system. More important, the fact that Mexican cartel leaders such as Joaquin "El Chapo" Guzman, Jorge Eduardo Sanchez, and others are imprisoned in the United States while the corporate banking executives who laundered their criminal proceeds saw no jail time gives added meaning to the sentiment that corporations are not only too big to fail but also too big to jail.

Like the Obama administration, the Trump administration continues to adhere to the prohibition belief of the drug enforcement regime. This belief is based on the assumption that robust drug enforcement can significantly reduce the supply of illicit narcotics entering into the United States, which will in turn increase street prices and reduce illicit drug consumption (Reuter and Kleinman 1986). Given this logic, comprehensive legalization of all narcotics would simply increase the supply of drugs available to drug users and increase drug abuse. However, graph 9.1 shows that, regardless of the steady increase in federal drug enforcement expenditures, illicit drug use, whether measured in terms of the number of users or as a percentage of the population, has continued to increase in the United States.

Clearly, more drug enforcement does not translate into less drug consumption, an empirical observation that has led students of drug enforcement to

Graph 9.1. Drug enforcement expenditures and drug users in the United States, 2002–2015. *Source*: National Survey on Drug Use and Health n.d.; Office of National Drug Control Policy n.d.

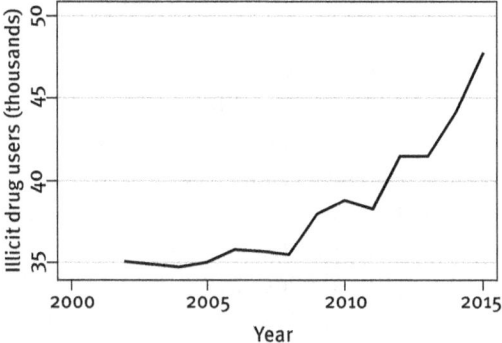

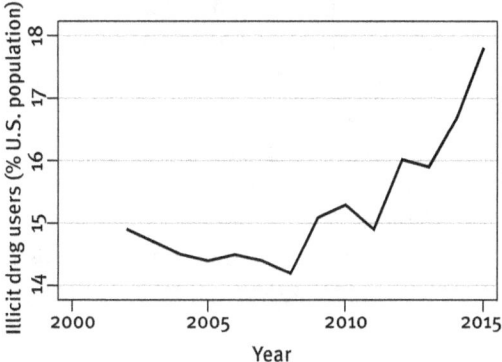

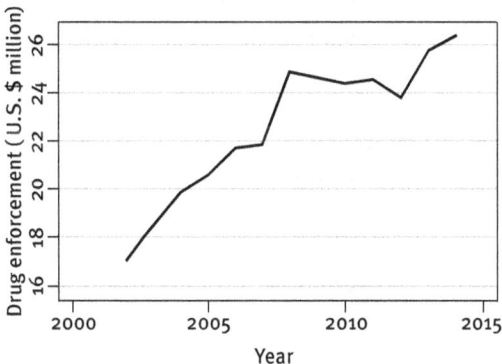

conclude, incorrectly, that the drug war's failure over the past forty-eight years proves that American policy makers are addicted to its failed policies (Loveman 2006). *Failure* is determined by the definition of *success*. Those who conclude that the U.S. war on drugs has failed logically evaluate the policy on the basis of its stated objective, which is to reduce the consumption and abuse of illicit narcotics in the United States. The facts that this objective has not been achieved, that drug enforcement expenditures today relative to their levels in 1971 when President Nixon declared the war on drugs have quadrupled, and that the regime has also become far more extensive with the inclusion of more international partners in the prosecution of the drug war suggest that once the regime is constructed it is difficult to deconstruct even if it fails to realize its overt raison d'être. The regime's endurance and success are based at least partly on its ability to distribute the benefits of capital accumulation—an economic residual of drug enforcement—to the various domestic and international members of the regime. The research presented in this book has demonstrated systematically that the drug war has not failed; rather, it has been remarkably successful for the corporations and their domestic and international political allies that drive its budgetary increases.

American corporations, along with their domestic political allies, not only drove legislation that secured congressional funding for Plan Colombia and the Mérida Initiative but also drive drug enforcement policy to countries beyond the Americas. The drug war is an important mechanism through which American corporations accumulate capital. Well-funded corporate lobbies, corporate-funded think tanks that shape the ideological environment that sustains domestic and international prohibition, corporate financing of federal elections, and corporate elite networks with the federal government and the military are important components of the embedded corporatist regime, which drives the drug war in order to secure government contracts, finance the security of overseas corporate assets, and facilitate the expansion of corporate investments into foreign markets. In the United States, with the support of some civil society organizations and particularly the Congressional Black Caucus (CBC), support for strong drug enforcement is seen as a way to stop the flow of drugs into urban communities and as a conduit for attracting private investment to promote economic development in the black community as well as in the Afro-Latino and Afro-Caribbean communities in countries that partner with the United States in prosecuting the drug war overseas. Domestic support for the embedded corporatist regime has led to the unintended consequence of mass incarceration in the United States and the creation of an internal "third world" labor market where corporate profits are extracted by exploiting cheap convict labor from the prison-industrial complex. Even when the policy preferences of some members of the regime change, the benefits of capital accumulation to other members far outweigh the policy incentive to dismantle the regime.

Drug War Policy Reforms and the Endurance of the Drug Enforcement Regime

In recent years, regime members have modified or advocated for drug war policy reforms to change the tactics of drug enforcement. But changes in tactics do not change the underlying prohibitive norm of drug enforcement, and in many ways these tactical changes strengthen the perceived legitimacy of the regime. For example, the Obama administration's approach to drug enforcement placed greater emphasis on treatment-and-prevention programs. Obama championed legislation that funded mental health and addiction treatment programs and research. In 2016 he signed into law the Twenty-First Century Cures Act (P.L. 114-255) and the Comprehensive Addiction and Recovery Act (P.L. 114-198), which provides funding for state and community prevention and treatment efforts. The Affordable Care Act, which was Obama's landmark legislation, mandated that insurance plans cover treatment for mental health and drug addiction. And notwithstanding President Trump's bluster about being tough on crime, during the 2016 presidential campaign he promised to increase funding and comprehensive Medicare coverage for drug addiction treatment. And despite former attorney general Jeff Sessions's directive to federal prosecutors to lock up low-level drug offenders, as well as his decision to end the Obama-era "safe harbor" federal policy, which provided legal shelter for marijuana sales in California and five other states where marijuana is legal for recreational purposes, like Eric Holder he admitted, during a House Judiciary Committee Oversight Hearing, that marijuana is not as dangerous as heroin and that it should be rescheduled (U.S. House of Representatives 2017).[2]

The health care approach to drug enforcement that the Obama administration promoted and the Trump administration has promised to continue legitimates the drug war without questioning the underlying premise of prohibition and, in the words of Eric Holder, continues "the battle against the narcotics problem" in the United States. Although Holder and Sessions agree in principle that marijuana is not as dangerous as heroin, neither of them used the office of the attorney general to formally lobby Congress to pass legislation to reschedule the drug. In fact, before California legalized marijuana for recreational use in 2018, in 2010 while he was attorney general Eric Holder strongly opposed California's Proposition 19, a referendum to legalize marijuana, and promised that the Obama administration would continue to vigorously prosecute federal marijuana possession cases. In speeches in Cartagena, Colombia, in 2012, and at a Town Hall meeting with Young Leaders of the Americas at the University of the West Indies in Kingston, Jamaica, in 2015, President Obama affirmed the importance of maintaining drug prohibition in the Americas and specifically rejected the idea of legalizing marijuana in the Caribbean.

The source of the endurance of the embedded corporatist drug enforcement regime is not limited to the policy continuity of the Obama and Trump administrations or to the benefits of capital accumulation enjoyed by some members of the regime; it is also a product of the incongruent drug war policy reforms that reflect the changing preferences of some of its domestic and international members. In the United States, racial disparities in drug enforcement sentencing laws and the associated rise in mass incarceration have led civil society organizations to advocate various drug war policy reforms that are in conflict with one another. In consequence, there is no consensus regarding a set of policy reforms around which disparate civil society groups can mobilize and coordinate their political activities to effectively change the prohibition norms of the embedded corporatist drug enforcement regime.

Different physician organizations advocate conflicting policies to reform the drug enforcement regime. The AMA, for example, considers marijuana a dangerous drug and a public health concern but argues that federal enforcement efforts to reduce marijuana use have been ineffective. The AMA supports policies that continue the criminalization of marijuana but suggests that marijuana use be treated with a public health approach rather than incarceration (Nelson 2013). The organization also argues that marijuana's status as a federal Schedule 1 controlled substance should be reviewed with the goal of facilitating the conduct of clinical research and development of cannabinoid-based medicines (American Medical Association 2009). Doctors for Cannabis Regulation (DFCR), a group of fifty physicians who represent the California Medical Association, became the first major physician association to endorse the full legalization and regulation of marijuana for adult recreational use—a significant departure from the policy preference of the AMA. DFCR argues that prohibition and the criminalization of marijuana perpetuate racial and economic disparities in drug enforcement while keeping marijuana prices high and lucrative for drug trafficking organizations. The organization argues that a legal and regulated marijuana market is the most effective way to ensure public safety and reduce the negative consequences of drug enforcement on disadvantaged communities (Ingraham 2016).

While some religious civil society organizations support maintaining the prohibition status quo of the drug enforcement regime, other organizations offer policy reforms that range from comprehensive legalization to the decriminalization of marijuana. The National Black Church Initiative (NBCI), a coalition of 34,000 African American and Latino churches, formally opposed California's Proposition 19. NBCI president Rev. Anthony Evans viewed Proposition 19 as an "unconscionable move that would weaken the Black Church, the Black community and the Black family" (National Black Church Initiative 2010). In 2015, the New England Conference of the United Methodist Church, representing more than 600 congregations, voted to end the war on drug through legalization. In Illinois, the Unitarian Universal Association, a coalition of Protestant pastors and Jewish rabbis, lobbied Illinois law makers to decriminalize marijuana (Pasman 2015). White evangelist conservative minister Pat Robertson supports marijuana legalization, stating that "we're locking up people who are taking a couple of puffs of marijuana. . . . We've got to take a look at what we're considering crimes. I'm not exactly for the use of drugs, don't get me wrong, but [incarcerating marijuana users is] costing us a fortune and it's ruining young people" (Hemingway 2010).

The different attitudes toward drug war policy reforms among white and black religious civil society organizations reflects a larger racial divide concerning the issue of drug abuse in the United States. A University of Michigan poll found that 49 percent of Hispanic parents and 44 percent of African American parents list drug abuse as a major risk to their children's health, as opposed to just 28 percent of whites (C. S. Mott Children's Hospital 2011). Since communities of color, relative to the white community, see drug abuse as a major threat to the health of their children, they are more likely to support the prohibition policies of the regime as opposed to reforming them.

In Latin America, the perpetual violence and growing human rights repression that has emerged from the prosecution of the drug war have led foreign members of the regime to advocate for policy reforms that are also incongruent with one another. Although American policy makers continue to hail Colombia as the model in the overseas war on drugs, President Juan Manual Santos has consistently insisted that the twenty-eight-year-old U.S.-sponsored drug war in his country has largely been ineffective. In consequence, the Colombian government in 2013 expanded existing marijuana and cocaine decriminalization to include methamphetamine and ecstasy (Isacson et al. 2013). In Bolivia, President Evo Morales has rejected comprehensive legalization of drugs but implemented an alternative model to combat drug trafficking, which allows 20,000 hectares of coca to be grown for traditional uses (Neuman 2012). Uruguay has moved to a state-regulated marijuana market where the government has regulatory control over its production and distribution. The law permits adults to purchase forty grams of marijuana per month and to cultivate six plants and authorizes cooperatives of fifteen to forty-five members to cultivate up to ninety-nine plants (Cave 2012; Isacson et al. 2013, 4). While Mexico rejects comprehensive drug legalization, in 2009 the government decriminalized possession of small amounts of marijuana, cocaine, heroin, and methamphetamine. While the threshold for determining personal possession is set very low, the Mexican government continues to emphasize criminalization and incarceration as policy responses to the country's drug problem (Associated Press 2009). Peru, Brazil, and Nicaragua remain opposed to the legalization or decriminalization of any drug (Archibold 2013). While Latin American leaders have called for policy changes in the existing drug enforcement regime, the lack of consensus on an alternative policy undercuts their ability to effectively change the prohibition norms of the regime.

Decriminalization, Legalization, and the Pathologies of the Drug War

The drug enforcement regime is also likely to endure because the policy alternatives to prohibition do not effectively eliminate the existing pathologies of the drug war. As discussed in chapter 4, the underlying contradiction of decriminalization or depenalization "is that it gives consumers permission to buy what dealers are forbidden to sell" (Kleiman et al. 2011, 27). Because decriminalization removes criminal penalties against drug users, it is likely to have a significant impact in reducing mass incarceration in the United States. However, since criminal penalties against producers, traffickers, and distributors of illicit narcotics would still be in effect, decriminalization would have no effect in reducing drug-related violence and human rights repression that have now become the collateral damage of the drug war (Bartilow 2014; Bartilow and Eom 2009a). Moreover, under a decriminalized drug enforcement regime, the raison d'être for the drug-war national security state and the illiberal nature of democracy in Latin America would continue since the existential threats against the state from drug cartels and narcoterror organizations would also continue.

Would the comprehensive legalization of drugs be more effective in eliminating the pathologies of the drug war? Comprehensive legalization would remove the system of capital accumulation embedded in the incentive structure of the corporatist drug enforcement regime. And since counternarcotic aid is shown to drive foreign direct investment (FDI) in Latin America, legalization has the potential to reduce, but not eliminate, the threat of displacement faced by Indigenous peoples. Legalization would certainly reduce mass incarceration in the United States and the associated income inequality. It would reduce but not eliminate income inequality and its associated repression of the rights of workers in Latin America. And while it would reduce regime transitions from liberal to illiberal governments, it would not eliminate illiberal democracies in the region. The research presented here has shown that, even in the absence of U.S. drug enforcement aid, illiberal democracy would still exist. And while counternarcotic aid is a significant accelerator of illiberal democracy, it is certainly not the cause of the phenomenon. A significant aspect of illiberal democratic development in Latin America is driven purely by structural economic factors and the agency of local political elites in the region.

The current opioid crisis, as well as the various societal costs of alcoholism and nicotine addiction, demonstrates that the legalization of drugs, even when rigorously regulated, is not a panacea for the negative externalities of drug consumption and controlled enforcement. The problems of drug abuse, whether facilitated by an illicit or licit drug industry, is rooted in the fragility of the human condition, which is made worse in the absence of a more equitable, humane, and democratic society. While egalitarian and democratic societies are difficult to build and even harder to maintain, they may be our best defense against the challenges associated with drug abuse and drug trafficking.

Chapter 1

Table 1.1A. Data measurements and sources

Indicator	Operationalization	Source
Polity index	Measures the institutional authority characteristics of regimes on a 21-point scale ranging from −10, regions with consolidated autocracies, to +10, regions with consolidated democracies	Marshall et al. 2013
Freedom House index	Measures the level of political freedom and civil liberties in countries; scores between 1 and 2.5 indicate "free"; between 3.0 and 5.5, "partly free"; and between 5.5 and 7.0, "not free"	Freedom House n.d.
FDI	Measured in terms of millions of U.S. dollars as a percentage of a country's GDP	World Bank 2016
PTS	Ranges from level 1, where citizens' human rights are secure under law, to level 5, where state repression is at its highest encompassing a country's entire population where leaders place no limits on the means through which they pursue personal and ideological goals.	Gibney and Dalton 1996
CIRI human rights data index	Additive index constructed from torture, disappearances, extrajudicial killing, and political imprisonment indicators; ranges from 0, no government respect for physical integrity rights, to 8, full government respect for these rights	Cingranelli and Richards 1999
U.S. counter-narcotic aid	Measured in millions of U.S. dollars	USAID n.d.

Chapter 3

Table 3.1A. Data measurements and sources

Variable	Operationalization	Source
Dependent variables		
U.S. counternarcotic aid (in selection stage)	Coded 1 if a country received counternarcotic aid in given year, 0 otherwise	USAID n.d.
U.S. counternarcotic aid (in amount stage)	Measured in millions of U.S. dollars; logged to improve the normality of its distribution	USAID n.d.
Explanatory variables		
Corporate lobbying expenditures	Total yearly corporate congressional lobbying expenditures (in millions of U.S. dollars) reported on the lobbyists' disclosure forms filed with the clerk of the House of Representatives	Open Secrets: Center for Responsible Politics, "Lobbying Database." (The annual corporate lobbying expenditures of the 33 corporations in the data set can be individually accessed by typing "lobbying expenditures of [name of the corporation]" into the database's search engine.)
AFL-CIO lobbying expenditures	Total yearly congressional lobbying expenditures (in millions of U.S. dollars) reported on the AFL-CIO's disclosure form filed with the clerk of the House of Representatives	Open Secrets: Center for Responsible Politics, "Annual Lobbying by AFL-CIO."
Amnesty International lobbying expenditures	Total yearly congressional lobbying expenditures (in millions of U.S. dollars) reported on Amnesty International's disclosure form filed with the clerk of the House of Representatives	Open Secrets: Center for Responsible Politics, "Annual Lobbying by Amnesty International USA."
Human Rights Watch lobbying expenditures	Total yearly congressional lobbying expenditures (in millions of U.S. dollars) reported on the Human Rights Watch disclosure form filed with the clerk of the House of Representatives	Open Secrets: Center for Responsible Politics, "Annual Lobbying by Human Rights Watch."

Table 3.1A. (*continued*)

Variable	Operationalization	Source
CIRI human rights index (rescaled)	Ranges from 0, full government respect for physical integrity rights, to 8, no government respect for these rights	Cingranelli and Richards 1999
Presence of narcoterror organizations	Coded 1 if a country has an indigenous narcoterrorist organization or an indigenous international drug cartel, 0 otherwise	Gleditsch et al. 2002; see also various issues of the U.S. Department of State, *International Narcotics Control Strategy Report.*
BFTIA with the United States	Coded 1 if a country has a BFTIA, 0 otherwise	U.S. Department of Commerce, International Trade Administration n.d.; U.S. Department of State, "United States Bilateral Investment Treaties"; Office of the U.S. Trade Representative, Executive Office of the President n.d.
Latin America and the Caribbean Basin	Coded 1 for countries in the region, 0 otherwise	
Presidential ideology	Coded 0 for the conservative years of the Bush administration, 1 for the liberal years of the Obama administration	Keefer 2012
Organizational inertia	A 1-year lag in the dependent variable: U.S. counternarcotic aid	USAID n.d.
Federal government revenues	Revenue, excluding grants, as percentage of GDP	World Bank 2016
Federal government debt	Measured as gross debt as percentage of GDP	Office of Management and Budget n.d.

Table 3.2A. Drug-war-aid recipient countries: Bilateral trade and investment agreements with the United States

| Region | Country | Agreement with the United States | |
		Bilateral investment treaty	Trade agreement
Latin America and the Caribbean	1. Antigua and Barbuda	No	CBTPA
	2. Argentina	Yes	—
	3. Bahamas	No	—
	4. Barbados	No	CBTPA
	5. Belize	No	CBTPA
	6. Bolivia	Yes	FTAª
	7. Brazil	No	—
	8. Chile	No	FTA
	9. Colombia	No	FTA
	10. Costa Rica	No	CAFTA-DR
	11. Dominica	No	CBTPA
	12. Dominican Republic	No	CAFTA-DR
	13. Ecuador	Yes	FTAª
	14. El Salvador	No	CAFTA-DR
	15. Grenada	No	CBTPA
	16. Guatemala	No	CAFTA-DR
	17. Guyana	No	CBTPA
	18. Haiti	No	CBTPA
	19. Honduras	Yes	CAFTA-DR
	20. Jamaica	Yes	CBTPA
	21. Mexico	No	NAFTA
	22. Nicaragua	No	CAFTA-DR
	23. Panama	Yes	CBTPA
	24. Paraguay	No	—
	25. Peru	No	TPA
	26. St. Kitts and Nevis	No	CBTPA
	27. St. Lucia	No	CBTPA
	28. Suriname	No	—
	29. Trinidad and Tobago	Yes	CBTPA
	30. Uruguay	Yes	—
	31. Venezuela	No	—

Table 3.2A. (*continued*)

Region	Country	Agreement with the United States	
		Bilateral investment treaty	Trade agreement
Middle East and North Africa	32. Algeria	No	—
	33. Egypt	Yes	—
	34. Iraq	No	—
	35. Israel	No	FTA
	36. Jordan	Yes	FTA
	37. Lebanon	No	—
	38. Morocco	No	FTA
	39. West Bank/Gaza	No	—
	40. Yemen	No	—
Sub-Saharan Africa	41. Botswana	No	—
	42. Ghana	No	—
	43. Kenya	No	—
	44. Guinea-Bissau	No	—
	45. Liberia	No	—
	46. Nigeria	No	—
	47. South Africa	No	—
	48. Sudan	No	—
	49. Uganda	No	—
	50. Zambia	No	—
Asia	51. Afghanistan	No	—
	52. Bangladesh	Yes	—
	53. Cambodia	No	MFN
	54. China (P.R.C.)	No	—
	55. India	No	—
	56. Indonesia	No	FTA[a]
	57. Laos	Yes	—
	58. Nepal	No	—
	59. Pakistan	Yes[a]	TIFA
	60. Philippines	No	FTA[a]
	61. Sri Lanka	Yes[a]	FTA[a]
	62. Thailand	No	FTA[a]
	63. Timor-Leste	No	—

Table 3.2A. (*continued*)

Region	Country	Agreement with the United States	
		Bilateral investment treaty	Trade agreement
Eurasia	64. Armenia	Yes	—
	65. Azerbaijan	Yes[a]	—
	66. Georgia	Yes	FTA[a]
	67. Kazakhstan	Yes	MFN
	68. Kyrgyzstan	Yes	—
	69. Moldova	Yes	—
	70. Russia	No	—
	71. Tajikistan	No	—
	72. Turkmenistan	No	—
	73. Ukraine	Yes	TIFA
	74. Uzbekistan	No	—
	75. Albania	Yes	—
	76. Bosnia and Herzegovina	No	—
Eastern Europe	77. Bulgaria	Yes	—
	78. Hungary	No	—
	79. Kosovo	No	—
	80. Romania	Yes	—

CAFTA-DR, U.S.–Central America–Dominican Republic Free Trade Agreement; CBTPA, Caribbean Basin Trade Partnership Act; FTA, free trade agreement; MFN, most favored nation and nondiscriminatory treatment status; NAFTA, North American Free Trade Agreement; TIFA, trade and investment framework agreement; TPA, trade promotion agreement. *Source*: Office of the U.S. Trade Representative, Executive Office of the President n.d.

[a]Under consultation as of 2016.

The Theoretical Rationale for Selecting the Corporations in the Sample

The corporate political behavior literature shapes the logic of the sampling procedure used in selecting the corporations analyzed in this study. Drawing on this literature, I argue that companies who are members of the same industry or have subsidiaries in Latin America are more likely to engage in similar types of political behavior, such as support for drug enforcement (Mizruchi 1992, 80; Lorrain and White 1971; White et al. 1976; DiMaggio and Powell 1983). There are two reasons for this phenomenon. The first is that government policies most often affect entire industries. The second is that, given the logic of structural equivalence, it is expected that firms with similar patterns of intraindustry relationships and subject to similar regional constraints will demonstrate similar types of political behavior (Lorrain and White 1971; White et al. 1976). Moreover, firms in the same industry will often mimic the political behavior of other firms that they see as peers (DiMaggio and Powell 1983).

Corporations were selected into the sample if they were in similar and/or related industries with international subsidiaries and influenced U.S. policy in Latin America and the Caribbean through lobbying. As a result, I selected thirty-three corporations into the sample. The policy preferences of these corporations are consistent with the predictions of corporate political behavior literature. Of these corporations, five are members of the USCBP, a consortium of American companies that promotes U.S. business interests in Colombia and also lobbied for counternarcotic-aid to the Colombian government (Ripley 2014). Twelve companies were members of NACC, a corporate advisory group to the U.S., Canadian, and Mexican governments comprising members of the now defunct Security and Prosperity Partnership of North America (SPP) (Marshall 2008; Fogal et al. 2010).

While the prosperity component of the SPP sought to deepen patterns of trade and investment, which would increase the comparative advantage that American corporations enjoyed under NAFTA, it was recognized that further regional integration was not possible without greater regional security, especially in the post-9/11 environment when the escalation of cartel and narcoterrorist violence undermined investor confidence in some countries in Latin America (Council on Hemispheric Affairs 2014). The security component of the SPP was formalized with the passage of the Mérida Initiative in 2007 (Fogal et al. 2010). The remaining sixteen companies in the sample formed coalitions that lobbied in support of Plan Colombia (Ripley 2014, 14–21) and the Mérida Initiative (Ridgeway 2010). Many of these companies lobbied the U.S. Congress for the purpose of providing services or selling products needed for the prosecution of the drug wars in Mexico and Colombia. Others lobbied for greater security for their investments and for greater access to markets in Latin America.

As demonstrated in chapters 5 and 6, American counternarcotic aid is often used to finance countries' infrastructure development, which in turn facilitates the expansion of American and other transnational corporate investment in aid-recipient countries throughout Latin America. Counternarcotic aid is also used to leverage free trade agreements with recipient countries (Perl 1992). For example, the Andean Trade Promotion and Drug Eradication Act (ATPDEA), enacted in 2002, allowed Bolivia, Colombia, Ecuador, and Peru to have duty-free access to a wide range of exports to the United States. The main Andean exports to the United States under ATPDEA increased the comparative advantage of American oil and mining companies, which benefited from the elimination of tariffs on imported oil and natural gas, as well as copper products destined for the U.S. market (Ehlers 2008). Since American defense contractors receive government contracts to supply foreign governments with the military hardware to execute the drug war, it is expected that the political activities of these companies will be oriented toward increasing counternarcotic aid flows. Finally, because counternarcotic aid is used to increase free trade and FDI, it is expected that American corporations that are not defense contractors will also support increases in counternarcotic aid since drug enforcement has now become a vehicle for capital accumulation.

Table 3.3A. The sample of American corporations

Corporation	Industry	Lobbying objectives and policy preferences
1. Occidental Petroleum[a]	Oil	1. Plan Colombia Aid Package 2. Improved commercial ties with Colombia 3. Against Colombia sanctions 4. Supplemental aid to Colombia 5. Investment issues in Colombia 6. General trade issues in Latin America
2. BP-Amoco Corp.[a]	Oil	1. Plan Colombia aid package 2. Against Colombia sanctions 3. U.S.-Mexico relations
3. Unocal/Chevron[a]	Oil	1. Plan Colombia aid package 2. Against Colombia sanctions 3. Counternarcotic certification process 4. U.S. policy in Mexico 5. NACC member and corporate adviser to the SPP 6. NAFTA
4. ExxonMobil[a]	Oil	1. Plan Colombia aid package 2. Against Colombia sanctions 3. U.S. policy in Mexico 4. NACC member and corporate adviser to the SPP 5. NAFTA
5. Drummond Coal Mining	Mining	1. Plan Colombia aid package
6. Newmont Mining	Mining	1. Peru drug enforcement 2. Investment issues in Peru 3. General trade issues in Latin America
7. United Technologies	Defense	1. Plan Colombia 2. Colombia aid programs 3. Mérida Initiative
8. Textron	Defense	1. Plan Colombia aid package
9. Northrop Grumman	Defense	1. Plan Colombia aid package 2. Western Hemisphere Drug Elimination Act 3. Supplemental appropriations for FY1999 drug interdiction provisions—sensor upgrades 4. Alliance with Colombia and the Andean Region Act of 1999
10. Lockheed Martin	Defense	1. Plan Colombia aid package 2. P-3 AEW aircraft modification for counter-drug operations 3. U.S. policy on arms transfers to Latin America 4. NACC member and corporate adviser to the SPP

Table 3.3A. *(continued)*

Corporation	Industry	Lobbying objectives and policy preferences
11. Boeing	Defense	1. Plan Colombia aid package 2. Mérida Initiative
12. Raytheon	Defense	1. Plan Colombia aid package
14. General Dynamics	Defense	1. Plan Colombia aid package
15. BAE Systems	Defense	1. Mérida Initiative
16. MPRI	Defense	1. Plan Colombia aid package
17. SAIC	Information technology	1. Plan Colombia aid package
18. Hewlett Packard	Information technology	1. NACC member and corporate adviser to the SPP
19. Monsanto	Biotech	1. Plan Colombia aid package
20. General Electric	Manufacturing	1. NACC member and corporate adviser to the SPP 2. Defense appropriations and authorizations to supply parts for the Black Hawk and Apache helicopters used in Latin America
21. Deer and Co.	Manufacturing	1. Plan Colombia aid package
22. General Motors Corp.	Manufacturing	2. U.S.-Brazil trade 3. Western Hemisphere trade issues 4. NAFTA
23. Ford Motor Co.	Manufacturing	1. SPP
24. Caterpillar, Inc.[a]	Manufacturing	1. Plan Colombia aid package 2. National security waiver for Colombia 3. Drug certification for Mexico
25. Whirlpool Corp.	Manufacturing	1. NACC member and corporate adviser to the SPP
26. Bank of America	Banking and finance	1. Plan Colombia aid package
27. J. P. Morgan Chase	Banking and finance	1. Western Hemisphere trade and investment issues—Andean, Central America, and Caribbean regions
28. Merck and Co., Inc.	Pharmaceutical	Western Hemisphere trade and investment issues—Andean, Central America, and Caribbean regions1.
29. Pfizer[a]	Pharmaceutical	1. Plan Colombia aid package 2. U.S. foreign aid to Colombia
30. FedEx Corp.	Air delivery and cargo	1. NACC member and corporate adviser to the SPP 2. Western Hemisphere trade issues

Table 3.3A. (continued)

Corporation	Industry	Lobbying objectives and policy preferences
31. United Parcel Service[a]	Air delivery and cargo	1. NACC member and corporate adviser to the SPP 2. Free Trade Area of the Americas
32. Wal-Mart Stores, Inc.	Retail and consumer	1. NACC member and corporate adviser to the SPP 2. Western Hemisphere trade issues
33. Proctor and Gamble	Retail and consumer	1. NACC member and corporate adviser to the SPP 2. Western Hemisphere trade issues

Sources: For the list of American companies that were corporate advisers to the SPP, in which the security component was later formalized into the Mérida Initiative, see U.S. Chamber of Commerce 2007. For the list of companies that supported drug enforcement in Colombia and free trade in the Americas, see Ripley 2014. For a list of private contractors that operate in Colombia, see also Center for International Policy's Latin America Security Program 2003.

[a]Member of the U.S.-Colombian Business Partnership (USCBP).

Chapter 4

Table 4.1A appears on pages 229–30.

Table 4.1A. Data measurements and sources

Variable	Operationalization	Source
Dependent variables		
U.S. counternarcotic aid (in selection stage)	Coded 1 if a country received counternarcotic aid in given year, o otherwise	USAID n.d.
U.S. counternarcotic aid (in the amount stage)	Measured in millions of U.S. dollars; logged to improve the normality of its distribution	USAID n.d.
Main explanatory variables		
Corporate campaign contributions	Measured in millions of U.S. dollars: 1. Total corporate contributions 2. Corporate contributions to PACs 3. Individual contributions to Democratic and Republican candidates for the House and Senate during election year cycles	Open Secrets: Center for Responsible Politics, "Top Organization Contributors." (The annual corporate campaign contributions of the 33 corporations in the study's data set can be individually accessed by typing "[corporation name] campaign contribution" into the database's search engine.)
Corporate–think tank interlock	Aggregate of three measures (higher values indicate increasing levels of interlocks): 1. Number of corporations that made financial donations, in any given year, to think tanks 2. Number of corporations in the data set that made financial donations to the same think tanks in a given year; captures the idea that increasing corporate connections through financial donations to the same think tanks increase the likelihood of corporate collusion in influencing think tank research and policy recommendations 3. Number of corporations, in a given year, whose board members are also think tank board members	McGann 2013, 2015
Corporate board member–think tank interlock	Number of corporate board members who are also board members of the think tanks in the data set; higher values indicate increasing levels of interlock	McGann 2013, 2015; annual reports of the 33 corporations included in this study

Table 4.1A. (continued)

Variable	Operationalization	Source
Corporate board member interlock	Number of corporate board members who are also board members of other corporations in the data set; higher values indicate increasing levels of interlock; given its skewed nature, this indicator is transformed as a natural log	Annual reports of the 33 corporations included in this study
Corporate-government interlock	Number of corporations in the data set whose board members held prior positions in the federal government or the military; captures the revolving door between corporations and the federal government; higher values indicate increasing interlock; given its skewed nature, this indicator is transformed as a natural log	Annual reports of the 33 corporations included in this study
Interlocking directorate	Compiled from the following variables (higher values indicate increasing levels interlock): 1. Corporate-government interlock 2. Corporate board member–think tank interlock 3. Corporate board member interlock	McGann 2013, 2015; annual reports of the 33 corporations included in this study. The data set and the coding rules that guided the construction of this variable and the variables it comprises are available from the author upon request.
Dependent variable		
Corporate revenues	Measured in millions of U.S. dollars	Annual reports of the 33 corporations included in this study
Main explanatory variables		
U.S. counternarcotic aid	Measured in millions of U.S. dollars; logged to improve the normality of its distribution	USAID n.d.
Prior levels of corporate revenues	A 1-year lag in the dependent variable: corporate revenues	
Average effective U.S. corporate tax rate	Average rate at which corporations are taxed on pretax revenues made in the U.S.	Hungerford 2013; Pomerleau 2014
Average effective foreign corporate tax rate	Average rate at which corporations are taxed on pretax revenues made in foreign countries	Hungerford 2013; Pomerleau 2014
Economic growth of drug-war aid-recipient countries	Countries' annual percentage growth rate of per-capita GDP at constant 2005 U.S. dollars	World Bank 2016

Chapter 6

Table 6.1A. Data measurements and sources

Variable	Operationalization	Source
Latent variable repression		
PTS	Ranges from level 1, where citizens' human rights are secure under the law, to level 5, where state repression is at its highest encompassing a country's entire population where leaders place no limits on the means through which they pursue personal and ideological goals	Gibney and Dalton 1996
CIRI physical integrity rights (rescaled)	For ease of statistical interpretation and to ensure that the direction of the scale is similar to the PTS, rescaled to range from 0, full government respect physical integrity rights, to 8, no government respect for these rights	Cingranelli and Richards 1999, 2010; Bartilow 2014
CIRI civil liberties index	An additive index constructed from the freedom of movement, freedom of speech, workers' rights, political participation, and freedom of religion indicators; for ease of statistical interpretation and to ensure the direction of the scale is similar to the PTS, it is rescaled to range from 0, full government respect for these five rights, to 10, no government respect for these rights	Cingranelli and Richards 1999, 2010; Bartilow 2014
Main explanatory variables		
U.S. counternarcotic aid	Measured in millions of U.S. dollars	USAID n.d.
U.S. FDI (foreign direct investment)	Measured in millions of U.S. dollars on a historical-cost basis	Bureau of Economic Analysis n.d.
Pro-government paramilitaries	For each country, for any given year, coded 1 if pro-government paramilitary groups are active, 0 otherwise	Carey et al. 2013
Control variables		
Independence of judiciary	Coded 0, nonindependent (judges experience significant executive influence or interference, or high levels of corruption); 1, somewhat independent (judges experience some executive pressure, with occasional reports of corruption); or 2, independent (judges are generally independent from outside influences, with no mention of corruption)	Keith 2011
Economic development	Countries' GDP per capita (Poe and Tate 1994; Henderson 1991, 130; Hibbs 1973, 25–26; Dye and Zeigler 1988, 48–49)	World Bank 2016

Table 6.1A. (*continued*)

Variable	Operationalization	Source
Population	Natural logarithm of countries' total national population (Poe and Tate 1994; Poe 1990, 1991; Poe et al. 1999; Mitchell and McCormick 1988)	World Bank 2016
Military regime	Governments that have come to power "as a consequence of a successful coup d'état, led by the army, navy or air force, that remained in power with a military person as the chief executive, for at least six months in a given year" (McKinlay and Cohan 1976, 61) The variable is coded 1 for a military regime (a regime that came to power via a successful coup d'état) and 0 otherwise	Marshall and Marshall 2018
Democracy	Measured by the Polity index; ranges from −10, regions with consolidated autocracies, to +10, regions with consolidated democracies	Marshall et al. 2013
Presence of narcoterror organizations	Coded 1 if a country has an indigenous narcoterrorist organization or international drug cartel, 0 otherwise	Gleditsch et al. 2002; various issues of the U.S. State Department's *International Narcotics Control Strategy Report (INCSR)*

Chapter 7

Table 7.1A. Data measurements and sources

Variable	Operationalization	Source
Dependent variables		
Illiberal democracy	Coded 1 if a country in any given year is an illiberal democracy, 0 otherwise	Data was adapted from Smith and Ziegler (2008, 51–52), for the years 1978 to 2004. This data was recoded and expanded to the year 2011 by the author using the same sources as Smith and Ziegler (2008). These included: the Freedom House index and the CIRI human rights index
Regime transitions	Three transition measures, coded as follows: 1. Toward greater democracy: coded 0 if there were no transitions in that year, or 1 if there was a transition that moved in the direction of liberal democracy 2. From illiberal to liberal democracy: coded 0 if there were no transitions in that year, or 1 if there was a transition from illiberal to liberal democracy 3. From liberal to illiberal democracy: coded 0 if there were no transitions in that year, or 1 if there was a transition from liberal to illiberal democracy	Data was adapted from Smith and Ziegler (2008, 53) for the years 1978 to 2004. This data was recoded and expanded to the year 2011 by the author using the same sources as Smith and Ziegler (2008). These included: the Freedom House index and the CIRI human rights index
Main explanatory variable		
U.S. counternarcotic aid	Measured in millions of U.S. dollars; logged to improve the normality of its distribution	USAID n.d.
Control variables		
Economic growth	Countries' annual growth rate of GDP at constant 2005 U.S. dollars	World Bank 2016
Economic development	Countries' per-capita GDP	World Bank 2016
Inflation	Countries' annual growth rate of the GDP deflator	World Bank 2016

Table 7.1A. (*continued*)

Variable	Operationalization	Source
Debt crisis	Proxies whether countries are under an IMF structural adjustment program; coded 1 if in any given year a country is under an IMF program, 0 otherwise	Adapted from Vreeland 2003, for the years 1978–1989 and extended to 1990–2011 using the IMF Annual Report, the same source used by Vreeland 2003.
Duration of military rule	Number of years a country was ruled by a military government	Calculated based on data from Keefer 2012
Presidential election	Percentage of population voting in the presidential election; larger percentages indicate citizens exercising their rights and increased participation in the political process	Adapted from Keefer 2012
Post–Cold War changes in U.S. geopolitical and economic interests	Coded 1 for post-Cold War years, 0 otherwise	
Prior experiences with illiberal democracy	A 1-year lag of the dependent variable: illiberal democracy	
Duration of democracy	Number of years a country has been an electoral democracy	Freedom House n.d.
Social upheavals	Coded 1 if in any given year a country experiences an organized nonviolent protest or an organized violent opposition against the government, 0 otherwise	Adapted from Keith 2011

Chapter 8

Table 8.1A. Data measurements and sources

Variable	Operationalization	Source
Dependent variables		
Income inequality in Latin America and the Caribbean	Gini index; ranges from 0, perfect equality, to 100, perfect inequality	World Bank 2016
Income inequality in the United States	Gini index; ranges from 0, perfect equality, to 100, perfect inequality	Atkinson and Morelli 2014
Percentage of Americans below the poverty line		Atkinson and Morelli 2014
Top 1% share of gross income in the United States		Atkinson and Morelli 2014

Table 8.1A. (*continued*)

Variable	Operationalization	Source
Top 0.1% share of gross income in the United States		Atkinson and Morelli 2014
Top decile as percentage of median income in the United States		Atkinson and Morelli 2014
Income inequality among white, black, Asian, or Hispanic Americans (individual variables)	Gini index for each of the four groups	U.S. Census Bureau 2018
Main explanatory variables		
U.S. counternarcotic aid	Measured in millions of U.S. dollars; logged to improve the normality of its distribution	USAID n.d.
CIRI workers rights index (rescaled)	Extent to which workers have freedom of association at their workplace, the right to engage in collective bargaining with their employers, and other internationally recognized rights at work; measured on a three-point scale, recoded for ease of interpretation: 0, rights are fully protected; 1, rights somewhat restricted, or 2, rights severely restricted	Cingranelli and Richards 1999
U.S. counternarcotic aid × rights of workers interaction	Computed by multiplying U.S. counternarcotic aid by CIRI workers rights index (rescaled)	
Federal government domestic drug control expenditures	Measured in millions of U.S. dollars; includes expenditures *only* for domestic law enforcement, interdiction, and crop eradication; excludes expenditures on drug treatment and education designed to reduce the demand for narcotics	Office of National Drug Control Policy n.d.
Control variables		
GDP annual growth	Annual percentage growth rate of countries' GDP at constant 2005 U.S. dollars	World Bank 2016; Barro 2000; Li et al. 1998; Gustafsson and Johansson 1999

Table 8.1A. (*continued*)

Variable	Operationalization	Source
International economic integration	The level of countries' integration into the international capitalist economy, measured in terms of the KOF Swiss Economic Institute (n.d.): • Provides a comprehensive measure of international economic integration based on trade, FDI, portfolio investment, and income payments to foreign nationals (all as a percentage of GDP), which proxies the extent to which countries employ foreigners in their productive processes • Also includes measures of the restrictions on trade and capital, using hidden import barriers, mean tariff rates, taxes on international trade (as a share of current revenues), and an index of capital controls Higher values indicate more international economic integration	Dreher 2006, 1092–93
Index of economic freedom	Based on 10 quantitative and qualitative factors, grouped into four categories: 1. Rule of law (measures for property rights and freedom from corruption) 2. Limited government (measures of fiscal freedom and government spending) 3. Regulatory efficiency (measures of regulation of capital markets, labor markets, and private business) 4. Open markets (measures of trade freedom, investment freedom, and financial freedom) Each of the ten economic freedoms is graded on a scale of 0 to 100, then averaged to produce a country's overall score; higher values indicate greater levels of economic freedom.	Heritage Foundation 2016

Table 8.1A. (*continued*)

Variable	Operationalization	Source
Democracy	Measured by the Polity index, ranging from −10, regions with consolidated autocracies, to +10, regions with consolidated democracies	Marshall et al. 2013
Central explanatory variables in the SEM		
Rate of incarceration	Number of sentenced prisoners in state and federal prisons, per 100,000 persons.	Carson and Mulako-Wangota n.d.
Corporate lobbying expenditures	Total yearly corporate congressional lobbying expenditures reported on the lobbyists' disclosure forms filed with the clerk of the House of Representatives	Open Secrets: Center for Responsible Politics, "Lobbying Database."
Corporate revenues	Measured in millions of U.S. dollars	Annual reports for 2000–2012 for the 33 corporations represented in the study
Percentage of Americans below the poverty line		Atkinson and Morelli 2014
Federal government domestic drug control expenditures	Measured in millions of U.S. dollars; includes expenditures *only* for domestic law enforcement, interdiction, and crop eradication; excludes expenditures on drug treatment and education, designed to reduce the demand for narcotics	Office of National Drug Control Policy n.d.

Graph 8A. Annual GDP growth and income inequality in Latin America.
Source: Author-generated LOWESS scatter plot of data from World Bank 2016.

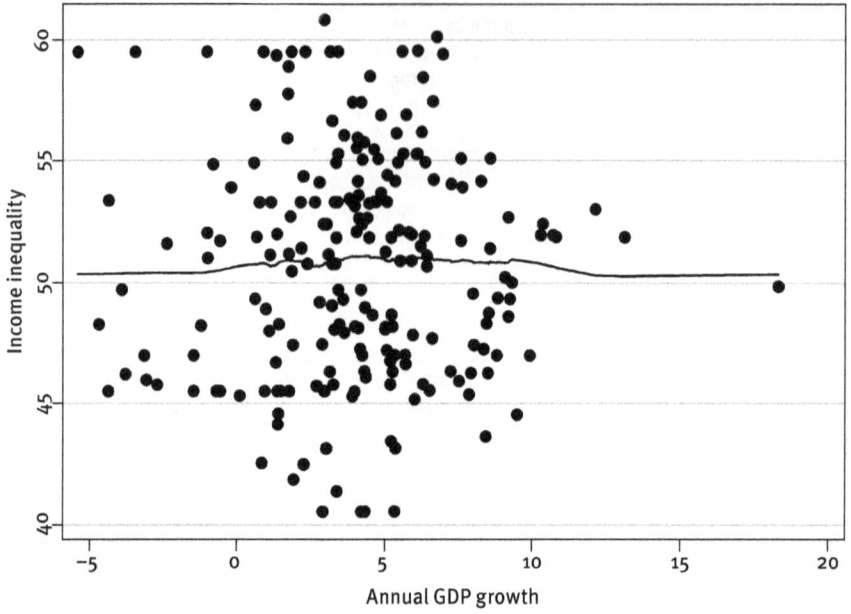

Chapter 1

1. It is important to acknowledge that other global powers, such as the European Union (discussed in chapter 3; see table 3.2A in the data appendix), and other countries, such as Canada and the United Kingdom, have enacted policies that promote the drug prohibition regime.

2. See Table 1.1A in the data appendix. The data appendix contains a full description of all the variables that are used in this study and how they are measured.

3. The measurements and sources of all the indicators used in this study are discussed in the data appendix.

4. Not all repression is a consequence of government's drug enforcement policies in the region, and this analysis does not pretend to account for all repression that is exogenous of the drug war, but as chapter 7 demonstrates, repression is also endogenous to countries in the region.

Chapter 2

1. Vice President Gore avoided federal ethics laws that safeguard against conflicts of interest by claiming that he was merely acting as executor of Occidental Petroleum stocks whose proceeds went to his mother. See Electronic Code of Federal Regulations, 2018.

2. In 2010, BAE Systems "pleaded guilty to knowingly and willfully . . . providing false statements to circumvent U.S. export laws and to defraud the U.S. Government" and was fined U.S. $400 million (U.S. Department of Justice 2010).

Chapter 3

1. The theoretical rationale that guides the sample selection of the corporations included in the data analysis is discussed in the data appendix. Table 3.3A in the data appendix provides a list of the thirty-three corporations in the sample and a summary of their policy preferences for supporting counternarcotic aid flows. Table 3.2A in the data appendix lists countries included in the data set. The availability of relevant data (corporate lobbying expenditures and important control variables) limits the analyses to the years 2003–12.

2. In chapter 4, I show how corporate funding and leadership of think tanks influence their policy reports that consistently support drug prohibition.

3. Maximum likelihood estimation was used to generate estimates in the first-stage, selection equation and produced the nonselection hazard rate or the reciprocal of the Mills ratio, which represents "the instantaneous probability of being excluded from the sample

conditional upon being in the pool at risk" (Berk 1983, 391). The second-stage equation was estimated by ordinary least squares, and the hazard rate was added as a variable. The Heckman estimator provides consistent estimates for the second-stage amount equation by normalizing the mean of the errors to zero and allowed the error terms of the first-stage and second-stage equations to be correlated.

4. Based on my calculations; see table 3.2A in the data appendix for the list of trade and bilateral investment agreements with the United States.

5. Table 3.1A in the data appendix contains a full description of all the variables used in this chapter and how they were measured.

6. Regression analyses also assumed that the error terms for different observations were uncorrelated, and therefore, including organizational inertia, which is a one-year lag in U.S. counternarcotic aid, in the second-stage equation also controlled for autocorrelation in the error term (Baltagi 2005, 12; Berry 1993).

7. Predicted probabilities of the selection equation were generated by STATA's Margins command.

Chapter 4

1. The term *military-industrial complex* refers to the interconnected interests of legislators, the military, and defense contractors for maintaining high levels of military spending. President Dwight D. Eisenhower popularized the term in his farewell address to the American people on January 17, 1961, in which he warned the public that the collusion of these groups threatens democracy. See Eisenhower 1961.

2. My calculations of data taken from these think tanks, which rank among the top ten think tanks in the world (McGann 2013, 2015), are used to illustrate the interlocking corporate directorate.

3. The names and biographical information of the individuals represented in figures 4.1–4.4 are available from the author upon request.

4. Corporate campaign contribution data for the thirty-three corporations in the data set were extracted from the Center for Responsible Politics. Table 4.1A in the data appendix provides a full description of how corporate campaign contributions were measured.

5. Data used in the construction of corporate–think tank interlocks, corporate-government interlocks, and an interlocking directorate were extracted from the yearly annual reports of the thirty-three corporations in the data set, as well as from the yearly annual reports of the think tanks ranked as the world's ten most influential (McGann 2013, 2015). Table 4.1A in the data appendix describes how these variables were measured.

6. An Excel spreadsheet that contains the results for the Plan Colombia votes is available at http://www.drcnet.org/wol/july23-yesno.xls.

7. House members who voted no who received campaign contributions from corporations that lobbied for Plan Colombia include Bud Cramer (D-AL), Ellen Tauscher (D-CA), Gene Taylor (D-MS), Jo Bonner (R-AL), Terry Everett (R-AL), Dennis Hastert (R-IL), Ernie Fletcher (R-KY), Cass Ballenger (R-NC), and Paul Ryan (R-WI). A list of these names is available at http://www.drcnet.org/wol/july23-yesno.xls. A list of the corporations that provided campaign contributions is available at https://www.opensecrets.org/members -ofcongress/contributors?cid=N00003350&cycle=2002&type=I. This information can be

accessed by typing the name of the individual House member, contributors, and the 2002 electoral cycle in the search bar.

8. See table 3.3A in the data appendix for a list of American corporations that lobbied against the decertification of Colombia. All these companies are members of the U.S.-Colombia Business Partnership, a corporate consortium that promotes U.S. business interests in Colombia.

9. Table 4.1A in the data appendix describes how these variables are measured.

10. Regression analysis also assumed that the error term for different observations are uncorrelated, and therefore, including prior corporate revenues, which represents a one-year lag in corporate revenues, also controls for autocorrelation in the error term (Baltagi 2005, 12; Berry 1993).

11. Because of space constraints, fixed effects estimates for differences in country and corporations are not shown in tables 4.5 and 4.6. They are available from the author upon request.

Chapter 5

1. Social infrastructure is a subset of the infrastructure sector and typically includes assets that accommodate social services. Social infrastructure assets include schools, universities, hospitals, prisons, and community housing.

2. See the data appendix for a description of the measurements for U.S. FDI and U.S. counternarcotic aid and the sources from which these indicators were adopted.

3. While dependency theory as an explanation for developing countries' relations with the international capitalist economy is widely viewed as outdated, it remains a useful theoretical alternative to neoclassical liberal theories of repression and is used here and in chapter 6 as a theoretical framework to analyze how transnational corporations interact with domestic political actors to affect human rights repression in developing countries.

Chapter 6

1. Table 6.1A in the data appendix describes how all the variables in this chapter were measured.

2. Data on U.S. FDI in the petroleum and mining industries are available from the U.S. Department of Commerce. See Bureau of Economic Analysis. "U.S. Direct Investment Abroad." However, petroleum and mining data are missing for most years for 50 percent and 40 percent, respectively, of the countries in the data set because conglomerates in these industries choose to suppress information to avoid disclosing data for individual companies.

3. In the previous section I argued that paramilitary organizations are reliable proxies for the military since, in many instances, these organizations are often created and given logistical and financial support by countries' militaries.

Chapter 7

1. The Latinobarómetro is available from 1995 for Argentina, Bolivia, Brazil, Chile, Colombia, Costa Rica, The Dominican Republic, Ecuador, El Salvador, Guatemala, Honduras, Mexico, Nicaragua, Panama, Paraguay, Peru, Uruguay, and Venezuela. Data are not available for Caribbean countries. See Latinobarómetro 1995.

2. The regional averages and graphs are the author's calculations. For the complete database see World Bank, "Intentional Homicides (per 1000,000 people)."

3. See the Drug Abuse Act of 1986 (P.L.99-570), Foreign Operations Appropriations for FY 2002 (HR. 2506/P.L. 107-115), and Foreign Operations Appropriations for FY 2003 (H.R. 1646/P.L. 107-228).

4. Table 7.1A in the data appendix describes how the dependent and contextual variables are measured.

5. The dependent variable was lagged to control for autocorrelation in the error term (Baltagi 2005, 12; Berry 1993).

6. Table 7.1A in the data appendix describes how the dependent and contextual variables were measured. Also following Smith and Ziegler (2008), a lagged dependent variable was not used in regime transitions models as autocorrelation poses less of a problem when estimating rare event data. However, to make sure that the reported results were not affected by autocorrelation, robustness checks were performed using the lagged dependent variable, and the results did not change. These estimates are available from the author upon request.

7. Rare event logit is used to estimate the data because regime transitions are infrequently occurring events, and under these conditions logistic regression will sharply underestimate the probability of such events and will produce bias. The rare events method significantly outperforms traditional logistic regression in estimating rare events data (King and Zeng 2001a, 2001b).

Chapter 8

1. Table 8.1A in the data appendix describes how the dependent and contextual variables were measured.

2. Since there is no variation in the Polity indicator for the United States, it is not included in models that provide estimates of the drug war's effect on income inequality in the United States.

3. Because of space constraints, the estimates with year and country fixed effects in model 3 are not shown. These are available from the author upon request.

4. In tables 8.2 and 8.3 the dependent variable is not lagged. Achen (2000) has shown that estimates will be biased where serial correlation is present in the main variable of theoretical interest (federal drug enforcement expenditure) and when this variable and other exogenous variables in the model are seriously trended. Achen (2000, 7) concludes that "when a lagged dependent variable is entered into a regression equation with serial correlation, it acts as a proxy, picking up some of the effects of unmeasured variables. However, the autoregressive term does not conduct itself like a decent, well-behaved proxy. Instead, it is a kleptomaniac, picking up the effect, not only of excluded variables, but also included variables if they are sufficiently trended. As a result, the impact of the included substantive variables is reduced, sometimes to insignificance." Consequently, three tests for serial correlation was conducted and in all tests, when federal drug enforcement expenditure is lagged by 1 or 2 years the statistically significant p-values indicate that serial correlation is indeed present. In addition, time series plots of federal drug enforcement expenditure, index of economic globalization, and index of economic freedom show that these variables are heavily trended upward. These results are available from the author upon request.

5. All the goodness-of-fit statistics that support the findings in table 8.5 are excellent and similar to those reported in table 8.4.

Chapter 9

1. Even when banking executives did not knowingly launder drug proceeds, Mexican cartels, according to the FBI, have used Bank of America accounts to invest drug money in the U.S. horse-racing industry (Fitzpatrick 2012).

2. Attorney General Jeff Sessions's directive to end the Obama-era "safe harbor" federal policy has been recently undercut by President Trump's own directive that the Justice Department would not prosecute marijuana infractions in states where the drug is legal for both medical and recreational use, effectively continuing the Obama-era safe harbor marijuana policy. In fact, President Trump has been assuring congressional lawmakers in these states that the Department of Justice's rescission of the Cole memo outlining the Obama-era safe harbor policy will not impact the legal marijuana industry and that he supports a federal-based legislative solution to this issue, which he considers to be the rights of states (Smith 2018).

Abbott, Jeff. 2014. "Mayan Q'eqchi' Communities Violently Evicted in Alta Verapaz, Guatemala." Upside Down World, September 16. http://upsidedownworld.org/main /guatemala-archives-33/5048-mayan-qeqchi-communities-violoently-evicted-in -alta-verapaz-guatemala.

———. 2015. "Indigenous Campesinos in Guatemala Demand an End to Violent Evictions." Upside Down World, April 27. http://upsidedownworld.org/main/guatemala -archives-33/5303-indigenous-campesinos-in-guatemala-demand-an-end-to-violent -evictions.

ABColombia. 2010. *Caught in the Crossfire: Colombia's Indigenous Peoples*. London: ABColombia, October 31. https://www.abcolombia.org.uk/caught-crossfire-colombias -indigenous-peoples/.

———. 2011. "Mandé Norte Mining Project in Embera Indigenous Peoples Land." August 31. https://www.abcolombia.org.uk/mande-norte-mining-project-embera -indigenous-peoples-land/.

Achen, Christopher H. 2000. "Why Lagged Dependent Variables Can Suppress the Explanatory Power of Other Independent Variables." Paper presented at the annual meeting of the American Political Science Association, Political Methodology Section, Los Angeles, CA, July 20–22.

Akinkugbe, Oluyele. 2004. "Flow of Foreign Direct Investment in Developing Countries: A Two-Part Econometric Modelling Approach." In *External Finance for Private Sector Development: Appraisals and Issues*, edited by M. Odedokun, 180–206. London: Palgrave Macmillan.

———. 2005. "A Two-Part Econometric Analysis of Foreign Direct Investment Flows into Africa." *Journal of World Trade* 35 (5): 907–23.

Akinkugbe, Oluyele, and Pender Gbenedio. 2004. "Explaining Foreign Direct Investment Flows to Developing Countries." *Business Review, Cambridge* 3 (1): 219–26.

Alexander, Michelle. 2012. *The New Jim Crow: Mass Incarceration in the Age of Colorblindness*. New York: New Press.

Alfa Bank. 2003. "Proctor and Gamble Russia—Key Facts." July 28. https://alfabank.com /news/procter-gamble-russia-key-facts/.

Allison, Graham. 1969. "Conceptual Models of the Cuban Missile Crisis." *American Political Science Review* 63 (3): 869–718.

———. 1971. *Essence of Decision: Explaining the Cuban Missile Crisis*. Boston: Little, Brown.

Alsema, Adriaan. 2015. *Colombia Government Asks for Forgiveness for 1988 Paramilitary Massacre.* Medellín, Colombia: Colombia Reports, December 21. https://colombia reports.com/160585-2/.

Ambito.com. 2014. "Corte de EEUU rechazó demanda contra automotriz por desaparecidos." January 14. https://www.ambito.com/corte-eeuu-rechazo-demanda-contra -automotriz-desaparecidos-n3824383.

Ambrosio, Tara-Jen, and Vincent Schiraldi. 1997. *From Classrooms to Cell Blocks: A National Perspective.* Washington, DC: Justice Policy Institute.

American Medical Association. 2009. *AMA Policy: Medical Marijuana.* Chicago: American Medical Association.

American Watch Report. 1990. *The "Drug War" in Colombia: The Neglected Tragedy of Political Violence.* New York: Human Rights Watch.

Amin, Samir. 1977. "Capitalism, State Collectivism and Socialism." *Monthly Review* 29 (2): 25–41.

Amnesty International. 2010. "U.S. Policy in Colombia." http://www.amnestyusa.org /our-work/countries/americas/colombia/us-policy-in-colombia. Accessed June 10, 2015.

Amnesty International, and Fellowship of Reconciliation. 2008. *Assisting Units That Commit Extrajudicial Killings: A Call to Investigate US Military Policy toward Colombia.* New York: Amnesty International.

Andreas, Peter, and Ethan Avram Nadelmann. 2006. *Policing the Globe: Criminalization and Crime Control in International Relations.* Oxford: Oxford University Press.

Apodaca, Clair. 2001. "Global Economic Patterns and Personal Integrity Rights after the Cold War." *International Studies Quarterly* 45 (4): 587–602.

Archibold, Randal C. 2013. "In Americas, Resistance to Legal Marijuana." *New York Times,* June 6.

Arias, Enrique Desmond, and Daniel M. Goldstein, eds. 2010. *Violent Democracies in Latin America.* Durham, NC: Duke University Press.

Arlacchi, Pinto. 1986. *Mafia Business: The Mafia Ethic and the Spirit of Capitalism.* London: Verso.

Associated Press. 2009. "Mexico Legalizes Drug Possession." *New York Times,* August 21.

Atkinson, Anthony B., and Salvatore Morelli. 2014. *Chartbook of Economic Inequality.* Oxford: Society for the Study of Economic Inequality. http://www.chartbookof economicinequality.com.

Aviles, William. 2006. *Global Capitalism, Democracy, and Civil Military Relations in Colombia.* Edited by J. N. Rsenau. Albany: State University of New York Press.

Azarvan, Amir. 2009. "Investing in Repression? Foreign Direct Investment and Human Rights in Poorer Countries." PhD diss., Georgia State. University.

Bacon, David. 2012. "Canadian Mining Goliaths Devastate Mexican Indigenous Communities and Environment." Truth-Out.Org, July 25. http://www.truth-out.org/news /item/10501-canadian-mining-goliaths-devastate-mexican-indigenous-communities -and-environment.

BAE Systems. 2015. "BAE Systems U.S. Board of Directors." http://www.baesystems.com /our-company-rus/bae-systems-inc-rus/inc-board-of-directors. Accessed April 3, 2015.

Baken, Abigail B., David Cox, and Colin Leys, eds. 1993. *Imperial Power and Regional Trade: The Caribbean Basin Initiative.* Waterloo, ON: Wilfrid Laurier University Press.

Baker, David R. 2013. "Chuck Hagel's Chevron Tie Not Criticized." SFGate, January 15. http://www.sfgate.com/business/article/Chuck-Hagel-s-Chevron-tie-not-criticized -4197225.php.

Baker, Peter. 2009. "Obama to Use Current Law to Support Detentions." *New York Times*, September 23.

Ballvé, Teo. 2011. "Territory by Dispossession: Decentralization, Statehood, and the Narco Land-Grab in Colombia." Paper Presented at the 65th Annual International Conference on Global Land Grabbing, April 6–8, University of Sussex, UK: Land Deals Politics Initiative, 1–21.

Baltagi, Badi H. 2005. *Econometric Analysis of Panel Data*. 3rd ed. New York: Wiley.

Baram, Marcus. 2010. "Fear Pays: Chertoff, Ex-Security Officials Slammed for Cashing In on Government Experience." *Huffington Post*, November 23. http://www.huffington post.com/2010/11/23/fear_pays_chertoff_n_787711.html.

Barlett, Donald L., and James B. Steele. 2007. "Washington's $8 Billion Shadow." *Vanity Fair*, February 6. http://www.vanityfair.com/news/2007/03/spyagency200703.

Barro, Robert J. 2000. "Inequality and Growth in a Panel of Countries." *Journal of Economic Growth* 5 (1): 5–32.

Bartilow, Horace A. 1997. *The Debt Dilemma: IMF Negotiations in Jamaica, Grenada and Guyana*. London: Macmillan Caribbean.

———. 2000. "Compliance under C-Type Coercive Diplomacy: Theoretical Insights from Haiti, 1991–1994." *Journal of Conflict Studies* 20 (1): 74–104.

———. 2001. "Diplomatic Victory Misunderstood: A Two Level Game Analysis of U.S. Policy Toward Haiti." *Security Studies* 10 (3): 115–52.

———. 2007. "Does Drug Enforcement Reduce Crime? An Empirical Analysis of the Drug War in Central America and Caribbean Countries." In *Crime, Delinquency and Justice: A Caribbean Reader*, edited by R. Deosaran, 555–77. Kingston, Jamaica: Ian Randle.

———. 2014. "Drug Wars Collateral Damage: US Counternarcotic Aid and Human Rights in the Americas." *Latin American Research Review* 49 (2): 24–46.

Bartilow, Horace, and Kihong Eom. 2009a. "Busting Drugs While Paying with Crime: The Collateral Damage of U.S. Drug Enforcement in Foreign Countries." *Foreign Policy Analysis* 5 (2): 93–116.

———. 2009b. "Free Traders and Drug Smugglers: Does Trade Openness Weaken or Strengthen States' Ability to Combat Drug Trafficking?" *Latin American Politics and Society* 51 (2): 117–45.

———. 2012. "Shirkers and Drug Runners: The Limits of U.S.-Bilateral Counter-narcotics Cooperation in the Caribbean Basin." *National Political Science Review* 14: 57–77.

Baumgartner, Frank R., Jeffery M. Berry, Marie Hojnacki, David C. Kimball, and Beth L. Leech. 2009. *Lobbying and Policy Change: Who Wins, Who Loses, and Why*. Chicago: University of Chicago Press.

BBC News. 2010. "Canadian Mining Firm Sued over Role in DR Congo Conflict." BBC News Service, November 10. https://www.bbc.com/news/world-africa-11725651.

Bedoya, Nicholas. 2014. "Why Drummond and Glencore Are Accused of Exporting Colombian Blood Coal." Colombia Reports, July 2. http://colombiareports.com /drummond-glencore-blood-coal/.

Beittel, June S. 2012. *Colombia: Background, and U.S. Relations, Congressional Interest.* Washington, DC: Congressional Research Service.

Bell, Larry. 2013. "The Greening of Gore's Bank Account." *Forbes*, May 21. http://www.forbes.com/sites/larrybell/2013/05/21/the-greening-of-gores-bank -account/.

Bennett, Wells C., and John Walsh. 2014. *Marijuana Legalization Is an Opportunity to Modernize International Drug Treaties.* Washington, DC: Brookings Institution, Center for Effective Public Management.

Bergen, Peter. 2012. "Drone Is Obama's Weapon of Choice." CNN, September 19. http://www.cnn.com/2012/09/05/opinion/bergen-obama-drone/.

Berk, Richard. 1983. "An Introduction to Sample Selection Bias in Sociological Data." *American Sociological Review* 48: 386–97.

Berle, Adolph A. 1963. *The American Economic Republic.* New York: Harcourt, Brace and World.

Berry, William D. 1993. *Understanding Regression Assumptions.* Edited by M. S. Lewis-Beck. Newbury Park, CA: Sage.

Berry, William, and Stanley Feldman. 1985. *Multiple Regression in Practice.* Beverly Hills, CA: Sage.

Bertram, Eva, Morris Blachman, Kenneth Sharpe, and Peter Andreas. 1996. *Drug War Politics: The Price of Denial.* Berkeley: University of California Press.

Bevan, Anna-Claire. 2013. "Tortured, Killed and Branded a 'Terrorist'—for Being a Trade Unionist in Guatemala." Equaltimes.org. http://www.equaltimes.org/tortured-killed -and-branded-a?lang=en#.VwWC-MegPHQ. Accessed April 17, 2013.

Bhavan, T. 2014. "Effectiveness of Foreign Aid in Facilitating Foreign Direct Investment: Evidence from Four South Asian Countries." *Asian Economic and Financial Review* 4 (12): 1770–83.

Bhavan, T., Changsheng Xu, and Chunping Zhong. 2011. "The Relationship between Foreign Aid and FDI in South Asian Economies." *International Journal of Economics and Finance* 3 (2): 143–49.

Blanton, Shannon Lindsey. 2000. "Promoting Human Rights and Democracy in the Developing World: U.S. Rhetoric versus U.S. Arms Exports." *American Journal of Political Science* 44 (1): 123–31.

———. 2005. "Foreign Policy in Transition? Human Rights, Democracy, and U.S. Arms Exports." *International Studies Quarterly* 49 (4): 647–67.

Blanton, Shannon L., and Robert Banton. 2007. "What Attracts Foreign Investors? An Examination of Human Rights and Foreign Direct Investment." *Journal of Politics* 69 (1): 143–55.

———. 2009. "A Sectoral Analysis of Human Rights and FDI: Does Industry Type Matter?" *International Studies Quarterly* 53 (2): 469–93.

Blasi, Gerald J., and David L. Cingranelli. 1997. "Do Constitutions and Institutions Help Protect Human Rights?" In *Human Rights and Developing Countries*, edited by D. L. Cingranelli, 125–46. Greenwich, CT: JAI Press.

Bluestone, Barry, and Bennett Harrison. 1982. *The Deindustrialization of America: Plant Closings, Community Abandonment, and the Dismantling of Basic Industry.* New York: Basic Books.

Bohoslavsky, Juan Pablo, and Veerle Opgenhaffen. 2010. "The Past and Present of Corporate Complicity: Financing the Argentinean Dictatorship." *Harvard Human Rights Journal* 23: 157–203.

Bonner, Robert C. 2010. "The New Cocaine Cowboys: How to Defeat Mexico's Drug Cartels." *Foreign Affairs* 89 (4): 35–47.

———. 2012. "The Cartel Crackdown: Wining the Drug War and Rebuilding Mexico in the Process." *Foreign Affairs* 91 (3): 12–16.

Bonner, Robert C., and Gillian Horton. 2015. "Get Shorty: After Catching El Chapo, Mexico Should Extradite Him to the United States." *Foreign Affairs* 90 (2): 1–5.

Booth, William, and Steve Fainaru. 2009. "U.S. Drug Aid Delays in Drug War Criticized." *Washington Post*, April 5. http://www.washingtonpost.com/wp-dyn/content/article/2009/04/04/AR2009040402593.html?sid=ST2009040402864.

Boswell, Terry, and William J. Dixon. 1990. "Dependency and Rebellion: A Cross-National Analysis." *American Sociological Review* 55 (4): 540–59.

Bricker, Kristin. 2009. "Plan Mexico: U.S. Congress Abandons Human Rights Posturing in Favor of Black Hawk Helicopters." *Narco News*, May 12. http://narcosphere.narco news.com/notebook/kristin-bricker/2009/05/plan-mexico-us-congress-abandons-human-rights-posturing-favor-black.

Brinded, Lianna. 2013. "HSBC Tackles Money Laundering Scandal with Former US Deputy Attorney General Hire." *International Business Times*, January 30. http://www.ibtimes.co.uk/hsbc-james-brien-comey-jr-money-laundering-429453.

Briody, Dan. 2004. *The Halliburton Agenda: The Politics of Oil and Money*. Hoboken, NJ: Wiley.

Brookings Institution. 2014. *Brookings: Annual Report 2014*. Edited by R. Moore and H. Gibbs. Washington, DC: Brookings Institution.

Brown, William O., Eric Helland, and Janet Kiholm Smith. 2006. "Corporate Philanthropic Practices." *Journal of Corporate Finance* 12: 855–77.

Brownfield, William R. 2007. "Endorsement Memo for Director of U.S. Foreign Assistance Henrietta Fore." Bogota, Colombia: U.S. Embassy.

Brumley, James. 2018. "Ten Companies Making Huge Stock Buybacks in 2018." *Kiplinger*, March 5. https://www.kiplinger.com/slideshow/investing/T052-S001-10-companies-making-huge-stock-buybacks-in-2018/index.html.

Brzezinski, Zbigniew. 1983. *Power and Principle: Memoirs of the National Security Adviser, 1977–1981*. New York: Farrar Straus and Giroux.

Bureau of Economic Analysis. n.d. "U.S. Direct Investment Abroad: Balance of Payments and Direct Investment Position Data." http://www.bea.gov/international/di1usdbal.htm. Accessed June 20, 2015.

Burfisher, Mary E., Sherman Robinson, and Karen Thierfelder. 2001. "The Impact of NAFTA on the United States." *Journal of Economic Perspectives* 15 (1): 125–44.

Busse, Matthias, Peter Nunnenkamp, and Mariana Spatareanu. 2011. "Foreign Direct Investment and Labor Rights: A Panel Analysis of Bilateral FDI Flows." *Applied Economics Letters* 18 (2): 149–52.

C. S. Mott Children's Hospital. 2011. *National Poll on Children's Health: Drug Abuse Now Equals Childhood Obesity as Top Health Concern for Kids*. Ann Arbor: University of Michigan.

Caldeira, Teresa P. R. 2000. *City of Walls: Crime, Segregation, and Citizenship in Sao Paulo.* Berkeley: University of California Press.

Caldeira, Teresa P. R., and James Holston. 1999. "Democracy and Violence in Brazil." *Comparative Studies in Society and History* 41 (4): 691–729.

Calleros, Juan Carlos. 2009. *The Unfinished Transition to Democracy in Latin America.* New York: Routledge.

Campbell, Bonnie. 2006. "Good Governance, Security and Mining in Africa." *Minerals and Energy—Raw Materials Report* 21 (1): 31–44.

Campbell, James E. 2015. *The Presidential Pulse of Congressional Elections.* Lexington: University Press of Kentucky.

Caracol Radio. 2012. "Fiscalía tiene listas 19 acusaciones contra palmicultores por desplazamiento forzado." Colombia Reports, July 30. http://www.caracol.com.co /noticias/judiciales/fiscalia-tiene-listas-19-acusaciones-contra-palmicultores-por -desplazamiento-forzado/20120730/nota/1732208.aspx.

Cardoso, Fernado Henrique. 1972. "Dependency and Development in Latin America." *New Left Review* 74: 83–95.

Cardoso, Fernado Henrique, and Enzo Faletto. 1973. *Dependencia e dessenvolvimento na America Latina: Ensaio de interpretacao sociologica.* Rio de Janeiro: Editora Zahar.

Carey, John M., and Mathew Soberg Shugart. 1998. *Executive Decree.* Cambridge: Cambridge University Press.

Carey, Sabine C., Neil J. Mitchell, and Will Lowe. 2013. "States, the Security Sector, and

Carnegie Endowment for International Peace. 2014. "Contributors and Funders 2014." http://carnegieendowment.org/about/development/index.cfm?fa=funders. Accessed March 3, 2015.

Carson, E. Ann. 2014. *Prisoners in 2013.* Washington, DC: U.S. Department of Justice.

———. 2015. *Prisoners in 2014.* Washington, DC: U.S. Department of Justice.

Carson, E. Ann, and William J. Sabol. 2012. *Prisoners in 2011.* Washington, DC: U.S. Department of Justice.

Carson, E. Ann, and Joseph Mulako-Wangota. Bureau of Justice Statistics. n.d. Imprison-ment Rates of Total Jurisdiction Population, 2000–2012. Generated using the Correc-tions Statistical Analysis Tool (CSAT)—Prisoners. https://www.bjs.gov/index.cfm?ty =nps. Accessed July, 7, 2015.

Catton, William Robert. 1982. *Overshoot: The Ecological Basis of Revolutionary Change.* Champaign: University of Illinois.

Caulfield, Norman. 2010. *NAFTA and Labor in North America.* Urbana: University of Illinois Press.

Caulkins, Jonathan P. 2000. *Do Drug Prohibition and Enforcement Work?* Santa Monica, CA: RAND Corporation.

Cave, Damien. 2012. "South America Sees Drug Path to Legalization." *New York Times,* July 29.

Center for International Policy's Latin America Security Program. 2003. *Report to Congress, Certain Counternarcotic Activities in Colombia.* Submitted to the Congress by the Secretary of State Pursuant to Section 694 (b) of the Foreign Relations Authori-zation Act, PL 107-228, Fiscal Year 2003, April 14. https://adamisacson.com/files /old_cip_colombia/03041401.htm.

Center for Responsive Politics. 2000a. "Corporate Lobbying on Latin America Jan. 1, 1996 through Dec. 31, 2000." http://www.public-i.org/Latam_Wash_tables.htm. Accessed March 5, 2015.

———. 2000b. "Top Contributors to Federal Election Campaigns 1995 to 2000." http://www.public-i.org/Latam_Wash_tables.htm. Accessed March 5, 2015.

Center for Strategic and International Studies. 2016. "Corporation and Trade Donors." http://csis.org/support-csis/our-donors/corporations. Accessed March 4, 2016.

Central Intelligence Agency. 1986. *Bolivia: The Impact of Blast Furnace.* Washington, DC: CIA.

Centro de Información Judicial. 2013. "Lesa humanidad: Procesaron a ex directivos de la empresa Ford 2016." May 21. http://www.cij.gov.ar/nota-11452-Lesa-humanidad--procesaron-a-ex-directivos-de-la-empresa-Ford.html.

Chaiken, Jan M., and Marcia R. Chaiken. 1982. *Varieties of Criminal Behavior.* Santa Monica, CA: RAND Corporation.

Chalk, Peter. 2011. *The Latin American Drug Trade: Scope, Dimensions, Impact and Response.* Santa Monica, CA: RAND Project Air Force.

Chen, Winny. 2010. Ties That Bind: *U.S.-Taiwan Relations and Peace and Prosperity in East Asia.* Washington, DC: Center for American Progress.

Chevron Corporation. 2015. "Kazakhstan Fact Sheet." Almaty, Kazakhstan: Chevron Eurasia Business Unit.

Chicaiza, Gloria, and Willi Hass. 2013. "The Mining Enclave of the Cordillers del Condor." In *Ecological Economics from the Ground Up: Keep the Oil in the Soil and the Coal in the Hole,* edited by H. Healy, J. Martinez-Alier, L. Temper, M. Walter, and J. -F. Gerber, 55–80. New York: Routledge.

Cingranelli, David L., and Thomas E. Pasquarello. 1985. "Human Rights Practices and the Distribution of U.S. Foreign Aid to Latin American Countries." *American Journal of Political Science* 29 (3): 539–63.

Cingranelli, David L., and David L. Richards. 1999. "Measuring the Level, Pattern, and Sequence of Government Respect for Physical Integrity Rights." *International Studies Quarterly* 43 (2): 407–18. http://www.humanrightsdata.com/p/data-documentation.html.

———. 2014. "The Cingranelli-Richards (CIRI) Human Rights Data Project Coding Manual Version." May 20. https://drive.google.com/file/d/0BxDpF6GQ-6fbWkpxTDZCQ01jYnc/edit.

———. 2010. "The Cingranelli and Richards (CIRI) Human Rights Data Project." *Human Rights Quarterly* 32: 395–418.

Claps, Luis Manuel. 2013. "Peru: Police Abuse in the Pay of Mining Companies." North American Congress on Latin America, December 16. https://nacla.org/blog/2013/12/16/peru-police-abuse-pay-mining-companies.

———. 2014. "Police Repression Legalized as Mining Protests Grow in Peru." North American Congress on Latin America, February 13. https://nacla.org/blog/2014/2/13/police-repression-legalized-mining-protests-grow-peru.

Colectivo de Abogados José Alvear Restrepo. 2007. "Fiscalia general de la nación, frente al caso de Jorge Noguera Cotes ex director del DAS, debe actuar con decisión y celeridad." *Afiliaciones,* June 20. http://www.colectivodeabogados.org/FISCALIA-GENERAL-DE-LA-NACION.

Collier, Robert. 2000. "Costly Drug War Backed by Fragile Consensus." *San Francisco Chronicle*, December 20.

Confessore, Nicholas, Sarah Cohen, and Karen Yourish. 2015. "Buying Power: The Families Funding the 2016 Presidential Election." *New York Times*, October 10.

Cook, Collen W., and Clare Ribando Seelke. 2008. *Mérida Initiative: Proposed U.S. Anti-crime and Counterdrug Assistance for Mexico and Central America*. Washington, DC: Congressional Research Service.

Coordinator for the Rights of Indigenous Peoples. 2014. "Another Massacre of Indigenous People in Guatemala." Upside Down World, October 2. http://upsidedownworld.org /archives/guatemala/another-massacre-of-indigenous-people-in-guatemala/.

CorpWatch. 2002. "Latin America: Enron Fallout Is a Hot Issue." March 4. http://www .corpwatch.org/article.php?id=1949.

Council on Foreign Relations. 2015. *2015 Annual Report*. New York: Council on Foreign Relations.

Council on Hemispheric Affairs. 2014. "Violence in Mexico and Latin America." http:// www.coha.org/violence-in-mexico-and-latin-america/. Accessed March 18, 2014.

Crandall, Russell. 2008a. *Driven by Drugs: U.S. Policy toward Colombia*. 2nd ed. Boulder, CO: Lynne Rienner.

———. 2008b. *The United States and Latin America after the Cold War*. Cambridge: Cambridge University Press.

Crawford, G. B., Peter Reuter, K. Isaacson, and P. Murphy. 1988. *Simulation of Adaptive Response: A Model of Drug Interdiction*. Santa Monica, CA: RAND Corporation.

Cross, Frank B. 1999. "The Relevance of Law in Human Rights Protection." *International Review of Law and Economics* 19: 87–98.

Cruz, Consuelo, and Rut Diamint. 1998. "The New Military Autonomy in Latin America." *Journal of democracy* 9 (4): 115–27.

Cummings, Richard. 2007. "U.S.: Lockheed Stock and Two Smoking Barrels." CorpWatch, January 16. http://www.corpwatch.org/article.php?id=14307.

Currie, Elliott. 1993. *Reckoning: Drugs, the Cities, and the American Future*. New York: Hill and Wang.

Dahl, Robert A. 1961. *Who Governs? Democracy and Power in an American City*. New Haven, CT: Yale University Press.

———. 1971. *Polyarchy: Participation and Opposition*. New Haven, CT: Yale University Press.

Dallin, Alexander, and George W. Breslauer. 1970. *Political Terror in Communist Systems*. Stanford, CA: Stanford University Press.

Davenport, Christian. 1995. "Multi-dimensional Threat Perception and State Repression: An Inquiry into Why States Apply Negative Sanctions." *American Journal of Political Science* 39 (3): 683–713.

David, Edeli, and Kyle Richardson. 2002. "The Battle for Putumayo." *Cultural Survival Quarterly* 26 (4). https://www.culturalsurvival.org/publications/cultural-survival -quarterly/battle-putumayo.

Defensoría del Pueblo. 2013. *Adjuntía para la prevención de conflictos sociales y la gobern-abilidad*. Reporte de Conflictos Sociales no. 115. Lima, Perú: Defensoría del Pueblo.

Delegation of the Order of Preachers to the United Nations. 2000. "Item 7: Human Rights of Indigenous Peoples." Dominican Network. http://un.op.org/en/node/2004. Accessed June 5, 2015.

del Prado, Jose Luis Gomes. 2008. *Report of the Working Group on the Use of Mercenaries as a Means of Violating Human Rights and Impeding the Exercise of the Right of Peoples to Self-Determination*. New York: U.N. Human Rights Commission.

Devereaux, Ryan. 2010. "Is Obama's Use of State Secrets Privilege the New Normal?" *Nation*, September 29.

DeYoung, Karen, and Greg Jaffe. 2010. "U.S. "Secret War' Expands Globally as Special Operations Forces Take Larger Role." *Washington Post*, June 4.

DiMaggio, Paul J., and Walter W. Powell. 1983. "The Iron Cage Revisited: Institutional Isomorphism and Collective Rationality in Organizational Fields." *American Sociological Review* 50: 150–60.

Ditta, Elise. 2016. "ELN_FARC Battle Urabeños in Colombia." InSightCrime: Organized Crime in the Americas, April 13. http://www.insightcrime.org/news-briefs/eln-farc -battle-urabenos-in-colombia.

Domestic Council Drug Abuse Task Force. 1975. *White Paper on Drug Abuse*. Washington, DC: U.S. Government Printing Office.

Domhoff, G. William. 1967. *Who Rules America?* Upper Saddle River, NJ: Prentice Hall.

———. 1983. *Who Rules America Now?* Upper Saddle River, NJ: Prentice Hall.

———. 1996. *State Autonomy or Class Dominance? Case Studies on Policy Making in America*. New York: Aldine De Gruyter.

Downie, James. 2016. "Obama's Drone War Is a Shameful Part of His Legacy." *Washington Post*, May 5.

Dreher, Axel. 2006. "Does Globalization Affect Growth? Evidence from a New Index of Globalization." *Applied Economics* 38 (10): 1091–1110.

Drug War Chronicle. 2003. "House Defeats Effort to Divert Colombia Military Aid, Barely." July 25.

Drug War Facts. n.d. "Estimated Federal Drug Control Spending by Fiscal Year, 2003– 2017." https://drugwarfacts.org/node/2365#sthash.7Bgjb1QD.dpuf=&overlay=table /fedspending_trends. Accessed March 15, 2016.

Drutman, Lee. 2015. *The Business of America Is Lobbying: How Corporations Became Politicized and Politics Became More Corporate*. New York: Oxford University Press.

Duke, Steven, and Albert Gross. 1993. *America's Longest War: Rethinking Our Tragic Crusade against Drugs*. New York: Putnam.

Dye, Thomas R., and Harmon Zeigler. 1988. "Socialism and Inequality in Cross-National Perspective." *PS: Political Science and Politics* 21 (1): 45–56.

DynCorp International Inc. 2009. *Annual Report 2009*. Falls Church, VA: DynCorp International Inc.

ECLAC (Economic Commission for Latin America and the Caribbean). 2010. *Foreign Direct Investment in Latin America and the Caribbean*. New York: United Nations.

———. 2012. *Foreign Direct Investment in Latin America and the Caribbean*. New York: United Nations.

————. 2013. *Foreign Direct Investment in Latin America and the Caribbean*. New York: United Nations.

Ehlers, Freddy. 2008. *The Andean Trade Promotion and Drug Eradication Act: Impact on the U.S. and Andean Economies*. Washington, DC: Andean Community General Secretariat.

Ehrlich, Paul R., and Anne H. Ehrlich. 1990. *The Population Explosion*. New York: Simon and Schuster.

Eisenhower, Dwight D. 1961. "The Farewell Address." January 17. https://www.eisenhower .archives.gov/research/online_documents/farewell_address/Reading_Copy.pdf.

Electronic Code of Federal Regulations. 2018. "Standards of Ethical Conduct for Employ- ees of the Executive Branch: Subpart D, §2635.402, Disqualifying Financial Interests." December 20. http://www.ecfr.gov/cgi-bin/text-idx?c=ecfr&SID=06f812f26e7ed9f364b b87944757b912&rgn=div5&view=text&node=5:3.0.10.10.9&idno=5.

El Tiempo. 2003. "Mientras yo sea presidente no seran suspendidas las fumigaciones, advierte Alvaro Uribe." June 29.

Engler, Robert. 1977. *The Brotherhood of Oil: Energy Policy and the Public Interest*. Chicago: University of Chicago Press.

Epstein, Edward. 1984. "Legitimacy, Institutionalization, and Opposition in Exclusionary Bureaucratic Authoritarian Regimes." *Comparative Politics* 17: 37–54.

Epstein, Edwin M. 1969. *The Corporation in American Politics*. Englewood Cliffs, NJ: Prentice-Hall.

Escuela National Sindical. 2010. "Impunity and Violation of the Human Rights of Trade Unionists in Colombia: 2009–2010 and 2002–2010." In *Note Book of Human Rights*, 1–76. Medellín, Colombia: Comisión Colombiana de Juristas.

Evans, Michael. 2011. "Colombia and the United States: Political Violence, Narcotics, and Human Rights, 1948–2010." In *The Chiquita Papers*, 1–4. National Security Archive Briefing Book no. 340. Washington, DC: National Security Archive.

Evans, Peter. 1979. *Dependent Development: The Alliance of Multinational, State and Local Capital in Brazil*. Princeton, NJ: Princeton University Press.

Exxon-Mobil. 2016a. "Azerbaijan." http://corporate.exxonmobil.com/en/company /worldwide-operations/locations/azerbaijan. Accessed January 27, 2016.

————. 2016b. "Russia." http://corporate.exxonmobil.com/en/company/worldwide -operations/locations/russia. Accessed January 27, 2016.

Felbab-Brown, Vanda. 2010. *Shooting Up: Counterinsurgency and the War on Drugs*. Washington, DC: Brookings Institution Press.

————. 2012a. "Drug Policy: How to Solve the Problem without Generating Even Greater Violence." *World Today*, August–September, 19.

————. 2012b. "The Predicament in Afghanistan." In *U.S. Policy in Afghanistan and Iraq*, edited by S. Brown and R. H. Scales, 139–74. London: Lynne Rienner.

————. 2013. *Aspiration and Ambivalence: Strategies and Realities of Counterinsurgency and State Building in Afghanistan*. Washington, DC: Brookings Institution Press.

————. 2014a. "Crime, Low-Intensity Conflict, and the Future of War in the Twenty-First Century." In *Failed States and Fragile Societies: A New World Disorder?*, edited by I. Trauschweizer and S. M. Miner, 89–115. Athens: Ohio University Press.

———. 2014b. "Improving Supply-Side Policies: Smarter Eradication, Interdiction and Alternative Livelihoods—and the Possibility of Licensing." In *Ending the Drug Wars: Report of the LSE Expert Group on the Economics of Drug Policy*, 41–48. London: London School of Economics and Political Science.

Fellner, Jamie. 2009. "Race, Drugs, and Law Enforcement in the United States." *Stanford Law and Policy Review* 20 (2): 257–92.

Fellowship of Reconciliation. 2010. *Military Assistance and Human Rights: Colombia, U.S. Accountability, and Global Implications.* Nyack, NY: Fellowship of Reconciliation and U.S. Office on Colombia.

Fitch, J. Samuel. 1998. *The Armed Forces and Democracy in Latin America.* Baltimore, MD: Johns Hopkins University Press.

Fitzpatrick, Dan. 2012. "Bank Accounts Figure in Drug Probe: FBI Says Mexican Cartel Funneled Money through Bank to Horse-Racing Firm." *Wall Street Journal*, July 9. http://www.wsj.com/articles/SB10001424052702303292204577514773605576442#project%3DBOFAsub0708%26articleTabs%3Dinteractive.

Fleck, Robert K., and Christopher Kilby. 2006. "How Do Political Changes Influence U.S. Bilateral Aid Allocations? Evidence from Panel Data." *Review of Development Economics* 10 (2): 210–23.

Flounders, Sara. 2011. "The Pentagon and Slave Labor in U.S. Prisons." Global Research, June 23. http://www.globalresearch.ca/the-pentagon-and-slave-labor-in-u-s-prisons/25376.

Fogal, Constance, Laura Carlsen, and Stephen Lendman. 2010. "Security and Prosperity Partnership: Militarized NAFTA." Voltaire Network, March 27. http://www.voltairenet.org/article164650.html.

Forero, Juan. 2018. "Where Colombian Rebels Once Ruled, Drug Gangs Now Fight for Control." *Wall Street Journal*, July 16. https://www.wsj.com/articles/where-colombian-rebels-once-ruled-drug-gangs-now-fight-for-control-1531733400.

Forsythe, David P. 1987. "Congress and Human Rights in U.S. Foreign Policy: The Fate of General Legislation." *Human Rights Quarterly* 9 (3): 382–404.

Foster, Jennifer. 2012. *Income Inequality, Welfare Spending, and Globalization, Economics.* Logan: Utah State University.

Foweraker, Joe, and Roman Krznaric. 2009. "The Uneven Performance of Third Wave Democracies: Electoral Politics and Imperfect Rule of Law in Latin America." In *Latin American Democratic Transitions: Institutions, Actors, and Process*, edited by W. C. Smith, 53–77. Malden, MA: Wiley-Blackwell.

Fox News. 2010. "AP IMPACT: After 40 Years, $1 trillion, US War on Drugs Has Failed to Meet Any of Its Goals." May 13. http://www.foxnews.com/world/2010/05/13/ap-impact-years-trillion-war-drugs-failed-meet-goals/.

Frank, Andre Gunder. 1966. *The Development of Underdevelopment.* New York: Monthly Review Press.

Franklin, James C. 2008. "Shame on You: The Impact of Human Rights Criticism on Political Repression in Latin America." *International Studies Quarterly* 52 (1): 187–211.

Freedom House. n.d. "Freedom in the World Comparative and Historical Data: Country and Territory Ratings, 1973–2018 (Excel)." https://freedomhouse.org/report-types /freedom-world.

Freeman, Laurie, and Jorge Luis Sierra. 2005. "Mexico: The Militarization Trap." In *Drugs and Democracy in Latin America: The Impact of US Policy*, edited by C. A. Youngers and E. Rosin, 263–302. Boulder, CO: Lynne Rienner.

Frey, R. Scott, Khalid Al-Sharideh, Kent Bausman, Seifaldin DaNa, Robert Dunkley, Daphne Keboneilwe, Michael Kemeh, Laura Khoury, Sherry Laman, Janis Monier, Deborah Reyes, James Schraeder, and Alpha Sheriff. 1999. "Development, Dependence, Population Pressure, and Human Rights: The Cross-National Evidence." *Human Ecology Review* 6 (1): 49–55.

Friedland, Jonathan. 1999. "Wiley Labor Group Stymies Mexican Privatization Plan." *Wall Street Journal*, December 3.

Friedman, Milton. 1962. *Capitalism and Freedom*. Chicago: University of Chicago Press.

Friedman, Uri. 2011. "A Brief History of Plan Colombia." *Foreign Policy Magazine*, October 28. http://www.foreignpolicy.com/articles/2011/10/27/plan_colombia_a_brief _history.

Friends of Brad Will. 2008. "Opposition Growing to Bush's Proposed 'Mérida Initiative.'" May 8. http://friendsofbradwill.org/2008/05/opposition-growing-to-bushs-proposed -merida-initiative/.

Frontline World. 2005. "Peru: The Curse of the Inca Gold." PBS, October 2005. https:// www.pbs.org/frontlineworld/stories/peru404/thestory.html.

Gagne, David. 2016a. "BACRIM: Winner or Looser in Colombia Peace Deal?" InSight-Crime: Organized Crime in the Americas, July 1. http://www.insightcrime.org /news-analysis/bacrim-winner-or-loser-in-colombia-peace-deal.

———. 2016b. "On 15 Year Anniversary, Govt Asks for New Plan Colombia." InSight-Crime: Organized Crime in the Americas, February 2. http://www.insightcrime.org /news-analysis/on-15-year-anniversary-colombia-asks-for-new-plan-colombia.

Gasiorowski, Mark. 1995. "Economic Crisis and Political Regime Change: An Event History Analysis." *American Political Science Review* 89 (4): 882–97.

Gibbs, David N. 1991. *The Political Economy of Third World Intervention: Mines, Money, and U.S. Policy in the Congo Crisis*. Chicago: University of Chicago Press.

Gibney, Mark, and Mathew Dalton. 1996. "The Political Terror Scale." *Policy Studies and Developing Nations* 4: 73–84. http://www.politicalterrorscale.org/Data/Download. html.

Gilens, Martin. 2012. *Affluence and Influence: Economic Inequality and Political Power in America*. Princeton, NJ: Princeton University Press.

Gills, Barry, and Joel Rocamora. 1992. "Low Intensity Democracy." *Third World Quarterly* 13 (3): 501–23.

Gills, Barry, Joel Rocamora, and Richard Wilson. 1993. *Low Intensity Democracy: Political Power in the New World Order*. London: Pluto Press, with the Transnational Institute.

Giraldo, Javier. 1996. *Colombia: The Genocidal Democracy*. Monroe, ME: Common Courage Press.

Gleditsch, Nils Petter, Peter Wallensteen, Mikael Eriksson, Margareta Sollenberg, and Håvard Strand. 2002. "Armed Conflict 1946–2001: A New Dataset." *Journal of Peace Research* 39 (5): 615–37. http://ucdp.uu.se/downloads/#d3.

Glennon, Michael J. 2014a. "National Security and Double Government." *Harvard National Security Journal* 5 (1): 1–114.

———. 2014b. *National Security and Double Government.* New York: Oxford University Press.

Global Witness. 2009. "International Timber Company DLH Accused of Funding Liberian War." Business & Human Rights Resource Centre, November 18. https://www.globalwitness.org/en/archive/international-timber-company-dlh-accused-funding-liberian-war/.

Goldman, David. 2009. "United Technologies to Cut 11,660 Jobs." CNN Money, March 10. http://money.cnn.com/2009/03/10/news/companies/united_technologies/index.htm?postversion=2009031012.

Goldstein, Daniel M. 2012. *Outlawed: Between Security and Rights in a Bolivian City.* Durham, NC: Duke University Press.

Golubkova, Katya, and Denis Pinchuk. 2014. "Update 1—ExxonMobil Says Not Planning to Leave Sakhalin Project in Russia." Reuters, May 16. http://www.reuters.com/article/russia-exxon-mobil-sakhalin-idUSL6N0O22QG20140516.

Gosling, James J. 2009. *Budgetary Politics in American Government.* New York: Routledge.

Graham, Edward M., and Paul R. Krugman. 1995. *Foreign Direct Investment in the U.S.* Washington, DC: Institute for International Economics.

Gregory, Kathryn. 2009. *Backgrounder: Shining Path, Tupac Amaru (Peru, Leftists).* New York: Council on Foreign Relations.

Guaqueta, Alexander. 2005. "Change and Continuity in U.S.-Colombia Relations and the War on Drugs." *Journal of Drug Issues* 35 (1): 27–56.

Guerino, Paul, Paige M. Harrison, and William J. Sabol. 2011. *Prisoners in 2010.* Washington, DC: U.S. Department of Justice.

Gupte, Praney. 1984. *The Crowded Earth.* New York: Norton

Gustafsson, Björn, and Mats Johansson. 1999. "In Search of Smoking Guns: What Makes Income Inequality Vary over Time in Different Countries?" *American Sociological Review* 64 (4): 585–606.

Gyimah-Brempong, Kwabena. 2002. "Corruption, Economic Growth, and Income Inequality in Africa." *Economics of Governance* 3: 183–209.

Haggard, Stephan. 1990. *Pathways from the Periphery: The Politics of Growth in the Newly Industrializing Countries.* Ithaca, NY: Cornell University Press.

Hamburger, Tom, and Alexander Becker. 2014. "At Fast-Growing Brookings, Donors May Have an Impact on Research Agenda." *Washington Post*, October 30.

Hamilton, Alexander, Clinton Rossiter, James Madison, and John Jay. 1961. *The Federalist Papers.* New York: New American Library.

Hansia, Fatima. 2015. "French Tribunal Investigates Qosmos over Surveillance Software in Syria." CorpWatch, July 21. http://www.corpwatch.org/article.php?id=16044.

Hardin, Garrett. 1993. *Living within Limits: Ecology, Economics, and Population Taboos.* New York: Oxford University Press.

Hari, Johann. 2015. *Chasing the Scream: The First and Last Days of the War on Drugs.* New York: Bloomsbury.

Hartung, William D. 2012. *Prophets of War: Lockheed Martin and the Making of the Military-Industrial Complex.* New York: Nations Books.

Haugaard, Lisa, Adam Isacson, and Jennifer Johnson. 2011. *A Cautionary Tale: Plan Colombia's Lessons for U.S. Policy towards Mexico and Beyond.* Washington, DC: Latin America Working Group Education Fund Center for International Policy, and Washington Office on Latin America.

Hawkins, Robert G., Norman Mintz, and Michael Provissiero. 1976. "Government Takeover of U.S. Foreign Affiliates." *Journal of International Business Studies* 7 (1): 3–16.

Heckman, James. 1979. "Sample Selection Bias as a Specification Error." *Econometrica* 47: 153–61.

Hemingway, Mark. 2010. "The 420 Club? Pat Robertson Now Support Marijuana Decriminalization." *Washington Examiner*, December 23.

Henderson, Conway W. 1991. "Conditions Affecting the Use of Political Repression." *Journal of Conflict Resolution* 35 (1): 120–42.

———. 1993. "Population Pressures and Political Repression." *Social Science Quarterly* 74 (2): 322–33.

Henrichson, Christian, and Ruth Delaney. 2012. "The Price of Prisons: What Incarceration Cost Taxpayers." edited by The Pew Center on the States. New York: Vera Institute of Justice.

Heritage Foundation. 2016. "2016 Index of Economic Freedom." http://www.heritage.org /index/explore?view=by-region-country-year. Accessed April 21, 2016.

Hibbs, Douglas A. 1973. *Mass Political Violence: A Cross-National Causal Analysis.* New York: Wiley.

Hirschman, Albert O. 1969. *How to Divest In Latin America and Why.* Princeton, NJ: Princeton University Press.

Hodges, Sam. 2000. "Callahan Wins $1.7 Billion For Colombia." *Mobile Register*, March 31.

Holston, James. 2008. *Insurgent Citizenship: Disjunctions of Democracy and Modernity in Brazil.* Princeton, NJ: Princeton University Press.

———. 2009. "Insurgent Citizenship in an Era of Global Urban Peripheries." *City and Society* 21 (2): 245–67.

House Committee on Foreign Affairs. 2008. *Central America and the Mérida Initiative.* Hearing before the Subcommittee on the Western Hemisphere. Washington, DC: Committee on Foreign Affairs.

House Committee on the Budget. 2003–2012. https://budget.house.gov/publications /publications-archive?page=10. Accessed April 20, 2015.

Hristov, Jasmin. 2009. *Blood and Capital: The Paramilitarization of Colombia.* Athens: Ohio University Press.

Hudak, John, and Grace Wallack. 2015. *Ending the U.S. Government's War on Medical Marijuana Research.* Washington, DC: Brookings Institution.

Hufbauer, Gary Clyde, and Jeffrey J. Schott. 2005. *NAFTA Revisited: Achievements and Challenges.* Washington, DC: Pearson Institute for International Economics.

Hula, Kevin W. 1999. *Lobbying Together: Interest Group Coalitions in Legislative Politics.* Washington, DC: Georgetown University Press.

Human Rights Watch. 2000. "The Ties That Bind: Colombia and Military-Paramilitary Links." February 1. https://www.hrw.org/legacy/reports/2000/colombia/.

———. 2005. "A Bad Plan in Colombia." May 19. http://www.hrw.org/news/2005/05/19/bad-plan-colombia.

Human Rights without Frontiers, National Human Rights Coordinating Committee, GRUFIDES, and the Society of Threatened Peoples. 2013. *Police in the Pay of Mining Companies: The Responsibility of Switzerland and Peru for Human Rights Violations in Mining Disputes.* Cajamarca, Peru, and Ostermundigen, Switzerland: Society of Threatened Peoples Switzerland.

Hungerford, Thomas L. 2013. "Corporate Tax Rates and Economic Growth since 1947." Economic Policy Institute, June 4. http://www.epi.org/publication/ib364-corporate-tax-rates-and-economic-growth/.

Huntington, Samuel P. 1968. *Political Order in Changing Societies.* New Haven, CT: Yale University Press.

———. 1991a. "Democracy's Third Wave." *Journal of Democracy* 2 (2): 12–34.

———. 1991b. *The Third Wave: Democratization in the Late Twentieth Century.* Norman: University of Oklahoma Press.

———. 1997. "After Twenty Years: The Future of the Third Wave." *Journal of Democracy* 8 (4): 3–12.

Ingraham, Christopher. 2016. "More and More Doctors Want to Make Marijuana Legal." *Washington Post*, April 15.

International Center for Settlement of Investment Disputes. 2008. *In the Proceeding between Occidental Petroleum Corporation, Occidental Exploration and Production Company (Claimants) and the Republic of Ecuador (Respondent).* Quito, Ecuador: International Center for Settlement of Investment Disputes.

International Consortium of Investigative Journalists. 2001a. "The Helicopter War." September 26. http://www.icij.org/project/us-aid-latin-america/helicopter-war.

———. 2001b. "Narcotics and Economics Drive U.S. Policy in Latin America." September 26. http://www.icij.org/project/us-aid-latin-america/narcotics-and-economics-drive-us-policy-latin-america.

ILOSTAT (International Labor Organization). n.d. "Number of Strikes and Lockouts by Economic Activity." https://www.ilo.org. Accessed March 28, 2015.

International Monetary Fund. n.d. "IMF Annual Reports." https://www.imf.org/en/search#q=IMF%20Annual%20Reports&sort=relevancy. Accessed November 15, 2016.

———. n.d. International Financial Statistics database. http://data.imf.org/?sk=4C514D48-B6BA-49ED-8AB9-52B0C1A0179B.

International Rights Advocates. 2009a. *Balcero et al. v. Drummond Company, Inc.* http://www.iradvocates.org/case/latin-america-colombia/balcero-et-al-v-drummond-company-inc. Accessed June 5, 2015.

———. 2009b. *Mendoza Gomez et al. v. Dole Food Company, Inc.* http://www.iradvocates.org/case/latin-america-colombia/mendoza-gomez-et-al-v-dole-food-company-inc. Accessed June 5, 2015.

International Trade Union Confederation. 2013. "Countries at Risk: Violations of Trade Union Rights." October 10.

———. 2016. "Survey of Violations of Trade Unions Rights: Freedom of Association—Collective Bargaining—Strike." http://survey.ituc-csi.org. Accessed April 5, 2016.

Irwin, John, Vincent Schiraldi, and Jason Ziedenberg. 1999. *America's One Million Non-violent Prisoners*. Washington, DC: Justice Policy Institute.

Isacson, Adam. 2005. "The U.S. Military in the War on Drugs." In *Drugs and Democracy in Latin America: The Impact of U.S. Policy*, edited by C. A. Youngers and E. Rosin, 15–60. London: Lynne Rienner.

———. 2014. *Ending Fifty Years of Conflict: The Challenges Ahead and the U.S. Role in Colombia*. Washington, DC: Washington Office on Latin America.

Isacson, Adam, Lisa Haugaard, Abigail Poe, Sarah Kinosain, and George Withers. 2013. *Time to Listen: Trends in U.S. Security Assistance to Latin America and the Caribbean*. Washington, DC: Center for International Policy, Latin America Working Group, Education Fund, and Washington Office on Latin America.

Isikoff, Michael. 2000. "The Other Drug War." *Newsweek*, April 2. http://www.newsweek.com/other-drug-war-157827.

Jaccard, James J., and Robert Turrisi. 2003. *Interaction Effects in Multiple Regression*. London: Sage.

Jaumotte, Florence, and Carolina Osorio Buitron. 2015a. *Inequality and Labor Market Institutions*. Washington, DC: International Monetary Fund.

———. 2015b. "Power from the People." *Finance and Development* 52 (1): 29–31.

Johnson, Chalmers. 2003. "The War Business: Squeezing a Profit from the Wreckage in Iraq." *Harper's Magazine*, November, 53–58.

Johnson, Julie. 1988. "Reagan Signs Bill to Curb Drug Use." *New York Times*, November 19.

Johnson, Nicholas, Phil Oliff, and Erica Williams. 2011. *An Update on State Budget Cuts: At Least 46 States Have Imposed Cuts that Hurt Vulnerable Residents and Cause Job Loss*. Washington, DC: Center on Budget and Policy Priorities.

Johnston, David. 2009. "U.S. Says Rendition to Continue, but with More Oversight." *New York Times*, August 24.

Juhasz, Antonia. 2008. *The Tyranny of Oil: The World's Most Powerful Industry—and What We Must Do to Stop It*. New York: William Morrow–Harper Collins.

Justice for Colombia. 2016. "Trade Union Violence." https://justiceforcolombia.org/about-colombia/trade-unions//. Accessed January 15, 2019.

Kamphuis, Charis. 2012. "Foreign Investment and the Privatization of Coercion: A Case Study of the Foreza Security Company in Peru." *Brooklyn Journal of International Law* 37 (2): 529–78.

Kane, Alex. 2014. "Multi Billion Dollar Bonanza: Companies Which Make Money by Keeping Americans 'Terrified of Terror Attacks.'" Center for Research on Globalization, September 22. http://www.globalresearch.ca/multi-billion-dollar-bonanza-companies-which-make-money-by-keeping-americans-terrified-of-terror-attacks/5403341.

Kapfer, Steve, Rich Nielsen, and Daniel Nielson. 2007. "If You Build It, Will They Come? Foreign Aid's Effect on Foreign Direct Investment." Paper Presented at the 65th Annual Midwest Political Science Association Meeting, Chicago.

Kaplan, Fred M. 1980. *Dubious Specter: A Skeptical Look at the Soviet Nuclear Threat*. Washington, DC: Institute for Policy Studies.

Karakaplan, M. U., B. Neyapti, and S. Sayek. 2005. *Aid and Foreign Investment: International Evidence*. Ankara, Turkey: Bilkent University.

Katz, Alyssa. 2015. *The Influence Machine: The U.S. Chamber of Commerce and the Corporate Capture of American Life.* New York: Random House.

Kaufman, Robert. 1979. "Industrial Change and Authoritarian Rule in Latin America: A Concrete Review of the Bureaucratic-Authoritarian Model." In *The New Authoritarianism in Latin America,* edited by D. Collier, 165–253. Princeton, NJ: Princeton University Press.

———. 2007. *In Defense of the Bush Doctrine.* Lexington: University of Kentucky.

Keefer, Philip. 2012. *Database of Political Institutions: Changes and Variable Definitions.* Washington, DC: World Bank.

Keh, Douglas I. 1996. "Economic Reform and Criminal Finance." *Transnational Organized Crime* 2 (1): 66–80.

Keith, Linda Camp. 1999. "The United Nations International Covenant on Civil and Political Rights: Does It Make a Difference in Human Rights Behavior?" *Journal of Peace Research* 36 (1): 95–118.

———. 2002a. "Constitutional Provisions for Individual Human Rights (1977–1966): Are They More than Mere Window Dressing?" *Political Research Quarterly* 55 (1): 111–43.

———. 2002b. "Judicial Independence and Human Rights Protection around the World." *Judicature* 85 (4): 195–200.

———. 2011. *Political Repression: Courts and the Law.* Edited by J. Bert B. Lockwood. Philadelphia: University of Pennsylvania Press.

Keith, Linda Camp, C. Neal Tate, and Steven C. Poe. 2009. "Is the Law a Mere Parchment Barrier to Human Rights Abuse?" *Journal of Politics* 71 (2): 644–60.

Kenfield, Isabella. 2009. "Monsanto's Man in the Obama Administration." Counterpunch, August 14. http://www.counterpunch.org/2009/08/14/monsanto-s-man-in-the-obama-administration/.

Keohane, Robert O. 1984. *After Hegemony: Cooperation and Discord in the World Political Economy.* Princeton, NJ: Princeton University Press.

Kilmer, Beau, Jonathan P. Caulkins, Rosalie Liccardo Pacula, and Peter H. Reuter. 2012. *The U.S. Drug Policy Landscape: Insights and Opportunities for Improving the View.* Santa Monica, CA: RAND Drug Policy Research Center.

Kilmer, Beau, and Robert J. MacCoun. 2017. "Should California Drop Penalties for Drug Possession?" The RAND Blog, July 20. https://www.rand.org/blog/2017/07/should-california-drop-criminal-penalties-for-drug.html.

Kindleberger, Charles P. 1981. "Dominance and Leadership in the International Economy: Exploitation of Public Goods, and Free Rides." *International Studies Quarterly* 25: 245–54.

King, Gary, and Langche Zeng. 2001a. "Explaining Rare Events in International Relations." *International Organization* 55 (3): 693–715.

———. 2001b. "Logistic Rare Events Data." *Political Analysis* 9: 137–63.

Kinosain, Sarah. 2012. "Colombia to Indict 19 Palm Oil Companies for Forced Displacement." Colombia Reports, July 31. http://colombiareports.co/colombia-to-indict-19-palm-oil-companies-for-forced-displacement/.

Kirchhoff, Suzanne M. 2010. *Economic Impact of Prison Growth.* Washington, DC: Congressional Research Service.

Kirkpatrick, Jeane. 1982. *Dictatorships and Double Standards: Rationalism and Reason in Politics*. New York: Simon and Schuster.

Kirschke, Joseph. 2008. "State Department Pushing Aerial Poppy Eradication in Afghanistan." Worldpress.org, February 29. http://www.worldpress.org/Asia/3082.cfm.

Kleiman, Mark. 1992. *Against Excess: Drug Policy for Results*. New York: Basic Books.

Kleiman, Mark A. R., Jonathan P. Caulkins, and Angela Hawken. 2011. *Drugs and Drug Policy: What Everyone Needs to Know*. New York: Oxford University Press.

Kline, R. B. 2011. *Principles and Practice of Structural Equation Modeling*. 3rd ed. New York: Guilford Press.

Koening, Kevin. 2015. "The Chevron Tapes: Secret Videos Reveal Company Hid Pollution in Ecuador." Amazon Watch, April 8. http://amazonwatch.org/news/2015/0408 -the-chevron-tapes.

Koening, Thomas, Robert Gogel, and John Sonquist. 1979. "Models of the Significance of Interlocking Corporate Directorates." *American Journal of Economics and Sociology* 38 (2): 173–86.

KOF Swiss Economic Institute. n.d. KOF Globalization Index. http://www.kof.ethz.ch /globalisation/. Accessed May 20, 2015.

Kongsager, Rico, and Anette Reenberg. 2012. *Contemporary Land-Use Transitions: The Global Oil Palm Expansion*. Copenhagen: Global Land Project.

Kontos, Alex P. 2004. "'Private' Security Guards: Privatized Force and State Responsibility under International Human Rights Law." *Non-state Actors and International Law* 4 (3): 199–238.

Kornbluh, Peter. 2000. "Chile and the United States: Declassified Documents Relating to the Military Coup, September 11, 1973." National Security Archive, George Washington University. https://nsarchive2.gwu.edu//NSAEBB/NSAEBB8/nsaebb8i.htm. Accessed January 31, 2019.

———. 2013. *The Pinochet File: A Declassified Dossier on Atrocity and Accountability*. New York: New Press.

Kornblut, Anne E., and Carrie Johnson. 2010. "Obama Will Help Select Location of Khalid Sheik Mohammed Terrorism Trial." *Washington Post*, February 12.

Kosack, Stephen, and Jennifer Tobin. 2006. "Funding Self-Sustaining Development: The Role of Aid, FDI and Government in Economic Success." *International Organization* 60 (1): 205–43.

Koulish, Robert. 2010. *Immigration and American Democracy: Subverting the Rule of Law*. New York: Routledge.

Krasner, Steven D. 1976. "State Power and the Structure of International Trade." *World Politics* 28 (3): 317–47.

Kraul, Chris. 2009. "DEA Presence Ends in Bolivia." *Los Angeles Times*, January 30.

Kredo, Adam. 2013. "Borat, Chuck Hagel, and an Oil Company Walk into a Bar: Defense Nominee Chuck Hagel's Ties to Kazakhstan, Chevron, Atlantic Council under Fire." *Washington Free Beacon*, February 11. http://freebeacon.com/politics/borat-chuck -hagel-and-an-oil-company-walk-into-a-bar/.

Kruit, Dirk. 2001. "Low Intensity Democracies: Latin America in the Postdictatorial Era." *Bulletin of Latin American Research* 20 (4): 409–30.

Kuznets, Simon. 1955. "Economic Growth and Income Inequality." *American Economic Review* 45 (1): 1–28.

Lai, Brian. 2003. "Examining the Goals of U.S. Foreign Assistance in the Post-Cold War Period, 1991–96." *Journal of Peace Research* 40 (1): 103–28.

La Jornada. 2012. "'Failure of Anti-drug Fight Is Intentional,' Says Chomsky." December 21. http://diario.mx/Internacional/2012-05-13_de6ae7ea/fracaso-de-lucha-antinarco-es-intencional-asegura-chomsky/.

Latinobarómetro. 1995. "Opinion Publica LatinoAmericana." http://www.latinobarometro.org/lat.jsp. Accessed on April 20, 2013.

Lander, Mark. 2009. "Clinton Says Demand for Illegal Drugs in the U.S. 'Fuels the Drug Trade' in Mexico." *New York Times*, March 25.

Langdon, Shanna. 2000. *Peru's Yanacovha Gold Mine: The IFC's Midas Touch?* Berkeley, CA: Project Underground.

Langone, Alix. 2018. "Here's How America's Biggest Companies Are Spending Their Tax Cuts (It's Not on Jobs)." Time.com, May 17. http://time.com/money/5267940/companies-spending-trump-tax-cuts-stock-buybacks/.

LaSusa, Mike. 2016. "FARC Dissidents Forming Criminal Groups in Ecuador: Reports." InSightCrime: Organized Crime in the Americas, August 9. http://www.insightcrime.org/news-briefs/farc-dissidents-forming-criminal-groups-in-ecuador-reports.

Lawrence, Robert. 1996. *Single World, Divided Nations: International Trade and OECD Labor Markets.* Paris: Brookings Institution Press.

Ledebur, Kathryn. 2005. "Bolivia: Clear Consequences." In *Drugs and Democracy in Latin America: The Impact of U.S. Policy*, edited by Coletta A. Youngers and E. Rosin, 143–84. Boulder, CO: Lynne Rienner.

Lee, Hae-Young, Jongsung Kim, and Beom Cheol Cin. 2013. "Empirical Analysis on the Determinants of Income Inequality in Korea." *International Journal of Advanced Science and Technology* 52: 95–109.

Lemus, Marcia Clemencia Ramirez, Kimberly Stanton, and John Walsh. 2005. "Colombia: A Vicious Circle of Drugs and War." In *Drugs and Democracy in Latin America: The Impact of U.S. Policy*, edited by Coletta A. Youngers and E. Rosin, 99–142. London: Lynne Rienner.

Lendman, Stephen. 2010. "Security and Prosperity Partnership: Militarized NAFTA." Project Censored, April 30. http://www.projectcensored.org/2-security-and-prosperity-partnership-militarized-nafta/.

Leonning, Carol D. 2007. "In Terrorism-Law Case, Chiquita Points to U.S." *Washington Post*, August 2. http://www.washingtonpost.com/wp-dyn/content/article/2007/08/01/AR2007080102601.html?hpid=topnews.

Lessig, Lawrence. 2012. *Republic Lost: How Money Corrupts Congress—and a Plan to Stop It.* New York: Hachette.

Levine, Ross, Norman Loayza, and Thorsten Beck. 2000. "Financial Intermediation and Growth: Causality and Causes." *Journal of Monetary Economics* 46: 31–77.

Li, Hongyi, Lyn Squire, and Heng-fu Zou. 1998. "Explaining International and Intertemporal Variations in Income Inequality." *Economic Journal* 108 (446): 26–43.

Li, Quan, and Rafael Reuveny. 2003. "Economic Globalization and Democracy: An Empirical Analysis." *British Journal of Political Science* 33 (1): 29–54.

Lindblom, Charles E. 1977. *Politics and Markets: The World's Political and Economic Systems.* New York: Basic Books.

———. 1978. "Why Government Must Cater to Business." *Business and Society Review* (Fall): 4–7.

Linthicum, Kate. 2017. "Mexico's Bloody Drug War Is Killing More People than Ever." *Los Angeles Times*, July 22.

Lipson, Charles H. 1976. "Corporate Preferences and Public Policies: Foreign Aid Sanctions and Investment Protection." *World Politics* 28 (3): 396–421.

Liptak, Adam. 2013. "Justices Turn Back Challenge to Broader U.S. Eavesdropping." *New York Times*, February 26.

Lockheed Martin Corporation. 1995. *1995 Annual Report.* Bethesda, MD: Lockheed Martin Corporation.

———. 1999. *1999 Annual Report.* Bethesda, MD: Lockheed Martin Corporation.

———. 2014. *Lockheed Martin Corporation: 2014 Annual Report.* Bethesda, MD: Lockheed Martin Corporation.

Long, Heather. 2017. "U.S. Economy 'Performing Well' as Federal Reserve Hikes Rates." *Washington Post*, December 13.

Lopez, Aldo Orellana. 2012. "ICSID Orders Ecuador to Pay $1.7 Billion to Occidental Petroleum: Interview with the Ecuador Decide Network." Network for Justice in Global Investment, October. http://justinvestment.org/2012/10/icsid-orders-ecuador -to-pay-1-7-billion-to-occidental-petroleum-interview-with-the-ecuador-decide -network/.

Lorrain, François, and Harrison C. White. 1971. "Structural Equivalence of Individuals in Social Networks." *Journal of Mathematical Sociology* 1: 49–80.

Loveman, Brian. 1998. "When You Wish upon the Stars: Why the Generals and Admirals Say Yes to Latin American 'Transitions' to Civilian Government." In *The Origins of Liberty: Political and Economic Liberalization in the Modern World,* edited by Paul W. Drake and. Mathew. D. McCubbins, 115–45. Princeton, NJ: Princeton University Press.

———. 2006. *Addicted to Failure: U.S. Security Policy in Latin America and the Andean Region.* Lanham, MD: Rowman and Littlefield.

Lowery, Annie. 2011. "It's Mostly Wonks: Just How Tied In with Wall Street Is the Obama Administration?" Slate, January 6. http://www.slate.com/articles/business/moneybox /2011/01/its_mostly_wonks.html.

Lublin, Nancy. 2001. "Drug Trafficking in Central Asia: A Matter of Survival for Some." Eurasianet.org, January 27. http://www.eurasianet.org/departments/insight/articles /eav050901.shtml.

Lusane, Clarence. 1991. *Pipe Dreams Blues: Racism and the War on Drugs.* Boston: South End Press.

MacCallum, R. C., M. W. Browne, and H. M. Sugawara. 1996. "Power Analysis and Determination of Sample Size for Covariance Structure Modeling." *Psychological Methods* 1: 130–49.

Madland, David. 2015. *Hollowed Out: Why the Economy Doesn't Work without a Strong Middle Class.* Berkeley, CA: University of California Press.

Madland, David, and Keith Miller. 2013. "Three Charts Showing How Middle-Class Incomes Continue to Stagnate While Overall Inequality Grows." Center for American Progress, September 17. https://www.americanprogress.org/issues/labor/news/2013/09 /17/74489/3-charts-showing-how-middle-class-incomes-continue-to-stagnate-while -overall-inequality-grows-2/.

Magdoff, Harry. 1978. *Imperialism: From the Colonial Age to the Present*. New York: Monthly Review Press.

Mainwaring, Scott, and Mathew S. Shugart, eds. 1997. *Presidentialism and Democracy in Latin America*. Cambridge: Cambridge University Press.

Malthus, Thomas Robert. 1708. *An Essay on the Principle of Population*. London: J. Johnson.

Manufacturing.Net. 2009a. "United Technologies Says More Jobs Cuts Possible." March 16. http://www.manufacturing.net/news/2009/03/united-technologies-says -more-job-cuts-possible.

———. 2009b. "United Technologies to Layoff 1,500 in Connecticut." March 13. http:// www.manufacturing.net/news/2009/03/united-technologies-to-layoff-1500-in -connecticut.

Marshall, Andrew G. 2008. "Security and Prosperity Partnership of North America (SPP): Security and Prosperity for Whom?" Global Research, March 17. http://www .globalresearch.ca/security-and-prosperity-partnership-of-north-america-spp -security-and-prosperity-for-whom/8375.

Marshall, Monty G., Ted Robert Gurr, and Keith Jaggers. 2013. *POLITY IV Project: Political Regime Characteristics and Transitions, 1800–2012*. Vienna, VA: Center for Systemic Peace. http://www.systemicpeace.org/inscrdata.html.

Marshall, Monty G., and Donna Ramesy Marshall. 2018. *Coup D'état Events, 1946–2017*. Vienna, VA: Center for Systemic Peace. http://www.systemicpeace.org/inscrdata .html.

Martin, Michael. 2013. "Guantanamo Bay Still Unresolved." *Tell Me More*, National Public Radio, January 14. https://www.npr.org/2013/01/14/169334679/guantanamo-bay -still-unresolved.

Mauer, Marc, and Ryan S. King. 2007. *A 25-Year Quagmire: The Drug War and Its Impact on American Society*. Washington, DC: Sentencing Project.

Mayer, Lindsay Renick. 2007. "Money Divided House Vote to Tax Oil Industry." OpenSecrets.org, January 23. https://www.opensecrets.org/news/2007/01/money -divided-house-vote-to-ta/.

Mazzetti, Mark. 2013. *The Way of the Knife: The CIA, a Secret Army, and a War at the Ends of the Earth*. New York: Penguin.

Mazzetti, Mark, Charlie Savage, and Scott Shane. 2013. "How a U.S. Citizen Came to Be in America's Cross Hairs." *New York Times*, March 9.

McDermott, Jeremy. 2016. "Eight Reasons Why Colombia's Post-conflict Is Still a Ways Off." InSightCrime: Organized Crime in the Americas, June 23. http://www .insightcrime.org/news-analysis/eight-reasons-colombia-post-conflict-is-still-a -way-off.

McGann, James G. 2013. *2013 Global Go To Think Tank Index Report*. Philadelphia: University of Pennsylvania, Think Tanks and Civil Societies Programs.

———. 2015. *2014 Global Go To Think Tank Index Report*. Philadelphia: University of Pennsylvania, Think Tanks and Civil Societies Program.

McKinlay, Robert D., and Alvin S. Cohan. 1975. "A Comparative Analysis of the Political and Economic Performance of Military and Civilian Regimes." *Comparative Politics* 8: 1–30.

———. 1976. "Performance and Instability in Military and Nonmilitary Regimes." *American Political Science Review* 70 (3): 850–64.

McLennan, Rebecca M. 2008. *The Crisis of Imprisonment: Protest, Politics and the Making of the American Penal State, 1776–1941*. New York: Cambridge University Press.

Mejia, Daniel. 2012. "The War on Drugs under Plan Colombia." In *Rethinking the "War on Drugs" through the US-Mexico Prism*, edited by E. Zedillo and H. Wheeler, 19–32. New Haven, CT: Yale Center for the Study of Globalization.

Meriage, Lawrence. 2000. *Vice President, Executive Services and Public Affairs, Occidental Oil and Gas Corporation*. Testimony before the House Government Reform Subcommittee on Criminal Justice, Drug Policy, and Human Resources Hearing on Colombia, 106 Cong, 2d Sess. Washington, DC: U.S. Congress.

Mesler, Bill. 2000. "Al Gore: The Other Oil Candidate." CorpWatch, August 29. http://www.corpwatch.org/article.php?id=468.

Meyer, Peter J., and Clare Ribando Seelke. 2015. *Central American Regional Security Initiative: Background and Policy Issues for Congress*. Washington, DC: Congressional Research Services.

Meyer, William H. 1996. "Human Rights and MNCs: Theory versus Quantitative Analysis." *Human Rights Quarterly* 18: 368–97.

———. 1998. *Human Rights and International Political Economy in Third World Nations: Multinational Corporations, Foreign Aid, and Repression*. Westport, CT: Praeger.

Miliband, Ralph. 1969. *The State in Capitalist Society*. London: Weidenfeld and Nicolson.

———. 1982. *Capitalist Democracy in Britain*. New York: Oxford University Press.

Miller, Todd. 2009. "Mexico: A War against Organized Crime Becomes a War against Organized Labor." North American Congress on Latin America, November 15. https://nacla.org/news/mexico-war-against-organized-crime-becomes-war-against-organized-labor.

Mills, C. Wright. 1956. *The Power Elite*. Oxford: Oxford University Press.

Miraliyeva, Naila. 2007. "ExxonMobil Investments in Azerbaijan." *Journal of Turkish Weekly*, April 30. http://www.turkishweekly.net/2007/04/30/op-ed/exxonmobil-investments-in-azerbaijan/.

Miron, Jeffery A., and Katherine Waldock. 2010. *The Budgetary Impact of Ending Drug Prohibition*. September 27. Washington, DC: Cato Institute. https://www.cato.org/publications/white-paper/budgetary-impact-ending-drug-prohibition.

Mitchell, Neil J., and James M. McCormick. 1988. "Economic and Political Explanations of Human Rights Violations." *World Politics* 40 (4): 476–98.

Mizruchi, Mark S. 1992. *The Structure of Corporate Political Action: Interfirm Relations and Their Consequences*. Cambridge, MA: Harvard University Press.

———. 2013. *The Fracturing of the American Corporate Elite*. Cambridge, MA: Harvard University Press.

Moe, Terry M. 1984. "The New Economics of Organizations." *American Journal of Political Science* 28 (4): 739–77.

Mommsen, Wolfgang J. 1980. *Theories of Imperialism.* New York: Random House.

Mondragon, Hector. 2002. "U.S. Fuels the Fires in Colombia." Information Services Latin America. Special report. isla.igc.org/Features/Colombia/SR3mon-dragon.html. Accessed May 10, 2013.

Monopoly of Violence: A New Data Base on Pro-Government Militias. n.d. *Journal of Peace Research* 50 (2): 249–58. https://www.prio.org/JPR/Datasets/.

Monshipouri, Mahmood, Claude E. Welsh Jr., and Evan T. Kennedy. 2003. "Multinational Corporations and Ethics of Responsibility: Problems and Possibilities." *Human Rights Quarterly* 25 (4): 965–89.

Montero, David, and Kelly Whalen. 2002. "Global Reach: U.S. Corporate Interests in Colombia." Frontline World, November. http://www.pbs.org/frontlineworld/stories /colombia/corporate.html.

Moor, Marianne, and Joris van de Sandt. 2014. *The Dark Side of Coal: Paramilitary Violence in the Mining Region of Cesar, Colombia.* Utrecht: PAX.

Moore, William. 2011. "Para-Business Gone Bananas: Chiquita Brands in Colombia." Council on Hemispheric Affairs, August 18. http://www.coha.org/para-business-gone -bananas-chiquita-brands-in-colombia/.

Morini, Gabriel A. 2013. "Argentina, a un paso de investigar a bancos por creditos a la dictadura." infonews, September 9. http://www.infonews.com/nota/96709/argentina -a-un-paso-de-investigar-a-bancos.

Mosley, Layna, and Saika Uno. 2007. "Racing to the Bottom or Climbing to the Top? Economic Globalization and Collective Labor Rights." *Comparative Political Studies* 40: 923–48.

Moughty, Sarah. 2011. "Top CIA Official: Obama Changed Virtually None of Bush's Controversial Programs." Frontline, September 1. https://www.pbs.org/wgbh/frontline /article/top-cia-official-obama-changed-virtually-none-of-bushs-controversial -programs/.

Movement de Unidad Popular Argentina. 2013. "A 37 años de del apagón de Ledesma." July 23. http://www.mupargentina.com.ar/noticia_A-37-anos-de-del-apagon-de -Ledesma.html.

Mugge, Zachary P. 2005. "Plan Colombia: The Environmental Effects and Social Costs of the United States Failing War on Drugs." *Journal of International Environmental Law and Policy* 51 (2): 309–40.

Murch, Donna. 2015. "Crack in Los Angeles: Crisis, Militarization, and Black Response to the Late Twentieth-Century War on Drugs." *Journal of American History* 102 (1): 162–67.

Murphy, Dylan. 2013. "Money Laundering and the Drug Trade: The Role of the Banks." Global Research, May 13. http://www.globalresearch.ca/money-laundering-and-the -drug-trade-the-role-of-the-banks/5334205.

Nadelmann, Ethan A. 1990. "Global Prohibition Regimes: The Evolution of Norms in International Society." *International Organizations* 44 (Autumn): 512.

———. 1993. *Cops across Borders: The Internationalization of U.S. Criminal Law Enforcement.* University Park: Pennsylvania State University Press.

Nagle, Luz E. 2002. *Plan Colombia: Reality of the Colombian Crisis and Implications for Hemispheric Security.* Carlisle, PA: Strategic Studies Institute at the U.S. Army War College.

National Black Church Initiative. 2010. *National Black Church Initiative Joins Former DEA Leadership to Condemn Prop 19.* Washington, DC: National Black Church Initiative.

National Security Council. 2002. *The National Security Strategy of the United States of America.* Washington, DC: White House.

National Survey on Drug Use and Health: Substance Abuse & Mental Health Data Archive. n.d. https://www.datafiles.samhsa.gov/study-series/national-survey-drug -use-and-health-nsduh-nid13517. Accessed October 17, 2016.

Negretto, Gabriel L. 2004. "Government Capacities and Policy Making by Decree in Latin America." *Comparative Political Studies* 37 (5): 531–62.

Neild, Rachel. 2005. "U.S. Police Assistance and Drug Control Policies." In *Drugs and Democracy in Latin America: The Impact of U.S. Policy,* edited by C. A. Youngers and E. Rosin, 61–97. London: Lynne Rienner.

Nelson, Steven. 2013. "AMA Reaffirms Opposition to Marijuana Legalization." *U.S. News and World Report,* November 20. https://www.usnews.com/news/articles/2013/11/20 /ama-reaffirms-opposition-to-marijuana-legalization.

Nelson-Pallmeyer, Jack. 1992. *Brave New World Order: Can We Pledge Allegiance?* Maryknoll, NY: Orbis Books.

Neuman, William. 2012. "Coca Licensing Is a Weapon in Bolivia's Drug War." *New York Times,* December 26.

Northrop Grumman. 2010. *Northrop Grumman: Annual Report 2012.* Falls Church, VA: Northrop Grumman.

Obstfeld, Maurice. 1998. "The Global Capital Market: Benefactor or Menace?" *Journal of Economic Perspectives* 12 (4): 9–30.

O'Conner, James. 2001. *The Fiscal Crisis of the State.* New Brunswick, NJ: Transaction Publishers.

O'Donnell, Guillermo. 1973. *Modernization and Bureaucratic Authoritarianism.* Berkeley: University of California Press.

———. 1993. "On the State, Democratization and Some Conceptual Problems: A Latin American View with Glances at Some Post-communist Countries." *World Development* 21 (8): 1355–69.

———. 1994. "Delegative Democracy." *Journal of Democracy* 5 (1): 55–69.

Office of Management and Budget. n.d. Historical Tables. Table 7.1. Federal Debt at the End of Year: 1940–2023. https://www.whitehouse.gov/omb/historical-tables/.

Office of National Drug Control Policy. n.d. National Drug Control Budget, FY's 2000– 2015. https://drugwarfacts.org/node/2365#sthash.7Bgjb1QD.dpuf=&overlay=table /fedspending_trends. Accessed on March 16, 2016.

Office of the U.S. Trade Representative: Executive Office of the President. n.d. "Enforcement and Compliance." http://tcc.export.gov/Trade_Agreements/Bilateral _Investment_Treaties/index.asp. Accessed January 31, 2019.

Olcott, Martha Brill, and Natalia Udalova. 2000. *Drug Trafficking on the Great Silk Road.* Washington, DC: Carnegie Endowment for International Peace.

Olson, Eric L., David A. Shirk, and Andrew Selee, eds. 2010. *Shared Responsibility: U.S.-Mexico Policy Options for Confronting Organized Crime*. Washington, DC: Woodrow Wilson International Center for Scholars, and Mexico Institute.

Open Secrets: Center for Responsible Politics. n.d. "Annual Lobbying by AFL-CIO." https://www.opensecrets.org/lobby/. Accessed January 31, 2019.

———. n.d. "Annual Lobbying by Amnesty International USA. https://www.opensecrets.org/lobby/clientsum.php?id=D000047121&year=2018. Accessed January 31, 2019.

———. n.d. "Lobbying Database." https://www.opensecrets.org/lobby/. Accessed January 31, 2019.

———. n.d. "Top Organization Contributors." https://www.opensecrets.org/orgs/list.php?id=.

———. 2000a. "Oil & Gas: Top Recipients." https://www.opensecrets.org/industries/recips.php?cycle=2000&ind=E01. Accessed January 31, 2019.

———. 2000b. "Oil & Gas: Top PAC Recipients." https://www.opensecrets.org/industries/pacrecips.php?ind=E01&cycle=2000. Accessed January 31, 2019.

Otis, John. 2005. "Tree Oil Plan Tries to Bear Fruit." *Houston Chronicle*, February 6.

———. 2012. "Targeting Teachers: The 'Dirty War' against Colombia's Unions." Global Post, February 9. http://www.globalpost.com/dispatch/news/regions/americas/colombia/120207/colombia-unions-teachers-violence.

Paley, Dawn. 2014. *Drug War Capitalism*. Oakland, CA: AK Press.

Palmer, Mark J. 2002. "Oil and the Bush Administration." *Earth Island Journal*, Fall. http://www.earthisland.org/journal/index.php/magazine/entry/oil_and_the_bush_administration/.

Parra, Alberto de la. 2013. "Mexico: Mexican Congress Approves Bill to Open Mexico's Electricity Industry to Private Investors." Jones Day, December 30. http://www.mondaq.com/x/283456/Energy+Law/Mexican+Congress+Approves+Bill+To+Open+Mexicos+Electricity+Industry+To+Private+Investors.

Pasman, Manya Brachear. 2015. "Clergy Join Push to Legalize Marijuana in Mission of Social Justice." *Chicago Tribune*, June 2.

Patroni, Viviana, and Manuel Poitras. 2002. "Labour in Neoliberal Latin America: And Introduction." *Labour, Capital and Society* 35 (2): 207–20.

Payne, Leigh A., and Gabriel Pereira. 2016. *Corporate Complicity in Dictatorship*. Oxford: University of Oxford, Saïd Business School.

Pelaez, Vicky. 2014. "The Prison Industry in the United States: Big Business or a New Form of Slavery?" Global Research, March 31. http://www.globalresearch.ca/the-prison-industry-in-the-united-states-big-business-or-a-new-form-of-slavery/8289.

Pelaez, Victor, and Wilson Schmidt. 2004. "Social Struggles and the Regulation of Transgenic Crops in Brazil." In *Agribusiness and Society: Corporate Responses to Environmentalism, Market*, edited by K. Jensen and S. Vellema, 232–52. New York: Palgrave Macmillan.

Perl, Raphael F. 1992. "United States Andean Drug Policy: Background and Issues for Decisionmakers." *Journal of Interamerican Studies and World Affairs* 34 (3): 13–35.

Perlez, Jane, and Lowell Bergman. 2005. "Tangled Strands in the Fight over Peru Gold Mine." *New York Times*, October 25.

Peyrouse, Sébastien. 2012. *Drug Trafficking in Central Asia: A Poorly Considered Fight?* Washington, DC: PONARS (New Approaches to Research and Security in Eurasia).

Pincus, Walter. 2010. "White House Threatens Veto on Intelligence Activities Bill." *Washington Post*, March 16.

Plouffe, William C., Jr. 2011. "1909 Shanghai Conference." In *Encyclopedia of Drug Policy*, edited by Mark. A. R. Klelman and James E. Hawdon, 586–88. Thousand Oaks, CA: Sage.

Poe, Steven C. 1990. "Human Rights and US Foreign Aid: A Review of the Quantitative Studies and Suggestions for Future Research." *Human Rights Quarterly* 12 (4): 499–512.

———. 1991. "Human Rights and the Allocation of US Military Assistance." *Journal of Peace Research* 28 (2): 205–16.

Poe, Steven C., and James Meernik. 1995. "U.S. Military Aid in the 1980s: A Global Analysis." *Journal of Peace Research* 32 (4): 399–411.

Poe, Steven C., and C. Neal Tate. 1994. "Repression of Human Rights to Personal Integrity in the 1980s: A Global Analysis." *American Political Science Review* 88 (4): 853–72.

Poe, Steven C., Neal C. Tate, and Linda Camp Keith. 1999. "Repression of the Human Right to Personal Integrity Revisited: A Global Cross-National Study Covering the Years 1976–1993." *International Studies Quarterly* 43 (2): 291–313.

Pomerleau, Kyle. 2014. *How Much Do U.S. Multinational Corporations Pay in Foreign Income Taxes?* Washington, DC: Tax Foundation.

Popkin, Margaret. 2001. "Efforts to Enhance Judicial Independence in Latin America: A Comparative Perspective." In *Guidance for Promoting Judicial Independence and Impartiality*, by Office of Democracy and Governance, 100–132. USAID technical publication. Washington, DC: USAID.

Poulantzas, Nicos. 1976. "The Capitalist State: A Reply to Miliband and Laclau." *New Left Review* 95 (January–February): 63–83.

———. 1978. *Classes in Contemporary Capitalism*. London: NLB.

Prins, Nomi. 2015. *All the Presidents' Bankers: The Hidden Alliance That Drives American Power*. New York: Nation Books.

Project for the New American Century. 1997. *PNAC Statement of Principles*. Washington, DC: Project for the New American Century.

———. 1998a. *Neoconservative Think Tank Urges US to Attack Iraq*. Washington, DC: Project for the New American Century.

———. 1998b. *PNAC Calls on Republican Congressional Leaders to Assert US Interests in Persian Gulf*. Washington, DC: Project for the New American Century.

Przeworski, Adam. 2000. *Democracy and Development: Political Institutions and Well-Being in the World*. Cambridge: Cambridge University Press.

RAND Corporation. 2014. *@ RAND*. Annual report. Washington, DC: RAND Corporation.

Raskin, Marcus G. 1976. "Democracy versus the National Security State." *Law and Contemporary Problems* 40 (3): 189–220.

RAYCOM News Network. 2015. "South Carolina Business Used to Launder Billions to Drug Cartels, Terrorist." July 15. http://raycomgroup.worldnow.com/story/29046749 /south-carolina-businesses-used-to-launder-billions-to-drug-cartels-terrorists.

Reich, Robert B. 2007. *Supercapitalism: The Transformation of Business, Democracy, and Everyday Life*. New York: Knopf.

Remmer, Karen. 1990. "Debt or Democracy? The Political Impact of the Debt Crisis in Latin America." In *Financing Latin American Growth: Prospects for the 1990s*, edited by D. Felix, 63–78. Armonk, NY.: M.E. Sharpe.

Reuter, Peter H., and Jonathan P. Caulkins. 1995. "Redefining the Goals of National Drug Policy: Recommendations from a Working Group." *American Journal of Public Health* 85 (8): 1059–63.

Reuter, Peter, and Victoria Greenfield. 2001. "Measuring Global Drug Markets: How Good Are the Numbers and Why Should We Care about Them?" *World Economics* 2 (4): 159–73.

Reuter, Peter, and Mark A. R. Kleinman. 1986. "Risks and Prices: An Economic Analysis of Drug Enforcement." In *Crime and Justice: A Review of Research*, edited by M. Tonry and N. Morris, 289–340. Chicago: University of Chicago Press.

Reuters. 2004. "Newmont Scales Back at Blockaded Peru Gold Mine." September 17. http://www.minesandcommunities.org//article.php?a=5806.

———. 2010. "WalMart Eying Russia's Lenta." May 12. http://uk.reuters.com/article /idUKLDE64B2IM20100512?feedType=RSS&feedName=consumerproducts-SP.

Richani, Nazih. 2005. "Multinational Corporations, Renter Capitalism, and the War System in Colombia." *Latin American Politics and Society* 47 (3): 113–14.

Richards, David L, Ronald Gelleny, and David Sacko. 2001. "Money with a Mean Streak? Foreign Economic Penetration and Government Respect for Human Rights in Developing Countries." *International Studies Quarterly* 45 (2): 219–39.

Ridgeway, James. 2010. "The Airport Scanner Scam." *Mother Jones*, January 4. http:// www.motherjones.com/mojo/2010/01/airport-scanner-scam.

Ripley, Charles G. 2014. "Washington, Logrolling, and Plan Colombia: Rethinking U.S. Involvement in Colombia's Armed Conflict." *Ciencias Politicas y Relaciones Internacionales* 3 (3): 6–22.

Roberts, J. Timmons, and Nikki Demetria Thanos. 2003. *Trouble in Paradise: Globalization and Environmental Crises in Latin America*. New York: Routledge.

Robinson, Phyllis. 2009. "New Evidence Links Dole Food Company to Paramilitary Assassinations in Colombia." International Rights Advocates, December 7. http://smallfarmersbigchange.coop/2009/12/07/new-evidence-links-dole-food -company-to-paramilitary-assassinations-in-colombia/.

Rohrlich, Justin. 2011. "Why Are Prisoners Building Patriot Missiles?" Minyanville.com, March 7. http://www.minyanville.com/businessmarkets/articles/defense-industrial -base-defense-budget-defense/3/7/2011/id/33198?page=full.

Rojas, Isaias. 2005. "Peru: Drug Control Policy, Human Rights, and Democracy." In *Drugs and Democracy in Latin America: The Impact of U.S. Policy*, edited by C. A. Youngers and E. Rosin, 185–230. Boulder, CO: Lynne Rienner.

Rooney, Kate. 2018. "Trump's Tax Cut Windfall Lifts Stock Dividends to New Record." CNBC, April 3. https://www.cnbc.com/2018/04/03/trumps-tax-cut-windfall-lifts -stock-dividends-to-new-record.html.

Rose, Arnold Marshall. 1967. *The Power Structure: Political Process in American Society*. New York: Oxford University Press.

Rubin, Alissa J. 2009. "Afghans Detail Detention in 'Black Jail' at U.S. Base." *New York Times*, November 28.

Rudra, Nita. 2008. *Globalization and the Race to the Bottom in Developing Countries: Who Really Gets Hurt?* New York: Cambridge University Press.

Runde, Daniel F., and Julie Snyder. 2016. "Rebuilding the National and Global Consensus against Illicit Narcotics: An Agenda for the Next President." Center for Strategic and International Studies, January 13. http://csis.org/publication/rebuilding-national-and -global-consensus-against-illicit-narcotics-agenda-next-president.

Ruskin, Gary. 2010. "Obama Gives Key Agriculture Post to Monsanto Man." Global Research, March 27. http://www.globalresearch.ca/obama-gives-key-agriculture -post-to-monsanto-man/18499.

Ryan, Kevin F. 1998. "Clinging to Failure: The Rise and Continued Life of U.S. Drug Policy." *Law and Society Review* 32 (1): 221–42.

———. 2001. "Towards an Explanation of the Persistence of Failed Policy: Binding Drug Policy to Foreign Policy, 1930–1962." In *Drug War American Style: The International- ization of Failed Policy and Its Alternatives*, edited by J. Gerber and E. L. Jensen, 19–48. New York: Garland.

SAIC (Science Applications International Corporation). 2007. *SAIC Annual Report Fiscal Year 2007.* McLean, VA: SAIC.

Sandberg, Christin. 2014a. "Guatemalan Court Rules in Favor of Indigenous People over Goldcorp Mining in Sipacapa." Upside Down World, July 31. http://upsidedownworld .org/main/guatemala-archives-33/4963-guatemalan-court-rules-in-favor-of-indigenous -people-over-goldcorp-mining-in-sipacapa.

———. 2014b. "Mayan People's Movement Defeats Monsanto Law in Guatemala." Upside Down World, September 11. http://upsidedownworld.org/main/guatemala-archives -33/5042-mayan-peoples-movement-defeats-monsanto-law-in-guatemala.

Sanger, David E. 2013. *Confront and Conceal: Obama's Secret Wars and Surprising Use of American Power.* New York: Broadway Books.

Savage, Charlie. 2009a. "Obama Upholds Detainee Policy in Afghanistan." *New York Times*, February 21.

———. 2009b. "Obama's War on Terror May Resemble Bush's in Some Areas." *New York Times*, February 17.

———. 2011. "Secret U.S. Memo Made Legal Case to Kill a Citizen." *New York Times*, October 8.

———. 2012. "Judge Rejects New Rules on Access to Prisoners." *New York Times*, September 6.

———. 2013. "Robert's Picks Reshaping Secret Surveillance Court." *New York Times*, July 25.

Savage, Charlie, and Mark Landler. 2011. "White House Defends Continuing U.S. Role in Libya Operation." *New York Times*, June 15.

Savage, Charlie, and James Risen. 2010. "Federal Judge Finds N.S.A. Wiretaps Were Illegal." *New York Times*, March 31.

Schedler, Andreas. 2002. "Elections without Democracy: The Menu of Manipulation." *Journal of Democracy* 13 (2): 36–50.

Schlesinger, Arthur M. 1973. *The Imperial Presidency*. Boston: Houghton Mifflin.

Schlesinger, Stephen, and Stephen Kinzer. 1999. *Bitter Fruit: The Story of the American Coup in Guatemala*. Cambridge, MA: Harvard University Press.

School of the Americas Watch. 2007. "Colombian Paramilitary Leader Confirms Collusion with U.S. Trained Colombian Generals." March 27. http://www.soaw.org/news /news-alerts/3283.

Schumpeter, Joseph A. 1950. *Capitalism, Socialism and Democracy*. New York: Harper and Row.

Scott, Christine. 2013. *The Work Opportunity Tax Credit (WOTC)*. Washington, DC: Congressional Research Service.

Scott, Peter Dale. 2003. *Drugs, Oil and War: The United States in Afghanistan, Colombia, and Indochina*. Lanham, MD: Rowman and Littlefield.

Seelke, Clare Ribando. 2009. *Mérida Initiative for Mexico and Central America: Funding and Policy Issues*. Washington, DC: Congressional Research Service.

———. 2010. *Mérida Initiative for Mexico and Central America: Funding and Policy Issues*. Washington, DC: Congressional Research Service.

Seelke, Clare Ribando, and Kristin Finklea. 2014. *U.S.-Mexican Security Cooperation: The Mérida Initiative and Beyond*. Washington, DC: Congressional Research Service.

Seelke, Clare Ribando, Liana Sun Wyler, June S. Beittel, and Mark P. Sullivan. 2011. *Latin American and the Caribbean: Illicit Drug Trafficking and U.S. Counterdrug Programs*. Washington, DC: Congressional Research Service.

Selaya, Pablo, and Eva Rytter Sunesen. 2012. "Does Foreign Aid Increase Foreign Direct Investment?" *World Development* 40 (11): 2155–76.

Sellin, Thorsten. 1976. *Slavery and the Penal System*. New York: Elsevier.

Sentencing Project. 2013. *Fact Sheet: Trends in U.S. Corrections*. Washington, DC: Sentencing Project.

———. 2016. *Six Million Lost Voters: State-Level Estimates of Felony Disenfranchisement, 2016*. Washington, DC: Sentencing Project.

———. 2017. *Trends in U.S. Corrections*. Washington, DC: Sentencing Project.

Seraffino, Nina M. 2001. *Colombia: Plan Colombia Legislation and Assistance (FY2000–FY2001)*. Washington, DC: Congressional Research Service.

Shachtman, Noah. 2011. "Prisoners Help Build the Patriot Missiles." Wired.com, March 8. http://www.wired.com/2011/03/prisoners-help-build-patriot-missiles/.

Sheridan, Mary Beth. 2009. "On Mexico Trio, Clinton Criticizes U.S. Drug Policy." *Washington Post*, March 26.

Shorrock, Tim. 2008. *Spies for Hire: The Secret World of Intelligence Outsourcing*. New York: Simon and Schuster

Shugart, Mathew Soberg, and John M. Carey. 1992. *Presidents and Assemblies: Constitutional Design and Electoral Dynamics*. Cambridge: Cambridge University Press.

Sikkink, Kathryn. 2004. *Mixed Signals: U.S. Human Rights Policy and Latin America*. Ithaca, NY: Cornell University Press.

Silverstein, Ken. 2013. "The Secret Donors behind the Center for American Progress and Other Think Tanks." *Nation*, May 22.

Sisodia, Rajeshree, and Andrew Buncombe. 2009. "Burmese Villagers 'Forced to Work on Total Pipeline'." Independent, August 14. https://www.independent.co.uk/news/world/asia/burmese-villagers-forced-to-work-on-total-pipeline-1771876.html.

Sloan, Bob. 2015. "Identifying Businesses That Profit from Prison Labor." popular resistance.org, May 19. https://popularresistance.org/identifying-businesses-that-profit-from-prison-labor/.

Small, Albion, and G. Vincent. 1894. An Introduction to the Study of Society. New York: American Books.

Smith, Jennifer M. 2012. "Indigenous Communities in Mexico Fight Corporate Wind Farms." Upside Down World, November 1. http://upsidedownworld.org/main/mexico-archives-79/3952-indigenous-communities-in-mexico-fight-corporate-wind-farms.

Smith, Mark A. 2000. American Business and Political Power: Public Opinion, Elections, and Democracy. Chicago: University of Chicago Press.

Smith, Michael. 2010. "Banks Financing Mexico Drug Gangs Admitted in Wells Fargo Deal." Bloomberg.com, June 29. http://www.bloomberg.com/news/articles/2010-06-29/banks-financing-mexico-s-drug-cartels-admitted-in-wells-fargo-s-u-s-deal.

Smith, Peter. 2018. "Trump Cuts Legs out from under Sessions' War on Weed." Drug War Chronicle, April 15. https://stopthedrugwar.org/chronicle/2018/apr/15/trump_cuts_legs_out_under.

Smith, Peter H., and Melissa R. Ziegler. 2008. "Liberal and Illiberal Democracy in Latin America." Latin American Politics and Society 50 (1): 31–57.

Sokoloff, Kenneth L., and Stanley L. Engerman. 2000. "History Lessons: Institutions, Factors Endowments, and Paths of Development in the New World." Journal of Economic Perspectives 14 (3): 217–32.

Solano, Luis. 2015. "Guatemala: How a Pseudo-military Project Was Created to Protect the Escobal Mine." Upside Down World, April 9. http://upsidedownworld.org/main/guatemala-archives-33/5274-guatemala-how-a-pseudo-military-project-was-created-to-protect-the-escobal-mine-.

Sopko, John F. 2014. Poppy Cultivation in Afghanistan: After a Decade of Reconstruction and Over $7 Billion in Counternarcotics Efforts, Poppy Cultivation Levels Are at an All Time High. Office of the Special Inspector General for Afghanistan Reconstruction, October 14. https://apps.dtic.mil/dtic/tr/fulltext/u2/a610310.pdf.

Spar, Debora. 1999. "Foreign Investment and Human Rights." Challenge 42 (1): 55–80.

St. Clair, Jeffery. 1999. "The Monsanto Machine." In These Times, March 7. http://www.commondreams.org/headlines/090300-03.htm.

Stephan, James J. 2004. State Prison Expenditures, 2001. Bureau of Justice Statistics: Special Report, June. Washington, DC: U.S. Department of Justice.

Stirk, Chloe. 2013. "Colombia: Resources for Humanitarian Responses and Poverty Reduction." Global Humanitarian Assistance, April 29. http://devinit.org/wp-content/uploads/2013/04/Colombia-final-draft.pdf.

Stockholm International Peace Research Institute. 2015. SIPRI Arms Data Base. http://www.sipri.org/contents/armstrad/at_data.html. Accessed March 13, 2015.

Storrs, K. Larry. 2003. Drug Certification/Designation Procedures for Illicit Narcotics Producing and Transit Countries. Washington, DC: Congressional Research Service.

Taffet, Jeffrey. 2007. *Foreign Aid as Foreign Policy: The Alliance for Progress in Latin America*. New York: Routledge.

Tankersley, J., and M. Tackett. 2018. "Trump Tax Cuts Pays Dividends For the GOP." *New York Times*, August 18.

Telegraph. 2009. "U.S. Buys Mexico Helicopters to Fight Drug War Violence." March 26. http://www.telegraph.co.uk/news/worldnews/centralamericaandthecaribbean /mexico/5053823/US-buys-Mexico-Helicopters-to-fight-drug-violence.html.

Tielemans, Otto Raul. 2014. *Authoritarianism on the Rise: The War on Drug's Erosion of Mexican Democracy*. Washington, DC: Council on Hemispheric Affairs.

Timberlake, Michael, and Kirk R. Williams. 1984. "Dependence, Political Exclusion, and Government Repression: Some Cross-National Evidence." *American Sociological Review* 49 (1): 141–46.

Tonry, Michael. 2011. *Punishing Race: A Continuing American Dilemma*. New York: Oxford University Press.

Trevaskes, Susan. 2007. "The Private/Public Security Nexus in China." *Social Justice* 34 (3/4): 38–55.

Truman, David B. 1951. *The Governmental Process: Political Interests and Public Opinion*. New York: Knopf.

Tseblis, George, and Eduardo Aleman. 2005. "Presidential Conditional Agenda Setting in Latin America." *World Politics* 57 (3): 396–420.

Tulchin, Joseph S., and Gary Bland, eds. 2005. *Getting Globalization Right: The Dilemmas of Inequality*. Boulder, CO: Lynne Rienner.

Tuman, John, and Craig Emmert. 1999. "Explaining Japanese Foreign Direct Investment in Latin America, 1979–1993." *Social Science Quarterly* 80 (3): 539–55.

Ungar, Mark. 2007. "The Privatization of Citizen Security in Latin America." *Social Justice* 34 (3/4): 20–37.

U.N. Development Programme. 2008. *The European Union's Border Management Programme in Central Asia (BOMCA)*. Brussels, Belgium: European Union and U.N. Development Programme.

U.N. General Assembly. 2013. *Annual Report of the United Nations High Commissioner for Human Rights: Report of the United Nations High Commissioner for Human Rights on the Situation in Colombia*. New York City: U.N. General Assembly.

U.N. International Drug Control Programme. 1998. *Social and Economic Consequences of Drug Abuse and Illicit Trafficking*. Vienna, Austria: U.N. International Drug Control Programme.

United Nations. 1985a. "Resolution 40/32." General Assembly, November 29. New York: United Nations.

———. 1985b. "Resolution 40/146." General Assembly, December 13. New York: United Nations.

———. 2002. *Report of the International Conference on Financing for Development*. Monterrey, Mexico: United Nations.

———. 2008. *United Nations Declaration on the Rights of Indigenous Peoples*. International Labor Organization. New York: United Nations.

United Nations Conference on Trade and Development database. n.d. http://unctadstat .unctad.org/wds/ReportFolders/reportFolders.aspx?sCS_ChosenLang=en.

United Technologies Corporation. 2013. *Focused: 2013 Annual Report.* Hartford, CT: United Technologies Corporation.

UNODC (U.N. Office on Drugs and Crime). 2007. *Crime, Violence, and Development: Trends, Costs, and Policy Options in the Caribbean.* New York: UNODC and World Bank.

———. 2011. *2011 World Drug Report.* New York: UNODC.

———. 2013. *Citizen Security with a Human Face: Evidence and Proposals for Latin America.* New York: U.N. Development Programme.

———. 2014. *2014 World Drug Report.* New York: UNODC.

———. 2015. *Press Release: 2014 Bolivia Survey Reports Decline in Coca Cultivation for Fourth Year in a Row.* La Paz, Bolivia: U.N. Office on Drugs and Crime.

USAID (U.S. Agency for International Development). n.d. *The Green Book.* https://www .usaid.gov/developer/greenbookapi.

———. 2013. *USAID: Colombia.* Washington, DC: USAID.

———. 2016. *Assessment of the Caribbean Basin Security Initiative.* Washington, DC: USAID.

U.S. Census Bureau. 2018. Historical Tables: Income Inequality, Table F-4. Gini Ratios of Families by Race and Hispanic Origin Householder. https://www.census.gov/data /tables/time-series/demo/income-poverty/historical-income-inequality.html. Accessed January 20, 2019.

U.S. Chamber of Commerce. 2007. "North American Competitive Council (NACC): Enhancing Competitiveness in Canada, Mexico, and the United States—Private Sector Priorities for the Security and Prosperity Partnership of North America (SPP)." February. https://www.uschamber.com/sites/default/files/legacy/reports/070223nacc .pdf.

U.S.-Colombia Business Partnership. 1996. "U. S-Colombia Business Partnership." https://www.bloomberg.com/profiles/companies/0824355D:US-us-colombia-business -partnership. Accessed March 14, 2015.

U.S. Department of Commerce, International Trade Administration. n.d. *Free Trade Agreements.* https://www.trade.gov/fta/. Accessed April 30, 2016.

U.S. Department of Education. 2015. *Digest of Education Statistics, 2013.* Edited by National Center for Education Statistics. Washington, DC: U.S. Department of Education.

U.S. Department of Energy. 1998. "Sale of the Elk Hills Naval Petroleum Reserve." February 5. http://energy.gov/fe/sale-elk-hills-naval-petroleum-reserve. Accessed March 29, 2015.

U.S. Department of Justice, Office of Public Affairs. 2007. "Chiquita Brands International Pleads Guilty to Making Payments to a Designated Terrorist Organization and Agrees to Pay $25 Million Fine." March 19. http://www.justice.gov/archive/opa/pr/2007 /March/07_nsd_161.html.

———. 2010. "BAE Systems PLC Pleads Guilty and Ordered to Pay $400 Million Criminal Fine." March 1. http://www.justice.gov/opa/pr/bae-systems-plc-pleads-guilty-and -ordered-pay-400-million-criminal-fine.

U.S. Department of State. 2009a. "2009 Human Rights Report: Mexico." March 11. http:// www.state.gov/j/drl/rls/hrrpt/2009/wha/136119.htm.

———. 2009b. "The Central Asia Counternarcotic Initiative (CACI)." https://2009-2017 .state.gov/documents/organization/184507.pdf. Accessed January 17, 2019.

———. n.d. *International Narcotics Control Strategy Report (INCSR)*. https://www.state .gov/j/inl/rls/nrcrpt/. Accessed May 14, 2015.

———. n.d. "United States Bilateral Investment Treaties." http://www.state.gov/e/eb/ifd /bit/117402.htm. Accessed May 1, 2016.

U.S. Drug Enforcement Administration. 1990. *The History of the DEA: 1985–1990.* Washington, DC: U.S. Drug Enforcement Administration.

Useem, Michael. 1984. *The Inner Circle: Large Corporations and the Rise of the Business Political Activity in the U.S. and U.K.* Oxford: Oxford University Press.

U.S. Embassy Bogotá. 1997a. "Ambassador's January 12 Meeting with New MOD [Minister of Defense] Designate." Declassified document. Bogotá, Colombia: Declassified Document of the U.S. Department of State.

———. 1997b. "CODEL's Hastert's May 24–27 Visit to Colombia." Declassified document. Bogotá, Colombia: U.S. Department of State.

———. 1997c. "Hold on Sec. 506 Shipment for Colombian Military." Declassified document. Bogotá, Colombia: U.S. Department of State.

U.S. Embassy Mexico. 2010. *Mexico—Detailed Advanced Acquisition Plan.* Mexico City: U.S. Department of State.

———. 2012. *U.S.-Mexico Border Cooperation under the Mérida Initiative: Non-intrusive Inspection Equipment.* Mexico City: U.S. Embassy Mexico, Narcotics Affairs Section.

U.S. Foreign Intelligence Surveillance Court. 2013. *Application of the Federal Bureau of Investigation for an Order Requiring the Production of Tangible Things from Verizon Business Network Services, Inc on Behalf of MCI Communication Services, Inc. D/B/A Verizon Business Services.* Washington, DC: U.S. Foreign Intelligence Surveillance Court.

U.S. Government Accountability Office. 2008. *Plan Colombia: Drug Reduction Goals Were Not Fully Met, but Security Has Improved; U.S. Agencies Need More Detailed Plans for Reducing Assistance.* Washington, DC: U.S. Government Accountability Office.

———. 2010. *Mérida Initiative: The United States Has Provided Counternarcotics and Anticrime Support but Needs Better Performance Measures.* Washington, DC: U.S. Government Accountability Office.

U.S. House Committee on Foreign Affairs. 1990. *The Andean Initiative. Hearings before the Subcommittee on Western Hemisphere Affairs of the Committee on Foreign Affairs, House of Representatives,* 101st Cong., 2nd Sess., June 6 and 20, 1–147. Washington, DC: U.S. Government Printing Office.

U.S. House Committee on the Judiciary. 1984. *1984: Civil Liberties and the National Security State.* Washington, DC: U.S. Government Printing Office.

U.S. House of Representatives. 2005. "Building Better Relations with Afro-Colombians." *Congressional Record* 151 (12), 16212-13

———. 2008. *H.Res. 1504: Urging the President to Increase Efforts under the Border Initiative (TBI) to Deepen Cooperation and Collaboration with Caribbean Nations.* Washington, DC: U.S. Government Printing Office.

———. 2009. "Congressional Black Caucus." *Congressional Record* 155 (11), 15120.

———. 2017. *AG Jeff Sessions Testifies before the House Judiciary Committee.* Washington, DC: U.S. Congress.

U.S.-Mexico Chamber of Commerce. 2011. "Issue Paper 1: U.S.–Mexico Security Cooperation." August. http://www.usmcoc.org/papers-current/1-US-%20Mexico-Security -Cooperation.pdf.

U.S. Office on Colombia. 2013. *Large-Scale Mining in Colombia: Human Rights Violations Past, Present and Future.* Washington, DC: U.S. Office on Colombia.

U.S. Senate Committee on Homeland Security and Governmental Affairs. 2009. "Southern Border Violence Impels Hearings: Senate Committee to Examine Implications for U.S. Security." February 26. http://www.hsgac.senate.gov/media/majority-media /southern-border-violence-impels-hearings. Accessed March 30, 2015.

U.S. Senate Judiciary Subcommittee on Technology, Terrorism, and Government Information. 2002. *International Drug Trafficking and Terrorism.* Washington, DC: U.S. Senate Committee on the Judiciary.

Vacius, Ingrid, and Adam Isacson. 2000. "Plan Colombia: The Debate in Congress, 2000." Center for International Policy Brief, December 4. http://www.ciponline.org /research/html/plan-colombia-the-debate-in-congress-2000.

Verbitsky, Horacio, and Juan Pablo Bohoslavsky, eds. 2013. *The Economic Accomplices to the Argentine Dictatorship: Outstanding Debts.* Cambridge: Cambridge University Press.

Vivanco, José Miguel. 2015. "Mexico/U.S.: Letter to President Obama regarding President Peña Nieto Human Rights Record." Human Rights Watch, January 5. http://www .hrw.org/news/2015/01/05/mexicous-letter-president-obama-regarding-president -pena-nietos-human-rights-record.

Voss, D. Stephen. 2004. "Multicollinearity." In *Encyclopedia of Social Measurement,* edited by K. Kempf-Leonard, 759–70. San Diego, CA: Academic Press.

Vreeland, James Raymond. 2003. *The IMF and Economic Development.* Cambridge: Cambridge University Press.

Waldron, Travis. 2013. "Corporate Profits Have Risen 20 Times Faster than Workers' Income Since 2008." ThinkProgress, March 4. http://thinkprogress.org/economy/2013 /03/04/1665281/corporate-profits-worker-income/.

Wallerstein, Immanuel. 1974. *The Modern World System.* New York: Academic Press.

———. 1984. *The Politics of the World Economy.* Cambridge: Cambridge University Press.

Walmsley, Roy. 2013. *World Prison Population List.* 10th ed. UK: University of Essex, International Center for Prison Studies.

Walt, Stephen M. 2005. *Taming American Power: The Global Response to U.S. Primacy.* New York: Norton.

Washington Office on Latin America. 2008. "The Mérida Initiative and Citizen Security in Mexico and Central America." March 19. http://www.wola.org/publications/the _merida_initiative_and_citizen_security_in_mexico_and_central_america.

Waterhouse, Benjamin C. 2014. *Lobbying America: The Politics of Business from Nixon to NAFTA.* Princeton, NJ: Princeton University Press.

Weiss, Robert P. 2007. "From Cowboy Detectives to Soldiers of Fortune: Private Security Contracting and Its Contradictions on the New Frontiers of Capitalist Expansion." *Social Justice* 34 (3/4): 1–19.

Weiss, Thomas G. 1999. "Sanctions as a Foreign Policy Tool: Weighing Humanitarian Impulses." *Journal of Peace Research* 36: 499–509.

Western, Bruce, and Becky Pettit. 2010. "Incarceration and Social Inequality." *Daedalus*, Summer, 8–19.

White, Harrison C., Scott A. Boorman, and Ronald L. Breiger. 1976. "Social Structure from Multiple Networks. I. Blockmodels of Roles and Positions." *American Journal of Sociology* 81 (4): 730–80.

White House. 2001. *Fact Sheet: President's Speech at the Summit of the Americas*. Washington, DC: Office of the Press Secretary.

———. 2015. *The National Security Strategy*. Washington, DC: White House.

White House Office of National Drug Control Policy. 2003. *2003 National Drug Control Strategy*. Washington, DC: Office of National Drug Control Policy.

———. 2013. *2013 National Drug Control Strategy*. Washington, DC: Office of National Drug Control Policy.

———. 2014. *National Drug Control Budget: FY 2015 Funding Highlights*. Washington, DC: Office of National Drug Control.

———. 2016. *FY 2017 Budget and Performance Summary*. Washington, DC: Office of National Drug Control.

———. 2017. *National Drug Control Budget: FY 2018 Funding Highlights*. Washington, DC: Office of National Drug Control.

Williams, Daniel. 1998. "Oil-Soaked Azeris Find Affluence Elusive." *Washington Post Foreign Service*, September 7.

Williams, Mark Eric, and Vinay Jawahar. 2003. "When Rational Policy Making Fails: Plan Colombia and the Approaching Commitment Trap." *International Journal of Politics and Ethics* 3 (2): 159–72.

Wilson, Scott, and Anne Gearan. 2013. "Obama Didn't Know about Surveillance of U.S.-Allied World Leaders until Summer, Officials Say." *Washington Post*, October 28.

Wojciak, Piotr. 2014. "Sixteen Businessmen Sentenced to Prison for Paramilitary Ties." Columbia Reports, December 10. http://colombiareports.com/16-businessmen -sentenced-jail-criminal-associations-paramilitaries/.

Wolfe, Alan. 1984. *The Rise and Fall of the Soviet Threat: Domestic Sources of the Cold War Consensus*. Washington, DC: Institute for Policy Studies.

Woodrow Wilson International Center for Scholars. 2014. *Wilson Center FY 2014 Corporate Gifts*. Washington, DC: Wilson Center.

World Bank. 2016. *Databank: World Development Indicators*. http://databank.worldbank .org/data/reports.aspx?source=world-development-indicators. Accessed April 21, 2016.

World Bank and UN Office on Drugs and Crime's International Homicide Statistics database. "Intentional Homicides (per 1,000,000 people)." http://data.worldbank.org /indicator/VC.IHR.PSRC.P5. Accessed September 15, 2015.

Yagoub, Mimi. 2016. "'We Will Not Demobilize': First FARC Dissidents Won't Be

the Last." InSightCrime: Organized Crime in the Americas, July 6. https://www
.insightcrime.org/news/analysis/we-will-not-demobilize-first-farc-dissidents-wont
-be-the-last/.

Yardeni, Edward, and Debbie Johnson. 2016. "U.S. Economic Indicators: Corporate Profits in GDP." Yardeni Research, Inc., March 4. www.yardeni.com.

Young, Abe Louise. 2010. "BP Hires Prison Labor to Clean Up Spill While Coastal
Residents Struggle." *Nation*, July 21. http://www.thenation.com/article/bp-hires
-prison-labor-clean-spill-while-coastal-residents-struggle/.

Zakaria, Fared. 1997. "The Rise of Illiberal Democracy." *Foreign Affairs* 76 (6): 22–43.

Zanger, Sabine C. 2000. "A Global Analysis of the Effects of Political Regime Changes
on Life Integrity Violations." *Journal of Peace Research* 37 (2): 213–33.

Zelizer, Julian E. 2002. "Seeds of Cynicism: The Struggle over Campaign Finance,
1956–1974." *Journal of Policy History* 14 (1): 73–111

threats to, 149; Indigenous challenges to, 148; resistance to, 110, 126–35, 152

capitalism, 1–2, 139; drug war, 185–95

capitalist state, fiscal crisis of the, 57

Caribbean, 14, 37–38, 112; aid to fight drug war, 55; Caribbean Basin Security Initiative, 112; counternarcotic aid to, 58–60; foreign direct investment in, 114–16, 148; homicide rates in, 167; U.S.-funded drug war in, 119, 167; U.S. transnational corporate penetration into, 138

CARICOM, 38

Carnegie Endowment for International Peace, 86, 94

Carroll, Philip, 72

cartels, drug, 2, 20–22, 37, 41, 55, 57, 81, 94, 95, 111, 117, 147, 166, 168, 170, 172, 209–10, 216, 225, 243n1; power struggles within, 112

Carter, Jimmy, 162

Case, Francis, 71

Caspian Basin: oil companies interests in, 61

Caspian Pipeline Consortium, 61

Caterpillar, Inc., 33, 93, 95, 194

Center for American Progress, 74

Center for Responsible Politics, 240n4 (chap. 4)

Center for Responsive Politics, 71, 86

Center for Strategic and International Studies, 76, 77–78, 86, 95; corporate contributors to, 96

Central America: African palm oil cultivation in, 118; Central American Regional Security Initiative, 112; citizens' perceptions of democracy in, 157–58; foreign direct investment in, 114, 148; training of military and police officers in, 42; U.S. aid to fight drug war in, 37–39

Central Asia: American oil companies in, 61; Border Management Program, 63; Counternarcotics Initiative, 63; Drug Action Program, 63

Central Intelligence Agency, 42, 163; creation of, 160

CEO compensation, 189

Chalk, Peter, 88

Chaney, Dick, 76

Chertoff, Michael, 44

Chevron Corporation, 194

Chevron Oil Company, 37, 61, 72, 75, 83, 90, 93, 95, 96, 141; environmental contamination in Ecuador, 123

Chile, 76, 117, 140

China, 9; foreign direct investment in, 114

Chiquita, 7–8, 130–31

The Chiquita Papers, 7

Chomsky, Noam, 19

Christie, Chris, 72

churches, African American, 2

Cingranelli-Richards human rights data index, 5, 6

Cisco, 101

Citibank, 140

citizen insecurity: Latin American responses to, 5–8; vigilantism as response to, 7

citizens, 5, 9, 111, 138, 163; accused of committing acts of terror, 163; cultivation of support and cooperation of, 171; human rights and political freedoms of, 156, 176

citizenship, quality of, 6–7

Citizens United decision, 72, 85, 103

civilians, 20, 28, 131–33, 141, 147

civil society groups: lobbying expenditures of, 48–49, 52, 55–59; repression of, 126

Clarke, Yvette, 37

class bias, 202, 207, 208

cleavages, corporate, 50

Clinton, Hillary, 20, 21, 39, 74; campaign contributions to, 72

Clinton, William J., 30, 138

Clinton administration, 12, 26, 30, 34–36, 44, 74, 76, 81, 85, 102, 131

Clyburn, Jim, 26

CNN's *Zakaria GPS*, 73

coalition, political, 48

coal mines: in Colombia, 31

Coca-Cola, 120

cocaine, 20, 32, 86, 88, 89, 94, 131; crack cocaine, punishment for, 11

cocaine-producing countries, 167–68

Cold War, in aftermath of, 174
collective bargaining, 102, 139, 186, 189, 208
Colombia, 3, 5–6, 8, 88, 94, 102, 112, 117, 167, 215, 241n8 (chap. 4); Administrative Department of Security, 187; aerial crop fumigation program in, 171; African palm oil cultivation in, 118, 130; Afro-diaspora in, 27; air force, 33, 83; American corporate investments in, 29–32, 80; Andean Initiative in, 169; army's *convivir* system, 7–8, 133; Autodefensas Unidas de Columbia, 130; Chocó, 27, 130; Clean Energy Project, 118; cocoa operations in, 33–34, 88, 130; corporations that profited from, 31–36, 42–44; corporations' support for U.S. drug enforcement in, 90; creation of sustainable democracy in, 30; drug suppression efforts in, 91; drug war initiatives in, 14; economic development in, 25; environmental management plan in, 171; fact-finding delegation to, 83; House of Representatives, 27; human rights violations in, 27–28, 81, 130, 133; Indigenous people in, 124, 130–35; Inter-Church Justice and Peace Commission, 124; Justice and Peace process in, 131–32, 187; Mandé Norte Mining project, 124; marijuana and cocaine decriminalization in, 215; Marshall Plan, 25; militarized pattern of drug enforcement in, 34–35, 117; narco-security threats to, 169; oil field in, 30; paramilitary death squads in, 130, 187; peasant organizations in, 7; President Andrés Pastrana Arango, 25–26; sale of military and nonmilitary equipment to, 33; trade unionists in, 187, 189; U.S. aid to, 26, 28, 30–33, 60, 68, 83–85, 115; U.S. drug war in, 130, 215; U.S. embassy in Bogotá, 81; U.S. Special Forces training and equipment in, 117; U.S.-Colombia Business Partnership, 241n8 (chap. 4)
Colombian-Venezuelan border, 30
Colombia Strategic Development Initiative: and U.S. counternarcotic aid, 117–18, 169–70, 186

Comey, James, 210
Committee for the Liberation of Iraq, 77
Committee on Foreign Intelligence, 161
Committee on Transnational Threats, 161
Committees on Appropriations, 54
community: African American, 2, 11, 12, 89, 215; disadvantaged, 214; Hispanic, 11, 215
Compaq: work-release inmates hired at, 194
Comprehensive Drug Abuse and Prevention Act, 11
conflict, social and political, 145
conglomerates, 241n2 (chap. 6)
Congressional Black Caucus, 26–27, 36–38, 212
Congressional Leadership Fund: campaign contributions to, 101
ConocoPhillips, 72
conspiracy theory, 102–3
constitutionalism, democratic, 156
construction and engineering companies: construction contracts, 71
convict leasing system. *See* prison labor
corporate capitalism, 2, 11, 19
corporate revenues, 99–102, 191, 195, 204, 207, 241n10
corporate stock buybacks, 101–2
corporate taxes: in U.S., 99–102
corporations, 2, 3, 7, 13, 19, 22, 32, 34–36, 40, 90, 93, 202, 225, 239n1 (chap. 3); boards of directors of, 69, 77–79; campaign contributions from, 26, 32–33, 70–73, 74, 102–3, 188, 229, 240n4 (chap. 4); corporate congressional lobbying effects on counternarcotic aid flows, 62, 96; interlocking directorate, 74–99; lobbying expenditures of American, 48–49, 51, 53, 55–59, 61–67, 191; network of think tanks and foundations, 73, 94; political behavior of, 99–103; private, 24, 25; subcontracting, 127–35; transnational, 37, 120–27, 130, 138, 147, 241n3 (chap. 5); use of prison labor by, 193–95, 207; lucrative government contracts of, 20, 24, 31,

33, 34, 36, 40–45, 50, 56, 63, 64, 70, 71, 74, 75–83, 94, 120–24, 129, 134, 141, 148–49, 193–94, 212, 225–28

corporatism, 3, 13

Corrections Corporations of America, 194. *See also* prison labor

Costa Rica, 156; foreign direct investment in, 117

Council on Foreign Relations, 73, 76, 77, 78, 93; corporate donors to, 94, 96

counternarcotic aid, U.S., 5–8, 13, 19–21, 25–26, 28, 30, 47, 53–60, 68–103, 110, 115, 146–47, 150–53, 169–71, 173–75, 177–83, 198–99, 216–17, 225, 239n1 (chap. 3), 240n6 (chap. 3), 241n2 (chap. 5); compliance with U.S. human rights law, 54–55, 60, 84–85; and drug war in Mexico and Central America, 37; expenditures on, 20, 28, 33, 47, 57–60, 225; lobbying for, 61–64, 225; recipient countries of, 13, 31, 47, 55, 58, 60, 68–103, 112, 114–15, 117–18, 135, 149, 155, 169–71, 182, 186, 225; trade and foreign, 33, 225; U.S. drug enforcement and, 28, 109–35; U.S. military and, 26, 32–33, 37. *See also* Mérida Initiative; Plan Colombia

covert operations, 163–64

crimes: drug trafficking, 12, 86; organized, 90, 209

criminal justice system: in the United States, 9, 11; in Latin America, 112

criminal organizations, power struggles among, 90, 112

crisis: economic, 48; nation's drug, 12

crop eradication, 22, 28, 34, 91

cross-border: drug enforcement, 63; security arrangements, 64

Cruz, Ted, 72

Cuba, 9

Cuomo, Mario M., 122

cyber warfare, 164

Dahl, Robert, 23, 50, 156

dairy farming, 123

Daley, William, 75

D'Amato, Al, 40

deaths, drug-related, 95

debt crisis, 173

declaration of war, congressional, 163

decriminalization of drugs, 213–16

Deere and Company, 33, 64, 194

defense: security and national, 160–61

defense contractors, 33, 40, 42, 44, 76, 80, 83, 85, 94, 225, 240n1 (chap. 4); use of prison labor, 193–95

defense industry, 20, 32–33

Delahunt, William, 38

Dell: work-release inmates hired at, 194

democracy, 4, 13, 240n1 (chap. 4); American, 70, 162, 176; consolidated, 6, 8; delegative, 156; electoral, 156, 174; growth of, 138; illiberal and liberal, 154–60, 173, 216; Latin America's levels of, 5, 154, 175–76; low-intensity, 156, 159; pluralist, 24; promotion of, 54, 60; quality of, 157–58; violent, 6; world's leader of, 10

Democratic Party, 32

democratization, 4, 5, 169, 171, 174; literature on, 173–74

Democrats, 28; campaign contributions to, 72

dependency theory of state repression, 126–27, 136, 138, 139, 197, 241n3 (chap. 5)

Dependent Development (Evans), 126

developing countries: distribution of wealth and income in, 197

development aid, 113–14

dictatorships, 6, 156

digital surveillance, 129

directorate, interlocking corporate, 68–69, 74–99, 240n2 (chap. 4)

directors, corporate, 69, 92

disaster mitigation, 37

discrimination, racial, 11

disparities, class, 10

displacement, forced, 112, 131–33, 187, 216

distress, economic, 24

dividends, shareholder, 101

Doctors for Cannabis Regulation, 214

Dodd, Christopher, 32–33, 40

Dole, 7, 130–32; *Mendoza Gomez et al. v. Dole Food Company*, 132

House Oversight and Reform Committee, 83, 84
House Select Committee on Narcotics Abuse and Control, 12
House Subcommittee on International Organizations, Human Rights, and Oversight, 38
HSBC, 210
Hudak, John, 92
HudBay Minerals, 130
Humala, Ollanta, 129
human rights, 4, 5–9, 13, 27–28, 38, 51, 53, 81, 84, 103, 111, 129, 135, 137, 143, 173; advocacy groups for, 23–24, 26, 29, 38, 51, 74; U.S. lobbying expenditures for, 58–59; promotion of, 60; respect for, 144–45; violations of, 4, 39, 54–55, 77, 81, 129, 140–41, 147
Human Rights Report for Mexico, 39
Human Rights Watch, 39
human security, 13, 22
human trafficking, 90
Hunt, Ray Lee, 72
Huntington, Samuel P., 180
Hunt Oil, 72
Hussein, Saddam, 76, 77
Hutchinson, Asa, 54

Ibarguen, Julio, 27
IBM: work-release inmates hired at, 194
imperial presidency, as characteristic of national security state, 162–64
incarceration, mass: in the U.S., 9–10, 11, 12–13, 191; cost of, 192–93
incentives, economic, 4
income inequality: impact of international economic integration on, 197–98, 202; in Latin America, 8, 11, 189; in U.S., 10–11, 13, 14, 102–3, 185, 190, 200, 202, 207, 216
India, 114
Indigenous peoples, 119, 129–35; forced displacement of, 130–35, 216; foreign direct investment in, 119–25; resistance to corporation expansion on ancestral lands, 121–22; social mobilizations by, 124–25, 129
inducements, corporate, 24

industrialization, 23
industries, capital-intensive, 138
inflation, 24, 50, 173, 180
information technology: lobbying expenditures of, 64
infrastructure development, 110, 113, 241n1 (chap. 5); U.S. counternarcotic aid for, 116–17, 225
inmate education programs, 12
inner cities: gentrification of, 12
insecurity, citizen. *See* citizen insecurity
inspection systems: vehicle and cargo, 64
instrumental theory, 24–25, 29, 34, 36, 40, 42, 69, 78, 96 theory
insurgency, guerilla, 25, 31
insurgent groups: financial resources from drug trade, 91, 112
intelligence: security payments in exchange for, 7–8
Inter-American Development Bank, 26
Inter-Church Justice and Peace Commission, 124
interest groups, 23, 48, 50, 69
interlocks, corporate-government, 96, 240n4.5
Internal Revenue Service, 99
international drug control, 25, 90
international financial institutions, 70
international free trade, 197
International Monetary Fund, 70, 159, 160, 189
International Narcotics Control Report, 5
international relations, scholars of, 3, 57
International Red Cross, 163
International Security Assistance Force, 91
International Trade Union Confederation, 187
interstate conflict, 76
investments: corporate, 12, 27, 128; human capital, 113–14; overseas, 114; transnational corporate, 5, 117, 138
Iran, 9; cyberwarfare against, 164
Iraq: Committee for the Liberation of, 77; postwar oil industry of, 72; U.S. interventions in, 70, 72, 76
Israel, 26, 129
ITT, 140

MacCoun, Robert J., 89

Macquarie, 120

Maduro, Nicolás, 183

Malthusian catastrophic theory of state repression, 146

Mancuso, Salvatore, 187–88

manufacturing industry, 26, 29, 117, 126; lobbying expenditures of, 64; use of prison labor, 193–95

Marathon, 71

marijuana, 87–88, 89, 214–215; legalization of, 2, 92–93, 213; federal domestic policy on, 15, 213; medical research on, 92, 214; safe harbor policy for, 243n2

Marijuana Legalization Is an Opportunity to Modernize International Drug Treaties (Bennett and Walsh), 92

Marshall Plan. *See* Plan Colombia

Martin, Paul, 36

Marx, Karl, 185

mass incarceration, 89, 92, 185, 192–93, 204, 205, 212, 216

mass murder, 28

McCaffery, Barry, 36

McDonnell Douglas: work-release inmates hired at, 193

Mellman, Mark, 32

Melton, Timothy, 101

mental health and addiction treatment programs, 213

Mercedes Benz, 140

Mercer, Robert, 72

Merck and Company, 37, 194

Meriage, Lawrence, 30

Mérida Initiative, 13, 14, 19–23, 25, 36–45, 47, 68, 75, 88, 169, 188, 189, 212, 225; anticrime operations of, 40; border and maritime security of, 40; congressional support for, 40, 47, 49; corporations that profited from, 31–36, 42–44; drug war expenditures for, 41; funding for, 39, 47, 121; funding for infrastructure development, 118–19; military procurement for, 42; opposition to, 38; as security component of SPP, 37

Merkel, Angela, 164

Merrill Lynch, 140

Mexico, 3, 20, 21, 36–38, 40, 94–95, 111, 134, 216; African palm oil cultivation in, 118; American counternarcotic aid to, 68; commercialization of electric power in, 188; corporate lobbying expenditures for, 56; corporate support for U.S. drug enforcement initiatives in, 90; drug cartels in, 41, 95, 210, 243n1; drug trafficking organizations in, 112; FEMSA, 120; forced displacement of Indigenous peoples in, 134; human rights repression in, 39, 40, 41; Indigenous peoples' movements in, 119; Monsanto Law, 121; narcoguerrillas in, 94; trade unions in, 188–89; training of military and police officers in, 42; U.S. drug war initiatives in, 14, 36–37, 41, 60, 88, 170, 216; U.S. foreign direct investment in, 114, 117; U.S. military aircraft and defense equipment sold to, 40–42, 44

Mica, John, 28

Microsoft: work-release inmates hired at, 194

Middle East, 5, 13, 72, 77

military, 3, 6, 20, 29, 56, 77, 146, 156, 161, 162, 166, 169, 240n1; Colombian, 7–8, 27, 30–31, 33

military counternarcotic operation, U.S.-funded, 26, 83, 169. *See also* Andean Initiative; Plan Colombia; Mérida Initiative;

military-prison-industrial complex, 194, 240n1

Military Professional Resources Inc., 42

Mills, C. Wright, 25, 29, 68, 77

Mineta, Norman, 44, 77

mining, 225, 241n1 (chap. 6); environmental impacts of, 122–23; forced displacements from, 132–33; threats to, 129; by transnational corporations, 121

mining and hydrocarbon projects, transnational, 117, 134

missile defense, 76

Mitsubishi Corporation of Japan, 120

Mizruchi, Mark S., 50, 51

oil pipelines and facilities: security for, 30, 61, 83, 118
Olcott, Martha Brill, 94
Operation Iraqi Freedom, 77
opioids, 21, 217
opium, 21, 24, 61, 91
opium-producing countries, 167–68
Organization of American States, 131
organizations: civil society, 2, 15, 24, 48, 212, 214, 215; criminal, 90; drug trafficking, 111; foreign terrorist, 131; human rights, 3, 14, 37, 51, 60, 187; labor union, 38, 51, 186–87; narcoterrorist, 2, 146–47, 167, 216; paramilitary, 241n6.3; physician, 214; women's, 121
organized crime, 90; money laundering and, 210

Pakistan, 75, 114
Paley, Dawn, 110
palm oil business, 130
Panama, 31, 117, 131
Pan Am Systems, 101
Paraguay: U.S. counternarcotic aid to, 170
paramilitarism, 8
paramilitary groups, 25, 137, 147, 148; pro-government, 142
Pastrana plan. *See* Plan Colombia
Patriot Act, 163
Pelosi, Nancy, 28, 32
Pennzoil, 71
Pentagon, 166, 194
Pepsi, 101
Perry, Rick, 73
Peru, 5, 6, 112, 167, 216; Andean Initiative in, 169; drug suppression efforts in, 91; Minister of Interior, 128; Peruvian National Police, 128; Private Security Services Act, 127–28; privatization of national police force in, 127–28; protection of mining facilities in, 128; strike against Newmont Mining Corporation in, 121–22; U.S. counternarcotic aid to, 60, 170
Petroamazonas, 123–24
Pfizer, 64, 90, 194

PGGM, 120
pharmaceutical industries: lobbying expenditures of, 64
Phillips, 71
Plan Colombia, 13, 14, 19–23, 25–36, 37, 40, 47, 68, 75, 80, 189, 212, 225, 240n7 (chap. 4); budgetary deliberations for, 29, 31; Congressional Black Caucus's support for, 26–27; and coca eradication, 33, 34, 118; congressional funding for, 47, 49; corporate lobbying expenditures for, 56; corporations that profited from, 31–36, 42–44; development investments for, 117–18; fifteenth anniversary of, 169; infrastructure security of, 117; and military approach to drug enforcement, 31; and oil development, 30, 117; opposition to, 28, 38–39; supply-reduction strategy of, 29; U.S. counternarcotic aid for, 117; votes for, 240n6 (chap. 4)
pluralist theory of state repression, 29, 50–53
PNAC, 77
policing, democratic, 171
policy: American foreign and security, 160–61, 163; drug enforcement, 4, 13–14, 23–24, 68–103, 209–13; reforms in, 213–16; safe harbor, 15, 213, 243n2
policy makers, 19–25, 28, 39, 49, 52, 57, 85, 91, 147, 171, 197–98
policy papers, 86–99
policy think tanks, 2, 27, 69, 73–76, 85, 92, 239n2 (chap. 3), 240n2; corporate funding of, 3, 49, 73, 93–94, 212
Political Order in Changing Societies (Huntington), 180
Political Terror Scale index, 5, 6, 142
politics: transactional, 26–27, 38; pluralist, 37
Politics and Markets (Lindblom), 24
Polity index, 5, 6, 9, 198, 242n2 (chap. 8)
polling data, 32
post-9/11, 60, 225
post–Cold War era, 60
postwar military-industrial complex, 69–70

poverty: increasing levels of, 145, 185, 202, 204; Plan Colombia's aim to reduce, 25–26

power: American, 4, 22, 42–45; corporate, 3, 24–25, 29–36–37, 46, 67, 84–85, 97–99, 102; institutional, 23, 48; political, 126

powers, separation of, 9

President, Executive Office of the, 56, 84–85, 162

presidential elections, 70–71, 157–58

Prins, Nomi, 70

prison-industrial complex, 193–95, 204, 208, 212

prison labor: corporate use of, 193–95; corporate profits from, 195, 208, 212; corporations' use of, 110, 193–95, 207

prison populations, 9, 192–93

prisons: federal and state, 12, 192; correction expenditures for, 192–93

private armies, 126

private capital, 188

private corporations, 24, 25, 33, 72, 72, 113, 189, 195, 202

private direct investment, 113

private equity investments, 72

private investment, 2, 27, 113, 114, 118, 212; foreign, 109

private militaries, 134

private prison corporations, 194, 208

private property, protection of, 128

private security firms, 110, 127–35, 142, 148, 153

private shareholder, 61

private wealth, 202

privatization, threat to, 1–2

Proctor & Gamble, 64, 95, 194

Prodeco, 133–34

prohibitionist preferences in U.S. drug policy, 24–25

Project for the New American Century, 76

Promigas, 31

prosecutors, former government, 165

protesters, 121–23, 129

public health, 23, 190, 192

public housing, 190

public officials, 23–24; accountability of, 156

public opinion, 2, 70, 73

public policy, shaping, 23–25, 46–47, 48, 50, 51, 69, 73, 77, 85

Putumayo region, 30

Qosmos, 142

racial bias, 205, 207

racism, 11

radar planes, 32, 42, 44, 83

radars, ground-based, 83

radical theory of state repression, 25, 29, 36, 40, 48–49

Ralston, Joseph, 36

Ramstad, James, 28

RAND Corporation, 77–78; drug enforcement research of, 86–89

Rangel, Charles B., 12

Rapiscan, 40, 42, 44

Raytheon, 33, 80–81, 93, 94, 96

Reagan, Ronald, 12, 76, 138, 162

rebel forces, 141

"Rebuilding the National and Global Consensus Against Illicit Narcotics" (Runde and Snyder), 95

recession, 24, 41, 70, 102, 200

reforms: drug policy, 15; neoliberal, 2, 110, 121, 127

regime: anticommunist authoritarian, 158; anti-money-laundering, 209–10; corporatist, 2, 10, 14–15, 102–3, 135, 155, 191, 207–8, 212, 216; democratic, 146; drug enforcement, 11–13, 20–22, 36–38, 45, 46–52, 68–103, 171, 183, 191, 214; human rights, 60; military, 140, 146; objectives of the, 8; pathologies of the, 209, 216

Reich, Otto, 76

renewable energy, 118

rent assistance programs, 190

repression: acts of, 174, 239n4 (chap. 1); corporate-induced, 136, 137–42, 152–53; drug-induced, 208; human rights, 4, 9, 11, 14, 27, 60, 103, 109, 135, 137, 139, 142, 216, 241n3 (chap. 5); increasing levels

state, the: corporate dominance over, 29, 34–36, 70; national security, 155; operations of, 70–73, 102–3, 154; political decisions of, 23; theories of, 23–25, 29, 36, 40–41, 42, 46, 48, 67, 102

Stockholm International Peace Research Institute, 33, 41–42

sub-Saharan Africa, 5, 13; militarized, 35–36

Suriname, 117

surveillance: equipment, 142; satellites, 76, 88

surveillance systems: U.S. counternarcotics drug, 33, 88

Syria, 9

Tahoe Resources, 129

Taiwan: American Institute in, 74; U.S. relations in, 74

Tajikistan, 167

Talbott, Strobe, 93

Taliban: counterinsurgency against, 64, 91

task forces, counternarcotics, 63

Taylor, Michael, 36, 74

taxes: cuts, 24; rates, 99; reform, 101, 103

Tea Party, 72

Teets, Peter B., 76

Tenet, George, 42

Tengizchevroil, 61

terrorism: international, 161, 163; privatization of, 125–35; War on Terror, 90–91

Texas Eastern Transmission, 71

Texas Instruments: work-release inmates hired at, 194

Textron Corporation, 33, 41–42; work-release inmates hired at, 193

Thailand, 5, 6, 167

theories of state repression, 5–9. *See also specific theories*

Third Border Initiative, 37–38

Ties that Bind: U.S.-Taiwan Relations and Peace and Prosperity in East Asia (Chen), 74

Tobago, 117

Torres, Edgar, 27

torture, 39, 140, 163

Total SA, 141

trade: free, 50, 55, 225; international, 4, 64, 116

training, military and police, 37, 42

Transportation Security Administration, 40

trinational working group, 37

Trinidad, 117

Truman, Donald: as presidential candidate, 46; as president, 162, 213, 243n2

Trump administration, 15, 22, 102, 208, 210

Turkmenistan: drug-related homicide rates in, 167; oil and gas development in, 94

Udalova, Natalia, 94

UNICOR, 193–95

Union Oil Company of California, 94

unions, labor/trade, 3, 14, 24, 37–39, 48, 121, 126, 186–89; lobbying expenditures of, 48–49; repression of, 139, 186, 187

Unitarian Universal Association, 215

United Fruit Company, 140

United Kingdom, 239n1 (chap. 1); Atomic Weapons Establishment, 76; foreign direct investment in, 114

United Nations, 75, 128, 135; Basic Principles on the Independence of the Judiciary, 143–44; High Commission for Human Rights, 29; International Labor Organization's Convention on the Rights of Indigenous and Tribal Peoples, 120, 121, 135; Monterrey Consensus on International Financing for Development, 113; Office on Drugs and Crime, 111–12

United Parcel Service, 194

United States: bilateral trade and investment agreement with, 55, 57, 240n4 (chap. 3); budget for international drug control, 94, 161; class conflict in, 185–95; democratic creed of, 9; drug enforcement in, 190–92, 200, 209–13; drug policy in, 23–24, 56, 84–85; drug war in, 192, 212; exports to, 225; foreign economic policy, 25, 138; illiberal governance in, 208; income inequality

www.ingramcontent.com/pod-product-compliance
Lightning Source LLC
Chambersburg PA
CBHW020458270326
41926CB00008B/656